Business and Government
During the Eisenhower
Administration

Business and Government During the Eisenhower Administration

A Study of the Antitrust Policy
of the Antitrust Division
of the Justice Department

THEODORE PHILIP KOVALEFF

 OHIO UNIVERSITY PRESS | ATHENS

Library of Congress Cataloging in Publication Data
Kovaleff, Theodore Philip, 1943-
 Business and government during the Eisenhower
Administration.

 Includes bibliographical references and index.
 1. United States. Dept. of Justice. Antitrust
Division—History. 2. Antitrust law—United States—
History. I. Title.
KF1653.K68   338.8   79-25590
ISBN 0-8214-0416-4

TO MY MOTHER

Table of Contents

Preface

BOOKS that treat the subject of antitrust normally fall into one of two categories: Either they excoriate the concept of antitrust and then denounce "government meddling," or they expose the politics of the subject and endeavor to prove that the antitrust program is little more than rhetoric or response to various pressure groups. This book will disappoint the partisans of each, for in treating the topic—the actions of the Antitrust Division of the Department of Justice during the Eisenhower years—it takes neither side, but rather seeks to view the situation from a middle ground, one often occupied by the Antitrust Division itself. In brief, this volume is not meant to be a history of antitrust or business in the 1950s; instead it details the period's increasingly strong enforcement patterns in the antitrust field, activities not readily expected of a "business-oriented" administration. Not only should the work in this volume be useful to those studying the Eisenhower years, but the data on mergers should also aid the legal fraternity.

In these days of oil crises and OPEC price-fixing, some readers may search for a treatment of the oil cartel case. I have not dealt with this subject because Burton Kaufman covers it much more extensively in *The Oil Cartel Case: A Documentary Study of Antitrust Activity in the Cold War Era* (Westport, CT: 1978).

Much of the material used in preparing this book is drawn from primary sources such as documents, press releases, articles, and speeches by major figures; however, many of my ideas were formulated after having read the responses to my numerous questionnaires. To the many members and conferees of the Attorney General's National Committee to Study the Antitrust Laws who answered my questions, I would like to express my thanks. Many others took time from their busy schedules to reply to my sometimes prying questions. Especial thanks go to the former chiefs of the Antitrust Division of the Justice Department: H. Graham Morison, Stanley Barnes, Victor Hansen, Robert Bicks and Lee Loevinger, all of whom were extremely helpful. Baddia Rashid, the director of operations of the Antitrust Division, not only found time to give me a lengthy interview, but also answered countless questions which later arose. Keith Clearwaters, the

Assistant to the Assistant Attorney General in Charge of the Antitrust Division, aided me in overcoming many bureaucratic hurdles in my efforts to consult all the Antitrust Division files. Joe Sims and Robert Yahn kept me abreast of the alterations in regulations at the Justice Department and advised me how to conform best to the ever-changing strictures. James Layerzapf and his staff at the Eisenhower Library were especially helpful, enabling me to make the most of my research time in Abilene, Kansas. Milton Handler generously allowed me to audit his popular course on trade regulation at the Columbia University Law School and afterwards discussed in great detail his experience as a member of the Attorney General's National Committee and his subsequent role in the Electrical cases. I would also like to thank Raymond J. Saulnier for steering me in the direction of the topic. It would be impossible to express my gratitude to Vincent P. Carosso under whose guidance the study was completed. His advice, assistance and support were invaluable. Finally, a word of thanks to my mother, Barbara P. Kovaleff, who typed the work, first as a dissertation and then in its present form.

The merits of this study, then, are due to the aid and kindness of many people. Any errors, however, are my own.

Business and Government During The Eisenhower Administration

CHAPTER I

Introduction

ALTHOUGH antitrust has a bipartisan background, surprisingly some of its most effective proponents were members of Dwight Eisenhower's administration in the 1950s. Instead of relying on various regulatory agencies to control the actions of business, the Republicans depended to a great extent on antitrust, especially as enforced by the Justice Department.

Monopoly, price fixing and market division were not unknown in the American colonies, and almost from the start laws appeared against regrating, forestalling and engrossing.[1] One of the often-cited causes of the American Revolution was monopoly. Indeed, had it not been for the British East India Company's tea monopoly, and the ensuing Tea Party in Boston Harbor, the American Revolution might never have taken place.

The constitutions of many of the original states contained anti-monopoly clauses, and Thomas Jefferson, in a letter to James Madison explaining his opposition to the Constitution, complained that the document contained no restriction on monopolies.[2] This state of affairs persisted until after the Civil War when the American economy began to assume more national parameters; it was not until nearly the end of the nineteenth century that any need was manifested for a national antitrust law.

The first movements were usually grange-inspired and aimed at the regulation of railroads. The Anti-Monopoly Party ran a candidate in the 1884 presidential election and although it only garnered the minuscule total of 175,370 ballots, or a little less than two percent of the total vote, its influence was considerable, for, within four years, the Republicans declared their "opposition to all combinations of capital organized in trusts or otherwise to control arbitrarily the condition of trade among our citizens; . . . [recommending] to Congress and the State Legislatures . . . such legislation as will prevent the execution of all schemes to oppress the people."[3] The Democrats were less forceful but also included a statement opposing the trusts: "Judged by Democratic principles, the interests of the people are betrayed, when, by unnecessary taxation, trusts and combinations are

3

permitted and fostered, which, while unduly enriching the few that combine, rob the body of our citizens."[4]

Although between 1888 and the middle of 1890 many antitrust bills and petitions were submitted to Congress,[5] the Sherman Act was the one that was finally passed by an overwhelming vote in the nominally Republican Legislature and signed by the Republican President Benjamin Harrison. The House vote of 242 to 0, with 85 members abstaining, and the single "nay" vote in the Senate underline the bipartisan nature of the bill.[6]

In general, the act prohibited every contract, combination or conspiracy in restraint of interstate trade. While the possession of a monopoly was not deemed illegal, the attempt to gain monopoly power or the exercise thereof was a crime, and the government could obtain injunctive relief. Private parties were better treated; they were authorized to sue for treble repayment of damages incurred as a consequence of the illegal act. There were no exemptions included in the statute.

Shortly after the passage of the Sherman law, it was supplemented in 1894 by sections of the Wilson Tariff Act. Sections 73 through 77 extended the Sherman Act prohibitions to the importation of goods into a state from a foreign country. Provisions similar to those in the Sherman Act were made for treating the violators, including the proviso for private treble damage suits.[7] This extension and reaffirmation of the act by a Democratic Congress and President again emphasize the bipartisan heritage of antitrust.

Between 1908 and 1912 minor provisions were enacted to harass violators of the Sherman Act.[8] In 1908, an act to encourage the development of coal deposits in the territory of Alaska contained a section stipulating "If any of the lands or deposits leased are . . . so that they form part of or are in anywise controlled by any combination in the form of an unlawful trust . . . the lease shall be forfeited by appropriate court proceedings."[9] Two years later, part of an act to grant right of way over the public domain in the State of Arkansas for oil or gas pipelines provided that if any citizen, company, or corporation taking advantage of the provisions of the act were determined to violate the Sherman Act, he would automatically forfeit the benefits gained from the statute.[10] The Panama Canal Act, passed in 1912, contained a clause denying the use of the facility to any transgressor of the law.[11]

Neither the Sherman Act nor the Wilson Tariff Act offered any protection to organized labor or to farm cooperatives. Indeed, four of the eight cases filed by the Cleveland administration were against some aspect of labor union activity. The farm cooperatives fared little better in the courts. In the years prior to the passage of the Clayton Act in 1914, both groups would strive to obtain exemption from coverage by legislation, or by riders to appropriation bills, stating that the funds appropriated could not be employed to prosecute their organizations. Congress as a whole rarely voted on bills containing such clauses and only one was passed; even that did not become law because President Taft exercised his veto power.[12] Not until the passage of the Clayton Act would labor be able to bargain collectively without violating the law.

In 1912, the platforms of the three major parties all included planks advocating the strengthening of the antitrust laws which had been weakened by adverse Supreme Court decisions during the Taft administration. The Democratic platform, which branded private monopoly as indefensible and intolerable, backed vigorous enforcement and demanded "the enactment of such additional legislation as may be necessary to make it impossible for private monopoly to exist in the United States."[13] After claiming credit for having "placed upon the statute book . . . the antitrust act of 1890," the Republican platform proclaimed its support of "the enactment of legislation supplementary to the existing antitrust act which will define as criminal offenses those specific acts that uniformly mark attempts to restrain and to monopolize trade. . . . The same certainty should be given to the law prohibiting combinations and monopolies . . . in order that no part of the field of business opportunity may be restricted by monopoly or com-bination. . ."[14] Essentially President Taft did not aim to increase the severity of the Sherman Act; instead he wished to increase its coverage.[15] The Progressive Party also bluntly favored "strengthening the Sherman law" by prohibiting certain enumerated trade practices which were legal but "unfair."[16] Furthermore, both the Progressive and Republican Parties specifically urged the establishment of a strong federal administrative commission to maintain permanent active supervision over corporations engaged in interstate commerce, as, quoting the Progressive platform, "is now done for the railroads by the Interstate Commerce Commission."[17] Thus, the antitrust issue was not the handmaiden of any particular political party.

The Clayton Act, enacted in late 1914, supplemented and extended the Sherman Act. With the exception of the exemptions for farm and labor organizations, it did not alter the prohibitions of the Sherman Act, rather it interdicted activities which Congress felt were left uncovered by existing laws. The idea of halting problems in their incipiency was very important. Thus, while the Sherman Act was aimed at present evils, the Clayton Act was directed against potential problems, whether or not they were currently illegal. This goal was to be accomplished mainly by forbidding such activities as price discrimination, exclusive dealer contracts, certain types of stock acquisitions and interlocking directorates any of which could have the effect of lessening competition substantially or tending to create a monopoly. The treble damage recovery proviso was also included.

Almost simultaneously with approval of the Clayton Act, Congress passed the Trade Commission Act, creating the Federal Trade Commission (FTC) to serve as an administrative body. Congress also endowed it with certain quasi-legislative powers so that it could define what was unfair competition and thus determine the areas of its own jurisdiction. The FTC was also given the responsibility of enforcing various sections of the Clayton Act. Since the Department of Justice already had been assigned that task, the two bodies had to coordinate their enforcement activities.

Despite the fact that it was during the Wilson Administration that two important pieces of legislation, the Clayton Act and the Federal Trade Commission Act, were passed, Wilson cannot be described as the "father of anti-trust." The real parent was Theodore Roosevelt, who resurrected the Sherman Act and used it as part of his campaign to regulate big business.[18] William Howard Taft continued his predecessor's policy and during his administration, slightly more than half as long as that of TR, the government initiated twice as many anti-trust actions as it had during the previous administration. Almost as soon as Woodrow Wilson had signed the Clayton Act, his antitrust ardor cooled.[19] There appear to have been several reasons for this. First, it has been stated that antitrust was not high on the Wilsonian list of priorities. Much more important to him were tariff reduction and revision of the banking system.[20] Second, and perhaps more important, was the worsening situation in Europe. FTC critics in particular have noted, that, within hours of the birth of the commission, World War I began.[21] Finally, the increasingly deteriorating health of his wife may well have diverted his attention from any issues which did not have "priority" status.

During the Wilson Administration the first exemptions to the antitrust laws were granted.[22] According to Section 6 of the Clayton Act, "the labor of a human being is not a commodity or article of commerce." Also as a result of intense lobbying, not only labor but also agricultural and horticultural organizations "instituted for the purposes of self help," but not being "conducted for profit," were exempted from coverage by the Sherman Act.

The Webb-Pomerene Act of 1918 was the second act passed during the Wilson Administration that exempted an activity from being covered by the Sherman Act. It specified that nothing contained in the Sherman Act "shall be construed as declaring to be illegal an association entered into for the sole purpose of engaging in export trade." Next the Merchant Marine Act of 1920 contained a section exempting marine insurance from the coverage of the Sherman and Clayton acts.

The trend of granting exemptions to the antitrust laws, started during the Wilson Administration, continued during the 1920s with the passage of the Capper-Volstead Agricultural Cooperative Marketing Act, which sought to clarify the activities of agricultural cooperatives. Farmers, ranchers, dairymen, and nut or fruit growers may "act together in associations, corporate or otherwise . . . in collectively processing, preparing for market, handling and marketing in interstate and foreign commerce, such products of persons so engaged." The Cooperative Marketing Act of 1926[23] further delineated the scope of the legal joint activities of the cooperatives.

The Fishermen's Collective Marketing Act of 1934,[24] modeled along the lines of the Capper-Volstead law, authorized independent fishermen to form cooperative associations. They too were then able to overcome their disadvantage in bargaining for a better price for their commodity. In this way, fishermen obtained the same exemption that Congress had accorded to the nation's farmers a dozen years earlier.

The Depression was not likely to stimulate attitudes in favor of the existing economic system, which was essentially one of competition. Ellis Hawley has analyzed the reactions of Franklin Roosevelt and the New Deal to the problem of monopoly, and he suggests that the administration had, at best, an ambivalent attitude on the subject. "There was little agreement on the course" of action to be taken and "the result was an amalgam of conflicting policies and programs, one that might make sense to the politician, but little to the rational economist."[25] The general reaction, or perhaps even antipathy, toward the competitive system was capped by the National Industrial Recovery Act experiment in cartelization. In order "to remove obstructions to the free flow in interstate and foreign commerce" and to provide for the general welfare by promoting the "organization of industries" for "collective action," the National Recovery Administration (NRA) suspended many facets of the antitrust laws. It condoned or even encouraged trade associations, and it established and enforced Codes of Fair Competition. The 874 Codes approved by the NRA covered the areas of prices and production; some even divided the market among the various members of an industry. With the unanimous *Schechter* decision,[26] coinciding with a growing dissatisfaction toward many phases of the NRA movement, the National Recovery Administration "had done its part" and was gracefully retired. Roosevelt's attitude toward competition appears to have remained unchanged, however, for the number of exemptions to the antitrust laws continued to proliferate during his regime.[27]

Many of the acts that were passed during 1934-1935 were influenced by NRA philosophy. Special situations were singled out and efforts were made to suppress competition in such areas as farming, bituminous coal operations, oil production, trucking and labor.[28] Although many of the acts were later declared unconstitutional,[29] there was no fundamental change in the Roosevelt Administration's direction. What occurred was that subsequent legislation was more carefully drafted[30] and the special interests of farming, bituminous coal, oil and labor were again regulated.[31]

Two acts relating to transportation, the Motor Carrier Act and the Civil Aeronautics Act, illustrate that the anti-antitrust attitude permeated the Roosevelt Administration for longer than the First New Deal. The Motor

Carrier Act imposed rigid restrictions on entry into the industry, and it fixed prices below which a trucker could not charge. This type of regulation obviously suppressed competition. Those who voted for the Civil Aeronautics Act of 1938 were motivated by the same fear that had influenced the framers of the NRA: competition is wasteful and destructive. One of the aims of the act which established the Civil Aeronautics Board (CAB) was to circumvent, by means of regulation, the uneconomical duplication of routes.

Two other bills were passed during the New Deal that have been the focus of much controversy. The Robinson-Patman Act, actually an amendment to the Clayton Act, and the various Fair-Trade bills were in many respects opposed to the philosophy. Described by some as the "Wrong-Way Corrigan" of our antitrust laws, the Robinson-Patman Act later was accused of moving in the opposite direction from the objectives of the antitrust laws.[32] One of its clauses required an identical price to all buyers, except for provable cost savings. This had the effect of encouraging uniform prices and of discouraging differences in prices which might be accomplished by a better or more forceful buyer. Passed as a reaction to the growth of chain stores, the Robinson-Patman Act[33] thus set up boundaries limiting one aspect of the competitive system. Perhaps luckily for competition in distribution, the act was never fully enforced.[34]

Much more antithetical to the concept of free competition than the Robinson-Patman bill was the Miller-Tydings Act passed in 1937 as an amendment to Section 1 of the Sherman Act. It exempted from the antitrust laws contracts or agreements prescribing minimum prices for the resale of a trademark-protected brand name commodity. What resulted is known by the euphemistic term, "fair trade." Had the concept been described as "resale price maintenance," its tenure might well have been either abbreviated or aborted. The law was not repealed; indeed, when the Supreme Court in the *Schwegmann*[35] decision of 1951 jeopardized effective fair trade, a Democratic Congress and a Democratic President passed and signed the McGuire amendment to the Federal Trade Commission Act. In this manner the loophole was filled, and it was up to individual states to decide whether or not there would be resale price maintenance within their boundaries.

The many laws and amendments passed during the FDR era opposed to the concept of antitrust suggest that the administration had, at best, a schizoid attitude toward the subject. While the achievements of Thurman Arnold's term as Assistant Attorney General in charge of the Antitrust Division and the Temporary National Economic Commission (TNEC) were important, they have been overemphasized.[36] The commission did not play an important role in the renaissance of antitrust enforcement; however, the outbreak of World War II in Europe, barely a year after Roosevelt signed the bill creating the TNEC, undoubtedly contributed to its failure to justify the hopes of those responsible for its inception. Nevertheless, despite the 37 volumes comprising some 17,000 pages, there was nothing new in the report of the TNEC.[37] Its real significance lay in its influence on the American mind. Antitrust was no longer a "dead letter."

It is noteworthy that when Arnold was appointed Assistant Attorney General, no one expected he would accomplish much. Corwin Edwards states that Arnold's selection "was widely regarded as a cynical recognition of the futility of antitrust enforcement."[38] However, by the time he had left his post to accept the position of Associate Justice in the United States Court of Appeals in the District of Columbia, he had instituted 44 percent of all the proceedings that had ever been undertaken by the Department of Justice during the more than half a century of the Sherman Act's existence.[39] Yet, despite the number of cases filed, and even taking into account the large percentage of victories won during his tenure, Arnold's major contribution was not any special case or group of cases, but rather his reawakening of the nation's interest in the antitrust laws.[40] As in the case of the TNEC, however, Arnold's activities clashed head on with the expansion of industry for war purposes. Thus, once again, consolidation, coordination, central management and monopolies became the watchwords of the Roosevelt Administration, and Arnold's trust policies were quietly retired for the duration of the crisis.[41] Little of major import in the antitrust field was accomplished during the war.

During the Truman Administration, there were only two items in the field of antitrust law that merit mention. On the negative side, after the *Schwegmann* decision, the McGuire Act had revitalized resale price maintenance; but in a positive vein, a very important change was made in the Clayton Act. The original Section 7 of the law had been aimed primarily at holding companies which, as the Alabama Democratic Representative Henry D. Clayton had stated, was a "common and favorite method of promoting monopoly."[42] Consequently the scope of the act had been limited, for while it had embraced the purchase, either directly or indirectly, of the stock of one corporation by another corporation, organizations such as partnerships were not covered. The most obvious defect of Section 7, however, was its confinement to stock acquisitions. It was easy to avoid that proscription simply by acquiring the assets of the other company. Furthermore, the interdict did not apply to purchases made solely for investment purposes, or to situations in which the acquisition did not substantially lessen competition between the acquiring and acquired corporation.

The "assets loophole" was utilized successfully almost at once as, in 1916, the FTC had declined to act in a merger case. According to its opinion, the commission believed it had been given no jurisdiction over the question of the legality of a purchase of one corporation by another.[43] The original section was further weakened in 1926, when the Supreme Court ruled that the FTC did not have the power under Section 7 to order the defendant corporation to divest itself of property even though it had been acquired by an illegal purchase of stock.[44] The problem of enforcement was further aggravated by the Court's interpretation of the phrase "substantially lessen competition between the acquired and the acquiring corporation." To the nonlegal student of antitrust, this would appear to rule out all mergers between companies which compete, no matter how small the market share might be. But the Court interpreted the phrase as treating the effect of merger on the rest of the industry.[45]

As early as 1927, the FTC noted that mergers were being accomplished more and more by means of acquisition of stock, and from that time onward, the commission urged an amendment stating that asset acquisitions should be handled in the same way as stock acquisitions.[46] More than a decade later, the *Final Report of the TNEC* recommended that asset acquisitions be included in the domain of Section 7.[47] Before the 1950 amendment had been passed, congressmen of both major parties had introduced nearly a score of bills to amend the original Section 7. No wonder that from 1914 until 1950 the Department of Justice had used the section alone only four times. If the number of actions in which multiple charges were made—that is, the Sherman Act as well as the Clayton Act, Section 7— are counted, the total then rises to 16.[48]

Besides the obvious lacunae in the law itself, there was also the issue of the expansion of United States Steel. In what charitably can be described as an action contradictory to the antitrust philosophy, as part of the industrial demobilization at the end of World War II, the federal government sold facilities in Utah known as Geneva Steel to United States Steel. Despite the fact that others had bid for the property, Geneva was sold to the largest steel producer in the nation because it could better expand steel production in that section of the country.[49] Slightly more than two years later, the Supreme Court upheld the purchase by Columbia Steel, a subsidiary of United States Steel, of the assets of the Consolidated Steel Corporation.[50]

The 1950 Celler-Kefauver Amendment to the Clayton Act wrought several other changes. The most expected and obvious was the inclusion of the acquisition of assets within the scope of Section 7 of the Clayton Act. The statute also prohibited a merger if it lessened competition substantially in any line of commerce or tended to create a monopoly in any section of the country. The old test of the illegality—the lessening of competition between the acquired and acquiring corporations—was dropped, and in its stead, the lessening of competition (or tendency to monopoly) in any line of commerce was substituted. In one way, the criteria were less restrictive, for under the revised section some mergers became legal which previously had been forbidden because the companies, no matter how small, had been competitors. On the other hand, the substitution of the modifying phrase, "in any line of commerce in any section of the country," aiming the act at "all mergers and acquisitions, vertical and *conglomerate* as well as horizontal" offered all sorts of possibilities for extending the scope of the law.[51]

Despite the modification of the Clayton Act, the record of the Truman Administration in the antitrust field was not outstanding. During World War II, antitrust enforcement had been deemphasized; even during reconversion, the Antitrust Division concentrated on gathering material for several big cases, such as the ones against Du Pont.[52] This led, at best, to an uneven enforcement program. The Korean War affected the Truman policy in two ways. Not only was there the question of effective mobilization with its attendant implications for antitrust enforcement, but there was also an economy drive, and the appropriations for the Antitrust Division of the Justice Department in fiscal year 1952 were slashed by $500,000. This necessitated that the Division function with approximately 100 fewer attorneys.[53] Yet, in spite of these problems, the Truman antitrust program was not stilled completely. Thirty cases were filed by the Antitrust Division against some of the largest corporations in the nation, such as International Business Machines Corporation. However, according to Stanley Barnes, the first head of the Antitrust Division in the Eisenhower regime, several cases were filed with the intent of "embarrassing" the succeeding administration.[54]

In 1952 both major political parties incorporated in their campaign platforms the standard homage to antitrust. The Republican Party platform stated, "We will follow principles of equal enforcement of the antimonopoly and unfair competition statutes and simplify their administration to assist the businessman who, in good faith, seeks to remain in compliance. At the same time, we shall relentlessly protect our free enterprise system against monopolistic and unfair trade practices. . . ."[55] There was considerable doubt in some quarters about how strong the commitment of the Republican Party was to antitrust regulation. During the campaign, the Democrats had raised the specter of a Republican repeal of the antitrust laws, or at the very least, nonenforcement. The Republican standard bearer, Eisenhower, vigorously denied this possibility and, with equal vigor supported the concept of antitrust in various statements and communications, such as his letter of October 16, 1952 to the National Association of Retail Druggists:

I favor with equal vigor the maintenance and effective enforcement of the necessary basic safeguards to free American enterprise. They are provided in our antitrust laws and in those laws supporting fair competitive pricing practices. I shall oppose any legislation which will weaken them.

American business cannot prosper and contribute in growing measure to our national wellbeing unless the opportunity to engage in business and to provide customers with new and better products and services is vigilantly preserved. Our laws against unfair and destructive pricing practices as well as other practices leading to monopoly must be fearlessly, impartially and energetically maintained and enforced.

I am for such necessary rules of fair play because they preserve and strengthen free and fair competition, as opposed to monopolies which mean the end of competition. I am for a realistic enforcement of them which they have not had during the past twenty years.

> Sincerely,
> Dwight David Eisenhower[56]

Despite such professions of faith in the antitrust laws, many observers continued to expect that the Eisenhower Administration would be a businessman's administration that would do little of positive value in the antitrust field.[57] Even in the Antitrust Division itself, there was some uncertainty about the future course of enforcement.[58] It was in this context that the Attorney General's National Committee to Study the Antitrust Laws took on great importance. The attitude of the Eisenhower Administration toward antitrust activity remained essentially unchanged from the attitude professed by the Republican Party during the 1952 campaign.

The concept of antitrust cannot be understood without grasping two opposing themes which run dichotomously through its entire history. On the one hand we have the prohibition of all restraints of trade, and the principle, often called the "rule of reason," which limits the scope of the prohibition. Section 1 of the Sherman Act states in apparently explicit terms, "*Every* contract, combination in the form of trust or otherwise, or conspiracy, in restraint of trade or commerce among the several states, or with foreign nations, is declared to be illegal.[59] On the other hand, however, also extant is the common-law principle that, in some circumstances, a showing of reasonableness will legalize some restrictions on competition.

The conundrum appeared to be resolved in the first *Standard Oil* case, in which the court stated that the Sherman Act prohibited only contracts or acts which "in the light of reason" unreasonably restrict competition. The court continued in its effort to reconcile common law and the Sherman Act by stating that the same standard of reasonableness had been applied to the judgments of restraints of trade in the common law.[60] This holding established parameters for interpretation and application of the Sherman Act that have lasted since 1911.

The adoption of the rule of reason in the *Standard Oil* case led every other antitrust defendant to endeavor to justify his action in a like manner—in the economic context and in light of certain conditions, that the attacked practice was reasonable. The courts responded to this by developing another doctrine: certain violations are illegal *"per se"* and are interdicted by antitrust laws regardless of any peripheral reasonableness.

There are six practices that have been found to be unreasonable and therefore *per se* illegal, agreements not to compete being one of them. When not ancillary to a legitimate contract, these agreements have been held illegal since the nineteenth century.[61] Second, collusive price-fixing was made illegal; this holds true whether the agreement was between horizontal or vertical competitors. A third type of illegality involved boycotts of almost any nature. With the exception of such action being employed in certain labor disputes, they were considered illegal.[62] Fourth, some combinations which foreclose competitors from any share of the market by tie-in arrangements fell into the category of *per se* illegal arrangements. The exact parameters of this category have not yet been fully delineated. Fifth, agreements by which competitors promise to pool either profits or losses were deemed restrictive of competition.[63] Finally, agreements between competing companies on the subject of market division have been castigated and adjudged comparable to price-fixing accords.[64]

NOTES

1. A person who forestalled was one who intercepted goods on the way to market in order to fix the price when he arrived there to sell his newly purchased goods. An engrosser purchased a commodity wholesale (in gross) and later sold it at a profit, although the goods were still in a wholesale lot. Regrating was buying a necessity in one market for the purpose of selling it again at a profit in another market.
2. Thomas Jefferson to James Madison, Dec. 20, 1787, in *The Papers of Thomas Jefferson*, ed. Julian P. Boyd, (Princeton, 1950—), XII, 440.
3. Kirk Porter and Donald Bruce Johnson, comps., *National Party Platforms 1840-1956* (Urbana, Ill., 1956), p. 80.
4. Porter and Johnson, p. 78.
5. Hans Thorelli, *The Federal Antitrust Policy: Origination of an American Tradition* (Baltimore, 1955), p. 176. It is interesting to note that Senator John Sherman (Republican, Ohio) had very little to do with the framing of the act. According to Thorelli, the Republican Senator George F. Edmunds of Vermont drafted Sections 1, 2, 3, 5, and 6; Senator James Z. George (Democrat, Mississippi) was responsible for Section 4, while Senator George F. Hoar, the Republican Senator from Massachusetts, contributed Section 7 and the Republican Senator John J. Ingalls of Kansas, Section 8 (Thorelli, p. 212). This situation prompted Senator Hoar to write, "In 1890 a bill was passed which was called the Sherman Act, for no other reason that I can think of except that Mr. Sherman had nothing to do with framing it whatever." (Thorelli, p. 210, quoting from George F. Hoar, *Autobiography of Seventy Years*, [New York, 1903], II, 363).
6. The single dissenter was Senator Rufus Blodgett, a Democrat from New Jersey. The *Congressional Record* recorded no explanation for his vote. *Congressional Record*, 51st Cong., 1st Sess. (Washington, D.C., 1889), p. 3153.
7. 28 *Stat.* 570 (1894).

8. John E. Schefter, "Historical Policy of the United States Toward Monopoly," *North Dakota Law Review*, 43 (Fall 1966), 25.

9. 48 U.S.C. 443 (1934 edition); after Alaska gained statehood, many of the territorial statutes were altered; see also 35 *Stat.* 424, sec. 3 (1908).

10. 36 *Stat.* 296 (1910); 43 U.S.C. 970 also includes the Clayton Act.

11. 15 U.S.C. 31.

12. John Noakes, "Exemptions for Cooperatives," *American Bar Association Antitrust Section*, 19 (Proceedings at the Annual Meeting, Aug. 7-11, 1961), 411. Hereafter volumes will be cited according to the form adopted by the American Bar Association on Aug. 24, 1959; thus, for example, this citation would read 19 *A.B.A. Antitrust Section* (Aug. 7-11, 1961), 411.

13. Porter and Johnson, p. 169.

14. Porter and Johnson, p. 178.

15. William Howard Taft, *The Anti-Trust Act and the Supreme Court* (New York, 1914), pp. 132-133.

16. Porter and Johnson, 178.

17. Porter and Johnson, p. 178.

18. Thurman Arnold, "Fair Fights and Foul," *The Antitrust Bulletin*, 10 (Sept.-Dec. 1965), 655.

19. Arthur S. Link, *Woodrow Wilson and the Progressive Era: 1910-1917* (New York, 1954), p. 75.

20. Dow Votaw, "Antitrust in 1914: The Climate of Opinion," 24 *A.B.A. Antitrust Section* (Apr. 16-17, 1964), 24.

21. Lowell B. Mason to author, April 22, 1971.

22. A patent could be treated as an exemption to the anti-trust laws, for it provides an inventor with a 17-year monopoly on his discovery. An inventor is allowed to do many things with his patented invention that would otherwise be deemed illegal. The right is guaranteed by the Constitution and thus antedates the Sherman Act by roughly a century; hence it cannot be described as vitiating the thrust of the antitrust laws.

23. 7 U.S.C. 451-457.

24. 48 *Stat.* 1213 (1934); 15 U.S.C. 521-522.

25. Ellis Hawley, *The New Deal and the Problem of Monopoly: A Study in Economic Ambivalence* (Princeton, 1966), pp. vii-viii.

26. Schechter Poultry Corp. v. U.S., 295 U.S. 495 (1935).

27. This interpretation of the New Deal's trust policies was suggested to the author in a discussion with Professor W. K. Jones of the Columbia Law School, Columbia University, Jan. 20, 1971.

28. Agricultural Adjustment Act, 48 *Stat.* 31 (1933); Agricultural Adjustment Act Amendments, 49 *Stat.* 750 (1935); Guffey-Snyder Act or Bituminous Coal Conservation Act, 49 *Stat.* 991 (1935); Connally Hot Oil Act, 49 *Stat.* 30 (1935); Interstate Oil Compact, 49 *Stat.* 939 (1935); Motor Carrier Act, 49 *Stat.* 543 (1935); National Labor Relations Act, 49 *Stat.* 449 (1935).

29. U.S. v. Butler et al., 297 U.S. 61 (1936); Carter v. Carter Coal Company, 298 U.S. 269 (1936); Panama Refining Company v. Ryan, 293 U.S. 388 (1935).

30. Henry Bamford Parkes and Vincent P. Carosso, *Recent America: A History*

(New York, 1963), II, III, quoting Merlo J. Pusey, "F.D.R. vs. The Supreme Court," *American Heritage*, 9 (Apr. 1958), 24.

31. Agricultural Marketing Agreement Act, 50 *Stat.* 246 (1937); 52 *Stat.* 31 (1938); Guffey-Vinson Act or Bituminous Coal Act, 50 *Stat.* 72 (1937); Interstate Oil Compact, 50 *Stat.* 617; 53 *Stat.* 10171 (1939); Fair Labor Standards Act, 52 *Stat.* 1060 (1938).
32. Thomas E. Sunderland, "The Robinson-Patman Act: Go Out and Compete But Don't Get Caught At It," *Chicago Bar Record*, 34 (Sept. 1953), 447.
33. 15 U.S.C. 13, 13a, 13b, 21a.
34. Earl W. Kintner, "The Federal Trade Commission and the Automotive Industry," speech delivered to the Southwestern Automotive Wholesalers Association, Kansas City, Mo., on Sept. 26, 1960; "The Role of Robinson-Patman in the Antitrust Scheme of Things—The Perspective of Enforcement Officials," speech delivered to the Section of Antitrust Law of the American Bar Association, Washington, D.C., on Aug. 30, 1960; "Pointers for Purchasers," statement to the meeting of Fifth District National Association of Purchasing Agents, Washington, D.C., on Oct. 14, 1960.
35. Schwegmann Bros. v. Calvert Distillers Corp., 341 U.S. 384.
36. *The New York Times*, Feb. 2, 1954. After describing the TNEC as a pageant, the piece continued: "This investigation was staged at great expense and amid enormous fanfare in an attempt to show that monopoly was the villain behind the business 'recession' of 1937-1938." Hammond Chaffetz described the Arnold era as having made more noise, but "I am not sure that there were any greater results [than during the Eisenhower era]." Hammond Chaffetz to author, Apr. 7, 1971.
37. David Lynch, *The Concentration of Economic Power* (New York, 1946), p. 356.
38. Corwin Edwards, "Thurman Arnold and the Antitrust Laws," *Political Science Quarterly*, 58 (Sept. 1943), 338.
39. Edwards, p. 339.
40. Oppenheim to author, Apr. 23, 1971.
41. Rexford G. Tugwell, *The Democratic Roosevelt: A Biography of Franklin D. Roosevelt* (Baltimore: Penguin, 1969), p. 563n.
42. House of Representatives Rep. #627. 63rd Cong., 2nd Sess.; series 6559 (1914).
43. Conference Ruling 1 FTC 541 (1916).
44. F.T.C. v. Western Meat Co., 272 U.S. 554 (1926).
45. Milton Handler, "Industrial Mergers and the Antitrust Laws," *Columbia Law Review*, 32 (1932), 179-180, 204.
46. U.S. Federal Trade Commission, *Annual Report* (Washington, D.C., 1927), pp. 13-15.
47. U.S. Temporary National Economic Committee. *Investigation of Concentration of Economic Power, Final Report and Recommendations* . . . (Washington, D.C., 1941), pp. 38-39.
48. William H. Orrick, Jr., "The Clayton Act: Then and Now," 24 *A.B.A. Antitrust Section* (April 16-17, 1964), 44-45. At this time, Orrick was the Assistant Attorney General in charge of the Antitrust Division.
49. *The New York Times*, June 8, 1948.
50. U.S. v. Columbia Steel Co., 334 U.S. 495 (1948).

51. House Rep. #1191, 81st Cong., 1st Sess., 11 (1949) (emphasis mine). H. Graham Morison, who became the Assistant Attorney General in charge of the Antitrust Division in January 1951, helped the Democrats Emanuel Celler and Estes Kefauver draft the bill to include the conglomerate merger within its scope. (Morison to author, July 15, 1971).
52. See below, Chapter V.
53. "Annual Report of Assistant Attorney General H. G. Morison Antitrust Division for fiscal year ending June 30, 1952," p. 222. Typed manuscript in U.S. Justice Department Library, Washington, D.C.
54. Stanley Barnes to author, May 7 and 14, 1971.
55. Porter and Johnson, p. 500.
56. Reprinted in the United States House of Representatives, 84th Cong., 1st Sess., Select Committee on Small Business, *Hearings Pursuant to House Resolution 114* (Washington, D.C., Oct. 31-Nov. 4, 1955), p. 319.
57. "Mr. Barnes Surprises Business," *America*, 93 (May 28, 1955), 228.
58. Robert Bicks to author, June 10, 1971.
59. 15 U.S.C. 1 (emphasis mine).
60. The Standard Oil Co., et al. v. U.S., 221 U.S. 1 (1911).
61. U.S. v. Joint Traffic Association, 171 U.S. 505 (1898).
62. Klor's v. Broadway-Hale Stores, 359 U.S. 207 (1959).
63. United States v. Paramount Pictures, Inc., 334 U.S. 131 (1948).
64. *A. G. Report*, 26; U.S. v. Consolidated Laundries Corp., 291 Fed. 2d. 563 (1961).

CHAPTER II

The Attorney General's National Committee to Study the Antitrust Laws

WHEN the Eisenhower Administration took office in early 1953, the climate of opinion was not favorable to antitrust. During the Depression, the government had experimented by first substituting the Blue Eagle of the NRA for much of the antitrust corpus; and then, when that failed, it tried a vigorous policy of trade regulation using the tools of the TNEC. Neither was successful in prodding the economy forward. With the advent of peace and the concomitant reorientation of national priorities after World War II, many people began to look at the antitrust laws very carefully. An accumulation of proposed amendments to the antitrust corpus awaited action in Congress.[1] Law and business journals presented articles on the subject, and even popular mass-culture periodicals treated the topic from every possible perspective. Perhaps the only point of agreement among all the authors was that the antitrust laws were not understandable and that something should be done.[2]

Of all the studies, the most important was the seminal contribution of S. Chesterfield Oppenheim entitled "Federal Antitrust Legislation: Guideposts to a Revised National Antitrust Policy."[3] A clarion call for a reexamination and reappraisal of American antitrust policy, the author began by enumerating the various antitrust statutes, and then he carefully noted that within the corpus there were "inconsistencies and compromises"; some of the provisions even "softening" the "hard" competition of other statutes.[4] Citing the unevenness of coverage, the debates over procedures, the overlapping responsibilities of the FTC and the Department of Justice, and the many questions about the relevance of the laws to the present situation, Professor Oppenheim noted that no attempt "has yet been made by the Congress to survey the entire field of antitrust law with a view toward comprehensive revision and coordination of these basic laws. Yet the wisdom and, indeed, the

17

irresistible necessity, of such fundamental inquiry into the question of where the country is heading in enforcing the antitrust laws, and what changes are needed in national antitrust policy, appears undeniable."[5] Therefore, the author proposed guideposts for just such an appraisal. The evaluation would be accomplished by a completely private body called the Committee on Revision of National Antitrust Policy.[6] It would be supported by grants from foundations.

It was in this context that on June 26, 1953, Eisenhower's Attorney General, Herbert Brownell, addressed the Judicial Conference of the Court of Appeals for the Fourth Circuit at White Sulphur Springs, West Virginia. His speech entitled "Our Antitrust Policy" was the first antitrust policy statement by the new administration, and it provided important indications of what would be its attitude on this question. Although many had felt that the 1952 Republican antitrust plank had been pure campaign rhetoric, Brownell endeavored to refute the charge by quoting the section and enunciating the broad outlines of coming actions: first, equality of enforcement; second, simplification of administration; third, assistance to those wishing to act within the law; fourth, "*an uncompromising determination* that there shall be no slackening of effort to protect free enterprise against monopoly and unfair competition; and . . . no winking at violations of the law and no wholesale dismissal of pending suits."[7] Brownell then proposed to establish "the Attorney General's National Committee to Study the Antitrust Laws" to determine "how the new administration might best answer the insistent public demand for review and clarification of the Federal Antitrust Laws and Policies . . . ."[8] While acknowledging that the areas of research were endless, the Attorney General did single out specific important topics which he felt needed consideration: first, the nature and measurement of monopoly, and how to distinguish market areas; second, the possible extension of or alternatives to the rule of reason and the *per se* rule; third, the action to be taken in regard to the Robinson-Patman Act; fourth, the overlapping jurisdiction of the Federal Trade Commission and the Department of Justice and how to deal with that overlap; fifth, the issue of patents and trademarks and their treatment in the antitrust laws; sixth, the exemptions to the antitrust corpus; seventh, the question of how to strengthen the laws. The proposed committee and its project had the total support of the President, to the extent that he requested all departments and agencies of the federal government to "give full cooperation to insure its [the committee's] success."[9]

The leadership of the committee was vital. Since it was to be a governmentally sponsored group, as opposed to the private one outlined in Oppenheim's influential article, Stanley Barnes, the Assistant Attorney General in charge of the Antitrust Division, was chosen to be one of the co-chairmen. Upon his shoulders fell the burden of persuading Oppenheim to be the other co-chairman.[10] On July 9, after a check by the Federal Bureau of Investigation, and less than two weeks after the Brownell speech, Oppenheim consented.[11]

With the question of leadership solved, the membership of the committee assumed paramount importance. In his White Sulphur Springs speech, Brownell had emphasized the need for the broadest possible viewpoint to be represented on the committee. With four exceptions— Barnes, head of the Antitrust Division: Edward Howrey, chairman of the Federal Trade Commission; Sinclair Weeks, Secretary of Commerce; and Wendell Barnes, an administrator in the Small Business Administration—there were no current governmental officials on the committee. This type of staffing was adopted because it was express administration policy that there be liaison with the various branches of government.[12] Eager to avoid political controversy and interested in seeing "to it that it[the report of the committee] was an executive product," no congressmen were included as members.[13]

Although the number of those involved in the antitrust field was far fewer in the early 1950s than it is today, there was still a large body of highly competent personnel from which Oppenheim could draw. Not only did the co-chairmen plan to include lawyers on the committee, they also intended to invite law professors, economists and counsel for business firms to be members.

The roster included men who had already served many years in diverse phases of national government.[14] Several had played roles in the NRA; a sizable number had served in the Department of Justice, and many even had experience in the Antitrust Division. With such backgrounds these individuals were expected to supplement the four government members.

The committee was not restricted to full-time lawyers. Several were academicians, and others both taught and practiced. The mix ranged from those professors who were counsel to a firm to those who were members of a firm and taught an occasional course.

Of equal luster was the array of economists on the committee. In keeping with the policy and chosen after lengthy conferences with Professor Alfred Kahn of Cornell University and A.D. Kaplan of The Brookings Institute, the economist members comprised a wide philosophical spectrum. Not only was ideological outlook important, but the various branches of the social sciences were also represented.

The largest group on the committee was comprised of important lawyers practicing in the field of antitrust. On the roster were both members of influential law firms and counsel for important companies. As most of the major companies had their headquarters in the northeastern megalopolitan area, it was not surprising that a large percentage of the personnel came from the same region. The committee was also supposed to be a national committee in geographic terms, and it was on this point that the Eisenhower

Administration made its only request—that the number of committeemen from the New York-Washington area be diminished while the number from the rest of the country be augmented.[15] According to the testimony of Stanley Barnes before Representative Patman's Select Committee on Small Business, the President "suggested no names."[16] Nevertheless there are communications which indicate that several on the White House staff did press for the appointment of specific people to the committee.[17] With the exception of Stephen P. Ladas, who was named as a "conferee" and not as a member, no White House-backed personnel were chosen.[18] It is interesting that Bob Ladd of Richard Nixon's office left a message for Oppenheim stating that "[Nixon] would appreciate it if you could give him [Robert Graham] extra special consideration."[19] Graham *was* appointed.

Not everyone who was asked to be a member of the committee accepted. Bernard Baruch declined membership because of the heavy load of his current duties, most of which, he emphasized, were of a public-service variety.[20] Former Justice of the Supreme Court, Owen Roberts, wrote to Oppenheim that he had been ordered by his doctors to reduce his work schedule. Dean Neil Jacoby of the University of California did not wish to be included since he was "about to undertake another Federal government service at the request of the President." Dean Donald K. David of the Harvard Law School refused because of "conflict of interest," and George Stocking, an eminent professor of economics wrote to Oppenheim that he needed the "time for research and writing." Later he explained that his research project treated antitrust problems and he preferred to deal with the subject unencumbered by association with the committee. He felt that his criticisms would be more effective from the "outside."[21]

At first glance, some notable absences from the membership list are obvious. The most blatant is that of Thurman Arnold. The man "who had helped put antitrust back on the map," according to Oppenheim, was at the time not only in less than optimum health but he was also an extremely busy partner in one of the preeminent Washington law firms, Arnold, Fortas and Porter. Although it is difficult to believe, there are no letters recommending Arnold in the committee files, and this absence of recommendations was cited as one reason for not including him. His views on the subject of antitrust, however, were already well known, and, in addition, there was the possibility of personality problems. Therefore, the co-chairmen decided to invite Wendell Berge, Arnold's successor as head of the Antitrust Division of the Justice Department. Since Berge and Arnold were like "Siamese twins" on the subject, Berge, who could better spare the time, became "the spokesman for the Arnold viewpoint."[22] The policy that not more than one person in a given firm appear on the roster of members eliminated Carl Newton, a brilliant partner in Donovan, Leisure, Newton, Lombard and Irvine, because Breck

McAllister, another partner, was already on the committee. Warren Berger, the future Chief Justice of the Supreme Court, appears to have ruled out Lee Loevinger, a future chief of the Antitrust Division, with the statement, "Loevinger has been a borderline left-winger all his life. I would have little confidence in his views on anything." "Personality problems" precluded the inclusion of John Caskey of Dwight, Royall, Harris, Kogel and Caskey, an outstanding New York and Washington, D.C., law firm.[23]

Upon the announcement of the composition of the committee, there were rumblings, mostly from Democrats, to the effect that the committee was "stacked."[24] Those who hurled this charge said that the membership of the group was very heavily weighted in favor of those who had opposed the antitrust laws. Scrutiny of the background of the membership appears to substantiate the charge that a considerable number had indeed represented defendants rather than plaintiffs in antitrust cases. But according to Baines it did not necessarily follow that a lawyer who had represented a defendant would let a client's interests influence his thinking on the committee.[25] In addition, the committee was formed when private treble damage suits were still in their infancy. Thus, to avoid a committee staffed with lawyers of whom more than 50 percent were defense attorneys, it would have been necessary to compose the membership with nonentities who had never been involved in antitrust suits at all.

Most of the adverse reaction to the staffing seems to have been political. Of the 33 responses to a questionnaire sent to the 45 living members of the committee, only one expressed any doubt in answer to the question, "Were all shades of opinion adequately represented?" Another questionnaire sent to the surviving officers and members of the nine committees of the Section of Antitrust Law of the American Bar Association in 1954 elicited a similar though not as unanimous reply. One would have expected that the latter group of respondents would have been more likely to object to the selection since they had not been chosen. Therefore, the large majority of positive answers appears to quash the charge of stacking the committee.

Ironically, Barnes was worried that since he had "been unable to ascertain the exact percentage of membership along political lines," it might be necessary to check them "so we don't appoint a committee predominantly democratic."[26] His fears appear to have been unfounded as the composition of the committee was closely balanced between Democrats and Republicans.

Members of the committee received no salary. They remained private citizens and were in no sense government employees; they did not even have to take the customary oath. The only monies available to them were for travel expenses and a small $12 per diem expense allowance for food and hotel room. Although travel expenses were covered, the cost of deluxe accommodations was only reimbursed if more spartan hotel facilities were already filled. In the final accounting, only the professors and a few lawyers were reimbursed, the others paid their expenses out of their own pocket or were recompensed by their law firms.[27] Despite the demands of committee work, all members had to remain employed. For some this entailed more of a burden than for others. For Oppenheim the task was monumental. In order to earn his salary from Michigan State University Law School, he had, by necessity, to teach his full complement of classes. Consequently, he taught on Fridays and Saturdays, and then traveled to Washington to fulfill his many duties as the committee's co-chairman.

After a great deal of consultation, the co-chairmen divided the membership into six work groups.[28]

I.   Legal and Economic Concepts of Competition and Monopoly
       George E. Hale, chairman
       Walter Adams
       Morris Adelman
       John M. Clark
       Clare Griffin
       Milton Handler
       Alfred Kahn
       Kenneth Kimble
       David Robinson
       Eugene Rostow
       Sumner Slichter
       Blackwell Smith
       John Paul Stevens
       George Stigler

II.   Foreign Commerce
       Charles Rugg, chairman
       Cyrus Anderson
       Wendell Berge
       Walter Derenberg
       Gilbert Montague
       Louis Schwartz
       David Searles
       Whitney N. Seymour (Sr.)
       Gerald Van Cise

III.   Patents
       Lawrence Wood, chairman
       Walter Derenberg
       George Frost
       Fred Fuller
       Richard McDermott

IV. Administration and Enforcement
    Breck McAllister, chairman
    Bruce Bromley
    Hammond Chaffetz
    Herbert Clark
    Robert Graham
    Edward Johnston
    Kenneth Kimble
    Francis Kirkham
    Bernard Segal
    Morrison Shafroth
    George Stigler
    Gerald Van Cise
    Curtis C. Williams, Jr.
V. Distribution
    Jack Levy, chairman
    Morris Adelman
    Cyrus Anderson
    H. Thomas Austern
    Cyrus Austin
    Thomas Daly
    Charles Dunn
    Parker McCollester
    James Rahl
    Albert Sawyer
    William Simon
VI. Exemptions
    John Paul Stevens, chairman
    Robert Graham
    Charles Gregory
    Clare Griffin
    Sherman Peer
    Sumner Slichter

The economists on the committee also formed a unit and were available for consultation with the work groups.[29] Those who were not assigned to any specific assemblage worked on smaller topics, such as mergers, or they offered advice when called upon to do so.[30] Like the committee itself, the work groups were for study; their aim was not to add to the already voluminous stores of statistical data or measure the economic effects of the antitrust applications to specific industries or companies. There were no hearings. No one on the committee had subpoena power, nor did the committee have a large research staff. The group, instead, was expected to build upon already existing research.[31]

To avoid the risk of compromising the various members, the composition of the work groups was not to be revealed to the public, or even to the entire committee. While there were certain leaks, it was actually only after some very vigorous questioning and the threat of a contempt citation by Texas Congressman Wright Patman, that part of the work-group membership lists became known.[32] The position of a specific member on a given topic, and whether or not to identify him with that opinion was left up to the individual member himself.

Also confidential was the composition of the work group's draft reports because they were simply tentative submissions for consideration by the entire committee. After the membership evaluated the draft reports, they were rewritten by Oppenheim and subsequently submitted again to the full committee.[33] Dissents could be registered within a specified period, and they could be either signed or anonymous. As there were 61 members on the committee, obviously the length of individual dissents had, by necessity, to be limited. By taking part in the committee work, a member signified that he had agreed to the rules.[34]

The group's findings appear to have been uninfluenced. Nowhere in the entire file is there a communication suggesting any pressure by the government. Rather the committee influenced the administration. The Attorney General, Herbert Brownell, stated that antitrust was "the most important and difficult problem" facing him and that he looked to the committee "for help and guidance."[35] Eisenhower also indicated the significance he attached to the findings when he urged the committee "to get going on it [the report]."[36] The administration followed the deliberations closely, and, to help avoid any outside pressure on the members of the committee, it made very diligent efforts to avoid any premature release of information.[37] Further illustrating the importance of the committee is the fact that the White House made it a policy not to support proposed changes in the antitrust corpus until after the publication of its report,[38] an advance summary of which the administration requested and received.[39] Thus the administration was able to reply on "expert advice."[40] Since it submitted or backed bills implementing many of the 86 proposals made by the committee, the influence of the group on the antitrust policy of the new administration is evident.

Because it advocated a stricter enforcement of the antitrust laws, and since most of the changes it recommended strengthened the corpus, the *Report of the Attorney General's National Committee to Study the Antitrust Laws*[41] was a smashing victory for antitrust. The most striking feature of the entire *Report* was its endorsement of the Sherman Act: "The Committee unanimously adheres to antitrust fundamentals with full vigor. Although many forces and other Government policies have materially promoted our creative American economy, we believe the antitrust laws remain one of the most important."[42] In the context of the multiphased attacks on antitrust and the campaign rhetoric questioning the Republican Party's devotion to the principle, the *Report's* vigorous reassertion of the fundamental antitrust philosophy was of major significance. Nevertheless, it would be incorrect to assume that the *Report* provides a blueprint for the future antitrust policies of the Eisenhower Administration. While the work supplies clues, it is not a key, especially in the field of mergers;[43] because with the passage of time and the accumulation of precedent the Antitrust Division was able to widen the scope of the coverage of the laws. By the end of Eisenhower's second term, the antitrusters were able to interdict corporate marriages which five years earlier few would have believed to have been within their grasp.

If there was one theme which can be said to run through the *Report*, it was the advocacy of the pragmatic "rule of reason" approach. Whether it was the first topic, Sections 1 and 2 of the Sherman Act, or the last subject, private antitrust suits, the *Report* espoused the determination of justice by the application of the rule of reason to each specific situation.

The *Report* comprised eight chapters, each treating an aspect of what were commonly considered to be basic antitrust issues.

1) A policy against "Undue Limitation on Competitive Conditions"
2) "Trade or Commerce *** with Foreign Nations"
3) Mergers
4) Antitrust Policy on Distribution
5) Patent Antitrust Problems
6) Exemptions from Antitrust Coverage
7) Economic Indicia of Competition and Monopoly
8) Antitrust Administration and Enforcement

Chapter 1[44] treated Sections 1 and 2 of the Sherman Act. When dealing with Section 1, agreements concerning prices or competition, there were few problems, and what the work essentially did was illuminate the various concepts. Turning to Section 2, the committee treated the important question of monopoly. It found that more important than mere size was the question of *relative* size. To ascertain that, it was necessary to discover what was the market, which the *Report* defined as the "area of effective competition within which the defendants . . . operate."[45] It is important to note that the *Report* did not set down a specific percentage guideline; it went so far as to emphasize that the mere possession of over 50 percent of a market did not prove monopoly. Needed was the proven intent to exercise the power. A monopoly was also legal if it had been achieved by superior technique.

Rather than making any suggestions which would result in vitiating the antitrust laws, Chapter 2 of the *Report* aimed instead at clarifying and improving the criteria for interpreting the existing statutory standards. Even in assaying foreign commerce, the rule of reason was much in evidence. Viewed as important were not only the government programs to expand trade but also those to protect the national security. Avoiding restraints of trade at home was essential, and thus the Webb-Pomerene Act, which had helped spur international cartels, was criticized but also credited with aiding small business in its efforts to gain a part of the export trade.

Perhaps the most important section of the whole work was the short chapter on mergers, Chapter 3, which was written mostly by Stanley Barnes.[46] His first point was that one clear object of the Congress in amending Section 7 was to strengthen prior limitations on mergers.[47] A second intent was to strike down some mergers beyond the reach of the Sherman Act.[48] The objective was to deal with mergers in their incipiency rather than to wait until the combinations had attained such effects as would justify a Sherman Act proceeding. Emphasizing that the Section 7 amendment, unlike the Sherman Act, required not findings of actual anti-competitive effects, but merely the reasonable probability of a substantial lessening of competition or tendency toward monopoly, the chapter set forth the meager precedents available and from those derived the essential legal tests. For acquisitions which involved noncompeting firms in related markets—known as vertical acquisitions—the legality might well turn on whether or not there was a reasonable probability that the corporate marriage would significantly restrict access to needed supplies or would notably limit the market. In short, would the merger foreclose a *substantial* share of the market? It is most conspicuous that the word "substantial" was not defined—in other words, there was no quantitative substantiality rule. Different market factors might be equally important in different cases in determining whether or not Section 7 had been violated in a vertical merger suit. Similarly, in treating the legality of horizontal integration, Barnes provided no simple formula. It "will always be necessary," he said, "to analyze the effect of the merger on relevant markets in sufficient detail . . . to permit a reasonable conclusion as to the probable economic effect."[49]

Sometimes very small mergers might be seen as illegal, while far larger ones could be viewed as beneficial by the Department of Justice and the Federal Trade Commission. A small acquisition might be attacked if it were interpreted as part of a series of acquisitions whose cumulative effect was an appreciable movement toward monopolistic power. Contrarily, however, a much larger acquisition might well be condoned by the government if it resulted in no dominance or if it aided a failing company.[50]

The last section of the chapter gave guidelines, some or all of which might be relevant in a merger case. Inquiring into the character of the acquiring and the acquired company would be necessary. Of obvious importance would be the size of both companies; this evaluation included calculation of their assets, sales and capacity. The products they sold and the location of their plants and the geographic parameters of their market would also be key factors. After a study of the companies and the relation of the products of each, it would then be possible to determine whether or not they belonged in the same market or how the market would be affected, especially if a horizontal merger were in question. Here, too, a picture of the market was a requirement. Of importance would be how many companies bought and sold in the market, and what was the share of each. What were the end uses of the products? How were the products sold? The question of ease of entry into the market was a factor whose salience could not be overestimated. This consideration subsequently would be one of the reasons for the government's objection to the Bethlehem-Youngstown Sheet and Tube merger (see Chapter 4).

A third question that had to be answered concerned the immediate competitive effects of the merger or acquisition. An obvious change was the size and structure of the newly integrated company, but a merger might have much broader ramifications. Even in a horizontal combination when a supplier was acquired, there were antitrust problems, for the market patterns usually were greatly altered. When it was a vertical merger and both companies operated in the same markets, the chapter emphasized that the effects on the other companies must be measured, and if they proved too great, then the corporate marriage would certainly be attacked.

Finally, the long-range competitive consequences of the acquisition had to be assessed. Here the inquiry had to treat the long-term effects for both buyers and sellers in the affected market. Did the acquisition stifle the incentive for improvement, new markets, lower prices and expansion? If the answer was positive, then the merger was likely to be seen as substantially lessening competition or tending toward monopoly and thus be assailed as illegal.[51]

Chapter 4 of the *Report* treated the problems of antitrust policy in the distributive area of the economy. Fair trade was subjected to the harshest possible treatment. With several members dissenting and Berge "reserving his position," the committee urged its repeal.[52] The *Report* then proceeded with a lengthy exegesis of the Robinson-Patman Act. While not urging the repeal of the Robinson-Patman Act, it specified numerous improvements which could be effected in order to make the bill comport "with overall antitrust policy."[53]

The section on patents, Chapter 5, emphasized that a patent was a legal monopoly which lasted for a specified period of time and which had the attributes of personal property. As such, a patent achieved its social and economic worth by its transferability as well as by its existence. Stressing that part of the philosophy sustaining the concept that a patent encouraged invention, the study group noted that punishment of a patent holder for "monopolization" was a "paradox." It concluded that to violate the Sherman

Act, a patentee had to abuse his grant.[54] In deciding what was abuse of a patent grant, the committee for the most part adopted the "rule of reason."

After having considered the major substantive antitrust problems, the study group next turned in Chapter 6 to antitrust exemptions for certain types of conduct by labor unions, agricultural cooperatives, and various regulated industries. Accepting that the "policy of the United States" is to encourage collective bargaining and to protect the right of workers to organize "for the purpose of negotiating terms and conditions of their employment," the study treated only those union activities not directed at such established ends; thus it aimed at restraints on competition. Agreeing unanimously, the committee went on record that union actions directed at fixing "the kind or amount of products which may be used, produced or sold, their market price, the geographical area in which they may be used, produced or sold, or the number of firms which may engage in their production or distribution are contrary to antitrust policy."[55] It stressed the need for new laws on the subject. Regarding regulated industries, the group concurred that unless Congress had otherwise so specified, the philosophy of the antitrust laws should be maintained and upheld. Although they did not suggest a more activist role for the antitrusters, the Antitrust Division did expand its power in the field during the Eisenhower administration.

Chapter 7, entitled "Economic Indicia of Competition and Monopoly," was written from an economic and not a legal perspective. The economists on the committee composed a section that defined and described the various shades of competition, and the concepts of market and monopoly. As the work of some of the leading economic thinkers of the period, the chapter is still of great value today, to both lawyers and economists.

In the final chapter, in delineating the mechanism of antitrust enforcement, the *Report* made several major recommendations. Perhaps the most important was that of "civil investigative demand." Recognizing that the Justice Department was handicapped in a civil investigation because it could not compel production of evidence, the group proposed the civil investigative demand which compelled the defendant to supply relevant documents. Essentially conservative, the scheme contained numerous safeguards. First, the demand had to emanate from the Attorney General, and it had to describe the requisite documents with "reasonable specificity" so as to identify the demanded material. In order to insure secrecy, the committee suggested that the Justice Department create an Office of Custodian of Documents. The court should have the power to modify or set aside the "demand" should it not conform to the bounds of the projected statue. As proposed it would cover all corporations, partnerships or associations subject to the jurisdiction of the United States. The committee also recommended that the maximum fine for a criminal violation of the Sherman Act be raised from $5,000 to $10,000, thus keeping the penalty in line with the shrinking value of the dollar. But the *Report* also correctly noted that the possibility of subsequent treble damage suits was really more important than the level of governmental fines.

The chapter also considered the negotiated settlement. The committee approved of the consent decree, suggesting that sometimes the government had asked too much in consent decree negotiations, thus forcing a lengthy and costly trial. Recommending several procedural mechanisms to stimulate negotiated settlements,[56] it emphasized that the job of the Division was efficient enforcement. The *Report* also considered the Antitrust Division's clearance procedure designed to halt violations before they occurred. It noted with approval that although the Department of Justice had been granted no authority to give advisory opinions, under the so-called *railroad release* program, it could bind itself not to resort to a criminal action under certain conditions.[57] In the area of mergers, it asserted that both the Department and the FTC had a procedure for giving a type of clearance. The committee also recognized the value of off-the-record discussions between counsel for the Department of Justice and private parties; however, it did not advocate any change in the existing procedures.

There were ground rules for dissent. Each member of a work group had many opportunities to persuade his colleagues to adopt his line of reasoning—in the work group meetings when the group's report was formulated and also at the two general meetings of the full committee. If still unsuccessful, a member had the right to write a dissent. Although it had originally been planned that dissents be anonymous in order to protect the impersonality of the document, the practice was changed so that a member could decide for himself whether or not to instruct the co-chairmen to identify the author of the dissent. If more than one member disagreed on the same point, then one of the co-chairmen, after consultation with the objectors, would either ask them to formulate a common statement expressing their recusancy, or he would draft a proposed statement, giving each a chance to approve it. Each of the dissents was to be printed in the final report and they would appear in the chapter dealing with the topic. There was a gentleman's agreement concerning the length of the protestations—they had to be brief. Oppenheim emphasized that after the *Report* was published, each dissenter could and should write a law-review article explaining the rationale for any difference of opinion. Finally, there was a deadline for the submission of dissents.[58]

Only two members took exception to the ground rules, Professors Eugene Rostow and Louis B. Schwartz. Rostow asked that his partial dissent to the *Report* as a whole be included *in toto* at the end of the document. While his request was not heeded, he came to believe that the dissents were handled correctly.[59] On the other hand, Schwartz wrote a letter dated March 9, 1955 (received on March 13), to Oppenheim, stating that he was writing a long dissent which would not be ready until the last minute. When the piece was delivered, it was so messy that it could not be photocopied; it was necessary to retype it before distribution to all the other members. Their reaction was almost immediate. Stanley Barnes at once telephoned Oppenheim, complaining that Schwartz had "abused the right of dissent." Several agreed with Griffin that if everyone on the committee were to have written such a diatribe, there would have been at least 2000 pages of commentary. In asking for a space limitation on dissents, he humorously added that on this subject, too, "the 'rule of reason' must be applied!" Frost suggested that "if Mr. Schwartz is entitled to about 30 printed pages, the rest of us are, too." Others were willing to let the work be included if they could write a "dissent from the dissent," but the co-chairmen ruled that since the deadline for dissents had passed, they could not be accepted.[60] Therefore, one member answered the Schwartz apostasy in *The Antitrust Bulletin*.[61]

According to the regulations, the Schwartz disagreement was split into parts and included with the pertinent sections of the *Report*. Where his dissent paralleled those of others, it was synthesized with them. This led to his charges of dismemberment, condensation and distribution throughout the report.[62]

In order that his dissent could appear in full, Schwartz printed his statement privately and then distributed it himself. The possibility of gaining publicity might have influenced him into taking this course of action, for, as a well-known professor, he could have been reasonably certain that his work would have been published by any one of the leading law reviews. Indeed, despite the private printing, *The Antitrust Bulletin* published it,[63] the Celler Committee included it in the transcript of its hearings, and the Patman Committee did likewise.[64] Federal Legal Publications, one of the largest publishers of legal works, included an advertisement for The Schwartz Dissent in its periodical, *The Antitrust Bulletin*. According to the notice, Schwartz's work had been printed so it could be bound "with your copy of the *Report of the Attorney General's National Committee to Study the Antitrust Laws*."[65]

Although there is conflicting evidence concerning the exact cost of the entire project, each of the final stated figures is less than $80,000.[66] Of that amount, $19,000 was spent on printing the *Report*, but that was entirely recouped because the book sold so well. The committee was allowed to borrow stenographic services from other departments of the Antitrust Division.[67] Those sections continued to pay the stenographers' salaries. Robert Bicks, the executive secretary of the operation, was placed on the Justice Department payroll as Special Assistant to the Assistant Attorney General in charge of the Antitrust Division, Stanley Barnes, a position he would keep after the publication of the *Report*. The salaries of Bicks and the secretarial help amounted to $28,000.[68] The government received a bargain, for it is more than likely that had it had to purchase the services of the committee, it would have had to pay at least $80,000 per person. The extent of the bargain received is all the more evident when the cost of the committee is compared to the nearly three-quarters of a million dollars spent by Congress to investigate the committee.[69]

In some circles there was strong opposition to the Attorney General's Committee to Study the Antitrust Laws even before the group had presented its report. It is perhaps significant, however, that there was little written in the way of conjecture regarding what would emanate from the committee. Interest in the subject of antitrust was not lacking; it was just that most of the popular magazines preferred to analyze what was occurring at the Antitrust Division of the Justice Department.[70]

After the publication of the *Report*, there was much more reaction. Despite partisan fears, the *Report* was a victory for antitrust belief. The central theme of the whole work was a unanimous reaffirmation of the philosophy of antitrust.[71] One commentator said: "Whether one agrees with the majority in its recommendations to strengthen the antitrust laws, or with a few dissenters that the Report weakens the antitrust laws, it is nevertheless true that the Report does not substantially alter the basic antitrust policy. Several recommendations for legislative action are made, but they are mostly peripheral and are not directed at the fundamentals."[72] Politics dictated that the *Report* be attacked from every possible angle, but there really was not that much to condemn.[73]

Almost immediately following publication of the *Report*, various congressional committees decided to investigate it. The Sub-committee on Antitrust and Monopoly of the Senate Committee on the Judiciary was the first to make an examination. On May 3, 1955, its first witness was the Assistant Attorney General in charge of the Antitrust Division, and former co-chairman of the study group, Stanley Barnes.

The chairman of the committee and also of the subcommittee, Democratic Senator Harley Kilgore of West Virginia, courteously questioned him concerning the *Report*.[74] Much of Barnes' testimony was an explication of the proposals of the study group. Only on the topic of dissents did the inquiry appear to become a little stiffer. Before it had finished collecting testimony on the subject, the Kilgore Committee would also hear from 11 other members or conferees of the study group.[75]

Almost concurrently, the Antitrust Subcommittee of the Committee on the Judiciary of the House of Representatives held hearings. Under the chairmanship of Emanuel Celler, the committee heard testimony from a large number of witnesses including nine members of the study group.[76] The attitude toward the co-chairman of the study group was very cordial and began with Representative Celler, the chairman of the committee, going on record with the statement, "I have a very high respect for your abilities."[77] Oppenheim was questioned vigorously on the subject of dissents, especially the Schwartz one, and, although Chairman Celler held the co-chairman in high esteem, it was evident that the congressman sympathized with the Schwartz stance.[78]

Since the *Report* had not been favorably disposed toward the Robinson-Patman Act, it was inevitable that Representative Patman would seek to discredit the work. As chairman of the Select Committee on Small Business of the House of Representatives, he held a series of hearings pursuant to a House resolution creating a committee to study and investigate the problems of small business.

On the second day of the hearings, Oppenheim was invited to testify. After the normal introductory questions and eight other queries, Chairman Patman asked about the work groups. As soon as mention was made of the group that had treated the topic of distribution, Patman demanded to know its composition. In accordance with his agreement with co-chairman Barnes and his promise to the other members, Oppenheim "respectfully" declined to answer the question. After hearing his refusal described as "fascist" and "totalitarian," he was told that if he did not name the members, the committee would "take action."[79] The following day, after a recess, he was again questioned relentlessly about the make-up of the work groups, especially the distribution section. This time, under threat of a contempt citation, he supplied the Patman Committee with the membership list of various work groups. Although it was not complete, it was the most comprehensive one available to the public until this publication.[80]

In the process of deciding on the personnel of the study group, Oppenheim and Barnes had solicited suggestions for prospective members. Countless people were recommended, but only Col. Harry Aubrey Toulmin, Jr., had "volunteered." An ex-Army friend of Eisenhower, he zealously pressed his case, having innumerable people write letters to the President and the Attorney General as well as to Barnes and Oppenheim.[81] After he had discovered that he was not going to be a member of that select group, he set out to disparage it by releasing a statement that it was stacked with corporation lawyers. When the *Report* was published, he attacked it in an extraordinary statement to the Patman Committee.[82] The only person who included an autobiographical summary, Toulmin made a great effort to impress upon the representatives his knowledge of antitrust, claiming that he had written an authoritative seven-volume work on the subject. To be sure, he had done so, but the work was cited infrequently by other writers. In addition, he was not popular with his peers, for when a rumor circulated that he would be appointed Commissioner of Patents, it "caused consternation among patent attorneys."[83]

The *Report* of the committee was also the subject of scholarly symposia, many of which were fully covered in law reviews[84] and individual articles.[85] While these were slightly more negative toward the *Report* than most other commentaries, many of the faults cited in the reviews can be attributed to the proclivity of these authors to lament, "he didn't do it the way I would have done it."

One of the oft-repeated criticisms of the *Report* was that it made very few recommendations and that most of the suggestions it did make had the effect of watering down the antitrust laws. There were actually two different types of advice from the study group. First, there was what could be described as "general guides"; these were proposed for the benefit of various enforcement agencies and courts. Careful scrutiny of the *Report* yields 74 suggestions. While many of the items advocated do not lend themselves to classification, the number of recommendations intended to strengthen the antitrust corpus outnumbers by more than 3 to 1 those which might weaken it. The committee also proposed 12 statutory changes. In five instances, the *Report* recommends legislative changes that would fortify antitrust statutes, while in three instances it suggests alterations that might weaken the laws. On closer inspection, however, the record is weighted heavily in favor of strong antitrust enforcement. Two of its recommendations, while cited often as debilitating, actually were not. The suggestion to double the Sherman Act fine from $5,000 to $10,000 might have been viewed as a positive recommendation had Congress not already set the machinery in motion to raise the penalty to $50,000. Secondly, the proposed amendment to Section 5 of the FTC Act, repealing the $5,000 per day ceiling on fines for violating orders and substituting instead one of $5,000 per violation was not an appreciable dilution of the law since the impost had never been levied.

The principal task of the Attorney General's National Committee to Study the Antitrust Laws was "to analyze the main course of . . . antitrust policy, its interpretation, and decisions. From this analysis, an evaluation of antitrust developments is made in light of established antitrust goals."[86] The value of the *Report* has been fully recognized by the Antitrust Section of the American Bar Association (ABA). In 1968, it endeavored to bring the *Report* up to date, and, with the help of a much larger but less illustrious staff, produced another volume, *Antitrust Developments 1955-1968: A Supplement to the Report of the Attorney General's National Committee to Study Antitrust Laws, March 31, 1955* (Chicago, 1968). The Antitrust Section planned to keep this work up to date; and it did so with its first addenda, *Antitrust Developments: 1968-1970*. In 1975, it published a full-scale update.[87]

In both the 1955-1968 supplement and subsequent addenda, the outline of the Attorney General's *Report* has generally been followed. A minor deviation resulted from the fact that extra space was allotted to merger and private damage litigations. The authors emphasized that since 1955 when the original *Report* was published, these two types of litigation experienced gigantic growth, and thus more precedents had to be included.

Of perhaps even greater importance than the reaction of the ABA was the attitude of the individual antitrust lawyer. When the conferees and members of the Attorney General's Committee, and the members of the various committees of the Antitrust Section of the ABA for the years 1954 and 1968 were asked, "Should another study be started now?" about half of those who replied in the negative emphasized that another study would only duplicate the work of the Antitrust Section. Charles B. Wallace, a Democrat from Dallas, Texas, opposed the formation of another study group for another reason:

It is not likely that such talent could now be assembled, it is not likely that the amount of agreement could now be obtained, and it is not likely that the quality of the report could be as good.[88]

The business community, as represented by the National Association of Manufacturers, found the study useful, stating that "while the quest for certainty in the antitrust laws is not ended by the filing of the Committee's Report . . . a contribution to that end . . . [has] been made."[89] Internationally, too, it is still important. As late as 1970, the Spanish Ministry of Commerce requested copies of the work.[90]

Even more significant are the countless legal opinions in which the *Report* has been cited. The members of the Antitrust Division still regard it as a valuable reference work. Additionally, the document is required reading for all new lawyers in the Division;[91] even the top men keep it within easy reach.

ROSTER OF THE COMMITTEE

Name	1953 Position	Home	Other Qualifications
Walter Adams	Professor of Economics, Univ. of Michigan	E. Lansing, Mich.	Author, numerous articles.
Morris A. Adelman	Professor of Economics, Massachusetts Inst. of Technology	Cambridge, Mass.	Author, numerous articles.
Cyrus Anderson	Asst. Counsel: Pittsburgh Plate Glass Co.	Pittsburgh, Penna.	Leader in field of antitrust compliance, Antitrust Division Authority on Clayton Act.
Douglas Arant	Partner: White, Bradley, Arant, All & Rose	Birmingham, Ala.	Chief counsel for Petroleum Admin. Ed. (NRA) Member, Regional Labor Bd. (NRA) also other labor boards.
H. Thomas Austern	Member: Covington & Burling	Washington, D.C.	Chairman, Trade Assoc. Committee of Antitrust Section of ABA Author, numerous articles.
Cyrus Austin	Partner: Appell, Austin & Gay	New York, N.Y.	Author of authoritative book on Robinson-Patman Act.
Wendell Barnes	Administrator: Small Business Administration	Washington, D.C.	General Counsel for Small Bus. Admin. (1946-53) Special Attorney Oklahoma Tax Commission (1935-39).
Wendell Berge	Partner: Berge, Fox & Arent	Washington, D.C.	Special Assistant to Attorney General (1930-35) Chief of Appellate Section, Antitrust Div., (1935-37) First Asst. to Asst. Attorney General in charge of Antitrust Division (1937-40) Asst. Attorney General in charge of Antitrust Div. (1943-47) Alternate member, TNEC.

Name	1953 Position	Home	Other Qualifications
Bruce Bromley	Partner: Cravath, Swaine & Moore	New York, N.Y.	Associate Judge N.Y. State Court of Appeals (1949). Author, numerous articles. Authority on international restrictive business practices.
Hammond Chaffetz	Member: Kirkland, Fleming, Green, Martin & Ellis	Chicago, Ill.	Staff, Antitrust Div. of the Dept. of Justice (1930-38). Chairman, Clayton Act Committee of Antitrust Section of ABA.
Herbert W. Clark	Partner: Morison, Rohfeld, Foerster & Clark	San Francisco, Cal.	Special Asst. to U.S. Attorney General (1927-28). Chairman, Committee of Bar Examiners of California (1941-42).
John Maurice Clark	Retired	Westport, Conn.	Member of Council, Antitrust Section of ABA. Consultant, NRA (1934-35). Honorary President, International Economic Assn. Member, OPA and predecessor agency (1940-43). Author, 9 books.
Thomas F. Daly	Member: Lord, Day & Lord	New York, N.Y.	Authority on Sherman Act.
John W. Davis	Partner: Davis, Polk, Wardwell, Sunderland & Kiendle	New York, N.Y.	Ambassador to Great Britain (1918-21). Democratic candidate for President, 1924. President, American Bar Assn.
Walter J. Derenberg	Partner: Alexander, Maltitz, Derenberg & Daniels	New York, N.Y.	Authority in field of industrial property. Professor, New York University.
Raymond Dickey	Partner: Danzanski & Dickey	Washington, D.C.	Expert, Antitrust Division of Department of Justice (1938-40). Counsel, Senate Small Business Comm. (1947-49).
Charles W. Dunn	Retired	New York, N.Y.	Professor of Law, New York University. Counsel to various food and pharmaceutical groups. President, ABA. Author, numerous books.

George E. Frost	Associate: Bair, Freeman & Molinare	Chicago, Ill.	Author, numerous articles on trademarks and patents. General Counsel, Owens Illinois Glass
Fred E. Fuller	Partner: Fuller, Harrington, Seney & Henry	Toledo, Ohio	General Counsel, Glass Container Manufacturers Institute. Author, numerous articles.
Robert W. Graham	Member: Bogle, Bogle & Gates	Seattle, Wash.	Long experience in field, and recommended by Federal District Court Judge.
Clinton S. Golden	Retired labor official. Lecturer: Harvard Univ. Graduate School of Business Administration	Solebury, Penna.	Regional Director, NLRB (1935-36) Regional Director, SWOC (1936-42) Vice-President, United Steelworkers (1942-46) Labor advisor to Pres. Truman.
Charles O. Gregory	Professor: Univ. of Virginia Law School	Charlottesville, Va.	Private law practice. Author, numerous articles especially in field of labor law.
Ewald T. Grether	Dean: School of Business Administration, Univ. of California (Berkeley)	Berkeley, Cal.	Consultant to NRA (1935-36) Chairman, various California governors' study groups. Director of Econ. Mgt., Natl. Security Resources Board (1948-49) Author, numerous articles.
Clare Griffin	Professor: School of Business Administration, Univ. of Michigan	Ann Arbor, Mich.	Consultant to cement and meat industry trade organizations. Economist who had given special attention to antitrust.
Milton Handler	Counsel: Kaye, Scholer, Fierman & Hays	New York, N.Y.	Author, *TNEC Monograph 38 Cases and Materials on Trade Regulation*. General Counsel, NLRB (1933-34) Professor of Law, Columbia University. Author, numerous articles.

Name	1953 Position	Home	Other Qualifications
George E. Hale	Member: Wilson & McIlvaine	Chicago, Ill.	Author, numerous articles.
Edward F. Howrey	Chairman: Federal Trade Commission	Washington, D.C.	Lawyer, Department of Justice (1927-29) Author, numerous articles.
Edward R. Johnston	Partner: Johnston, Thompson, Raymond & Mayer	Chicago, Ill.	First chairman of Antitrust Section of ABA (1952-53) One of the earliest practitioners in the field of antitrust Author, numerous articles.
Alfred Kahn	Professor: Dept. of Economics, Cornell Univ.	Ithaca, N.Y.	Antitrust Div. of Department of Justice (1941-42) Author, numerous articles.
A. Stewart Kerr	Member: Crawford, Sweeny & Dodd	Detroit, Mich.	Lecturer on law, Walsh Institute of Accounting
Kenneth Kimble	Member: McFarland & Sellers	Washington, D.C.	Special Attorney, Antitrust Div. (1934-39) Special Asst. to Attorney General of United States (1939-48) First Asst. Antitrust Div. of Department of Justice (1945-47).
Francis R. Kirkham	Member: Pillsbury, Madison & Sutro	San Francisco, Cal.	Extensive antitrust practice Practice and procedure authority.
George P. Lamb	Partner: Kittelle & Lamb	Washington, D.C.	Authority on trade association law.
Jack I. Levy	Member: Sonnenschein, Berkson, Lautmann, Levinson & Morse	Chicago, Ill.	Corporation executive Active in field Author, numerous articles.
Mason A. Lewis	Partner: Lewis, Grant, Newton, Davis & Henry	Denver, Colo.	Admitted to bar 1910.
Benjamin Long	Member: Dykema, Jones & Wheat	Detroit, Mich.	Member: War Dept. Board of Contract Appeals (1944-46).

Breck P. McAllister	Member: Donovan, Leisure, Newton & Irvine	New York, N.Y.	Special Asst. to Attorney General (1927-29) Member of faculty of Univ. of Washington, Univ. of North Carolina, Yale University, and Univ. of California Author, numerous articles.
Parker McCollester	Member: Lord, Day & Lord (retired)	New York, N.Y.	Practiced law with Louis Brandeis (1914-16) Chief, U.S. Economic mission to France (1944) Author, numerous articles.
Richard B. McDermott	Partner: Williams, Boesche & McDermott	Tulsa, Okla.	A successful plaintiff in major private antitrust case Authority on patent antitrust Author, numerous articles.
Gilbert Montague	Retired	New York, N.Y.	Special examiner for U.S. Government (1908-10) in antitrust suits NRA Advisor to Natl. Assn. of Manufacturers on antitrust Author, numerous articles.
Sherman Peer	Professor of Law, Cornell Univ.	Ludlowville, N.Y.	Private law practice President: Tompkins County Bar Assn. Counsel to GLF (1934- 47) Provost of Cornell University.
James A. Rahl	Professor: School of Law, Northwestern Univ.	Chicago, Ill.	Private law practice Author, numerous articles Contributor to symposia.
David W. Robinson	Partner: Robinson, Robinson & Dreher	Columbia, S.C.	General counsel: Federal Power Commission (1939- 40).
Eugene Rostow	Professor: School of Law, Yale Univ.	New Haven, Conn.	Background in economics Author, numerous articles.

Name	1953 Position	Home	Other Qualifications
Charles B. Rugg	Partner: Ropes, Gray, Best Coolidge & Rugg	Boston, Mass.	Admitted to bar 1914.
Albert Sawyer	Office at 56 Beaver Street	New York, N.Y.	Active in FTC aspects of antitrust Author, articles on accounting.
Louis B. Schwartz	Professor: Univ. of Pennsylvania Law School	Philadelphia, Penna.	Professor of Law Author, numerous articles.
David T. Searls	Partner: Vinson, Elkins, Weems & Searls	Houston, Tex.	Chairman, Antitrust Section of ABA (1953-54).
Bernard Segal	Partner: Schnader, Harrison, Segal & Lewis	Philadelphia, Penna.	Authority on Sherman Act Deputy Attorney General of Pennsylvania (1933-35) Chancellor, Philadelphia Bar Assn. (1952-53). Author, numerous articles.
Herman Selvin	Member: Loeb & Loeb	Los Angeles, Cal.	Member: Council, Antitrust Section of ABA.
Whitney North Seymour, Sr.	Member: Simpson, Thacher & Bartlett	New York, N.Y.	Authority on antitrust problems in international trade.
Morrison Shafroth	Partner: Grant, Shafroth & Toll	Denver, Colo.	Professor of law Active in Antitrust Section of ABA Chief Counsel: Bureau of Internal Revenue (1936-37).
William Simon	General Counsel: Advisory Committee on Foreign Trade to Senate Banking & Currency Committee	Washington, D.C.	General Counsel, Trade Policies Subcommittee, Senate Interstate & Foreign Commerce Committee (1948- 49). General Counsel, Petroleum Admin. for Defense (1952-53). Chairman, Antitrust Section of ABA (1954-55).

Sumner Slichter	Professor of Economics, Harvard Univ.	Cambridge, Mass.	Brookings Institute staff (1925-30) Chairman, Advisory Council on Social Security to Senate (1947-48) Author, numerous articles.
Blackwell Smith	Partner: Smith, Sargent, Doman, Hoffman & Grant	New York N.Y.	General Counsel and Member of National Industrial Recovery Board (1934-35) Professor, New York University Wrote Antitrust Report for Business Advisory Council of the Dept. of Commerce Author, numerous articles.
John Paul Stevens	Partner: Rothchild, Stevens & Barry	Chicago, Ill.	Counsel: Subcommittee to study Monopoly Power House Committee on Judiciary 1951 Lecturer on antitrust law, Northwestern Law School (1953) Author, numerous articles.
George Stigler	National Bureau of Economic Research	New York, N.Y.	Author, numerous articles.
Jerrold G. Van Cise	Member: Cahill, Gordon, Reindel & Ohl	New York, N.Y.	Chairman, Information and Education Committee of Antitrust Section of ABA Author, numerous articles.
Sinclair Weeks	Secretary of Commerce	Washington, D.C.	Manufacturer; of Hornblower and Weeks.
Curtis Williams, Jr.	Member: Jones, Day, Cockley Cockley & Reavis	Cleveland, Ohio	Chairman, FTC Committee of Antitrust Section of ABA.
Lawrence I. Wood	Counsel: General Electric Co.	New York, N.Y.	Chairman, Committee on the Sherman Act of the Antitrust Section of ABA Author, numerous articles.

Clinton Golden and Mason Lewis did not participate in the committee deliberations and therefore did not sign the *Report*.
John W. Davis and Parker McCollester died before the composition of the final draft.

The Attorney General's National Committee
to Study the Antitrust Laws

1. Sawyer
2. Handler
3. Barnes (Stanley)
4. Bicks
5. Oppenheim
6. Unidentified
7. Daly
8. Fuller
9. Dickey
10. Levy
11. Unidentified
12. Barnes (Wendell)
13. Lamb
14. Adelman
15. Wood
16. Graham
17. Howrey
18. Kerr
19. Unidentified
20. Anderson
21. Adams
22. Montague
23. Frost
24. McDermott
25. Rowe (a conferee)
26. Chaffetz

27. Kimball
28. Stevens
29. Austern
30. Unidentified
31. Kahn
32. John Kilcullen
33. Grether
34. Hale
35. Rostow
36. Searles
37. van Cise
38. Kintner
39. Frost
40. Simon
41. David Murchison
42. Johnson
43. Schwartz
44. Williams
45. McAllister
46. Clark
37. Derenberg
48. Kirkham
49. Unidentified
50. Arant
51. Dunn
52. Smith

NOTES

1. Herbert Brownell to author, April 11, 1974.
2. Benjamin Wham, "The Growth of Antitrust Law: A Revision Is Long Overdue," *American Bar Association Journal,* 38 (Nov. 1952), 934-935; H. Graham Morrison, "Is the Sherman Act Outdated?" *Journal of Public Law,* 1 (Fall 1952), 323-334; John McDonald, "Businessmen and the Sherman Act," *Fortune,* 41 (Jan. 1950), 104-114. See also the five-part series by David Lilienthal in *Collier's Weekly,* 129 (May 31-June 28, 1952); John McDonald, "Businessmen and the Sherman Act," *Fortune,* 41 (Jan. 1950), 104-114; unsigned section of *Fortune* Perspective, "A Note to Mr. Brownell," *Fortune,* 51 (Feb. 1953), 107-108. Stanley N. Barnes, "Background and Report of the Attorney General's Committee," *University of Pennsylvania Law Review,* 104 (Nov. 1955), 147.
3. *Michigan Law Review,* 50 (June 1951), 1139-1244. Hereafter cited as Oppenheim, "Guideposts."
4. Oppenheim, "Guideposts," p. 1114.
5. Oppenheim, "Guideposts," p. 1142.
6. Oppenheim, "Guideposts," p. 1143.
7. Herbert Brownell, "Our Antitrust Policy" (June 26, 1953). The papers of the Attorney General's National Committee to Study the Antitrust Laws are part of the Records of the Antitrust Division of the Dept. of Justice housed in the Federal Records Center, Suitland, Md. They are Acc. #70A4771 (unless otherwise designated), file 60-414-0. Dept. of Justice Papers will be cited as "Antitrust Papers: Topic or Subject." A copy of the Brownell speech is included in Antitrust Papers: Attorney General's National Committee to Study the Antitrust Laws (AGNC), sec. 123, "Antitrust Investigations," and another is in sec. 172, "Committee History and Operations."
8. Brownell to Oppenheim, July 2, 1953, Antitrust Papers: AGNC, section 432, "Antitrust Committee: General #1."
9. Brownell, "Our Antitrust Policy," and quoted in *A. G. Report,* p. iv.
10. Stanley Barnes to author, May 7, 1971.
11. J. Edgar Hoover to Barnes (May 30, 1953), Antitrust Papers: AGNC, sect. 431 (no title). The date of the memo is significant for it emphasizes that the study was one of the first items on the new administration's list of priorities. U.S. House, Select Committee on Small Business, 84th Cong., 1st Sess. *Price Discrimination: The Robinson-Patman Act and Related Matters: Hearings* . . . (Washington, D.C., 1955), p. 808. (Hereafter cited as *Patman Committee Hearings.*)
12. S. Chesterfield Oppenheim to author (Apr. 23, 1971); also S. Chesterfield Oppenheim, "The Organization of the Attorney General's National Committee to Study the Antitrust Laws," 3 *A.B.A. Antitrust Section* (Aug. 26-27, 1953), 24.
13. Brownell to author, Apr. 11, 1974.
14. See chart at end of chapter.
15. Oppenheim to author, Apr. 23, 1971.
16. *Patman Committee Hearings,* pp. 810-812.
17. Eisenhower Papers (Abilene, Kansas), General File 15-M-1, Box 285, "Endorsements, Members"; see also Antitrust Papers: AGNC, sect. 431, "Correspondence #2: Antitrust Committee."

18. Antitrust Papers: AGNC, sec. 19, "Advisory Committee: Suggestions for membership" and sec. 313, "Foreign Commerce Group: AG's Committee."

19. Memo dated Aug. 7, 1953, Antitrust Papers: AGNC, sec. 431, "Correspondence #2: Antitrust Committee."

20. Oppenheim to author, Apr. 23, 1971.

21. Neil Jacoby to author, Feb. 11, 1974. Papers of Neil Jacoby 1952-1963, "National Highway System," Box 3; "Antitrust," letter declining dated Aug. 26, 1953. Other letters in Antitrust Papers: AGNC, sec. 25, "Refusal or Undecideds"; letter from George Stocking to Wright Patman dated Jan. 3, 1955, reprinted in *Patman Committee Hearings*, p. 1169.

22. Oppenheim to author, Apr. 23, 1971; memo, "Those not named," Antitrust Papers. AGNC, sec. 416, "Misc. A G Rep."

23. Memo, "Those Not Named," Antitrust Papers: AGNC, sec. 416, "Misc A G Rep, also sec. 19, "Advisory Committee, Suggestions for membership (file 1)."

24. Stephen J. Spingarn to author (Apr. 22, 1971). Mr. Spingarn had been a member of the FTC from Oct. 25, 1950, to Sept. 25, 1953. During the illnesses of Chairman James Mead, he had been Acting Head.

25. While Stanley Barnes acknowledged that a client's interest could play a small part in determining a lawyer's attitude, he emphasized that social and political affiliations also might be determinant factors "Background and Report of the Attorney General's Committee," *University of Pennsylvania Law Review*, 104 (Nov. 1955), 149.

26. Barnes to Brownell, Aug. 14, 1953; Antitrust Papers: AGNC, sect. 416, "Misc. A G Rep"

27. Oppenheim to author, Apr. 23, 1971; Antitrust Papers: AGNC, sect. 56, "Travel"; sect. 331, "Herbert W. Clark: AG Comm. Member"; sect. 332, "Robert Graham."

28. The lists cited below are culled from the individual files of the various members; also, Antitrust Papers: AGNC, sec. 141 "Foreign Commerce Group;" sec. 134, "Corrsp."; sec. 431, "Corresp. II AG Committee"; sec. 456, "Misc AG Rep."

29. Antitrust Papers: AGNC, sec. 210, "Economic Committee."

30. The co-chairmen also added 14 others to the committee and thus to the work groups. Designated as "conferees," they were younger and slightly less well known. One conferee, Frederick Rowe, was building a reputation in the field of the Robinson-Patman Act and by the end of the decade was universally regarded as one of the nation's leading authorities on the subject. Another, Donald F. Turner, later became the head of the Antitrust Division of the Justice Department in the 1960s.

31. U.S. Senate, Subcommittee on Antitrust and Monopoly of the Committee on the Judiciary, 84th Cong., 1st Sess., *A Study of the Antitrust Laws: Hearings. . .* (Washington, D.C., 1955), Pt. I, 11-12. (Hereafter cited as *Kilgore Committee Hearings.*)

32. *Patman Committee Hearings*, pp. 234-239.

33. S. Chesterfield Oppenheim, "What Business Should Know about the Attorney. General's National Study Committee" speech delivered to The Trade and Professional Association Workshop of The Chamber of Commerce of the United

States in Washington, D.C., on Apr. 26, 1954. Copies are included in Antitrust Papers: AGNC, sect. 43, 172 and 457.

34. S. Chesterfield Oppenheim to author (Apr. 23, 1971); Stanley Barnes' letter to Eugene Rostow, dated Mar. 23, 1955, reprinted in U.S. House, Antitrust Subcommittee of the Committee on the Judiciary, 84th Cong., 1st Sess., *Current Antitrust Problems: Hearings.* . . (Washington, D.C., 1955), Pt. III, 2128-2129. (Hereafter cited as *Celler Committee Hearings.*) But see below, p. 29.

35. Memo dated Oct. 16, 1953, Antitrust Papers: AGNC, sec. 354, "Administrative and Enforcement Group: Attorney General's Committee."

36. Transcript of the meeting of Attorney General's Committee, Oct. 14, 1953, pp. 92-3, Antitrust Papers: AGNC, sec. 16.

37. See, for instance, "Preview of the Antitrust Report" (for the Cabinet). Written on the cover is "Recipients of this paper are requested to take special measures to protect its contents from premature release." (Mar. 16, 1955; Antitrust Papers: AGNC, sec. 1-B.

38. See memorandum to Arthur Burns from Melvin De Chazeau and Fritz Machlum. Eisenhower Papers, Official File 149-A, "Monopolies: Antitrust (1)."

39. Papers of the President of the United States: 1953-61, Ann Whitman File, Cabinet Series, Box 5, "Cabinet Meeting Mar. 18, 1955"; White House Office, Cabinet Secretariat, Records: 1953-1960, "Preview of the Antitrust Report (Mar. 16, 1955)."

40. Herbert Brownell to author, Apr. 11, 1974.

41. Washington, D.C., 1955. (Hereafter cited as *A.G. Report*).

42. *A.G. Report*, p. 2.

43. Handler to author, Apr. 20, 1971.

44. The material selected for treatment below was chosen to provide the parameters for understanding the policies of the Eisenhower administration. It is not an all-encompassing summary; for that, the reader should consult the testimony of Oppenheim and Barnes before the Celler, Patman and Kilgore Committees. Also see notes 72, 84, 85 below.

45. *A. G. Report*, p. 44.

46. Handler to author, Apr. 6, 1971.

47. *A. G. Report*, p. 115.

48. *A. G. Report*, p. 117.

49. *A. G. Report*, p. 123.

50. *A. G. Report*, pp. 123-125.

51. *A. G. Report*, pp. 125-127.

52. *A. G. Report*, p. 154.

53. *A. G. Report*, p. 219.

54. *A. G. Report*, p. 226.

55. *A. G. Report*, pp. 293, 4.

56. It is noteworthy that the group clearly stated that the Department of Justice should not seek relief that could not reasonably be expected after litigation. (*A. G. Reports*, pp. 360-1.), but see the statement of Stanley Barnes, below, 53.

57. The term "railroad release" is derived from a Department of Justice statement in the Association of American Railroads case of 1913, which explained why the

Government had not brought an antitrust suit. It had indicated certain conditions under which it would waive the right to initiate a criminal suit, and the Association had complied. Morrison Shafroth, "Enforcement of Compliance Procedures Other Than by Prosecution or by Formal Procedures" (First Draft of section for the Attorney General's National Committee to Study the Antitrust Laws [Feb. 13, 1954]), p. 14. Copy in possession of Mr. Morrison Shafroth. See also *A. G. Report*, p. 368.

58. Oppenheim to author, Apr. 23, 1971.
59. Eugene Rostow to author, Apr. 29, 1971.
60. Schwartz to Oppenheim, Mar. 9, 1955; Griffin to Oppenheim, Mar. 18, 1955; Frost to Barnes, Mar. 2, 1955; the dissent with its many inked corrections is also included in Antitrust Papers. AGNC, sec. 35, "The Schwartz Dissent"; Oppenheim to author, Apr. 23, 1971.
61. Mark Adelman, "General Comment on the Schwartz Dissent," *The Antitrust Bulletin*, 1 (Apr. 1955), 71-79.
62. *Celler Committee Hearings*, pp. 294-295.
63. Louis B. Schwartz, "The Schwartz Dissent," *The Antitrust Bulletin*, 1 (Apr. 1955), 37-70.
64. *Celler Committee Hearings*, pp. 247-264; *Patman Committee Hearings*, pp. 73-90.
65. *The Antitrust Bulletin*, 2 (Sept. 1956), 40.
66. In testimony before the Patman Committee, Barnes cited the costs as $78,179.40; the Appropriation-Allotment Balance Sheet of the committee shows expenses of $77,087, Antitrust Papers: AGNC, sec. 435, "AT Comm. file #4"; Barnes reported in a memo of Apr. 11, 1955, to Brownell that the total cost was $76,772.
67. James O'Donnell to author, July 8, 1971.
68. *Patman Committee Hearings*, p. 814.
69. Oppenheim to author, Apr. 23, 1971.
70. "The United States and Business: Era of Good Feelings?" *U.S. News and World Report*, 35 (July 24, 1953), 69-73; "What the Merger Law Means," *Business Week* (Oct. 9, 1954), pp. 25-27; "Government: Quick Action," *Newsweek*, 45 (Jan. 3, 1955), 49-50.
71. S. Chesterfield Oppenheim, "Highlights of the Final Report of the Attorney General's National Committee to Study the Antitrust Laws," *The Antitrust Bulletin*, 2 (Apr. 1955), 35.
72. Glen E. Weston, "Restatement of Antitrust Law: Salient Features of the Attorney General's Committee Report," *The George Washington Law Review*, 24 (Oct. 1955), 4.
73. Oppenheim to author, Apr. 23, 1971.
74. *Kilgore Committee Hearings*, pp. 4-32.
75. M. A. Adelman, Wendell Berge, Clare Griffin, Milton Handler, Edward Howrey, Carl Kaysen, Eugene Rostow, Louis Schwartz, Donald F. Turner, Walter Adams, and William Simon.76. Walter Adams, M. A. Adelman, Stanley Barnes, Milton Handler, Edward Howry, Alfred Kahn, S. Chesterfield Oppenheim, Eugene Rostow, William Simon, and Louis Schwartz.
77. *Celler Committee Hearings*, p. 203.

78. *Celler Committee Hearings*, pp. 1865-1910.
79. *Patman Committee Hearings*, pp. 191, 202.
80. See above, p. 20.
81. Eisenhower Papers, 9F-15-M-1, Box 285, Endorsements, "Members"; Antitrust Papers. AGNC, sec. 19, 21, "Advisory Committee Suggestions for Membership"; Oppenheim to author, Apr. 23, 1971.
82. *Kilgore Committee Hearings*, pp. 551-591.
83. *Journal Herald* (Dayton, Ohio) Dec. 6, 1952, clipping in Antitrust Papers: AGNC, sec. 21, "Advisory Committee, suggestions for membership."
84. For example, see *Northwestern University Law Review*, 50 (July-Aug. 1955), 305-348; *George Washington Law Review*, 24 (Oct. 1955), 1-107; *University of Pennsylvania Law Review*, 104 (Nov. 1955), 145-310; *Michigan Law Review*, 53 (June 1955), 1033-1152.
85. For example, see Edgar Buttle, "Analysis of the Antitrust Laws," *Bar Bulletin*, 13 (Sept. 1955), 44-50; John Stedman, "New Look at Antitrust: The Report of the Attorney General's Committee," *Journal of Public Law*, 4 (Fall 1955), 223-284; George W. Stocking, "The Attorney General's Committee Report: The Businessman's Guide through Antitrust," *Georgetown Law Journal*, 24 (Nov. 1955), 1-57.
86. *A. G. Report*, p. 3.
87. *Antitrust Law Developments*.
88. Charles Wallace to author, Apr. 17, 1971.
89. National Association of Manufacturers' Papers, folder 100-NN: 1955: Publications: Antitrust Laws: "The NAM Law Department Reviews the Antitrust Laws: The Report of the Attorney General's Committee." (The Papers of the NAM are located in the Eleutherian Mills Historical Library in Greenville, Wilmington, Del.)
90. "Attorney General's National Committee to Study the Antitrust Laws," File 4, 60-414-0. Department of Justice files, Records Administration Office Washington, D.C.
91. Baddia Rashid to author, July 8, 1971; Keith Clearwaters to author, Aug. 23, 1973.

CHAPTER III

Early Enforcement: The Sherman Act

WHEN Dwight Eisenhower took the oath of office on January 20, 1953, almost everyone expected that the administration would be "pro-business." Although few people could agree about exactly what "business" was, and even fewer could agree on what would be the consequences of this attitude, it did appear that in the field of antitrust, the new government would be more amenable to the wishes of the "business" community. For those expecting a holiday from antitrust enforcement, the eight years of the Eisenhower Administration were to prove a rude shock indeed, for in that area the period was one of movement and innovation.

The first move by the administration seemed to bear out the contentions of those who foresaw a term of lax policy. The choice of Stanley N. Barnes for the position of Assistant Attorney General in charge of the Antitrust Division of the Justice Department did not augur well for future enforcement. Recommended for the position by the man he had helped get a start in public life,[1] Vice-President Richard Nixon, Barnes had little else in the way of qualifications for the position.[2] Nevertheless he was acceptable to both factions of the Republican Party in California since the new trustbuster had been urged by Governor Earl Warren to accept the proffered post.[3] A successful lawyer, in 1929 he had been instrumental in forming the Los Angeles law firm of Chase, Barnes and Chase. In 1946, he had been appointed Superior Court Judge of Los Angeles County, and he had done such a good job that in 1948, he was elected to the post. Promotion came quickly, for in 1950, he became Presiding Judge of the Criminal Department, and in 1952 he was named Presiding Judge of the 80 Superior Courts of Los Angeles County. Obviously, Barnes had a stellar legal record, but there was nothing in his past to recommend him to head the Antitrust Division.

Replacing the Assistant Attorney General Edward P. Hodges, a member of the Truman Administration and interim member of the Eisenhower

Administration, on May 1, 1953, Barnes immediately set himself to work. His first task was to learn all about the antitrust laws. This task he accomplished by means of a systematically formulated schedule of reading. With the basic knowledge acquired, he then undertook a journey to the ten sub-offices of the Antitrust Division,[4] where he met with all the regional chiefs. He felt he could obtain a better picture of the local situation on the scene. His objective of first understanding the local needs as a means of grasping what must be done in the Washington headquarters was very successful. Not only did Barnes obtain valuable insights, but his method proved to be a great morale booster. Two of the offices had never been visited by any of his predecessors, and his appearance would subsequently be rewarded with increased output. Additionally, Barnes' consummate skill in handling people assured his high standing with lawyers and others who later evaluated his performance. Even the Nader Report on Antitrust was generally complimentary about the Barnes tenure.[5]

From his readings and consultations, the Assistant Attorney General was able to evolve a tentative antitrust philosophy. Perhaps the most important pillar of Barnes' antitrust faith was the one he stated first: "There exists almost universal recognition among the American people that that 'charter of freedom,' known as the Sherman Act, and to a lesser or greater extent, its thirty-odd supplemental related laws, are 'a part of the warp and woof of our economic life.' Furthermore, it is the means chosen by the people of America to confirm and preserve private competitive enterprise existing under limitations placed on freedom of commercial action." His second and third tenets emphasized the need for simplicity and flexibility: "If there is to be any change with regard to enforcement of fundamental law that approaches in many minds the dignity of Constitutional amendment it should be our constant *purpose* to accomplish this change by express legislative enactment, sufficiently general in terms to accommodate itself to differing economic pressures, but constant in theory, certain in interpretation, uniform in application, and simple enough to guide industry and commerce, acting in good faith, past courts of law. . . . Despite our quest for certainty there will and must always be room for *judicial*, and, to a more limited extent, *administrative*, interpretation and choice." While Barnes included it among his beliefs, his fourth precept belonged less in the category of philosophy than in that of future policy: "Certain cases that have been brought in the past by the Division may not fall within the category of violations of well-defined and recognized legal prohibitions, but are on the periphery of the law, and contemplate possible extensions of legal theories, based on political or sociological doctrines and beliefs. . . . It is for that reason that I propose to continue our review of every one of the one hundred and thirty-nine cases pending in my Division, with the purpose of seeing if there are cases pending which neither I nor my staff would, in the first place, have recommended filing."[6]

The aforementioned review of the cases pending implied to some that dismissal of several important suits might well be in the offing. Indeed, later in the same speech, the Assistant Attorney General announced that the suit begun in 1945 against the Cement Institute would be dropped. The Institute had dissolved itself in 1945, and since "no substantial benefit to the public could be expected from the trial of this case" and as it would take a great deal of time and cost a large sum of money, "Good sense demands its dismissal."[7]

Before instituting an action, Barnes wanted to know not only the answer to the simple "Can we win?" but also the answer to "What good can be obtained if the Department files suit?" and, conversely, "What harm could accrue?" Important, too, were speed and cutting of red tape. In certain unnamed instances he advocated negotiations before filing a suit in the hope that the parties involved might consent to a solution at that time.

When Barnes turned from the theoretical concepts to the cases themselves, he found that the Division was in a dismal state of disarray. There had been an almost continual shuffling of the leadership of the Division. In October 1950, William A. Underhill had been appointed to the position of Assistant Attorney General in charge of the Antitrust Division. Not remaining long enough even to be confirmed by the Senate, he was replaced in less than 100 days by H. Graham Morison, who headed the Division until July 1952. After Morison's exit, little progress was made in the field of antitrust, as Newell A. Clapp and Edward P. Hodges administered the department in quick succession. In scarcely more than two years, four men held the title Assistant Attorney General in charge of the Antitrust Division.

Although the revolving leadership did not hinder the filing of actions against alleged violators, it deterred settlements and left a sizable backlog of cases. When Barnes assumed his position in 1953, there were 12 cases that dated back to before 1946, the oldest one, the Columbia Gas and Electric case, having been filed on November 4, 1938. As any good judge should, he moved to clear up the docket.[8]

The housecleaning began not with the wholesale liquidation of suits prophesied by the Democrats, but instead with a bare handful of dismissals. Out of 144 pending cases when Barnes took the helm in 1953, only five were discarded. Perhaps the action most obviously in need of closing was that against Columbia Gas and Electric Corporation. According to Justice Department records, nothing had been done on the case since August 1943.[9] After discarding the outdated actions, Barnes concentrated on injecting a new vitality into the program. Taking dead aim at the oldest cases, usually the hardest to win, he succeeded, among other accomplishments, in closing out eight of the twelve pre-1946 cases in his first year on the job. Although he partially accomplished this feat by dismissing two of the most ancient, that concerning the Cement Institute and the one against Columbia Gas and Electric, still his record is distinguished. With the other cases, every effort was made to speed up the trials, including the use of stipulations concerning undisputed facts, and simple agreements with the defense counsel on statements of facts. These two minor innovations often cut weeks from the duration of a trial.[10] Not only was the handling of the individual cases expedited,[11] but also the total number of cases terminated rose significantly. From May 1, 1953, when Barnes became Antitrust Division chief, until January 20, 1954, a period of less than nine months, a total of 42 actions was concluded. To put the figure into perspective, the number was 60 percent higher than that for the corresponding nine months of the previous year. For the fiscal year 1954, the figures were more impressive; more than twice as many cases were terminated as had been in 1952.

The Division was also able to make a great deal of headway in solving the problem of delay when dealing with its own cases. The first time-saving device was the utilization of "prefiling conferences." Under this policy, after having investigated a particular situation and having prepared a proposed complaint, the Department notified the prospective defendant of the Division's intention of filing a complaint. It then summarized the nature and groups of the charges to provide the defendants with some frame of reference. If they wished to start negotiations towards a possible decree, prior to the filing of the complaint, Barnes' Division was ready to meet with them at the conference table in an effort to work out an acceptable solution. The agreement would dispose of the problems raised in the complaint, while safeguarding both the public and corporate interest. Although most companies were willing to negotiate before the filing of the suit, settlements did not always come that easily. For Barnes, a case settled quickly by prefiling negotiations had many advantages. First and most important, it enabled the government to obtain relief, thus restoring the previous competitive situation. Second, the promotion of competition was achieved much more rapidly than was otherwise attainable. Third, not only was the delay of litigation avoided, but so too was the expense.[12] For the defendants, the same savings of time and money accrued.

Prefiling was not new; it had been employed sporadically in the late 1920s, and, while it had fallen into disuse in the early 1930s, during the Arnold period it had been used often in conjunction with criminal suits. Throughout the Eisenhower era, however, it was utilized only when a civil suit was contemplated, and hence there could be no opportunity for blackmail.[13]

The second means of speeding up the workings of the Antitrust Division was recourse to consent decrees. A product of negotiation and a certain amount of compromise between the government and the defendant party, the decree once entered carried with it the essential force of litigated judgment.

Not only did it treat a current situation, it also could and often did include clauses which covered possible future situations. Of great importance, too, was the fact that in the field of antitrust, double jeopardy was impossible and thus a consent decree dealing with a certain topic stopped future proceedings on the same subject. To be effective, there were obligations on both government and defendant: the government should not press its bargaining power arbitrarily, while the defendants had to be completely candid in disclosing facts. The consent-decree mechanism was an important tool for both sides: for the government, it provided effective enforcement without the cost in time, manpower, and money of a protracted trial. During the Truman Administration, in contrast to 66.2 months, or over five and a half years from the time of the filing of the complaint until the final judgment, the time lapse for consent judgments averaged only 29.7 months, or less than half as long as a litigated case.[14] Beyond the savings to the government, the meetings negotiating the consent decree were informal. Under Barnes, the government's conferees were directed to appear in shirtsleeves; hopefully, such an unstudied atmosphere would lead to more give-and-take than might occur in the more formal court environment. Barnes emphasized that "the Division may strike down violations in areas otherwise, as a practical matter, beyond its reach."[15] All the advantages of consent decrees, however, did not redound to the government. From the defendant's viewpoint, perhaps the most important impetus for agreeing to such a judgment was supplied by Section 5 of the Clayton Act: "A final judgment or decree heretofore or hereafter rendered in any civil or criminal proceeding brought by or on behalf of the United States under the antitrust laws to the effect that the defendant has violated said laws shall be *prima facie* evidence against such defendant in any action or proceeding brought by any other party against such defendant under said laws or by the United States under section 4A, as to all matters respecting which said judgment or decree would be an estoppel as between the parties thereto: Provided, That this section shall not apply to consent judgments. . . ."[16] Thus, while government antitrust actions were *prima facie* evidence, consent decrees were not; and, consequently, any defendant who agreed to a consent decree greatly increased the work and sharply diminished the chances of success for any future treble damage claimant. Secondly, a consent decree did not garner as many headlines as did an antitrust conviction. By agreeing to such a judgment, a corporation was able to avoid a sizable portion of unfavorable publicity. Finally, just as for the government, there were the many savings connected with the acceptance.

The use of the consent decree by the Republican administration was not new. The first consent decree in the Sherman Act case was entered in 1906,[17] and after the enactment of Section 5 of the Clayton Act, the number filed swelled enormously. Used both by the Republicans in the 1920s and then by the Roosevelt Administration and lauded by the TNEC,[18] the instrument fell into disrepute in the waning years of the Truman term. The Celler Committee endeavored to manufacture a political issue out of the use of the consent decree by the Eisenhower Administration,[19] suggesting that revision of the consent decree procedure was essential.[20] Nevertheless, the mechanism was employed in a great many cases during Eisenhower's term; but, despite partisan rhetoric, the year in which the most consent decrees were ever entered was 1940 when 91.3 percent of all cases settled were so terminated.

The Eisenhower Administration refused to soft-pedal its use of the consent decree; instead, the Republicans considered its use a virtue.[21] Although some Democrats viewed the acceptance of a consent decree as a sign of weakness, admission that one does not think his case will stand up in court, the Republicans emphasized the importance of the tradeoff of perhaps a small amount in the decree in exchange for the time, money and staff to deal with another case. In addition, a consent decree did not consume much court time. To an administration so concerned with the problem of congestion in the courts that it sponsored the National Conference on Congestion in the Courts in 1956,[22] the chance to reduce judiciary backlog by the use of the consent decree was appealing.

A very valid criticism of the consent decree focused on the point that almost as soon as the decree had been entered, the issue was closed and little more was done on the matter. The problem had been recognized many years earlier and been lucidly described by Hamilton and Till: "A result has been reached, the zeal in the cause has been spent, interest moves on. If a decree provides for immediate changes, such as the sale of a property, a divestment of shares of stock, the dissolution of a trade association, the file is held open until such steps are taken. After that is done, the matter is adjudicated, the issues are removed from controversy. In the records of Justice the episode is closed; the case has gone to the hall of records; a fresh initiative is necessary to call it once more into action. Nor is an effort made to follow up a decree, observe success and shortcomings in operation, check practical result against intent, determine upon necessary revisions."[23] Despite the wide use of the consent procedure and criticisms such as those of Hamilton and Till, there were only ten instances until 1952 when the contempt power was used to enforce the injunctions under the Sherman Act.[24]

Both Barnes and Brownell recognized that the consent decree was only as effective as the follow-up policy. In speeches, they stressed that "Once decrees are entered, we see to it that they are lived up to."[25] The records of the Antitrust Division during the 1950s include many follow-up reports. Because the Department included clauses in consent decrees providing for proof of compliance by the company within a specified period or a changed market mix by a prearranged date, it was essential that the Division carefully monitor the actions of many companies. Although there was doubt about the number of contempt actions, the enforcement device was, without question, employed to a much fuller extent, under Barnes' leadership, for in his four-year tenure it was invoked nine times—somewhere between 50 percent and 33 percent of the total for the preceding 66 years!

Whereas the previous Democratic administration had concentrated on doubtful test cases, such as the Investment Banking case[26] (which the government lost), the Eisenhower Administration emphasized the more hard-core violations. What was important was not "mere doctrinal perambulation but . . . making real strides towards either cracking restraints on entry or controls on price."[27]

The 1954 Eastman Kodak case is important because it illustrates the operations and thought processes of the administration and the antitrusters. The action commenced with the use of the prefiling procedure, and from then on, negotiations moved smoothly, with both sides endeavoring to formulate a satisfactory solution as quickly as possible. Barnes subsequently became ebullient when he noted that the Kodak case was an example of how "good will and sincerity on both sides of the conference table" could ameliorate many difficult and complex problems. In short order, the government obtained a consent decree providing effective relief: the restoration of competition in the film-developing market without adversely affecting Kodak's profitability.

President Eisenhower was apparently convinced of the need for a vigorous antitrust enforcement policy, but the administration and the Justice Department papers indicate that he did not exercise rigid control over the Division. Instead, he seems to have been willing to let those he trusted carry out the day-to-day policy. He did, however, take a personal interest in several important cases.[28] Thus, while there are the standard memoranda informing the President of the filing or proposed settlement of cases, there are no other documents at all for most of them.[29] As an avid amateur photographer, Eisenhower was especially interested in the Kodak action, and on several occasions, he and Brownell discussed it at length over the telephone and in personal conferences.[30]

The Kodak case began with an investigation arising from a number of private complaints about the company's monopoly of amateur color film processing.[31] The findings suggested that Kodak had monopoly power in processing and that its practice of controlling the resale price of its color film under fair-trade laws amounted to an unfair trade practice since the price of developing was included in the cost of the film itself.[32] Thus, almost all Kodacolor and Kodachrome film sold in the United States was processed by Kodak after it had been exposed. Because the independent photo finisher had no opportunity to process the film, the public was paying the company a tariff for film development which was not determined by the competitive forces of the market place.

In July 1954, the Antitrust Division notified Kodak's officials of the intended complaint and furnished them with a copy. Shortly thereafter the company advised the Department that it wanted to try to work out a consent decree prior to the filing of the complaint.[33] By mid-August, the parameters of the negotiations had been set. At conferences lasting until early December, officials of both sides formulated the provisions included in the decree which was entered in the federal court at Buffalo on December 21, 1954, simultaneously with the filing of the complaint.[34]

Using the technique of prefiling, in less than six months and after 104 hours of negotiations,[35] the government was able to enter a decree which, saving the costs of time and trial, afforded satisfactory relief. The judgment required Kodak to cancel its fair-trade contracts covering its color film, and it enjoined the signing of any such new contracts in the future. Additionally, and a key factor for Barnes and Brownell, the decree prohibited Kodak from selling its color film with the processing charge included in the sales price or from tying together the price of the film and its subsequent processing in any other way. This clause of the decree would have been nearly meaningless had there not been an enabling section stating that independent film processors would obtain, upon written request, licenses at reasonable royalties under the Kodak processing patents. Since even the license to use certain techniques was useless without specific technical knowledge, the decree directed Kodak to make available scientific manuals which could be used by new entrants in the processing field. In order that Kodak not overlook any critical aspect of processing technique, the decree stipulated that the company must permit independent processors to send technical personnel to observe the methods and machines utilized at the Kodak plants in Rochester, Chicago, and Palo Alto. In addition, the company was required to make available all materials necessary for the processing of its amateur color film. To ensure that the independent film processors would be able to garner at least 50 percent of the market, part of the decree included the stipulation that seven years from the effective date of the judgment, Kodak would be forced to divest itself of a number of facilities so that it would ultimately control less than 50 percent of the domestic capacity for processing film. Illustrating the flexible attitude of the Eisenhower antitrusters, the decree also included a clause protecting the company: If, at the specified date, Kodak still controlled more than the agreed-upon market share, and if, at the same time, it could prove that it had taken no restrictive actions and that all purchasers had had the option of having their film processed by an independent company, the antitrusters would take no further action.[36]

The decree was far from popular. In the Justice Department files there are scores of letters attacking the settlement as "anti-business" and "communistic." Although understanding that certain dislocations were necessary to restore competition, according to Barnes, even "President Eisenhower . . . complained to me . . . about the inconvenience . . . of certain provisions of the Eastman Kodak decree."[37] Brownell asserts with pride that the great number of new entries in the processing field directly resulting from the decree established real competition in an industry where there had been none before.[38]

The Antitrust Division also terminated by a consent decree the 1949 civil suit against American Telephone and Telegraph Company (AT&T). The action was filed with three objectives: 1) that its supplier subsidiary, Western Electric, be divorced from AT&T and split into competing manufacturing concerns; 2) that AT&T and the various operating companies be compelled to buy equipment on a competitive bid basis; 3) that AT&T and Western Electric be required to license their patents to all applicants on a nondiscriminatory and reasonable royalty basis, and that there be available the necessary technical assistance and knowledge to apply the processes covered by the patents.

Almost immediately the case became enmeshed in politics, interdepartmental rivalries, and the need to rearm to pursue the Korean War. AT&T quickly recruited the aid of the Secretary of Defense, Robert Lovett, who wrote to the Justice Department emphasizing that the communications colossus had to expend all its energies on defense projects. Apparently, the Antitrust Division suspended activities on the case for a period of time.[39] When the Eisenhower Administration came to power, the conflicts still remained, but there was also a strong desire to clear up the held-over actions, and Brownell seems to have been especially anxious to end the telephone case. To expedite matters, the Attorney General placed Edward Foote in charge of the suit. The assignment was unfortunate; Foote had never tried an antitrust case, and he had "not very much" experience in the field as a whole.[40] His inadequate background cost the government a decree as strong as it might have been able to negotiate. Quiet pressure from the Federal Communications Commission led Brownell to feel that divestiture would lead to higher-priced service, and this possibility led to the abandonment of the divestiture demand by the government.[41]

The resultant decree, entered January 24, 1956, did not provide for breaking up the telephone company. AT&T did agree to leave the leasing and private communications maintenance business within a period of five years. What made the outcome a "victory" for the government was the inclusion of compulsory patent licensing provisions which, according to the Department of Justice, were "unprecedented in their breadth and duration."[42] The government did gain 1) the provisos that all patents belonging to the defendant companies, both at the time of judgment and in the future, would be made subject to compulsory licensing to all domestic applicants, and that there be no limits in the contract regarding time or use; 2) an agreement that approximately 8,600 patents which had been exchanged between AT&T, General Electric Company, Westinghouse Electric Corporation, and Radio Corporation of America would be licensed royalty-free to any domestic applicant; 3) the promise that companies already using the patents might renegotiate their contracts; and 4) the guarantee that to insure the patents being useful to all, technical knowledge and aid would be furnished at reasonable cost.[43] Despite these gains, the decree was not a victory for the government, for its achievements fell far short of what it had sought when it had first initiated the case, namely, the divestiture of Western Electric.

The very next day after the entrance of the telephone decree, the Justice Department announced that it had ended its case against International Business Machines (IBM). Although the Department had filed the action in January 1952, its origins were actually earlier. Thomas Watson, Sr., who led IBM to its position of world leadership in office machines, believed that the case had its roots in the World War II period.[41] In the years that followed, there were several opportunities to negotiate a consent decree, but Watson was convinced that no matter what the law said, consent decrees were admissions of guilt.

The government attacked several IBM practices; since 90 percent of all tabulating machines were leased, and since part of the leasing agreement called for the use of IBM-produced or approved supplies, including punch cards and IBM repair services, the Justice Department in January 1952 charged the company with restraints of trade and monopolization of the tabulating industry in the United States.

In the interval between the filing and settlement of the case, numerous changes transpired. The government stiffened its position, adding to its prayer of compulsory patent licensing the demand that IBM sell, as well as lease, its machines. The office-machine maker was also evolving; its planners were beginning to favor a more flexible policy regarding sales of equipment.[45] Furthermore, and of even greater import, Thomas Watson, Jr., had acquired the real power, and he was more interested in the future than in fighting an extended battle with the Justice Department. Thus negotiations, even in view of the firmer attitude of the government, could begin with an eye toward a consent decree.

The 1956 decree was a major victory for the government in that it struck hard at the practices in question. First, the company had to sell its equipment at a reasonable price to anyone; any lessor who had a machine had to be given an option to buy it. In line with eliminating the restrictive leasing practices, the company was enjoined from selling maintenance services with the machine. To insure that others would be able to repair the machines, the company was obliged to offer a manual and training to future competitors in the field of office-machine repair. Second, to encourage competition in the repair and service areas, the judgment included provisions giving all members of the tabulating industry complete access, at reasonable royalties, to all existing IBM electronic machine patents and also to those to be acquired by the company within five years. "To make this offer even more appealing,"[46] Barnes noted that the decree provided that if the applicant rejected the amount of royalty proposed by IBM, and if the parties were unable to agree on a reasonable rate with 120 days, the applicant or IBM might appeal to the court (in which the consent decree was filed) for determination of a reasonable royalty. Third, in an effort to open up the punch card business, the agreement stipulated that licenses under existing patents to manufacture tabulating cards should be royalty-free. In addition, in order to insure the growth of competition, IBM had to make available for sale the machinery, stock and technical knowledge to anyone who wished to enter the business. Should this not prove effective, the Department also included a "Sword of Damocles" provision requiring the company to divest itself of a part of its manufacturing facilities for tabulating cards so that it would control no more than 50 percent of the total capacity for manufacturing cards in the United States.[47] According to Barnes, as in the case of the Kodak and AT&T decrees, "The judgment . . . is designed to encourage the growth of competition in every phase of this important industry."[48] That the judgment was successful is evidenced by the number of computer-service-oriented companies listed on the New York, American, and regional exchanges, and in the over-the-counter market. For IBM, too, the agreement was very important, for it provided a set of rules to govern company conduct. Although on the surface the 1969 antitrust case against IBM appears to be a reopening of the one ended by the consent decree, in actuality it is not. The new action deals for the most part with computers which accomplish things that were scarcely dreamed of in the mid-1950s. It is significant, too, that the January 15, 1975, pretrial brief for the defendant makes very few references to the earlier decree.[49]

Often the actions of the Antitrust Division appear to be motivated by more than a simple desire to regulate trade. Any case which transcends the borders of the United States is, of necessity, tedious and involves careful diplomacy. Many of the problems arise from the singularity of the American antitrust corpus, but others are based on the sometimes contradictory aims of the different divisions of the government in Washington. The Swiss Watch Cases and the one against United Fruit Company illustrate these difficulties.[50]

While the Sherman Act applies to the activities of foreign firms acting within the borders of the United States, it is hard to obtain materials and to agree on a settlement over great distances. The Swiss Watch cases had their roots in an investigation begun in the summer of 1953 and in grand jury subpoenas issued in the fall of 1953 to some 50 companies.[51] Almost immediately, various spokesmen for the Swiss watch industry criticized the investigation and characterized it as an attempt to interfere with the internal activities of the private chronometer industry in Switzerland. Subsequently they assailed the suit as being designed to give the Sherman Act an extraterritorial application. The *Tribune de Geneve* classified it as "an attempt of the Government in Washington to destroy American markets for the Swiss watch industry."[52] In reality all the shouts of anguish were not based on any firm foundation; the defendant companies, most of whom were American subsidiaries, were private institutions operating in the United States, and, therefore, were of necessity bound by the American antitrust corpus. From the beginning, the State Department was "extremely interested" in the issue, especially because at the very same time, America was working on a revision of its tariff schedule and the subject of duties on watches and movements was being reevaluated.[53] The Defense Department was involved, too, because the "cases had a national security aspect, in that it was necessary for this country to have an adequate supply of watchmakers whose services were necessary in the development [of] warheads for our missile program."[54]

In an effort to lessen any misunderstandings, the Division met in Washington with representatives of the Swiss government and important relevant material was immediately forwarded in diplomatic pouches marked "air priority" to Ambassador Taylor.[55] Our diplomats endeavored to clarify the issues involved in the suit, to explain the antitrust laws, and to assure the Swiss delegation that the scope of the complaint was limited and not directed against operations of the industry in Switzerland.

Two separate complaints, filed October 19, 1954, and December 2, 1955, alleging violation of both the Sherman and Wilson Tariff acts, emphasized that the restraints related solely to the importation, exportation and domestic trade in jeweled watches, components and repair parts. In their press releases issued at the time of the filing, both Barnes and Brownell stressed that, "No attempt is made by this suit to regulate or control the operations of the Swiss watch industry in Switzerland. The complaint deals only with practices effectuated in the United States which relate to the domestic and foreign commerce of this country."[56] The actions attacked private agreements concerning such American commercial questions as:

1) The extent of watch manufacture permitted within the United States;
2) The extent to which United States businessmen can import watches from countries other than Switzerland;
3) The extent to which the exportation of Swiss-produced watch parts from the United States to countries other than Switzerland is to be permitted;

4) The agreed designation of large areas of the world in which United States businessmen are not permitted to sell Swiss-produced watches which they have bought and received in the United States;

5) The fixing and policing of minimum prices for watches sold within the United States;

6) The fixing and policing of maximum prices for watch parts sold within the United States;

7) The extent to which Swiss-manufactured watchmaking machinery may be used.[57]

In their investigation and their compilation of evidence, the antitrusters came upon some rather unique practices and events. They uncovered the practice of "up-jeweling," which consisted of declaring to customs that a watch movement being imported into the United States had fewer jewels than it really had. At other times "up-jeweling" took place in this country—movement was subsequently advertised as containing more jewels than it really had. This material was turned over to the Treasury Department.[58] Perhaps the most amazing item was turned up by the Federal Bureau of Investigation (FBI). In its inquiry into the suspected evasions of customs duty, the FBI found records of a Treasury Department investigation of the subject in 1939-40. The study allegedly was called off and remedial action blocked by Franklin D. Roosevelt. Hoover explained that "This was said to have been accomplished through a payoff of at least $5,000,000—a considerable portion of which was alleged to have gone to the 1940 campaign of former President Roosevelt."[59] No action was taken by Brownell because it was a "treasury matter" and, besides, the statute of limitations precluded prosecution.[60]

After a motion to dismiss the case was denied, all parties agreed to work toward a consent decree. The negotiations were broken into four separate sections: the first to work for a decree covering Swiss manufacturers and their association, Federation Suisse des Associations des Fabricants d'Horlogerie; the second to reach an agreement covering the American manufacturers; the third to prepare another to include the American importers and their association; and the fourth to draft still another covering the advertising agencies representing those involved in the other three sections. In time the American defendants negotiated acceptable decrees, but their Swiss counterparts did not appear to be as willing to work out a satisfactory agreement. In the process of forging a consent decree, the antitrusters always request detailed information, but the Swiss with their penchant for secrecy stalled, and there are memos in the Justice Department files questioning whether or not they really did want to work toward a consent judgment.[61] When the negotiations finally started, the Swiss manufacturers were unable to come to an agreement because the Justice Department "wanted too much,"[62] and that segment of the case was then tried in court, with the antitrusters prevailing.[63] While on appeal, the Federation retained Abe Fortas to try again to negotiate a consent decree. The distance and language differences were responsible for difficulties in negotiations; the time lapse inherent in checking back to Switzerland before and after each new proposal was especially cumbersome.[64] Although Fortas was no more successful than his predecessors in negotiating the decree, the break in the case came when Taylor cabled from his post in Switzerland, "The Swiss Embassy therefore hopes that the American authorities will take, in the very near future, the necessary steps to definitely clear up the situation."[65] This cable appears to have been the catalyst for new discussions in Washington between the Department of State, represented by the Under Secretary for Economic Affairs, Douglas Dillon, and the Ambassador of Switzerland, Henry de Torrente.[66] As a result of these discussions and meetings between the President and the Council of Economic Advisors, the decision was made to press for a resolution of the case; Victor Hansen (Barnes' successor as Assistant Attorney General in charge of the Antitrust Division) flew to Switzerland and, aided by Taylor, helped to hammer out an agreement. Taylor credits Hansen with having been very important in the solution and having played "a major part in the improvement of Swiss-American relations."[68] The watch companies were not as happy about the agreement as was the Swiss government and at first the manufacturers voted against the decree, but finally they settled because they were eager to be rid of the "expensive and time-consuming difficulty."[69]

In all likelihood, there were also more than just domestic reasons for the filing of another case, the antitrust suit against the United Fruit Company. In 1951, a left-wing government had taken power in Guatemala, and shortly thereafter it had begun a program of land reform which included the expropriation of some of the lands of the United Fruit Company.[70] That the Communists were a growing influence in the Jacobo Arbenez Guzman government was exemplified by the export of guns and munitions from Czechoslovakia to the tiny American republic. Although the menace of a Communist beachhead in the Western Hemisphere worried the United States and terrified the governments of Nicaragua and Honduras, it had been impossible to persuade the Pan-American Conference meeting in Caracas in March 1954 to do anything more constructive than go on record declaring international Communism a threat to the security of the hemisphere. When it became obvious that the hemispheric collective security system was ineffective in dealing with the Guatemalan problem, the Eisenhower Administration undertook unilateral action, and the Central Intelligence Agency aided a group of refugees in their effort to overthrow the Communist-inclined regime. In June 1954, under the leadership of Carlos Castillo Armas, the counter-revolution was successful; immediately Armas assumed the presidency and quickly abrogated the land-reform program, returning to the United Fruit Company its large holdings in the country.[71] Nearly instantaneously the cry was raised that the United States had backed the invasion to protect the interests of the monopolistic United Fruit Company. Almost simultaneously, on July 2, 1954, the Department of Justice announced the filing of a civil antitrust suit against the banana giant.

The "banana investigation" had its inception in the years before the Eisenhower Administration,[72] but little could be done until the left-leaning regime had been thrown out of power because "any antitrust proceedings against the United Fruit Company . . . would be playing into the hands of the Communists. They would take all the allegations as true and interpret the litigation as proof that the company is under attack by its own government and is ready prey for expropriation. The State Department would be seriously handicapped in its efforts to protect American interests and prevent the area from falling under the complete domination of the Communists."[73] Nevertheless, the Antitrust Division was busy preparing a case, and by February 1953, they had the proposed complaint ready to file.[74] The National Security Council then recommended that "the proceedings . . . be postponed, without prejudice to the Government, for one year." Furthermore it proposed that "the Attorney General should be directed to negotiate with the company, as a matter of urgency, for the elimination of practices deemed to be inconsistent with the U.S. anti-trust laws . . ." Although the President adopted this policy, Brownell was unsuccessful at the conference table.[75] Thus, when the new, more sympathetic regime was installed, the Antitrust Division was able to file the civil antitrust suit against United Fruit, alleging violations of both the Sherman and Wilson Tariff acts.[76]

Charging that the nation's leading banana importer had combined with or acquired many of its former competitors and that it had taken advantage of its dominance in the production, transportation and importation of this product in order to achieve a monopolistic position enabling it to control prices and exclude competitors, the government noted that since 1935, United Fruit had shipped in two-thirds of the total weight of bananas imported into the country. The suit then specified five of the exclusionary practices employed by the company: the company controlled almost all of Central American land usable for banana culture; as a major stockholder in International Railroads of Central America, it had obtained special transportation rights; it had preempted shipping space; it had cut prices in an effort to drive competition out of business; and it had endeavored to coerce customers with the threat of withdrawing the future supply of the product. Brownell never mentioned the Cold-War aspect of the suit. He stated that its purpose was "to restore conditions under which competition can flourish."[77]

Much of the next two years was spent in negotiation between company and

Justice Department lawyers. In an effort to speed negotiations or to strengthen the complaint should the matter go to trial, the government filed an amended complaint, charging that in acquiring the Cuyamel Fruit Company, United Fruit had attempted to eliminate competition, a Clayton Act Section 7 violation. While working on a consent judgment, the government made plans to go on to a trial, scheduled to begin on February 5, 1958.

The parties took nearly four years—until February 4, 1958—to work out a consent settlement. By that time Barnes had been appointed to the United States Court of Appeals, Ninth Circuit, and Victor Hansen had been named to fill his position. Hansen subsequently was criticized[78] for being less active in the field of antitrust than his predecessor.[79] Certainly the outcome of the United Fruit Company case cannot be cited as evidence for that charge.

To dissipate the power of United Fruit, the parties agreed in the judgment that a new company be formed, full-fledged like Athena, out of the assets and corporate structure of United Fruit. According to the provisions of the decree, the new entity should be capable of importing nine million stems of bananas, or 35 percent of the 1957 imports of United Fruit. To assure its ability to obtain the fruit, United Fruit had to supply banana-producing lands and the ships to transport the harvest. The company was granted eight years to draw up a plan of divestiture acceptable to the Antitrust Division. According to the agreement, three possible means of complying with this section existed: first, the United Fruit Company could create a new company which would hold the assets transferred to it, then the parent company could distribute stock in the new company in the form of a dividend to shareholders or a stock distribution of any other type. Second, the United Fruit Company could sell outright a requisite amount of assets to an "eligible person" who should not be connected with either the United Fruit Company or its competitor, Standard Fruit and Steamship Company. Third, also acceptable was any kind of combination of the two.[80]

In order to break down the monopoly power of United Fruit in the United States, the decree contained other important provisions. The company was enjoined from requiring any customer to buy all or any specified percentage of its supplies from United Fruit. The charge had been made that the company had forced purchasers to buy more bananas or a lower quality of bananas by threatening to refuse to sell to them in the future; the decree forbade such threats or other means of coercion. Numerous other clauses, all designed to widen the breach between the company and the ultimate consumers were also incorporated. The company was not allowed to ripen, process or sell bananas retail or wholesale within the United States; United Fruit was forced to agree that it would not acquire stock in a company engaging in such a business or in the transport of the fruit. The result would create three competing American entities in the banana business in Latin

America. Emphasizing the international aspects of the case upon the announcement of the decree, Hansen stated, "During the course of negotiations leading to this decree, the Department of Justice has remained in close touch with the Department of State."[81]

The full sanctions of the Sherman Act were employed for the first time during the Eisenhower Administration. Brownell issued a memorandum to all United States attorneys directing them not to consent to the acceptance of a *nolo contendere* plea by the court, except "where civil litigation is also pending." Feeling that "the plea has led to shockingly low sentences and insignificant fines which are no deterrent to crime,"[82] he was undoubtedly shocked by the fact that of the 298 criminal antitrust cases instituted between January 1, 1935, and January 1, 1950, only 48 had actually been tried.

Although in the criminal cases, incarceration is a possible sentence, until the 1950s no one had ever spent one day in jail as the result of a Sherman Act conviction.[83] In the Las Vegas Merchant Plumbers case, the defendants were found guilty and three of them were sentenced to imprisonment. This time there was no reduction or commutation of the judgment.[84] The outcome of the albeit unimportant case proved to be a landmark, for, by the end of the second Eisenhower term, a sizable number of corporation executives would be jailed for varying lengths of time.

During the Barnes-Hansen tenure, the Sherman Act was vigorously, if not always successfully,[85] enforced. The two men concentrated on cutting delay, introduced new methods, and endeavored to assess the full range of penalties as provided by the statutes.

NOTES

1. Brownell to author, April 11, 1974; "Antitrust: More Clamor to Come," *Newsweek*, 45 (June 13, 1955), 78.
2. "Government: The New Trust Buster," *Time*, 62 (Sept. 7, 1953), 86.
3. *The New York Times*, Apr. 4, 1953.
4. Philadelphia, Chicago, Detroit, Cleveland, New York, Boston, Los Angeles, San Francisco, Seattle, and Denver.
5. Mark J. Green, Project Editor and Director, *The Nader Study Group Report on Antitrust Enforcement: The Closed Enterprise System* (Washington, D.C., 1971), pp. 133-134.
6. Barnes, "The Judge Looks at Antitrust," speech delivered to the Section on Antitrust Law of the American Bar Association in Boston, Mass., on Aug. 27, 1953. (Reprinted in 3 *A.B.A. Antitrust Section* [Aug. 26-27, 1953], 13-19.)
7. The Cement Institute, Inc., was the principal motivating force behind the conspiracy to fix the price of delivered cement by means of the "basing point" system. Because of the filing of the complaint in 1945, the Institute dissolved itself in 1946. Although the challenged practices were subsequently abandoned, it

became possible for all to buy cement F.O.B. the mill, it was not until 1953 that the case was dismissed. Two memos dated Aug. 6, 1953, Antitrust Papers: Cement Institute, Acc. 64A580, file 60-10-27. (The use of the "basing point" system for determining prices was adjudged illegal in *Federal Trade Commission v. Cement Institute*, 333 U.S. 683 [1948]).

8. John Crider, "New Look at Antitrust: Mr. Barnes Speaks Softly but Carries a Big Stick," *Barron's* 34 (Aug. 23, 1954), 3.

9. Barnes memorandum to the Attorney General, June 8, 1953, Antitrust Papers: Columbia Gas and Electric, Acc. 64A580, file 60-156-16. The other cases which were dropped were: U.S. v. California Plumbing and Heating Wholesalers Association (dismissed Aug. 27, 1953, the records on this case have been lost); U.S. v. Du Pont (dismissed Oct. 7, 1953; while the records for this case are "lost," it is likely that they were misplaced, probably having been filed with any one of the other 23 cases or proposed actions of the government against Du Pont); U.S. v. Cement Institute (see above, note 7); U.S. v. Sunbeam Corporation (dismissed Dec. 11, 1953, Acc. 64A580, file 60-9-122).

10. Brownell, Address to the Section on Antitrust Law of the New York State Bar Association in New York, N.Y., on Jan. 28, 1954.

11. Antitrust litigation is not only time-consuming, it is also complicated and expensive. It has been estimated that it costs the government in the neighborhood of $200,000 to $250,000 to litigate a medium-sized antitrust suit. The Honorable Lamar Cecil, "Remedies in Antitrust Proceedings: Fines and Imprisonment," 5 *A.B.A. Antitrust Section* (Aug. 18-19, 1954), 123, and William D. Kilgore, "Antitrust Judgments and Their Enforcement," 4 *A.B.A. Antitrust Section* (Apr. 1-2, 1954), 105 note 3.

12. Barnes, "Antitrust in 1954," speech delivered to the Section on Antitrust Law of the New York State Bar Association in New York, N.Y., on Jan. 26, 1955.

13. Herbert Brownell, "Justice Policy: Vigorous Action," *Nation's Business*, 44 (Jan. 1956), 32.

14. Stanley Barnes, "The Businessman's Stake in the Antitrust Laws," speech to the Commonwealth Club at San Francisco, Calif., on Nov. 19, 1954.

15. Stanley Barnes, "Settlement by Consent Judgement," 4 *A.B.A. Antitrust Section* (Apr. 1-2, 1954), 10; Stanley Barnes, "The Trial of an Antitrust Case by the Department of Justice: Settlement by Consent Judgement" in Section of Antitrust Law, American Bar Association, *An Antitrust Handbook* (Chicago, 1958), p. 237.

16. 15 U.S.C. 16.

17. U.S. v. Otis Elevator Co., 9th Cir. (June 1, 1906), included in Roger Shale, comp., *Decrees and Judgments in Federal Antitrust Cases: July 2, 1890—Jan. 1, 1918* (Washington, D.C., 1918), 101. Cited in William J. Donovan and Breck McAllister, "Consent Decrees in the Enforcement of Federal Antitrust Laws," *Harvard Law Review*, 46 (Apr. 1933), 920.

18. U.S. Temporary National Economic Committee, *Monograph No. 16, Antitrust in Action* (Washington, D.C., 1940), 88-92. (Since the monograph was written by Walton Hamilton and Irene Till, it will be cited hereafter as *Hamilton and Till*.)

19. U.S. House, Antitrust Subcommittee of the Committee on The Judiciary, 85th

Cong., 1st and 2nd Sess., *Consent Decree Program of the Department of Justice: Hearings* . . . (Hereafter cited as *Consent Decree Hearings*.)

20. U.S. House, Antitrust Subcommittee of the Committee on the Judiciary, 86th Cong., 1st Sess., *Consent Decree Program of the Department of Justice: Report.* . . . (Washington, D.C., 1959), p. 27. (Hereafter cited as *Consent Decree Report.*)

21. "Consent Decree: Both Sides Win," *Business Week* (Mar. 3, 1956), p. 80.

22. The elimination of delay and the problem of congestion in the courts were topics of many of Attorney General Brownell's speeches. See, for example, his untitled addresses to the National Conference on Congestion in the Courts meeting, Washington, D.C., on May 21, 1956, and the Conference of United States Attorneys meeting, Washington, D.C., on July 16, 1956, and the National Conference of Bar Presidents of the American Bar Association meeting, Dallas, Tex., on Aug. 26, 1956. Also see William P. Rogers, "How Long Must a Person Wait to Have His Case Tried?" speech delivered to the Deep South Regional Meeting of the American Bar Association, New Orleans, La., on Nov. 28, 1955, and "Let's Eliminate the Delay in the Trial of Cases," speech delivered to the New York State Bar Association, Saranac, N.Y., on June 23, 1956. Copies of Brownell's and Rogers' speeches are housed in the Law Library of Columbia University, New York, N.Y.

23. *Hamilton and Till*, pp. 92-93.

24. *Consent Decree Hearings*, pp. 51-52. There appears to be a problem with the exact number of instances of contempt citations. While Victor Hansen gives the number as 18 for the period (*Hearings*, p. 434), *Fortune* credited 16. See editorial, "Antitrust: The Barnes Era," *Fortune*, 53 (Mar. 1956), 94.

25. Brownell, "Address," delivered to the 1956 Executive Conference on Administrative Policies and Problems in Philadelphia, Pa., on June 20, 1956.

26. *U.S. v. Henry S. Morgan, et al.*, 118 F. Supp. 621; Antitrust Papers, Investment Bankers, Acc. 64A580, file 60-391-0.

27. Barnes, "The Businessman's Stake in the Antitrust Laws," see above, note 14.

28. See below, for example, the Studebaker-Packard merger, the DuPont divestiture of General Motors securities, and the Electrical cases.

29. See, for instance, White House Office, Staff Research Group, Records.

30. Papers of the President of the United States: 1953-61, Ann Whitman File, Administration Series, Box 8, Brownell, Herbert, Jr. 1955-6[3]; DDE Diaries Series, Box 5, Phone calls, Jan. to July 1955(3), Jan. 21, 1955 [with Brownell].

31. See especially memo dated June 21, 1952, to William Dixon concerning complaint letter from a private citizen, William Drewry, Antitrust Papers: Kodak, Acc. 70A4771, file 60-42-18.

32. Fair-trade laws only cover commodities in "free and open competition with commodities of the same general class produced and distributed by others." The difficulty lay in the fact that processing is not a commodity, and "even if so, the processing aspect is not in free and open competition." Memo dated May 5, 1954, to Barnes, Antitrust Papers: Kodak.

33. Letter of Carl Nixon, General Counsel for Eastman Kodak, to Barnes, July 17, 1954, Antitrust Papers: Kodak.

34. Report of Barnes to files, Dec. 23, 1954, Antitrust Papers: Kodak.
35. Barnes to Frederick Mullen, Director of Public Information of the Department of Justice. (Dec. 23, 1954), Antitrust Papers: Kodak.
36. 1954 Trade Cases, par. 67,920; *Kodak News* (Dec. 21, 1954) (Distributed by Press Relations Department); Antitrust Papers: Kodak.
37. Barnes to author, May 7, 1971.
38. The Reminiscences of Herbert Brownell, 341, in the Oral History Collection of Columbia University.
39. Confidential source. The papers regarding this case are closed, as the Dept. of Justice is busy prosecuting another case against the company. The best material to be found on the subject is in *Consent Decree Hearings*, and the subsequent *Report*.
40. *Consent Decree Hearings*, p. 3648.
41. Confidential source. See also *Consent Decree Hearings*, pp. 3574, 3648-53; Barnes felt the government could not obtain divestiture in a court judgment, C. D. *Hearings*, 4091.
42. Dept. of Justice, "Immediate Release," Jan. 24, 1956, "Antitrusters Score a Patent Victory in AT&T Case," *Business Week* (Jan. 28, 1956), p. 160.
43. 1956 Trade Cases, par. 68,246.
44. Thomas and Marva Belden, *The Lengthening Shadow: The Life of Thomas J. Watson* (Boston, 1962), p. 297. Although there is little relation between the present antitrust case and the one in the 1950s, it is significant that both the government files and the records of IBM are closed. Nevertheless, Frank Cary, the new Chairman of the Board of IBM, asserts that in the current case "The Department of Justice has not alleged any violations of the Consent Decree." Frank Cary to author, Sept. 18, 1975.
45. Most of the planners believed that few would buy the machines anyway because the tax laws favored leasing, *Belden*, p. 309. They did not foresee, however, the growth of leasing firms.
46. Stanley N. Barnes, "The Consent Judgments against IBM and AT&T," in *Antitrust Law Symposium—1956* (Chicago, 1956), p. 49. The volume consists of most of the presentations delivered at the Eighth Annual Meeting of the Section on Antitrust Law of the New York State Bar Association, held on Jan. 25 and 26, 1956, in New York, N.Y.
47. 1956 Trade Cases, par. 68,245.
48. Dept. of Justice, "Immediate Release," Jan. 25, 1956.
49. Cary to author, Sept. 18, 1975, citing pp. 11-12, 60, 119, 330, 335, and 360.
50. Antitrust Papers: Swiss Watch, Acc. 70A4771, file 60-28-15; Antitrust Papers: United Fruit, Acc. 70A4771, files 60-166-56 and 60-166-56-1.51. Foote to Hoover, Director of the FBI, July 13, 1956, Antitrust Papers: Swiss Watch.
52. The Oct. 31, 1954, dispatch from Henry Taylor, ambassador to Switzerland, to John Foster Dulles includes a summary of newspaper opinion and quotations on the action, Antitrust Papers: Swiss Watch.
53. Internal memo (Dept. of Justice), July 13, 1954, Antitrust Papers: Swiss Watch.
54. Hansen to author, March 12, 1974.
55. A copy of Barnes' speech, "Current Antitrust Problems and Policies," to the

Metropolitan Economic Association meeting in New York, N.Y., on Oct. 27, 1954, was sent along with instructions to emphasize that the investigations had been initiated 18 months before the Tariff Commission hearings on watches. Both actions, the note continued, "are consistent with ultimate objectives: Prevention of serious injury [to our] domestic watch industry . . . and collaterally it will help safeguard [our] industrial base for defense purposes."

56. Dept. of Justice, "Immediate Release," Oct. 19, 1954.
57. Undated summary statement of the two pending cases relating to Swiss watches and watch machinery, Antitrust Papers: Swiss Watch.
58. "Up-jeweling," Nov. 12, 1954, Antitrust Papers: Swiss Watch.
59. Hoover to Brownell, Jan. 13, 1955, Antitrust Papers: Swiss Watch.
60. Brownell notation in note 59.
61. See memo of Mary Gardner Jones to files, Aug. 18, 1955, Antitrust Papers: Swiss Watch.
62. The author would like to express his appreciation to Mr. Eugene Gordon of Solinger and Gordon for describing his experiences on the case when he was a partner in the predecessor firm of Uhrenfabrik, Solinger and Gordon, which represented the Federation Suisse des Associations des Fabricants d'Horlogerie (Aug. 6, 1971).
63. 133 F. Supp. 40; 134 F. Supp. 710.
64. Eugene Gordon to author, Aug. 6, 1971; Gordon to Hollabaugh, Feb. 14, 1956, Antitrust Papers: Swiss Watch.
65. Unaddressed copy, Apr. 25, 1957, Antitrust Papers: Swiss Watch.
66. Douglas Dillon to Hansen, May 8, 1957; Hansen to Dillon, May 17, 1957, Antitrust Papers: Swiss Watch.
67. Papers of the President of the United States. 1953-61, Cabinet Series, Record of Action of the Cabinet, Jan. 24, 1958.
68. Taylor to Hansen, Sept. 30, 1958, Antitrust Papers: Swiss Watch.
69. Telegram to Secretary of State, Feb. 16, 1960, Antitrust Papers: Swiss Watch; Gordon to author, Aug. 6, 1971.
70. John Gerassi, The Great Fear: *The Reconquest of Latin America by Latin Americans* (New York, 1963), pp. 163-165.
71. Edwin Lieuwen, *U.S. Policy in Latin America* (New York, 1965), pp. 88-90.
72. "Banana Investigation," Sept. 28, 1951, Antitrust Papers: United Fruit.
73. Memo from the Executive Assistant to Newell Clapp, (Assistant Attorney General in charge of the Antitrust Division), Jan. 2, 1953, Antitrust Papers: United Fruit.
74. Proposed Complaint, Feb. 26, 1953, Antitrust Papers: United Fruit.
75. Papers of the President of the United States: 1953-61; NSC Series, Record of Activity, NSC, 1953 (2), #805, June 1, 1953. Joseph Rand Papers, Council on Foreign Economic Policy papers, folder 2(3), Kinter-World Report: United Fruit, May 7, 1955.
76. Dept. of Justice, "Immediate Release," July 2, 1954; *The Wall Street Journal*, Feb. 5, 1958.
77. Dept. of Justice, "Immediate Release," July 2, 1954.
78. Mark Green, *The Nader Study Group Report on Antitrust Enforcement*, 135,

213; also see Richard Austin Smith, "What Antitrust Means under Mr. Bicks," *Fortune*, 61 (Mar. 1960), 123.

79. For a more complete evaluation of Victor Hansen's tenure as Assistant Attorney General in charge of the Antitrust Division of the Justice Department, see below, Chapter 4.

80. 1958 Trade Cases, par. 68,941. Since management controlled very few shares of the stock, this solution was acceptable to the Justice Department. In most cases, management controls a much larger percentage of the float and the Justice Department would not have allowed the contingency. As an example, see Du Pont's divestiture of General Motors, below, Chapter 5. A decade later, the low percentage of stock controlled by the management of the United Fruit Company enabled the AMK Corporation to take over United Fruit. The successor company is now called United Brands.

81. Dept. of Justice, "Immediate Release," Feb. 4, 1958.

82. U.S. v. Jones, 119 F. Supp. 288, 289-90 (quoted in James M. Clabault and John F. Burton, Jr., *Sherman Act Indictments: 1955-1965*, [New York, 1966], pp. 28-29).

83. Section 2 of the Sherman Act provides for imprisonment of not more than one year (15 U.S.C. 2.). Until the Eisenhower era, unless a businessman had engaged in a violent act or had conspired within a labor union, he had no reason to fear being sentenced to a jail term. Twice, a person had been so sentenced but before the jailing, his punishment had been reduced to probation (in U.S. v. Trenton Potteries Company, 273 U.S. 392, and U.S. v. Gulf Coast Shrimpers and Oystermen's Association, S.D. Miss. 1953 and affirmed in 1956, 1956 Trade Cases, par. 68, 469).

84. 1954 Trade Cases, par. 67,673.

85. See the treatment of the Cellophane case, below, Chapter V.

CHAPTER IV

Early Enforcement: The Clayton Act

THERE can be no doubt that the Republican administration made a major imprint in the area of antitrust relating to mergers. Although Congress passed the Celler-Kefauver amendment to the Clayton Act in 1950, the improved instrument was unused until Eisenhower came into office. According to H. Graham Morison, a former chief of the Antitrust Division, during the last years of Truman's presidency, there was no occasion to use the bill;[1] however, the succeeding administration managed to find many opportunities, one even dealing with a situation that had its roots in the period before the Eisenhower incumbency.

In line with the Justice Department's policy of saving time, manpower and money by means of prefiling and by encouraging consent judgments, the Department promoted preclearance of mergers. This procedure entailed a thorough study in both a legal and economic framework of all the economic and competitive problems peculiar to the industry. Based on the voluntary disclosures of all pertinent information requested by the government, preclearance was tantamount to an assurance that the Antitrust Division would not institute proceedings at that time. The government, however, was not bound in any way since the standard letter of clearance contained a clause stating, "the Department reserves the right to take action in the event that other evidence . . . warrant[s] such action."[2] Furthermore, Barnes and Brownell both emphasized that "should the industry or relative market situation change after clearance, the Department reserves the right to proceed. Finally, even absent factual inaccuracy or market change, it should be kept in mind that strictly from a legal standpoint, a clearance granted by one attorney general has no binding effect on his successor."[3]

Pre-merger clearance played an important and growing role in the antitrust program of the Eisenhower Administration. In 1953, seven projected mergers were submitted to the Justice Department for clearance; five were allowed and were consummated; one was denied, and one was temporarily abandoned.[4] (Two years later the market was sufficiently altered, and the merger was allowed.) In 1954, of the 12 mergers submitted for clearance, seven were cleared, five were denied, and four of those were then abandoned.[5] The numbers continued to increase during the Eisenhower years.[6]

Beyond the clearance program, however, the Division also treated mergers not submitted for advance approval. To locate them the government had to consult the various trade journals, financial newspapers and other investment manuals. Initial investigation gauged the possible economic effect of the acquisition in question. If the Division had reason to believe that the merger might have the anti-competitive effects proscribed by Section 7, it would then seek additional detailed information from the parties involved.

The government considered many factors in deciding whether or not to institute a Section 7, Clayton Act proceeding. Information sought for the profile included a description of the physical location of the firm. The companies' financial health was a key determinant of legality. Ever since the *International Shoe Case*,[7] a "failing company" had been allowed to merge with another entity on the premise that consolidation was preferable to disappearance. Important, too, was whether or not the merging companies had a history of past acquisitions, or if their growth had been internally generated.

The study also included a precise inquiry into all the products of the two companies. The size and structure of the industry was important, and of even greater significance was the relative concentration of the industry. This consideration necessitated a description of the number of companies reported active in the industry, their respective size and relative standing in sales and total assets. An outline of the companies' relative positions was included, utilizing sales figures and breakdowns of the industry into definable market areas. If either of the companies held important patents, that fact was significant in a Justice Department decision because of the various possible antitrust problems in the patent field. Appended to the merger study were the annual reports of the merging companies, the contract terms and reasons of both parties for the merger or acquisition, plus a statement defining the mechanics of the merger. If a merger contract had been drawn up, it was also included. Finally, in the appendix were copies of the minutes of the board of directors' meetings of both companies on the topic. This is the context within which one must view the Clayton Act Section 7 enforcement during the Eisenhower presidency.

Although the administration followed the policy of delaying on any major antitrust action until the *Report of the Attorney General's National Committee to Study the Antitrust Laws* had been drafted,[8] the antitrusters were eager to act in the merger field. They wanted to find several cases which would help to delineate the exact coverage of the Clayton Act. In the papers of the Antitrust Division are countless entries such as "We need a better first case."[9]

Finally in early 1955 it was possible to act. The antitrusters quickly filed four separate complaints alleging violations of Section 7. Each presented "distinctive factual differences"[10] that could be useful in defining the limits of the amended law. Each helped illustrate the Justice Department's attitude toward mergers.

The first case filed by the Justice Department under the amended Section 7 was a suit directed against Schenley Industries for its "acquisition of a controlling interest of one of its prominent competitors, the Park & Tilford Distillers Corporation."[11] According to the complaint, which began with interesting background material on the industry, Schenley was one of the few companies engaged in the legal production of whiskey during Prohibition. In 1933, when the law was repealed, the defendant was in a good position to benefit from the change. Since that time, it had acquired more than 50 other companies involved in the production and distribution of alcoholic products. Not only had Schenley grown, but some other companies had also expanded, and the industry had become increasingly concentrated, with four big companies accounting for 75 percent of the spirituous liquor sales. This tendency had been worrying the antitrusters, and earlier, when Distillers Corporation-Seagrams Ltd. had considered acquiring Park and Tilford, the antitrusters indicated their opposition.[12] Perhaps they were guided by the fact that there had been a more rapid concentration in the liquor industry than in any other field in the preceding 50 years. Not only was the Justice Department interested in the possible effects of the merger on the industry itself, it was also concerned about its impact on the satellite fields, such as distribution and supply. In the case, statistics were an extremely important tool in establishing the government's proof:[13]

1) In 1953, Schenley had the largest annual capacity for producing whiskey (17 percent); Park & Tilford had 3 percent;
2) In 1953, Schenley was the second largest producer of whiskey—22 percent, Park & Tilford 4 percent;
3) In 1953, Schenley was the second largest bottler of whiskey (14 percent); with Park & Tilford's 3 percent, the total would exceed that of any other bottler;
4) In 1954, Schenley had 17 percent of the industry's storage capacity, and with Park & Tilford it would be 19 percent;
5) With Park & Tilford's inventory, Schenley's industry-leading number of barrels of whiskey in storage would rise to 22 percent of the total;
6) In 1953, Schenley's total sales were 17 percent of the industry's dollar volume; Park & Tilford's were 2 percent.[14]

In the Schenley case, the Antitrust Division attacked the acquisition of a small competitor by a major factor in an industry. The fact that Schenley had had a history of acquisitions did not make the Park & Tilford take-over illegal, but it did add to the impressive market statistics amassed by the Justice Department. Barnes therefore decided that the facts were indisputable and the situation was blatant enough to use the amended Section 7 for the first time.

The increasing concentration in the shoe business had been worrying the antitrusters since the Truman presidency, and in a report to Ephraim Jacobs dated May 18, 1953, Bernard Wehrmann wrote that "there is a pronounced merger movement in the field . . . [which], if permitted to run its natural course may destroy its [the industry's] traditional competitive structure. The problem posed by this development, . . . and a tendency to create an oligopoly embodying this concentration, may not lend itself to solution through orthodox or conventional approaches. It may even call for a re-interpretation of Section 7." Wehrmann then emphasized the necessity of taking action and using the Clayton Act to halt creeping acquisitions.[15] Of all the companies in the field, General Shoe had been the most active in its acquisitiveness. Although the Department had taken no action in early 1953 when General had moved to acquire stock in the Regal Shoe Company,[16] when apprised of the fact that it had taken over Delman, Incorporated, Barnes immediately contacted the companies and requested information concerning the details and mechanics of the merger.[17] After further study of the industry as a whole and inquiry into the effects of the series of vertical and horizontal mergers by General Shoe, Barnes wrote to Brownell explaining that "the theory of this case is slightly different from the customary case in that it alleges illegality with respect to a series of acquisitions, the first of which occurred in 1950, and the last of which [took place] in Dec. [sic] 1954. We do not contend that the latest acquisition is in itself substantial. We believe, however . . . that intervention in a series of acquisitions is permissible, if the overall effect may be to substantially lessen competition or tend to create a monopoly."[18]

In mid-1954, the major holders of the Hotels Statler Company, Inc., decided that because of family disunity and inheritance tax consequences, they should liquidate their shares in the company. Both the Sheraton Company and Webb and Knapp had also submitted bids, but the offer by the Hilton Hotels Corporation was the highest. When it became obvious that Hilton would acquire the Statler properties, the antitrusters began to study the situation. It was clear that the merger *should* be illegal yet even though the two companies were among the largest hotel chains in the world, their consolidation would not materially affect the hotel percentage of the entire industry. In their efforts to narrow the scope, the antitrusters formulated the "first-class hotel market" nationwide and also the "first-class hotel" market in the four cities in which the two companies were in direct competition:

Washington, New York City, Los Angeles, and St. Louis. Yet even this breakdown yielded figures which were too small, so the Justice Department finally based its complaint on the "convention hotel" market. The government prayed the court to order Hilton to divest itself of "the acquired properties" in the competing areas as well as any other properties necessary to "dissipate the effects of the violation of the law and to restore competitive conditions in the hotel industry."[19]

On November 30, 1954, Minute Maid Corporation announced that it had purchased the inventory and fixed assets of the Snow Crop Division of Clinton Foods Corporation; within a fortnight Barnes wrote to the companies to request a copy of the merger agreement and information such as plant output and locations.[20] After delving into the market structure and studying the statistics, the Division concluded that the action was illegal because orange juice was a separate line of commerce or market, and that as a result of the merger there would be three rather than four companies selling it nationwide. As Minute Maid was already a market leader, and as after the merger would have 31 percent of the juice market, there would be major effects on both producers and distributors. Minute Maid, which also wanted to expand into the frozen fruit and vegetable field, claimed that the acquisition would enable it to penetrate that market under the Snow Crop label. Although the antitrusters deemed this constructive, as it would enable the company to compete effectively with the major factors in that market they felt that overall the negative repercussions on the citrus concentrate field far outweighed the salutary ones in the other areas.[21] The more evidence that was gathered, the more ironclad the case appeared; and the Division quickly realized that it was a "fairly good case to try out the newly amended Section 7 of the Clayton Act."[22]

Minute Maid wanted to avoid publicity and to save the expense of a trial, so it cooperated fully with the government and worked toward a consent decree.[23] It became obvious that for Minute Maid, the rationale for the takeover was its desire to expand its product line beyond that of frozen juice concentrates. Although Snow Crop was a major factor in that field, it was also involved in the broader line of frozen fruits and vegetables. This was the attraction for Minute Maid, which was willing to consider divestiture of the Snow Crop juice assets. The negotiations were complicated by the government's contention that Minute Maid should divest itself not only of the frozen juice assets, but also of the Snow Crop trade name. Minute Maid felt that if there were two companies, both using the Snow Crop trade name, there would of necessity be difficulties over quality control, advertising costs and public recognition. It is likely that the Justice Department's lack of understanding of this difficulty was in part due to Minute Maid's non-use of pre-merger clearance.[24] Ultimately, the two parties worked out a consent decree which provided for the divestiture of three juice facilities and no future acquisitions by Minute Maid without Justice Department permission. The trademark question was to be settled within two years.[25] Within the allotted span of time, Minute Maid suffered serious financial reverses and was forced to sell the frozen food division to Seabrook Farms. The Antitrust Division took no action on the sale because of the precarious position of the juice company, and it closed the books on the Minute Maid case.[26]

None of the other three suits reached the decision stage in the courts. In the Statler Hilton Hotels merger case, after a series of meetings, a consent judgment was entered on February 6, 1956, in which the chain agreed to dispose of the Jefferson Hotel in St. Louis, the Mayflower in Washington, and either the New Yorker or the Roosevelt in New York City. As Hilton had already sold the Towne House in Los Angeles, no disposition was required in that city. Hilton additionally pledged not to acquire any other hotels in the four cities without first obtaining the government's permission. There was no relief secured from the company in the cities where there had been no competition with Statler. Finally Hilton agreed to submit reports to the government until the divestiture process was totally completed.[27]

At the same time, the Antitrust Division was also involved with the General Shoe case. After having been advised that the antitrusters had utilized the Federal Bureau of Investigation to gather additional materials, the company indicated that it was willing to discuss negotiating a consent judgment.[28] By February 1956, an agreement was reached, allowing the concern to keep Delman, but halting further acquisitions for five years, except with the approval of the court or the government. In only one instance could General Shoe take over companies without government approval—if the acquired corporation were facing imminent bankruptcy and had made efforts to sell out to other companies first. In order that markets not be foreclosed to smaller shoe companies, the judgment required that, for five years, General Shoe be bound to purchase 20 percent of its shoes from other manufacturers.[29]

The government saw to it that the provisions of the judgment were observed, both in letter and spirit. In 1957, when General Shoe requested permission to take over Laird Schrober and Company, a manufacturer of shoes, it was denied; however, in the following year the company was allowed to acquire another manufacturer, the Safety First Shoe Company, because in that case it would have gone bankrupt had the merger not been consummated.[30]

The last of the original Section 7 cases, the one challenging Schenley's acquisition of Park & Tilford Distillers, ended April 3, 1957, also with a consent judgment. Although at first glance the terms of the decree did not appear to have offered much relief—essentially an injunction against Schenley enjoining the company from making any acquisitions of any whiskey distiller or distributor—upon closer inspection, the agreement appears logical and appropriate. At the time of the takeover, Park & Tilford was losing money in the sale of domestic whiskey but it had a very lucrative import line. Within days of the consummation of the merger, Distillers Corp., Ltd. (DCL), informed Park & Tilford that it would lose its franchise to import and distribute VAT 69, House of Lords Gin, and Booth's High and Dry Gin because Schenley was already distributing competing brands such as Dewar's Scotch. Subsequently, John Harvey & Sons informed Park & Tilford that it was in danger of losing its franchise to distribute Harveys Bristol Cream Sherry because it was no longer large enough to do the job effectively. During the consent-degree negotiations, when Schenley explained the complex situation, it appeared to many in the Justice Department that the international Scotch whiskey cartel was transgressing American antitrust laws. Therefore, a grand jury was impaneled to investigate the sale of imported spirits in the United States. Schenley threatened to file a treble damage suit against DCL, claiming that the revocation of the franchises had materially affected Schenley's business. DCL, in turn, threatened Schenley with the loss of its Dewar's distributorship. Since the alleged infractions took place on foreign soil, they were beyond the jurisdiction of the American government and the grand jury was unable to uncover sufficient evidence to merit the filing of criminal charges. In the end, the grand jury investigation was dropped, Schenley was allowed to keep its Dewar's distributorship and Park & Tilford was given a "second line" Scotch to distribute.[31]

The government accepted the consent judgment fully aware that there had been a lessening of competition, but realizing that Park & Tilford, without the important distributorships, would be likely to go bankrupt. The company's fragile financial condition led some of the antitrusters to believe that, in a court test, the government might lose. Additionally, they became convinced that such an action would not utilize the Department's manpower to best advantage. The market was already glutted with items such as those which made up the bulk of the Park & Tilford assets, and thus the company was probably not salable. Furthermore, allowing Schenley to maintain the shell of Park & Tilford would result in the continued sale of its domestic product and thus would protect the jobs of the current employees of the company.[32] The Schenley-Park & Tilford decree illustrates the flexibility of the Eisenhower antitrusters, in sharp contrast to the rigidity displayed by some of their predecessors who, for instance, continued the case against the Cement Institute long after the organization had been dissolved.

While the amended Section 7 had been applied with a high degree of success in four cases by the Justice Department, legal scholars realized that although negotiated settlements were helpful as guidelines to other companies, consent decrees did not create legal precedent, and thus they were useless except for dealing with a specific problem. An adjudicated Section 7 judgment against a major company would be pivotal, for it would help establish legal parameters of the new law. Although the Hilton and Statler hotel chains were number one and two, respectively, in their industry group, and Minute Maid occupied a similarly high position, these corporations were not really sizable factors in American industry as a whole. Even the new case attacking the Brown Shoe Company, Inc.'s acquisition of all the stock of G. R. Kinney Company, Inc., was not large enough.[33]

To prove the strength of Section 7 the antitrusters recognized that it was necessary to use the statute against a merger of companies which made a sizable contribution to the gross national product of the United States. Hence, when the news of merger talks between Bethlehem Steel and Youngstown Sheet and Tube Corporation surfaced, there was no "jawboning" or threats; instead, Brownell practically dared the two companies to consummate what would have been, in terms of dollar assets, the largest merger in United States history.[34]

While the story of the romance between the two entities reaches back to the days of another Republican president, Herbert Hoover, the history of the rise of Bethlehem can be traced farther back to the days of Charles M. Schwab. Schwab had been an associate of Andrew Carnegie and had aided him in the amalgamation of his many properties into the first American billion-dollar corporation, United States Steel. Remaining for a few years as director of the colossus, Schwab wished for more competition and so acquired an interest in Bethlehem. In 1905, he resigned from U.S. Steel in order to devote full time to his new venture.[35]

Schwab's new company was extremely small, especially in comparison with Big Steel. Its ingot capacity was less than 1 percent of the nation's total, and measured against that of U.S. Steel it rang up a diminutive 1.5 percent.

Part of the growth of Bethlehem was the result of mergers. In 1922 it acquired Lackawanna Steel and its reserves of Michigan ore. Later in the decade it acquired a plant in Johnstown, Pennsylvania, and a half interest in a Mesabi ore lease from Midvale Steel. However, much of the expansion was self-generated. Between 1905 and 1925, while its assets grew from $44 million to $617 million, its debt ballooned from $9 million to $237 million.[36] In addition, it ploughed back much of its profits and acquired holdings in such diverse and far-flung locations as Cuba and Chile as well as many areas of the United States. By the mid-1920s, it was a large integrated steel company located primarily on the Atlantic and Pacific coasts; its only entry to the heartland was its holdings in Buffalo, New York.

As early as 1928, Bethlehem held exploratory merger talks with Youngstown, and in 1930 it believed that it had solved the problem of gaining access to the interior when the two agreed in principle to a corporate marriage.

The planners, however, had not reckoned with Cyrus Eaton, a larger holder of stock in Youngstown and Republic Steel, who had his own visions of forging a major steel empire in midland America by means of a three-way merger with Chicago's Inland Steel.[37] He sent emissaries to all those who owed him favors, including Francis Davis, Jr., the president of United States Rubber, who was closely allied with the du Pont interests. Davis then wrote to Irénée du Pont to persuade him to take a neutral or negative stand on the consolidation.[38] As another phase of an intense campaign to block the merger, he first hired the financial research and investment management company, United States Shares Corporation, to prepare a study of the matter.[39] Not surprisingly it found that the merger would be contrary to the interests of the Youngstown shareholders. One week later the Committee of Stockholders Opposed to Sale and Dissolution of Youngstown Sheet & Tube Company mailed a copy of the report to every Youngstown stockholder. Eaton subsequently employed the services of the accounting firm of Ernst & Ernst, which also found that the proposed merger formula offered insufficient compensation. When the proxies were counted, the two sides were nearly evenly divided and, on a legal technicality, Eaton succeeded in blocking the merger.[40] By the time the court ruled in its favor, the Depression had caught up with Bethlehem and the plan had to be abandoned. At no time did the Justice Department express any opposition to the proposed link-up; first the ambitions of Eaton and then the Depression thwarted the consolidation.

World War II ensued before the nation could recover from the economic disaster, and it was not until after the return to a type of "normalcy" that Bethlehem could contemplate expansion. By the advent of the Eisenhower Administration, the case for merging was much stronger. During the demobilization subsequent to World War II, U.S. Steel had been able to acquire facilities in the West, and furthermore, it had expanded into the area of Bethlehem's greatest strength, the Atlantic coast. In the eyes of the Bethlehem management, the argument for the merger was much more forceful.[41]

The environment had changed. In 1950, the Cellar-Kefauver amendment to Section 7 of the Clayton Act had been passed, and in November 1952 a Republican administration dedicated to vigorous enforcement of the antitrust laws had assumed office. Thus when, in mid-1954, Bethlehem announced its intention of merging with Youngstown, almost immediately the entire administration was interested. Eisenhower made a special request for information, and subsequently on September 10, 1954, a top secret meeting attended by Barnes and several cabinet members was held at the White House. In an administration that was dedicated to enforcing the antitrust laws, the opportunity of applying the amended law to a steel merger was most welcome, for it provided the vehicle by which the government could obtain a court interpretation of the scope and meaning of the amended Section 7.[43] The Justice Department appears to have decided to send a letter of disapproval in response to the two companies' request for pre-merger clearance. Opposition to the union then became a key factor in the anti-merger program of the Eisenhower Administration.[44]

In the interval between the first rumblings of the merger and its formal announcement in December 1956, the leadership of the Antitrust Division of the Justice Department changed. Stanley Barnes had wanted to return to the less hectic life of the bench, and so when offered a judgeship on the U.S. Court of Appeals for the Ninth Circuit, near his home in Los Angeles, he accepted it. Practically chosen by him, his successor, Victor Hansen, had a background very similar to that of Barnes. A California judge from the same part of the state, Hansen, like Barnes, had no particular knowledge of antitrust. Unlike Barnes, however, he had neither the personal magnetism nor the speaking ability which had served his predecessor so well. His poor public-speaking style often has been cited as one of the reasons why he was not given so high a rating as Barnes by those who judge performance in the antitrust field.[45] But Hansen did continue to follow the Barnes-Brownell antitrust enforcement policy, and a perusal of the cases filed during his term reveals little damping of the antitrust ardor so evident in the first years under Eisenhower. Hansen took a strong stand against the proposed Bethlehem-Youngstown merger. It was his belief that the merger should not be allowed and that if the present laws were inadequate to forestall the marriage, then Congress should be requested to strengthen the anti-merger provisions of the Clayton Act.[46]

The argument of each side was extremely simple. Bethlehem contended that the merger would increase competition because the new company would be able to compete more effectively with U.S. Steel, the giant in the field. It further noted that even after the merger, U.S. Steel would still be the largest steel company. Opposed to this stance was that of the federal government which, basing its case on the already high concentration in the steel industry, asserted that the merger would eliminate competition between the second largest steel maker—Bethlehem—and the fifth largest—Youngstown. In the process, the market share of Bethlehem would increase from 16 percent to 20 percent. These factors alone made the merger illegal *per se*.

Both sides were eager for a speedy decision. The steel makers had plans involving the consolidation properties; and, should the merger not be approved, they had contingency expansion programs. On the government side, there were other factors besides saving time, money, and manpower favoring a speedy resolution of the case. Hansen wanted to find out as quickly as possible about any limitations in the amended Section 7. Thus both parties adhered to agreements which were aimed at achieving a short trial. The merger agreement between Bethlehem and Youngstown was entered on

December 11, 1956, and in the same month the suit was filed. It was settled in December 1958 after a trial that lasted but 19 days. Each contestant restricted its stipulations to 140 pages, making the trial as well as the case a "classic example of streamlining."[47]

The critical phrases of Section 7 involved in the case were "any line of commerce" and "section of the country."[48] In terms of the lines of commerce, the companies argued for a broad market description applying a type of "reasonable interchangeability" argument to the production rather than to the market level. They maintained that producers could convert raw steel into various products, such as hot-rolled bars and track spikes, at the same mill, and therefore they should be included in the same "line of commerce." The court rejected this reasoning, stating, "The evidence establishes that the defendant's production flexibility or mill product line theory is indeed pure theory. In practice steel producers have not been quick to shift from product to product in response to demand." On the other hand, the government had divided the steel industry into eight different lines (see chart, following page) which it contended had peculiar characteristics and uses. This definition the court accepted.[49]

Essentially "section of the country" means an "area of effective competition." The steel companies split the country into three regional divisions in an effort to illustrate how little they were in competition with each other, citing the high cost of freight as a barrier to the shipment of products over any great distance. The Department of Justice maintained that the entire United States constituted a relevant market. Within this market, the government proposed other geographic breakdowns within which the two companies shipped substantial enough quantities of their products to be considered competitors.[50] The court, after an intensive analysis of the steel market and marketing practices, found "that the nation as a whole is an appropriate section of the country in which to assess the anti-competitive effects of the merger, the evidence justifies further findings that there are separate sections of the country—appreciable segments of the market—with respect to the iron and steel industry and other lines of commerce found by the Court, where the impact will also manifest itself."[51] The court then proceeded to accept the government's contention that the merger would definitely have an adverse effect on competition. Thus it found the merger to violate Section 7[52] and the companies abandoned the plans.

Antitrust doctrine has built into it considerations of a public interest nature; one example being the "failing company" concept.[53] Although not codified into the law, it is predicated on the belief that industries wax and wane just as the fortunes of individual companies rise and fall. To the antitrusters, it is preferable that a sick company merge with another rather than go out of business. Since the International Shoe case, in which the Court

GOVERNMENT'S LINE OF COMMERCE *Broad Line* *Iron and steel industry* *Separate Lines*	DEFENDANTS' LINE OF COMMERCE *Broad Line* *Common finished steel products* *Separate Lines*
1. Hot-rolled sheets. 2. Cold-rolled sheets.	1) sheet and strip mill products, including hot-rolled sheets, cold-rolled sheets, galvanized sheets and hot- and cold-rolled strip.
3. Hot-rolled bars. 4. Track spikes.	2) bar mill products, including merchant bars, hot-rolled bars, bar-size shapes, track spikes, cold-finished bars and sucker rods.
5. Tin plate.	3) tin mill products, including electrolytic and hot-dipped tin plate, hot-dipped terne plate and black plate.
6. Buttweld pipe. 7. Electricweld pipe. 8. Seamless pipe.	4) pipe, including buttweld pipe, electricweld pipe, seamless pipe, nonferrous metal and plastic pipe.

Source: 1959 Trade Cases, par. 69, 189.

stated that the anti-merger provisions of the Clayton Act did not apply to companies in distress,[55] this has been a guiding principle. A cursory perusal of Appendix A reveals that one of the most often employed reasons for allowing a merger was that one, or both, of the companies in question was in serious financial condition. A union between the two would strengthen them, thus guaranteeing that the facility remain in the market place and the workers hold their jobs.

For all their activism, the Eisenhower antitrusters did not attack every large merger. At almost the same time that it turned down the Bethlehem-Youngstown union, the Department granted pre-merger clearance to two consolidations in the automobile industry—that of the Packard Motor Car Company with the Studebaker Corporation into the Studebaker-Packard Corporation,[56] and the Hudson Motor Car Company and the Nash-Kelvinator Corporation into the American Motors Corporation.[57] The Justice Department reasoned that the small car makers were becoming relatively smaller and actually weaker: In 1949 they had had a meager 14.5 percent of the market; but by early 1954 that share had dwindled to slightly more than 4 percent, at which point some of the companies were actually operating at a loss. By giving them a broader asset base, allowing them to save money by eliminating duplicate facilities, and assuring them a wider dealer network, the Justice Department felt that the mergers would permit them to compete more effectively with the "Big Three." Although Bethlehem had used that same argument, emphasizing that merger with Youngstown would create a company of equal stature to United States Steel, in the automotive industry, in contrast to steel, there were no smaller firms that would be put to a competitive disadvantage by the corporate marriages. According to Brownell, these mergers actually intensified competition.[58]

Eisenhower himself was very worried about the situation. Paul Hoffman, a Republican stalwart and former chief of Studebaker, painted a bleak picture of the future for his old company. The President feared that if one of the small companies were to fail, "it might practically dry up the market" and lead to recession. Thus, while he feared possible political repercussions, he supported the mergers and the award of defense contracts to the newly merged entities.[59]

Apparently, the antitrusters would even have condoned a subsequent merger between Studebaker-Packard and American Motors Corporation if the carmakers had requested it. The grounds for allowing such a further concentration in the automobile industry would have been that "such action will increase rather than lessen competition. Furthermore, to permit further consolidation of independent companies will tend to lessen the control of the existing 'Big Three.' "[60]

The Antitrust Division was especially active in the packaging industry, carefully monitoring the unions which were taking place. When the American Can Company, the largest manufacturer of metal cans and a major producer of paperboard packaging materials, acquired the Dixie Cup Company, the largest manufacturer of disposable individual drinking cups, and then Marathon Corporation, a maker of foodwraps and various types of tissue paper, the Division acted quickly. It persuaded American Can to divest itself of portions of the Marathon business which were directly competitive with the canmaker's other facilities. Thus American Can sold Marathon's individual hot-cup line to Potlatch Forests, Inc., and later it disposed of a paperboard facility acquired in the Marathon transaction.[61]

When Owens-Illinois Glass Company, the largest manufacturer of bottles and glass containers, acquired National Container Corporation, a sizable producer of kraft paper, corrugated boxes and bags, the Antitrust Division was immediately interested, and on December 4, 1956, it filed a complaint to force Owens to divest itself of its recent acquisition. The antitrusters feared that the merger would significantly enhance the company's already dominant position because the bottle-maker would "become the only glass container producer having integrated facilities for the production of packaged glass containers."[62]

Almost simultaneously, Continental Can Company reacted to the increased competition from the glass-container manufacturers. It entered the field by the acquisition of the Hazel-Atlas Company. Since glassware is a fragile product, usually packaged in corrugated boxes, Continental, in an effort to round out its line fully, acquired the Robert Gair Company, a major manufacturer of paperware containers and flexible packaging products.

The response of the Justice Department to the container mergers illustrates the vigorous antitrust policy of the Eisenhower years and the more lax treatment afforded by the subsequent Kennedy and Johnson Administrations. There were thousands of companies in the packaging industry and one or two of them were major factors in each of the principal categories: glass, metal and paper. Drawing on the doctrine of "reasonable interchangeability," the antitrusters attacked the Hazel-Atlas takeover because, as Hansen remarked, "The consolidation of the second largest can manufacturer with the second largest glass manufacturer may give the resulting combination a decisive advantage over its less diversified competitors."[63]

The following month, the Justice Department filed another action against Continental for its acquisition of Robert Gair Company. Noting that in several minor fields the two companies were in direct competition, the complaint stated that the competitive position of Continental would be further strengthened by its acquisition of Robert Gair's facilities. Such a broadly based entity, with divisions in cans, glass jars, and cardboard would have an unfair advantage over the other less diversified container companies.[64]

In late 1960, the government received a setback when the District Court ruled that it had failed to prove its case against the merger of Continental and Hazel-Atlas. Thus the defense position that metal, glass and plastic containers have sufficiently peculiar characteristics and uses won out over the government's broader conception of the entire container market. But the antitrusters appealed to the Supreme Court and the decision was reversed on June 23, 1964. The government thereupon agreed that, if Continental would divest itself of eight of the ten Hazel-Atlas plants, it would be satisfied.

Perhaps it was more reasonable for the Hazel-Atlas plants to have been sold to another glass manufacturer, the Brockway Glass Company, for the former had yet to have turned a profit under the aegis of Continental and thus were not a viable entity. The manner of compensation, however, was highly dubious. For the eight plants, Continental received one million shares of nonvoting Class B stock in Brockway,[65] which represented nearly a 42 percent equity in the company.[66] Such a holding would appear to violate the Clayton Act as much as, if not more than, the original merger with Hazel-Atlas had. In September 1965 the Justice Department agreed to drop its suit against the acquisition of Robert Gair.

The government and Owens-Illinois negotiated a consent decree in 1963 calling for divestiture of most of the properties which had originally been acquired in the merger with National Container.[67] In 1965, the government accepted the Owens-Illinois plan: sale of the properties in question to the Alton Box Board Company.

The results of the deal were significant. The size of Alton Box Board more than doubled, and it was transformed from a regional to a nationwide enterprise. Nevertheless, in this settlement also, the means of financing the venture were questionable. Although a sizable portion of the purchase price was borrowed from banks and insurance companies, the rest was lent by Owens-Illinois. As part of the arrangement, Owens-Illinois received warrants to purchase Alton shares. Although the glassmaker already owned a substantial block of stock in Alton and while these securities had been placed in the hands of a trustee,[68] it is difficult to understand how the settlement can be regarded as a true divestiture.

The weak follow-through in the container industry cases was based on the premise that the companies were either failing or that they were too feeble to stand alone. In all three cases, the acquired companies had been making profits prior to merger. It seems reasonable to expect that, absent any major technological changes, a just settlement would have included divestiture of a viable company—even if that had entailed spinning off more assets than had been acquired in the first place. To endorse take-overs by companies already in the field appears highly suspect. Perhaps a consolidation of the three properties would have stimulated competition in the container industry. If that had not been possible, certainly the amalgamation of the Robert Gair and National Container facilities would have been preferable to the legitimized concentration which did take place.

Paralleling its activities concerning the Sherman Act, the Eisenhower Administration displayed firmness in enforcing the Clayton Act. During the Barnes-Hansen period, the boundaries of the 1950 Celler-Kefauver amendment were delineated. In both the area of preventing mergers and in that of sundering those which had already been consummated, the antitrust policy showed vigor, demonstrated strong initiative, and stood in sharp contrast to that of the succeeding administrations.

NOTES

1. H. Graham Morison to author, July 15, 1971.
2. Barnes to Cria Dobbins, president of Ideal Cement Company (undated) in Antitrust Papers: Ideal Cement, Acc 70A4771, file 60-0-37-39.
3. Brownell, untitled speech delivered Nov. 17, 1955, to the National Industrial Conference Board in Philadelphia, Pa.
4. For a complete list of the mergers investigated by the Division see Appendix A. Those allowed in 1953 were: the acquisition of the capital stock of the Florsheim Shoe Co. by International Shoe Co. (Acc 70A4771, file 60-0-37-11); the Congoleum-Nairn, Inc. takeover of Sloane Blabon Co. (Acc 64A580, file 60-0-

37-14); a verbal clearance was given to White Motor Company's merger with Autocar Co. (Acc 64A580, file 60-0-37-16); the sale by Mitchell & Smith of a division to Crown Cork and Seal Corp. (Acc 71A6389, file 60-0-37-17); a verbal clearance was probably given to Ross Carrier Co. to merge with Clark Equipment Co. (Acc 64A580, file 60-0-37-13). The antitrusters refused Westinghouse Electric Corporation's request to acquire Houghton Corp. (Acc 64A580, file 60-0-37-12). At first, the Division refused permission to American District Telegraph of Massachusetts (Grinnell) to take over General Alarm Co. because the transaction would lead to an excessive concentration in the Boston market; however, when Grinnell sold the Device Division, located in Boston, the antitrusters permitted the consolidation (Acc 70A4771, file 60-0-37-15).

5. Those mergers cleared were:

Nash-Kelvinator Corp. with Hudson Motor Car Corp. (Acc 64A580, file 60-0-37-21);

Allied Chemical & Dye Corp. with Mutual Chemical Co. of America (Acc 64A580, file 60-0-37-23);

Koppers Co., Inc., with American Lumber & Treating Co. (Acc 64A580, file 60-0-37-26);

Studebaker Corp. with Packard Motor Car Co. (Acc 70A4771, file 60-0-37-27);

Colson Corp. with Service Caster & Truck Co. (Acc 64A580, file 60-0-37-36);

Ideal Cement Co. with Spokane-Portland Cement Co. (Acc 70A4771, file 60-0-37-39);

American Linen Co. (via subsidiary Steiner Co.) with Paper Corp. of America (Acc 64A580, file 60-0-37-43).

Those disapproved and dropped were:

National Steel Corp. with Republican Steel Corp. (Acc 70A4771, file 60-0-37-30);

Republic Steel Corp.'s acquisition of assets of Follansbee Steel Corp. (Acc 64A580, file 60-0-37-32);

Koppers Co.'s take-over of Western Precipitation Corp. (Acc 68A580, file 60-0-37-33);

Bensing Bros. & Beeney, Inc.'s joint venture with California Ink Co. (Acc 64A580, file 60-207-2 [formerly 60-0-37-20]).

Bethlehem Steel Corp.'s merger with the Youngstown Sheet and Tube Co. was decided in the courts in the government's favor (see below, pp. 127-136).

6. For an example of Brownell's attitude, see his memo to the President dated October 22, 1956. (Papers of the President of the United States, 1953-61, Ann Whitman File, Administration Series, Box 8, Brownell, Herbert, Jr., 1955-6, [1].)

7. International Shoe Company v. F.T.C., 280 U.S. 291 (1930).

8. (Washington, D.C., 1955); Memorandum to Arthur Burns from Melvin de Chazeau and Fritz Machlum. Eisenhower Papers, Official File 149-A, "Monopolies: Antitrust (1)."

9. Barnes' inked comment on memo to himself concerning the acquisition by Harris Seybold of C.B. Cottrell & Sons Co., Dec. 1, 1954 in Antitrust Papers: Acc 72A7861, file 60-0-37-24.

10. U.S. Attorney General, *Annual Report . . . 1955* (Washington, D.C., 1955), p. 168.
11. Antitrust Papers: Schenley, Acc 70A4771, file 60-0-37-57; Dept. of Justice, "Immediate Release," Feb. 14, 1955.
12. Memo to Barnes, Jan. 31, 1955, Antitrust Papers: Schenley.
13. Milton Handler, "Annual Review of Antitrust Developments," *The Record of the Association of the Bar of the City of New York*, 10 (Oct. 1955), 338.
14. Handler, p. 339; 1957 Trade Cases, par. 68,664.
15. Antitrust Papers: General Shoe/Regal, Acc 64A580, file 60-0-37-22. (General Shoe is now known as Genesco).
16. The merger did not come to fruition, and in 1954 Regal was acquired by Brown Shoe Company.
17. Antitrust Papers: General Shoe/Delman, Acc 70A4771, file 60-0-37-53.
18. Mar. 22, 1955, Antitrust Papers: General Shoe/Delman. (On the following day Brownell advised Barnes to initiate the case.)
19. U.S. v. Hilton Hotels Corp. and Statler Hotels Delaware Corp., Civil No. 1889-55, filed April 27, 1955, copy in Antitrust Papers: Hilton, Acc 70A4771, file 60-0-37-48; Department of Justice, "Immediate Release," Apr. 27, 1955.
20. Barnes to Snow Crop Corp., Dec. 10, 1954, and Barnes to Minute Maid Corp., Dec. 10, 1954, Antitrust Papers: Minute Maid, Acc 70A4771, file 60-0-37-51.
21. Memo to Barnes, Dec. 15, 1954, Antitrust Papers: Minute Maid.
22. Edward Foote to Barnes, Jan. 21, 1955, Antitrust Papers: Minute Maid.
23. Jacobs to Barnes memo describing meeting with company officials, Feb. 2, 1955, Antitrust Papers: Minute Maid.
24. Memo to Jacobs, May 4, 1955, Antitrust Papers: Minute Maid.
25. Memo of consent decree, Sept. 7, 1955, Antitrust Papers: Minute Maid; Dept. of Justice, "Immediate Release," Sept. 7, 1955, Antitrust Papers: Minute Maid; Dept. of Justice, "Immediate Release," Sept. 7, 1955; 1955 Trade Cases, par. 68, 131.
26. John Wilson to Max Freeman, Nov. 22, 1957, and Max Freeman to Harry Burgess (Assistant Chief, Judgments and Enforcement Section, Antitrust Division) Nov. 25, 1957, Antitrust Papers: Minute Maid.
27. Consent judgment, Antitrust Papers: Hilton; Department of Justice, "Immediate Release," Feb. 6, 1956; 1956 Trade Cases, par. 68,253.
28. Barnes to J. Edgar Hoover, May 17, 1955, Antitrust Papers: General Shoe/Delman.
29. Material from preliminary consent agreement dated Feb. 17, 1956, (final agreement not in Dept. of Justice files), Antitrust Papers: General Shoe/Delman; Department of Justice, "Immediate Release," Feb. 17, 1956; 1956 Trade Cases, par. 68,271.
30. Hansen to James Withrow (Attorney for General Shoe), Apr. 13, 1956, Hansen to Withrow, Sept. 23, 1958, Antitrust Papers: General Shoe/Delman.
31. Memo dated Nov. 25, 1958, Antitrust Papers: Schenley.
32. "Reason for Settlement," Jan. 31, 1957, Antitrust Papers; Schenley; Dept. of Justice, "Immediate Release," Apr. 3, 1957.
33. Antitrust Papers: Brown-Kinney, Acc 70A4771, file 60-0-37-81. A confidential

88 | BUSINESS & GOVERNMENT DURING THE EISENHOWER ADMINISTRATION

source recounted that the antitrusters did not consider the case to be a very significant one while they were working on it. It assumed its importance from the Supreme Court decision, an event of the 1960s. The case is in 179 F. Supp. 721 and 370 U.S. 294 (1962).

34. "Bethlehem-Youngstown: Controversial Engagement," *Fortune*, 55 (June 1957), 145. (In constant dollars, however, the 1901 merger creating United Steel was bigger.) See also "The Reminiscences of Herbert Brownell," 340, in the Oral History Collection of Columbia University. Subsequently, Brownell slightly modified his stance. ("It wasn't a dare, it was a warning on what we felt was a serious violation of the law. . . . It was a real landmark case.") Brownell to author, Apr. 11, 1974.

35. Edmund F. Martin, "The Promise for the Future," speech delivered at the National Newcomen Dinner of the Newcomen Society in North America (Apr. 20, 1967). Copy at Watson Library of Business and Economics, Columbia University.

36. See the collection of prospectuses for Bethlehem Steel Corporation bonds housed in the Scudder File, Watson Library of Business and Economics, Columbia University.

37. "The Bethlehem-Youngstown Case," *Barron's*, 10 (Sept. 29, 1930), 24.

38. Davis to Irénée du Pont (Mar. 19, 1930), Series J, Acc. 1034, File 217, The Papers of Irénée du Pont, folder 3, "United States Rubber Company." (The papers are located in the Eleutherian Mills Historical Library, Greenville, Wilmington, Del.).

39. United States Shares Corporation, "Special Analysis on the Proposed Youngstown-Bethlehem Merger" (Mar. 22, 1930).

40. Wilder H. Haines, "Youngstown-Bethlehem and Other Proxy Contests," *Barron's*, 11 (Jan. 5, 1931), 20-21; "Billion Dollar Steel Merger Enjoined," *Barron's*, 11 (Jan. 5, 1931), 21.

41. John Chamberlain, "The Lost Merger: A Bethlehem-Youngstown Marriage Would Have Helped Steel Competition," *Barron's*, 44 (Oct. 11, 1954), 23.

42. Memo of call from White House, Aug. 3, 1954, Barnes' confidential memo of Sept. 2, 1954, Antitrust Papers: Bethlehem Youngstown, Acc 70A4771, file 60-0-37-29. Eisenhower Papers, Central Files: OF-5, Report of the Dept. of Justice—Apr. 21, 1954-Sept. 30, 1954. The President continued to be very interested in the suit, and received regular updates; see, for instance, John Lindsay to Toner, White House Office, Staff research Group, Records 1956-61, Box 12.

43. "What the Merger Law Means," *Business Week* (Oct. 9, 1954), p. 26.

44. Draft of letter of disapproval, Sept. 28, 1954, Antitrust Papers: Bethlehem-Youngstown; "Bethlehem-Youngstown Controversial Engagement," *Fortune*, 45 (June 1957), 145.

45. "The Changing of the Corporate Board," *Newsweek*, 47 (June 25, 1956), 77.

46. Victor Hansen to author (June 16, 1971); "Bethlehem-Youngstown: Controversial Engagement," *Fortune* 45 (June 1957), 145.

47. *The Wall Street Journal*, May 22, 1959.

48. 1958 Trade Cases, par. 69,189; see also 168 F. Supp. 576.

49. 168 F. Supp. 576, 592.
50. M. A. Adelman has noted the tautology intrinsic in the concept of different-sized markets encompassing the same area. He feels that only one of the concepts can be correct. Explaining why the court accepted the poly-market division of the United States, he posits that it would be harder to reverse the decision because, were the Supreme Court called upon to rule on an appeal no matter what definition it chose, the determination would have already been adopted by the lower court. "Economic Aspects of the Bethlehem Opinion," *Virginia Law Review*, 45 (June 1955), 694.
51. 168 F. Supp. 576, 601.
52. Although the decision was made by a district court, and thus did not have the status of a Supreme Court opinion, it was the first adjudicated use of the amended Section 7, and in their memoranda, the antitrusters cited it regularly. Later, when they had Supreme Court opinions to cite, such as the Brown Shoe case (see below, Appendix A, entry 81) they ceased alluding to the Bethlehem case.
53. Edwin M. Zimmerman, panelist in Symposium, "Regulated Industries and Antitrust." 32 *A.B.A. Antitrust Law Journal*, (Aug. 7-10, 1966), 243. (Vols. 1-31 were cited as *A.B.A. Antitrust Section*.) Mr. Zimmerman was the First Assistant to Donald F. Turner, Assistant Attorney General in charge of the Antitrust Division from 1965 until June 30, 1968. When Turner resigned, Zimmerman was promoted to Assistant Attorney General where he remained until the new President, Richard Nixon, replaced him with Richard W. McLaren.
54. But see U.S. Congress. House of Rep. *Report #191*, 81 Cong., 1st session, 6; Senate, *Report #1775*, 81 Cong., 2d session, 7.
55. International Shoe Company v. F.T.C., 280 U.S. 291, 302-3 (1930).
56. Memo to Ephraim Jacobs, June 18, 1954 (initialed by Barnes), Antitrust Papers; Studebaker-Packard, Acc 70A4771, file 60-0-37-27.
57. Memo to Jacobs, Jan. 7, 1954 (initialed by Barnes), Antitrust Papers: Nash-Hudson, Acc 64A580, file 60-0-37-21.
58. Brownell speech (no title) to the Small Business Administration National Council of Consultants in Washington, D.C., on July 14, 1955, and speech (no title) to The National Industrial Conference Board in Philadelphia, Pa., on Nov. 17, 1955.
59. Dwight David Eisenhower, Papers of the President of the United States 1953-61, DDE Diaries Series, Apr. 20, 1956; Ann Whitman Diary Series, Box 8; Apr. 1956(1).
60. Foote to Barnes, Aug. 19, 1954, Antitrust Papers: Studebaker-Packard.
61. Hansen to Brownell, Oct. 29, 1957, Antitrust Papers: American Can, Acc. 70A4771, file 60-0-37-142.
62. Hansen to Brownell, Nov. 26, 1956, Antitrust Papers: Owens-Illinois/National Container, Acc. 70A4771, file 60-0-37-118.
63. Dept. of Justice, "Immediate Release," Sept. 10, 1956.
64. Antitrust Division memo, July 3, 1956, Hansen to Brownell, Oct. 19, 1956, Antitrust Papers: CCC-Robert Gair, Acc. 70A4771, file 60-0-37-140.
65. CCC was allowed to keep two former Hazel-Atlas plants, both of which were

profitable. Compare this solution with that rejected by the Republican Antitrust Division for the divestiture of General Motors stock by the Du Pont Corporation (See below, Chapter V).

66. Thomas C. Fogarty, "The Outlook for 1965," speech to the annual meeting of Continental Can Company shareholders, Apr. 27, 1965.

67. 1963 Trade Cases, paragraph 70,808.

68. Memo to William Orrick, Jr., Apr. 9, 1965. Antitrust Papers: Owens-Illinois.

United States v. Du Pont

E. I. du Pont de Nemours and Company, Inc. (Du Pont) has been accused of violating the antitrust laws 24 times since 1939.[1] The alleged infractions have ranged from price-fixing to monopolization. Two of the most important were filed during the Truman presidency and were decided during the Eisenhower years. The first treated Du Pont's interest in cellophane, and the second involved the company's investment in the stock of General Motors Corporation and United States Rubber Company. Each action illustrates differences in approach by these two administrations.

The first entry in the Antitrust Division's files concerning cellophane, dated August 28, 1942, concluded that there was "extremely keen competition between the two companies [manufacturing cellophane] (Sylvania Corporation was the other)."[2] Others in the Division who felt differently described the cellophane market as "completely static" and suggested that since "new competition is virtually an impossibility," the Du Pont cellophane holdings should be "dissected into a suitable number of competitive and independent units."[3] Although the lattermost finding implied a criminal violation of the Sherman Act, little further was done while the nation was at war and Du Pont was helping develop the atomic bomb for the sum of one dollar. Perhaps as a result of the impaneling of a grand jury in August 1946, Du Pont indicated that it was willing to establish a competitor in the industry,[4] but Truman's antitrusters pushed forward anyway and initiated a civil action on December 13, 1947. In what quickly became known as the "Cellophane case,"[5] the Antitrust Division went all the way to the Supreme Court in search of victory.

Du Pont's involvement in cellophane began in 1923 when it entered into a series of agreements with a French company, La Cellophane. This firm, the world's only producer of cellophane, created a jointly owned subsidiary, the Du Pont Cellophane Company. As payment for patent rights, secret processes, technical information, and exclusive sales rights to North and

Central America, 48 percent of the stock in Du Pont Cellophane was transferred to La Cellophane. Du Pont Cellophane also granted back to the French company the right to use in the rest of the world any new cellophane patents it might obtain. In a short time it reached agreements with a German and an English firm. For several years, there was no competition in the field; but, in 1924, several former employees of the French firm helped to create a Belgian firm, Societe Industrielle de la Cellulose (SIDAC), and in 1929 it established an American subsidiary, Sylvania Industrial Corporation of America, to produce cellophane within the high tariff walls of the United States.[6]

The year 1929 was an important one for Du Pont. By means of a stock switch, the French company accepted stock in Du Pont in exchange for its holdings in the American joint subsidiary. Du Pont Cellophane thus became a wholly owned subsidiary in the Du Pont empire. Also it developed a moisture-proof product which enhanced marketability. Sylvania, however, was also engaged in perfecting a process which would make cellophane impermeable to water. After Du Pont had been granted its patents, it immediately filed suit against Sylvania for patent infringement. In 1933, they reached an out-of-court agreement in which Du Pont granted Sylvania an exclusive license to use Du Pont's moisture-proof patents. There were provisions stipulating that any subsequent patents in the field would be licensed only to the other firm. Included was a complicated royalty system in which Sylvania was to pay a base 12 percent fee. Should Sylvania's sales exceed a carefully calculated percentage of the total production, then an almost confiscatory fee schedule would be employed. It was never necessary to invoke the penalty provisions. In 1945 the two companies modified the terms, dropping all penalty provisions, making licensing nonexclusive, and excluding any stipulations regarding future patents.[7]

From the time Du Pont first embarked upon the production of cellophane until the proceedings in 1947, the sales of the product had enjoyed an explosive growth. In 1928, the company had sold $603,222's worth of moisture-proof cellophane; in 1950, it had sold nearly $89,850,416's worth.[8] During this period, Du Pont had greatly reduced the price of the product and had narrowed the gap between its price and the cost of other cheaper flexible packaging materials, which differed from Du Pont's in many respects. Few of the packaging materials had all like characteristics, and no other material had the identical features of cellophane. It could be manufactured to have any one or all of the following qualities: resistance to moisture, imperviousness to moisture, transparency, and the capacity to be heat sealed and to be colored. The specifications desired by the purchaser obviously played a part in his choice of a wrapping material and thus the specific characteristics.

Although the original suit had charged Du Pont with "monopoly, attempting to monopolize, and conspiracy to monopolize the manufacture and sale of cellophane and cellulose caps and bands"[10] in the United States, when the government appealed the adverse ruling of the lower court, the Supreme Court appeal was aimed only at "the ruling that du Pont has not monopolized trade in cellophane."[11] To prove their contention, the government maintained that cellophane and the other wrapping materials were neither substantially fungible nor like priced; and therefore the market for the other wrappings was distinct from the market for cellophane. Had the government won on this point, it would then have been necessary for it to establish the existence of monopoly. Even though the Court did not find for the government on the first issue, it did decide the additional question for the record: "even if du Pont (sic) did possess monopoly power over sales of cellophane, it was not subject to Sherman Act prosecution because (1) the acquisition of that power was protected by patents, and (2) that power was acquired solely through du Pont's business expertness. It [monopoly] was thrust upon Du Pont."[12]

Much more important than the findings for the record was the Court's interpretation of the "market." After much research into packaging, including a trip to a packaging exhibition and a local supermarket to view the various means of merchandising potato chips and frozen foods, the Court noted: "An element for consideration as to the cross-elasticity of demand between products is the responsiveness of the sales of one product to price changes of the other. If a slight decrease in the price of cellophane causes a considerable number of customers of other flexible wrappings to switch to cellophane, it would be an indication that a high cross-elasticity of demand exists between them and that the products compete in the same market. The court below held that the '[g]reat sensitivity of customers in the flexible packaging markets to price of quality changes' prevented du Pont from possessing monopoly control over price. [118 F. Supp., at 207]. The record contains these findings. . . . We conclude that cellophane's interchangeability with other materials mentioned suffices to make it a part of this flexible packaging market."[13]

"Reasonable interchangeability" produced new difficulties and opportunities for the antitrusters. First, it was a handicap in monopoly cases in which they endeavored to prove violation of Section 2 of the Sherman Act. Second, it allowed for competition among products that had not formerly been believed to be competitive, thus affording the government the opportunity to interdict more mergers under Section 7 of the Clayton Act. Finally, by widening the market, it made other Section 7 merger cases much harder to win.[14] After the Cellophane decision, one of the priorities of the Division was to make better use of economists and to employ their analyses in preparing cases.[15]

Although the government was unsuccessful in proving that Du Pont monopolized the cellophane market, it was able to persuade the court that Du

Pont's holdings of stock in General Motors violated Section 7 of the Clayton Act. The action was an outgrowth of an inquiry into the market power and actions of the General Motors Corporation.[16] As Du Pont owned more than a 20 percent equity in General Motors, the indagation was quickly expanded to ascertain the relationship between the two companies, "with particular strength being laid on the control which Du Pont exercises over General Motors and the economic and legal results flowing from such control."[17] Then the inquiry was split in order that the action would not interfere with other suits against General Motors. Various members of the Division also feared that, without the differentiation, a "District Court, and perhaps even the Supreme Court, might be reluctant both to dissolve General Motors and divorce it from Du Pont in one decree."[18] However, the investigation was hindered by lack of personnel, and it was not until the end of the year that, in order to compel the production of documents, a grand jury investigation of the relationship was initiated, necessitating a criminal action and the use of the Sherman Act. Nevertheless, the Division realized that "the type of relief needed to eliminate the abuses arising out of [Du Pont's] . . . control of General Motors" could best be secured by a civil action seeking complete divestiture.[19]

The grand jury impaneled to study the relationship between Du Pont, General Motors, United States Rubber Company (now Uniroyal), Ethyl Corporation, Bendix Aviation Corporation, North American Aviation Incorporated, and Kinetic Chemicals Incorporated, sent out its first subpoenas on August 20, 1948.[20] The political intent of the original suit, filed within weeks of the 1948 presidential election, was obvious to many observers.[21] Their suspicions were confirmed later by a speech delivered by a former Attorney General, Supreme Court Justice Robert Jackson, in which he admitted that antitrust actions had been initiated for political reasons during his own tenure.[2] Although 1948 was not supposed to be a "Democratic Year," there were two obvious benefits which could accrue to the party as a result of the suit. First, it improved the antitrust record of the Truman Administration. Second, if the Republicans were victorious, they would probably drop or lose the case, thus providing the Democrats with an example of the alleged Republican proclivity toward satisfying the wishes of big business.

When the government was unable to obtain an indictment from the grand jury, it filed a civil action[23] charging that the du Pont family's direct and indirect ownership of large blocks of stock in General Motors and United States Rubber gave them *de facto* control of the companies.[24] The resultant reciprocal dealings were in restraint of trade and thus violated Sections 1 and 2 of the Sherman Act and Section 7 of the Clayton Act.

On December 3, 1954, after extensive preparations and a lengthy trial,

Judge Walter J. LaBuy of the District Court for the Northern District of Illinois found that the defendants were not guilty. Had the Eisenhower Administration been soft on antitrust, as commonly alleged, it probably would have dropped the case and proceeded no further. Instead it appealed and on June 3, 1957, an Eisenhower appointee, Justice William J. Brennan, writing the majority opinion, reversed the lower court and ruled for the government in a 4 to 2 decision.[25] The unparalleled clamor arising from the decision was fairly evenly divided between jubilation and excoriation.[26] Such attitudes were perhaps understandable considering the strong dissents that had been registered in the Supreme Court.

The issues at the root of the Du Pont-General Motors case stretch back to the days before World War I. In 1908, Du Pont, a manufacturer of military and commercial explosives, sought to diversify because the United States Army and Navy had decided to undertake the production of smokeless powder.[27] To this end, Du Pont's board of directors appointed a committee to find new uses for guncotton and other products of the smokeless-powder plants. It found that the most important new outlets were celluloid, artificial leather, artificial silk, and lacquer. The company thereupon diversified into these areas, and in 1910 it purchased the Fabrikoid Company, the largest manufacturer of artificial leather in the United States.

During World War I, Du Pont made a sizable profit on its sales of powder and explosives. Some of this profit it immediately utilized in its expansion program. The company made it a policy to invest in concerns which would net more than a 10 percent return[28] and which were in growth areas. In late 1915 the firm purchased the Arlington Company, one of the two largest celluloid makers in the country and in 1916 it bought the Fairfield Rubber Company, which produced rubber-coated fabrics for automobile and carriage tops.[29] Fairfield was later completely absorbed into the Fabrikoid Division. Anticipating the end of the war with its attendant cessation of orders for powder and explosives, Du Pont's development department proposed to adapt some of its facilities to the manufacture of artificial silk, synthetic organic dyestuffs, vegetable oils, paints and varnish. It stressed the opportunity for synergism.[30]

Du Pont's executive committee believed that the paint and varnish industry offered attractive growth potential, and it recommended that the company diversify by acquiring several concerns in the field. In March 1917, Du Pont purchased Harrison Brothers and Company, a small factor in the industry but a good potential base for building up "a very satisfactory paint and varnish business." An additional consideration favoring the move at that moment was the belief that the paint and varnish business was counter-cyclical; that is, when business was booming there was little time for maintenance, much of which could be postponed until a slack period.[31] The newly acquired company held a 52 percent interest in Beckton Chemical Company; the other 48 percent was owned by Cawley Clark and Company, a color manufacturer, and within a few months that company was likewise purchased. Later in the same year Du Pont procured the Bridgeport Wood Finishing Company. By the end of 1917, and prior to any major investment in General Motors, Du Pont had acquired companies manufacturing artificial leather, celluloid, rubber-coated goods, paints and varnishes. Today, a company with such a product line would be classified as a conglomerate.

William C. Durant had formed the General Motors Company as a holding company to control the firms of Oakland, Cadillac, Buick and Oldsmobile. The company had had financial troubles and in 1910 had to seek a loan from a syndicate of bankers headed by the house of Lee, Higginson & Company. As part of the deal the bankers insisted on Durant's being replaced as president. He then organized the Chevrolet Motor Company, which was successful; with its profits Durant invested in the stock of General Motors. In early 1914, upon the recommendation of John J. Raskob, the treasurer of Du Pont, Pierre S. du Pont purchased 2,005 shares of General Motors for his personal account.[32] The paths of all the actors converged in 1915 at a stockholders' meeting at which Durant and the bankers deadlocked over the choice of directors for General Motors. As a compromise they invited Pierre du Pont to become chairman of the board. In May 1916, Durant regained the upper hand at General Motors, for by then through the Chevrolet Company he controlled 450,000 of the 825,000 General Motors shares. In February 1917, Raskob proposed that the Du Pont Company make an investment in General Motors, which it did on a sizeable scale. By 1920 the du Pont family and its company owned almost 24 percent of the outstanding stock of General Motors.[33]

This purchase was made after a report written by Raskob had been circulated among Du Pont executives. The report gave several reasons for making the investment, including the positive results that would accrue from a consolidation of the financial divisions of General Motors and Du Pont, the fact that the purchase price was less than the book value of General Motors, and finally the belief that "Our interest in the General Motors Company will undoubtedly secure for us the entire Fabrikoid, Pyralin, paint and varnish business of those companies, which is a substantial factor."[34] Raskob expected that in the future Du Pont would take over General Motors, Durant being bought out through the issuance of a new class of securities.[35] In his reminiscences, written in 1951, Pierre S. du Pont explained that his company needed to find an investment vehicle that was sufficiently developed so that it could compensate for the loss of munitions profits at the end of the war. Recognizing the prestige which would be gained from an undiminished and uninterrupted dividend during the conversion from a wartime to a peacetime economy, both he and Raskob believed that investment in the stock of

General Motors would "fill the breach" and enable their company to continue its liberal disbursement.[36]

In 1920, as part of the new financing for General Motors, managed by J. P. Morgan & Company, it was agreed to support the price of General Motors stock. A stock crash in the later part of the year caused those involved in the stabilization to lose a great deal of money. Independently, Durant had been speculating in the securities of his company and had become for $27 million indebted to various banks, with assets of only 2,700,000 shares of General Motors. The du Ponts, fearing what would happen to the value of their investment in General Motors if he was forced to liquidate his stock, organized the Du Pont Securities Company to borrow $20 million and take over most of the Durant indebtedness. The consequence of these operations was that the du Ponts came to own through Du Pont Securities and its other investments approximately 38 percent of all outstanding General Motors stock. Starting in 1923 they began to dispose of some of their holdings in General Motors, and by 1938 their holdings had again fallen to 23 percent of the motor company's outstanding stock.[37]

The investment in General Motors did not terminate the Du Pont expansion. In 1918, it purchased the largest manufacturer of paint and varnish in the world, the Flint Varnish and Color Works, and its allied company in Canada.[38] The initial impetus for the purchase did not, however, come from Du Pont; instead, it emanated from the president of Flint who knew that unless his company was consolidated with the Harrison Division of Du Pont, he would lose a valuable customer.[39] Du Pont subsequently sold the Canadian concern and amalgamated the Flint Harrison facilities.[40]

During the 1920s, the Du Pont Company made other acquisitions, many of them in the paint and varnish field. One of the most outstanding in mid-1927 was the company's purchase of 114,000 shares of United States Steel Corporation.[41] Although the financial community appears to have agreed that this move presaged some type of du Pont involvement if not control of the steel giant,[42] according to Pierre S. du Pont "[the] United States Steel purchase by DP [Du Pont] was for temporary investment of surplus cash and was sold when the cash was needed."[43] What actually occurred was that when Colonel William Donovan, the chief of the Antitrust Division of the Department of Justice, wrote to the company asking for information on the relationships between Du Pont, United States Steel and General Motors, Du Pont quickly liquidated its purchase.[44]

In the meantime, the du Ponts were also very actively investing in various companies,[45] among them the United States Rubber Company. In 1927, the family formed a syndicate for the purpose of acquiring enough stock in the company to obtain control.[46] United States Rubber was probably the weakest of the major rubber companies, but its sales were the highest and it was the best integrated. In addition, it had at least a six-year lead over the other rubber companies in the cultivation of a new "pedigreed" rubber tree which was supposed to be highly productive and more disease resistant.[47] Despite the fact that merging the concern with General Motors would have been advantageous, Irénée du Pont doubted its feasibility because of the objections of the Department of Justice and the Federal Trade Commission. Besides, as an astute businessman, he must have realized that there were other means of exercising effective control than recourse to corporate marriage. Although the du Ponts never owned as large an equity in the United States Rubber as they did in General Motors, in the suit the government averred that the du Ponts' holdings of 18 percent of common and the 11 percent of preferred stock (with voting rights) were enough to give them voting control of the corporations. This leverage allegedly obtained favored treatment for General Motors in the tire business and assured United States Rubber of a guaranteed market for a large percentage of its products.[48]

The original antitrust complaint, filed on June 30, 1949, was amended twice before it came to trial. Named as defendants were not only Du Pont, General Motors and United States Rubber, but also two Du Pont stock holding companies (Christiana Securities and Delaware Realty and Investment Corporation), a corporate trustee, the Wilmington Trust Company, and seven members of the du Pont family. Also included in the roster were 26 beneficiary defendants, all members of the du Pont family. It appeared to laymen that the Justice Department had been somewhat carried away in filing the case because ten of the last cited group were minors. To charge those under age (one of whom was only a few months old) guilty of violating Sections 1 and 2 of the Sherman Act and Section 7 of the Clayton Act seemed preposterous.[49] The Du Pont public relations department was keenly aware of this and supplied the press with photographs of the "culprits." The pictures received wide circulation.[50]

To support its accusation that there was a conspiracy to restrain and monopolize trade in the products of General Motors, Du Pont and United States Rubber, the government resorted to the most detailed forms of evidence. The respondents countered in kind with economic analyses and lists of goods that General Motors purchased from Du Pont's competitors. The Section 7 part of the charge was given minor attention; it was not even included in the government's opening statement[51] and in its closing argument, out of a total of 78 pages treating the legal aspects of the case, only eight dealt with the Clayton Act.[52] The defendants likewise paid it scant heed. Some analysts have even suggested that it was an "afterthought."[53] The District Court was not impressed by the government's claims. On December 4, 1954, Judge Walter J. LaBuy delivered an all-encompassing, detailed opinion finding for the defendants, bluntly stating that the government had failed to prove conspiracy, monopolization, restraint of trade, or any possible probability of restraint of trade.[54]

The Eisenhower Administration exercised its right of appeal, and the case was docketed for the October 1955 term of the Supreme Court.[55] In the final test, the roster of defendants was much more limited and United States Rubber was not included. The decision to abandon that phase of the case against the rubber company had a twofold rationale: first, the case against U.S. Rubber was the weakest aspect of the action; and second, the government knew that if it did prevail in the appeal, the question would become moot; for if the government was successful in its appeal, and if General Motors was to be divorced from Du Pont control, then there would be no further incentive to provide United States Rubber with the alleged sheltered market.[56]

On June 3, 1957, when the Supreme Court decided for the government, the shock was felt throughout the antitrust bar, the government and the public.[57] The Court found that the government had proved a violation of Section 7 of the Clayton Act. It continued with an astounding revelation: The unamended Section 7 applied to both vertical and horizontal lines of commerce and therefore to stock acquisitions. The Court explained: "Failure of the Federal Trade Commission to invoke Section 7 against vertical stock acquisitions is not a binding administrative interpretation that Congress did not intend vertical acquisitions to come within the purview of the Act."[58]

As the Court had widened the definition of the market in the Du Pont-cellophane case, so it narrowed the definition in the Du Pont-General Motors case, for it found automotive finishes and automotive fabrics to have sufficient peculiar characteristics and uses distinct from all other finishes and fabrics to make them a "line of commerce" within the meaning of the Clayton Act. Other finishes and fabrics should not be included in the market, the Court held, and the records showed that both in terms of quantity and percentage Du Pont supplied General Motors with the largest part of its requirements of fabrics and finishes. Du Pont thus was found to have a substantial share of the market. The Court also extended the old Section 7 tests, saying, "The test of a violation is whether, *at the time of suit,* there is any reasonable probability that the stock acquisition may lead to a restraint of commerce or tend to create a monopoly in the line of commerce."[59] It also held that a previously legal investment became unlawful if it brought about, or attempted to bring about, a substantial lessening of competition. Furthermore, the Court maintained that there were many documents refuting the "investment" theory, and that Du Pont had gained its position as a major supplier not simply on its own merits. Thus the findings of the lower court were reversed and the case had to be remanded to the lower court to determine the necessary remedies.

Many plans were proposed, and once again the Eisenhower Administration demonstrated its strong antitrust philosophy. The government had prayed first, that Du Pont, Christiana and Delaware be required to dispose of their General Motors stock by sale, not stock dividends, to avoid having many shares of General Motors pass to the du Pont family; and secondly, that the monies received from the sale be paid to the stockholders. Pending the disposal, the government also desired that Du Pont, Christiana and Delaware be enjoined from voting their stock; also that General Motors be given the option of purchasing the stock to be divested; that the defendants be enjoined perpetually from purchasing the stock; that the General Motors-Du Pont joint ventures be terminated; and that Du Pont be required to divest itself of the business of making tetraethyl lead and other products in that line. Additionally, the government had prayed that both Du Pont and General Motors be required to divest themselves of their respective shares of the Kinetic Corporation, an enterprise owned jointly by the two concerns.[60] The judgment proposed by the government modified these draconian measures slightly, suggesting that Du Pont pay to its shareholders stock dividends in the form of General Motors securities.[61]

Du Pont proposed that its shareholders be allowed to vote the General Motors stock held by the company. It stressed that this "pass-through" solution would obviate the disruptiveness of placing 63,000,000 shares of one company on the market and thereby spare many innocent stockholders a financial loss.[62]

Anticipating that some type of stock distribution would be necessary, however, all the parties contacted Russell Harrington, the Commissioner of Internal Revenue, requesting a ruling on the tax status of any General Motors shares dispersed as a result of the decision.[63] The Department of Justice predicated its proposed final judgment[64] on a favorable tax ruling by the Internal Revenue Service.[65] Everyone's hopes were dashed when, on May 9, 1958, in a lengthy letter, Harrington ruled that the proposed distribution would be treated by the Internal Revenue Service as dividends, making them taxable.[66]

On October 2, 1959, Judge Walter LaBuy made public the lower court ruling, noting that in framing a judgment the court should take into account the interests of all the stockholders and that the time lapse of 30 years between the original acquisition and the antitrust action had created a sizable group of shareholders who had purchased Du Pont believing that the General Motors holding was legal and proper. He stated that especially since the Clayton Act was not a "penal statute," the government plan without remedial tax arrangements would be "grossly unfair."[67] He ruled that Du Pont could keep its investment in General Motors provided that it did not vote the shares itself and it allowed its shareholders to vote the General Motors stock as they themselves saw fit. At that point it was calculated that each Du Pont proxy could vote 1.38 shares of General Motors. Judge LaBuy further ruled that no member of the du Pont family would be allowed to vote its General Motors stock; in addition, he held that Christiana and Delaware should be prohibited from voting their shares. Finally he decreed that directors of Du Pont, Christiana and Delaware must not vote any shares they held in General Motors. With the voting rights of the stock divested, as well as representation on the board of General Motors, the possession of the legal title to the stock by Du Pont left it with only three rights:

1) To receive dividends on the stock,
2) To share *pro rata* with other stockholders in the assets of General Motors in the event of liquidation,
3) To dispose of legal title.

Thus, by means of the "pass-through" and other provisions, Du Pont's holding in General Motors would be "sterilized" and the symbiotic relationship would no longer exist.[68] To guard further against ties between the two companies Judge LaBuy included conditions terminating any "requirements contracts, exclusive patent arrangements or arrangements relating to preferential use of discoveries which may exist between Du Pont and General Motors." The judgment also enjoined any commercial ventures between the two giants.[69]

The rationale for LaBuy's decision was that as they stood, the tax laws made the government's prayer "harsh and punitive."[70] Accepting the Du Pont argument, he noted that there had never been a distribution so large as the government had proposed, and that smaller ones had had adverse effects on the price of the equity involved in the offering. Besides, if the General Motors stock were to be distributed as a dividend, as the tax laws stood, it would be likely that a sizable percentage of the 63,000,000 shares of General Motors stock in question would have to be sold to cover the taxes. This would depress the price of General Motors stock, and it would impair the ability of the company to negotiate any equity offering that it might consider.[71]

The importance of the tax code in this case cannot be overemphasized. It was the ruling of Commissioner Harrington of the Internal Revenue Service, stating that any distribution of Du Pont stock would be treated as a dividend and hence taxable as ordinary income (at a federal rate of 20-91 percent plus state taxes), which forced LaBuy to reject the government's proposal and to adopt the "pass-through" option. The final judgment did, however, provide that in the event the tax laws should be changed to lessen the inequities, either party might apply for modification of the judgment.[72]

Judge LaBuy's determination was not the final solution. To decide whether or not the denouement was satisfactory was up to the Attorney General. If not, the government had the right to appeal the judgment back to the Supreme

Court. Since 1960 was a presidential election year, and since so many Americans held stock in General Motors and Du Pont, there was doubt that the government would remain steadfast in its prayer for complete divestiture. Many expected that the government would be satisfied with the outcome of the lengthy case and would claim a legitimate victory. But this is not what occurred. The financial community was stunned when on January 14, 1960, Robert Bicks, the new acting chief of the Antitrust Division, announced that the relief proposed by the District Court was not effective. The government thereupon served notice of its intention to appeal the District Court's plan and to ask the Supreme Court to rule in favor of outright divestiture.

On May 23, 1960, the Supreme Court's reply that it would consider the government's appeal led to its hearing more testimony from all sides. Not only were lawyers for Du Pont and General Motors involved, but also the Court had appointed two other lawyers to act as *amicus curiae*: Andrew J. Dallstream to represent the interests of the other Du Pont stockholders, and Manuel E. Cowen to guard the interests of the shareholders of General Motors. Each submitted an elaborate brief opposing divestiture. Most of the material had been covered in either the first trial, the first appeal, or the post-trial hearings and briefs; however, the government stressed that "common ownership of two companies, even if divorced from voting power" is not "effective divestiture," emphasizing that "the exercise of voting rights is but one of the avenues of influence over management." It cited instances in which individuals wielded great power over management without the right to vote a single share of stock; and it averred that "any conscientious management must . . . take into consideration the interests of those investors . . . even if formal power to direct them or fire them is absent."[73] Therefore, it stated that the only way for relief to be effective would be to remove any possibility of influence by means of a total divestiture of the stock.[74] On the subject of the hardship imposed by the high rate of taxes, the government was very blunt: "We believe that the impact of federal taxes is not a pertinent factor in ordering relief in an antitrust proceeding. What transactions shall be taxed, and how much, is a question of federal tax policy and it is not a proper function of the judiciary to tailor a decree either to add or to avoid federal taxes. . . . When the court gave such weight to the tax aspects of divestiture it was trespassing on the field reserved for Congress."[75]

After nearly a year, on May 22, 1961, the Court by a 4 to 3 vote[76] reversed the lower court's plan, stating that the proxy "pass-through" procedure was not an effective solution because it did not eliminate the violation of Section 7 of the Clayton Act. The Court, therefore, directed complete divestiture.[77]

The Supreme Court essentially vacated the judgment, except for the provisions enjoining Du Pont from exercising voting rights in respect to its General Motors stock, and remanded the case back again to the District

Court for a determination of the equitable relief necessary. The final judgment, written by Judge LaBuy included provisions that

1) Du Pont dispose of its stock in General Motors.
2) The divestiture be completed within 34 months.
3) Until divested, the stock be voted by means of the "pass through" method.
4) Christiana dispose of all its General Motors shares within three years.[78]

After the first Supreme Court decision, there were several unsuccessful attempts to pass legislation alleviating the tax burden in any divestiture of General Motors stock.[79] Since there appeared to be no sense of urgency, the bills never reached a vote in both houses of Congress. After the second Supreme Court decision overturning the "pass-through" formula and directing total divestiture, the action became more concerted. Apparently without the help of the Treasury and Justice Departments but supported by the President, Republican Senator John J. Williams of Delaware and Democratic Senator Harry F. Byrd of Virginia finally obtained passage of a statute (Public Law 87-403) providing that for tax purpose the market value of the General Motors shares received would be treated as a return of capital.[80]

The new statute was directly responsible for the divestiture timetable. Until passage of the bill, the government had sought distribution over a span of ten years to lessen the tax impact. Since the new law limited the tax liability at the time of dispersement of General Motors stock (unless the value of the stock received was greater than the original cost of the Du Pont stock), the pace was speeded up and divestiture was to be completed within less than three years.[81]

To lessen the disruption of the market in the two securities, the distribution was made in three installments totaling 1.36 shares of General Motors for each share of Du Pont.[82] During the divestment period, complying with Judge LaBuy's order, the du Pont family and their investment companies also made several large public offerings of General Motors stock. In March 1965 the last underwriting of 2,315,106 shares was made. Thus, after 16 years and four administrations, the government had finally accomplished what it had set out to do.

The "time of suit" concept appeared to offer fertile ground for other actions against large corporate concentrations. One of the first which the antitrusters considered was a suit against Du Pont for its acquisition of a controlling stock interest in the Remington Arms Company, Inc.[83] The proposed complaint charged that Du Pont had made its purchase to protect its market for smokeless powder and that Du Pont hoped to develop the company into a profitmaker by collaboration with other sporting-goods ammunition makers.[84]

In comparison to its relationship with General Motors, Du Pont's ties with

Remington were insignificant. In terms of total sales, the chemical giant's interest in Remington was less than one-half percent. There was also a national defense aspect to the case. In the mid-1950s, Du Pont considered withdrawing from the manufacture of smokeless powder, but it was induced by the federal government to remain in the field. The antitrusters believed that were the suit to be filed, Du Pont might well cease to manufacture that type of powder thus providing its one competitor, Hercules Powder Company, with a monopoly. Even if Du Pont were to continue to manufacture, the divestiture would not lead to a more competitive environment in the industry.

Apparently, the case was not filed because it was not large enough, and in several instances it was rather weak. Furthermore, the unfairness of applying the Du Pont-General Motors case's "time of suit" test of illegality against Du Pont before it was used against any other combination also might very well have influenced the antitrusters.[85]

The Du Pont cases assume their proper significance when viewed in full perspective. Despite the fact that the two were probably filed with partisan intentions by the Truman Administration, and although Charles Wilson, the first Secretary of Defense in the Eisenhower Administration, had previously been president of General Motors, the cases were vigorously fought throughout the courts. Although defeated in the Cellophane case, the antitrusters were provided with the tool of "reasonable interchangeability," a concept which would prove especially useful in evaluating the legality of subsequent mergers. The General Motors case is noteworthy, too, because the Eisenhower antitrusters fought for an unpopular concept right before the 1960 presidential election. It is important as well because it provided the opportunity, such as in the instance of the proposed Du Pont-Remington case, for other deconcentration actions. Significantly, subsequent administrations have not yet elected to use the tool.

Bibliography:

Government Antitrust Cases Against Du Pont

U.S. v. E.I. du Pont de Nemours and Company, et al.
  No. 280 in Equity, D.C. Del.
  Amended Petition filed 8/5/07
U.S. v. E.I. du Pont de Nemours & Company, et al.
  Cr. No. C106-15, D.C. S.D. N.Y.
  Indictment returned 9/1/39
U.S. v. Synthetic Nitrogen Products Corporation, et al.
  Cr. No. C106-16, D.C. S.D. N.Y.
  Indictment returned 9/1/39
U.S. v. Allied Chemical & Dye Corp., et al.
  C.A. No. 14-320, D.C. S.D. N.Y.
  Complaint filed 5/29/41
U.S. v. Allied Chemical & Dye Corp., et al.
  Cr. No. 753c, D.C. N.J.
  Indictment returned 5/14/42
U.S. v. E. I. du Pont de Nemours & Co., et al.
  Cr. No. 9733, D.C. E.D. Pa.
  Indictment returned 6/4/42
U.S. v. E.I. du Pont de Nemours & Co., et al.
  Cr. No. 1266, D.C. N.D. Ind.
  Indictment returned 6/26/42
U.S. v. E.I. du Pont de Nemours & Co., et al.
  Cr. No. 1268, D.C. N.D. Ind.
  Indictment returned 6/26/42
U.S. v. E.I. du Pont de Nemours & Co., et al.
  Cr. No. 1269, D.C. N.D. Ind.
  Indictment returned 6/26/42
U.S. v. Monsanto Chemical Co., et al.
  Cr. No. 1265, D.C. N.D. Ind.
  Indictment returned 6/26/42
U.S. v. E.I. du Pont de Nemours & Co., et al.
  Cr. No. 878-C, D.C. N.J.
  Indictment returned 8/10/42

U.S. v. Rohm & Haas Co., et al.
  Cr. No. 877-C, D.C. N.J.
  Indictment returned 8/10/42

U.S., ex rel. David Raider, and David Raider v.
E.I. du Pont de Nemours and Company, et al.
  C.A. No. 3105, D.C. E.D. N.Y.
  Complaint filed 1/21/43

U.S. v. National Lead Company, et al.
  Cr. No. C-114-455, D.C. S.D. N.Y.
  Indictment returned 6/28/43

U.S. v. Imperial Chemical Industries, Ltd., et al.
  C.A. No. 24-13, D.C. S.D. N.Y.
  Complaint filed 1/6/44

U.S. v. National Lead Company, et al.
  C.A. No. 26-258, D.C. S.D. N.Y.
  Complaint filed 6/24/44

U.S. (Counter-Claimant) *v. Wisconsin Alumni Research*
Foundation
  C.A. No. 43-704, D.C. N.D. Ill.
  Complaint filed 10/20/44

U.S. v. Bendix Aviation Corp., et al.
  C.A. No. 44-284, D.C. S.D. N.Y.
  Complaint filed 12/9/47

U.S. v. E.I. du Pont de Nemours and Company
  C.A. No. 1216, D.C. Del.
  Complaint filed 12/13/47

U.S. v. Sherwin-Williams, et al.
  Cr. No. 12, 789, D.C. W.D. Pa.
  Indictment returned 7/20/48

U.S. v. E.I. du Pont de Nemours & Company, et al.
  Cr. No. 12,790, D.C. W.D. Pa.
  Indictment returned 7/20/48

U.S. v. E.I. du Pont de Nemours & Company, et al.
  C.A. No. 49C-1071, D.C. N.D. Ill.
  Complaint filed 6/30/49

U.S. v. E.I. du Pont de Nemours and Company, et al.
  C.A. No. 70-829, D.C. N.D. Ohio
  Complaint filed 8/28/70

U.S. v. E.I. du Pont de Nemours and Company, et al.
  C.A. No. 74-1086, D.C. N.J.
  Complaint filed 7/18/74

U.S. v. E.I. du Pont de Nemours and Company, et al.
  Cr. No. 74-279, D.C. N.J.
  Indictment returned 7/18/74

NOTES

1. See appended chart at the end of the chapter. Note, for ease in differentiating DuPont denotes the company, du Pont means a member of the family.
2. "Additional Cellophane Price Information," Antitrust Papers: Cellophane, Acc. 70A4771, file 60-32-13. Note, Sylvania should not be confused with Sylvania Electric Products Corp. See Appendix A, entries 54, 63, 141, 228.
3. Memo for Attorney General Tom Clark, Nov. 13, 1942; see also "Program for relief envisioned when Government asks for same," Sept. 18, 1953, Antitrust Papers: Cellophane.
4. Memo of meeting with Du Pont officials, July 29, 1947, Antitrust Papers: Cellophane.
5. U.S. v. E.I. du Pont de Nemours and Company, 351 U.S. 377 (1956), affirming 118 F. Supp. 41 (D. Del. 1953).
6. Memo from Development Department to Executive Committee, Apr. 14, 1923, Records of E.I. du Pont de Nemours and Company, Series II, Part II, Film Department, Research Division, Patent Section, Acc. 1305. U.S. vs. [sic] Du Pont Cellophane Suit. The records of the Du Pont Company are housed in the Eleutherian Mills Historical Library.
7. "International aspects of the Cellophane Case," undated memorandum for the files: "Evidence in support of proposed complaint charging Du Pont with monopolization of the Cellophane Industry," July 3, 1947, Antitrust Papers: Cellophane; George W. Stocking and Willard F. Mueller, "The Cellophane Case and the New Competition," *The American Economic Review*, 45 (Mar. 1955), 29-44; Donald F. Turner, "Antitrust Policy and the Cellophane Case," *Harvard Law Review*, 70 (Dec. 1956), 281-285; Joel B. Dirlam and Irving M. Stelzer, "The Cellophane Labyrinth," *The Antitrust Bulletin*, 1 (Feb.-Apr. 1956), 633-651; George W. Stocking, "Economic Tests of Monopoly and the Concept of the Relevant Market," *The Antitrust Bulletin*, 2 (Mar. 1957), 479-493; Willard F. Mueller, "Du Pont: A Study in Firm Growth," unpublished doctoral dissertation (Nashville, Tenn., 1956); U.S. v. E.I du Pont de Nemours and Company, 351 U.S. 377, 382-385.
8. Records of E.I. du Pont de Nemours, Series II, Part II, Film Department Research Division, Patent Section. Acc. 1305, U.S. vs. [sic] "Du Pont Cellophane Suit, Current Situation: The field of commerce involved," Book I, and "Prices," Book XII, Cellophane—Preliminary Information, Sept. 28, 1948; U.S. v. E.I. duPont de Nemours and Co., 351 U.S. 377, 385.
9. "Historic samples of various film from different manufacturers the world over," Records of E.I. du Pont de Nemours, Series II, Part II, Film Department: Management Division, Acc. 1305.
10. Caps and bands are made from regenerated cellulose and are then extruded to form a covering which will shrink while drying to form a closure. Du Pont ceased manufacturing the caps the year that the suit was entered.
11. U.S. v. E.I. du Pont, 351 U.S. 377, 378.
12. U.S. v. E.I du Pont, 351, 381.
13. U.S. v. E. I. du Pont, 351, 400.

14. "Implications of Cellophane Decision," Mar. 11, 1957, Antitrust Papers: Cellophane, Acc. 71A6389, file 60-32-13, and Acc. 70A4771, file 60-32-13.

15. See especially "Economists and Economic Analysis in the Antitrust Division" a confidential report commissioned by Victor Hansen prepared by Professors E.T. Grether and Carl Kaysen. No copy is in Dept. of Justice files, incomplete copy in possession of author, courtesy of Victor Hansen; a fairly complete precis of the report, with names removed, can be found in E.T. Grether, "Economic Analysis in Antitrust Enforcement," *The Antitrust Bulletin* 4 (Jan.-Feb. 1959), 55-74; also see Rogers Papers: Box 29, Eisenhower Library, Staff Files.

16. Memo to Wendell Berge, Oct. 15, 1946, Antitrust Division of the Department of Justice Papers, Acc. 70A4771, file 60-107-37.

17. Memo to Melville Williams, Mar. 31, 1947 in Antitrust Papers: DuPont—General Motors.

18. Memo to Holmes Baldridge, Apr. 1, 1947, Antitrust Papers: DuPont—General Motors.

19. Memos to Holmes Baldridge, Apr. 29, 1947, and to John Sonnett, Nov. 6, 1947, Antitrust Papers: DuPont—General Motors.

20. The reason for the inclusion of the other companies was that the automotive giant owned positions in them until Jan. 1948, General Motors owned a substantial interest in Bendix Aviation Corporation. In June 1948, the motor company divested itself of its 29.1% equity in North American Aviation. While it is likely that their sales were a result of the antitrust inquiry, they were also part of a redeployment of capital to generate funds for post-war expansion. In the same period, General Motors also sold its interest in the Greyhound Corporation. The Ethyl Corporation was the result of a joint venture with the Standard Oil Company of New Jersey. Kinetic Chemicals was jointly owned with Du Pont: in Dec. 1949, General Motors sold its interest in the company to Du Pont, making the chemical manufacturer the sole owner of Kinetic.

21. See E.I. du Pont de Nemours & Co. Papers, Series II, Part 2: Acc. 1054, *Du Pont-General Motors Scrapbook*, vol. 1. The Du Pont papers are housed in the Eleutherian Mills Historical Library in Greenville, Wilmington, Del.

22. Speech to the New York State Bar Association, delivered Jan. 30, 1951, at the Harvard Club. The papers of Supreme Court Justice Jackson are in the possession of his son, William Jackson. It is noted in Ray Tucker, Feb. 1, 1951, "National Whirlagig" (Syndicated column) included in *Du Pont-General Motors Scrapbook*, I, 88.

23. *Quick Magazine*, July 11, 1949. (Included in *Du Pont-General Motors Scrapbook*, I, 22.)

24. Complaint at 26; Pretrial Brief for Plaintiff at U.S. v. Du Pont et al., 126 F. Supp. 235. Copies of all the court papers are also located in The Eleutherian Mills Historical Library. See also background memo to Newell A. Clapp (Acting Assistant Attorney General in charge of The Antitrust Division of the Justice Department), Dec. 17, 1952, Antitrust Papers: Cellophane.

25. U.S. v. E.I. Du Pont de Nemours and Company et al., 353 U.S. 586 (1957). Those justices voting with the majority were Justices Brennan, Black, Douglas and Chief Justice Warren. Those dissenting were Justices Burton and Frankfurter.

Justices Clark, Harlan and Whittaker took no part in the consideration or decision of the case. Clark had been the Attorney General when the case was filed, Harlan had helped form the defense for Du Pont, and Whittaker was appointed to the bench after much of the work on the case was already finished.

26. *Du Pont-General Motors Scrapbook*, IV; legal scholars who supported the decision included: George W. Stocking, "The Du Pont-General Motors Case and the Sherman Act," *Virginia Law Review*, 44 (Jan. 1958), 1- 40; Joel Dirlam and Irwin Stelzer, "The *Du Pont-General Motors* Decision: In the Antitrust Grain," *Columbia Law Review*, 63 (Jan. 1958), 24- 43. Those who opposed included: Jesse W. Markham, "The Du Pont-General Motors Decision," *Virginia Law Review*, 42 (Oct. 1957), 881-888; Blackwell Smith, "Precedent, Public Policy and Predictability," *The Georgetown Law Journal*, 46 (Summer 1958), 633-645; Milton Handler, "Annual Review of Recent Antitrust Developments," *The Record of the Association of the Bar of the City of New York* (Oct. 1957), pp. 411-443.

27. Argument for defendants at 7669; Alfred D. Chandler and Stephen Salsbury, *Pierre S. du Pont and the Making of the Modern Corporation* (New York, 1971), gives good background coverage.

28. Defendant Exhibit #48 (June 10, 1915, Development Department memo to Executive Committee signed by R.R.M. Carpenter, Director).

29. A major customer was the Ford Motor Company (126 F. Supp. 235, 266)!

30. P.S. du Pont, rough draft of a speech (undated), Group 10, Papers of P.S. du Pont, file 418: 1917-18, Box 3, folder "1918: Bonus: End of Wartime Contracts": Defendant Exhibit 59, "Proposed Utilization of Excess Plant Capacity" (memo dated Dec. 30, 1916): Defendant Exhibit 69, "Completed Recommendations of Excess Plant Utilization Division" (Nov. 23, 1917).

31. Defendant Exhibit 57 (memo dated Nov. 28, 1916) authorizing the Development Department to negotiate for the purchase of Harrison Brothers and Company.

32. P.S. du Pont, "Recollections," 10: File 418: 1917-18, Box 3, folder "Bonus, End of Wartime Contracts": Box 26, folder "Antitrust Suit"; Deposition for P.S. du Pont at 118-9.

33. In this and all further calculations, unless otherwise specified, the percentage control is the total family holdings plus that of the company.

34. Defendant Exhibit 85 (memo from the Du Pont Treasurer Raskob to the Finance Committee dated Dec. 19, 1917) "General Motors-Chevrolet Motor Stock Investment," 11.

35. "General Motors," p. 12.

36. The Longwood Manuscripts, Group 10, Papers of P.S. du Pont, Series B, folder 1203-63, "General Motors" p. 2a, 11.

37. Pierre S. du Pont to Irénée du Pont, Nov. 26, 1920, in Papers of John J. Raskob, Acc. 473, file 681, Box 1 of 2; folder: Pierre S. du Pont. The papers of John J. Raskob are located in The Eleutherian Mills Historical Library. Defendant Exhibit 110, (memo dated Aug. 17, 1921) "History of the du Pont Company's Investment in the General Motors Corporation"; cross examination of Pierre S. du Pont at 681.

38. Government Exhibit 69 (Apr. 17, 1918). Report on the Flint Varnish & Color

Works by the Development Department for R.R.M. Carpenter. Ironically, a minor stockholder in Flint was General Motors (Closing Argument on behalf of Government at 7588).

39. Government Exhibit #277, Transcript of Record, VI, Supreme Court of the United States, October term, 1956, No. 3, U.S. v. E.I. du Pont de Nemours and Company, et al., pp. 3696-3701.

40. Defendant Exhibit 110 (Aug. 17, 1921), "History of the du Pont Company's Investment in the General Motors Corporation," Cross Examination of Pierre S. du Pont at 681.

41. See letter of John Raskob to Pierre S. du Pont dated July 27, 1927 in Papers of John J. Raskob, Acc. 473, File 681, Box 2 of 2, folder: "P.S. du Pont."

42. *New York Evening Post* (July 30, 1927), *New York American* and *New York World* (Aug. 1, 1927), clippings in Raskob Papers, see preceding note.

43. Handwritten note in front cover of Pierre S. du Pont's personal copy of transcript, opening statement.

44. Longwood Manuscripts, Group 10, Papers of P.S. du Pont, file 229, Box 9, folder: Investments: 1903-1948.

45. Longwood Manuscripts, Papers of P.S. du Pont, Box 31: Investments, folders 1929-1931.

46. Defendant Exhibit 206 (letter dated Jan. 25, 1928 from Henry du Pont to Pierre S. du Pont).

47. Raymond Price to Irénée du Pont, Dec. 22, 1928; the Irénée du Pont Papers, Series J, Acc. 152, 228, file 217, folder 3. The papers of Irénée du Pont are located in The Eleutherian Mills Library.

48. Complaint of Government at 189, 251; Closing Argument of Government at 7198-99, 7440-7521.

49. Although, from a public relations perspective, the inclusion may have been a blunder, from a legal standpoint, it was essential since the government would only be able to obtain relief from those it had sued.

50. See *Du Pont-General Motors Scrapbook* for pages of clippings.

51. Opening Statement for Plaintiff at pp. 7-77.

52. Closing Argument for Plaintiff at pp. 7522-7600.

53. Irston Barnes, "Competitive Mores and Legal Tests in Merger Cases: The Du Pont-General Motors Decision," *The Georgetown Law Journal*, 44 (Summer, 1958), 571-573. E. Houston Harsha, who was in charge of the trial for the government in the proceedings in the District Court characterized the Section 7 charge as a "throw-in," noting that "the Government submitted a two-volume post-trial brief consisting of 777 pages, of which only two pages (the last two pages) were devoted to the Section 7 charge" (E. Houston Harsha to author, Aug. 27, 1971). Willis L. Hotchkiss, described by Harsha as the "father of the case," stated, "I personally was surprised that the Supreme Court based its decision on Section 7, and I think nearly everyone who had a hand in the trial and appeal was also surprised. When we drafted the complaint the Section 7 charge was included somewhat as a matter of course by way of touching all bases. At the trial stress was placed on the Sherman Act aspect of the case" (Willis Hotchkiss to author, Sept. 5, 1971). Victor Kramer, the most ardent advocate of including the Section

7 charge only believed that "there was a chance to win the case on Section 7" (Victor Kramer to author, Aug. 30, 1971).

54. Opinion of Judge Walter J. LaBuy at 219-220; also in 126 F. Supp 235, 335.

55. Mr. Dooley defined an appeal "whin you ask wan coort to show its contimpt f'r anither coort"; quoted in M.A. Adelman, "The Du Pont-General Motors Decision," *Virginia Law Review*, 43 (Oct. 1957), 873.

56. Memo to Simon Soboloff (Solicitor General), Jan. 28, 1955, Antitrust Papers.

57. See memo to Paul McCracken, June 17, 1957, entitled "A Note on the Supreme Court Decision in the Du Pont Case," in Staff Files, Papers of Philip Areeda: Box 5, Eisenhower Library. Also Walter Barthold to author, August 24, 1971. Mr. Barthold is a member of Arthur Dry, Kalish, Taylor and Wood (formerly Arthur Dry and Dole), one of the firms that represented United States Rubber in the District Court phase of the Case. In the antitrust area, the Supreme Court was beginning a period of deciding for the government on almost all appeals. Indeed, in the period 1962-1972 the Court backed the government in every instance on the antitrust field.

58. U.S. v. E.I. du Pont de Nemours and Company, et al., 353 U.S. p. 586.

59. U.S. v. E.I. du Pont, 586, 607 (emphasis in original). The retroactive implications of the phrase "time of suit" are tremendous. Although the concept could be used in many situations, it has never been employed.

60. Transcript of Record, vol. 1 at 256-260, U.S. v. E.I. du Pont, 353 U.S. 586.

61. Proposed Final Judgment for Plaintiff at 5.

62. See "Memorandum (by Victor Hansen, Assistant Attorney General in charge of the Antitrust Division) for the Attorney General," Apr. 1, 1958, Attachment, "The Adverse Effects of the Government's Plan," 19; also memo to George Reycraft, April 2, 1958, Antitrust Papers: Du Pont-General Motors.

63. Letter dated Dec. 16, 1957, to Russell Harrington from Daniel Gribbon, Attorney for du Pont de Nemours and Company; letter dated Jan. 16, 1958, to Russell Harrington from Leo Tierney, Attorney for General Motors. These and other letters bound in the Du Pont-General Motors Case material at the Eleutherian Mills Historical Library and in Antitrust Papers.

64. A copy of the proposed decree is in the Rogers Papers, Box 29, A67-6, "Antitrust Division" (Eisenhower Library).

65. Victor Hansen to Russell C. Harrington, Dec. 18, 1957. Antitrust Papers: DuPont-General Motors.

66. Harrington to Gribbon, May 9, 1958, Antitrust Papers: DuPont-General Motors.

67. Opinion of Judge Walter J. LaBuy at pp. 21-23 and 26 (Oct. 2, 1959).

68. La Buy, pp. 73-76.

69. La Buy, pp. 82-83.

70. La Buy, 99.

71. La Buy, pp. 97-101. For the Du Pont position see numerous press releases of the Public Relations Department, especially a 30-page memo dated May 31, 1962, by the director, Harold Brayman, Records of the Du Pont Company: Public Relations Department, Acc. 1111, Box 51, "Press Analysis, Reports, and Clippings" (Eleutherian Mills Historical Library).

72. Final Judgment at 13 (Nov. 17, 1959).
73. Brief for Plaintiff at 43-45, 54 (Oct. 1960).
74. Brief for Plaintiff, p. 45.
75. Brief for Plaintiff, pp. 59-61.
76. The majority decision was written by Justice Brennan with Warren, Black and Douglas concurring; Justices Frankfurter, Whittaker and Stewart dissented; and Justices Clark and Harlan abstained.
77. 366 U.S. 316, 331.
78. Final Judgment at 4-23 (Mimeographed copy). Also see section in *Du Pont-General Motors Scrapbook*, vol. VIII. Letter to the stock holders from Crawford H. Greenewalt, President of Du Pont (May 31, 1962), Scudder File, Watson Library of Business and Economics, Columbia University, New York, N.Y.
79. See, for example, memorandum for the Attorney General written by Victor Hansen discussing a conference between the staff of the Antitrust Division and the Under-Secretary of the Treasury, Fred Scribner, June 26, 1958. Staff Files: Papers of William Rogers: Box 29, Eisenhower Library.
80. *Du Pont-General Motors Scrapbook*, Vol. VIII and IX. Papers of the President of the United States: 1953-1961, Diaries Series, Box 33, Staff Notes August 1960 (1); Memorandum of Conference on FREAR Bill, June 28, 1960, Staff Notes, June 1960(1). It is interesting to note that on Aug. 25, 1960, Eisenhower met with Crawford Greenawalt of Du Pont.
81. According to PL-87-403, when the Du Pont stock was sold, the value of the General Motors equities received would be subtracted from the original cost of the Du Pont shares. The capital-gains taxes would be assessed on that cost figure.
82. On July 9, 1962, half a share of General Motors was dispersed to Du Pont stockholders of record June 8, 1962; the second allotment of .36 of a General Motors share was made on Jan. 6, 1964, to stockholders of record Nov. 26, 1963; the final parcel of half a share of General Motors stock was meted out on Jan. 4, 1965, to stockholders of record Nov. 24, 1964.
83. Memo, Nov. 28, 1958, Antitrust Papers: Du Pont-Remington, Acc. 71A6389, file 60-0-37-313.
84. "Proposed Complaint against E.I. du Pont de Nemours and Co. and Remington Arms Company, Inc.," Jan. 9, 1959, Antitrust Papers: Du Pont-Remington.
85. Unsigned, undated scrap of paper in Antitrust Papers: Du Pont-Remington.

CHAPTER VI

The Bicks-Rogers
Antitrust Policy

IN April 1959 Eisenhower chose Robert Alan Bicks to replace the retiring chief of the Antitrust Division, Victor Hansen. Bicks, who at thirty-one was the youngest man ever to be appointed to that position, brought to the post a vitality that he had been actively demonstrating in the antitrust field for the preceeding six years.

Born into a family of lawyers, he not surprisingly turned in the direction of jurisprudence. After being graduated *summa cum laude* from Yale and similarly distinguishing himself at that university's law school, he held the position of law clerk to Judge Stanley Fuld. Next he worked as legislative assistant to Irving Ives, the Republican Senator from New York. In 1953 he accepted the post of executive secretary of the Attorney General's National Committee to Study the Antitrust Laws—in which capacity he quickly demonstrated his ability both to Barnes and Brownell, and he mastered antitrust law. The job was actually a "19-month submersion in the antitrust complexities of monopoly, price fixing, etc."[1]

Upon completion of the study of the antitrust corpus, Barnes and Brownell wanted to keep Bicks in the Division; and since there were no openings that would be stimulating enough to insure his stay, they created the post of legal assistant to Barnes. It was in this position that Bicks most impressed his superior, and the two often worked together on cases late into the night after the rest of the staff had left. Toward the end of Barnes' tenure, Bicks handled many aspects of the running of the Antitrust Division.

When Hansen replaced Barnes as chief of the Division, Bicks was appointed his second assistant. The first assistant, Edward Foote, who had joined the Division in 1954, did not remain long. It came to the attention of some members of the House Antitrust Subcommittee that Foote (or his wife) had been speculating in stocks of companies having difficulties with the Antitrust Division. One outstanding example was his $65,564.58 purchase of

113

shares in the Warren Petroleum Corporation before the Department announced that it was not planning to investigate Warren's impending merger with Gulf Oil Company. Foote sold these shares right after the press release was published and just before the Federal Trade Commission declared its interest in the merger, and he thereby made a sizable profit. Foote resigned September 13, 1956, within eight days of the revelation of his activities, giving "family matters" as his reason for retirement.[2] Bicks was appointed acting first assistant in his stead; five months later, he became the first assistant. Bicks' tenure was not unsuccessful. Some observers have noted that he wielded a great deal of power; Richard Austin Smith stated, "It is somewhat of an open question whether or not Bicks actually ran the division for Hansen."[3] This was slightly unfair to Hansen. Rather, it was at this point that Bicks began to exhibit some of the qualities that were to create problems for him in the future. Sometimes tactless and overly assertive, he even filed one antitrust complaint while Hansen was out of town and only the following day did his boss become aware of the action from reading the newspapers. Technically, there was nothing out of order about the move because during Hansen's absence from his office, Bicks was the Acting Assistant Attorney General,[4] but it did serve to reinforce many people's attitudes toward him.

With the resignation of Hansen as chief on April 20, 1959, Bicks was named Acting Assistant Attorney General in charge of the Antitrust Division. It took 13 months for President Eisenhower to send Bicks' nomination to the Senate for confirmation, because, according to William Rogers, the Attorney General at the time, this delay would provide observers ample opportunity to see how well Bicks would do in the position. There was, Rogers said, "nothing abnormal" in waiting so long, "especially in the case of such a young man."[5] The full Senate never had a chance to vote on the nomination, for it remained bottled up in committee and Bicks continued to be Acting Assistant Attorney General until the end of Eisenhower's term. Since there was little overt resistance to the nomination and since Bicks received an unprecedented number of endorsements and considerable backing from both Democrats and Republicans, it seems safe to assume that most of the opposition to him was for personal reasons rather than from hostile reactions to his vigorous antitrust activities.

During Bicks' term as acting chief of the Antitrust Division there was no slowdown in antitrust activity; if there was any change, it was in the direction of intensified vigor in enforcement. The figures of cases filed during the period are impressive. Furthermore, the trend toward increasingly energetic enforcement of Section 7 of the Clayton Act's restrictions on corporate mergers and acquisitions continued unabated. It was in this phase that the Division under Bicks made its greatest advances. Convinced that Section 7 represented a prime weapon for "prophylactic" antitrust, he endeavored to implement the statute forcefully in those sections of the economy that were not already highly concentrated.[6]

It is in this framework then that the actions in the oil industry must be considered. Far from concentrated, the industry consisted of many competitive units at each level of operations—production, refining and retailing. It was Bicks' goal to preserve the existing structure by means of Section 7 because "we have a unique chance to apply Section 7 in the oil industry today so that in twenty-five years we do not have an industry like steel or aluminum."[7]

The treatment of the prospective merger between the Standard Oil Company of Ohio (Sohio) and Leonard Refineries illustrates the attitudes of the Justice Department. In mid-1955, when Leonard wanted to take over the assets of Mid-West Refineries, Inc., Roosevelt Oil and Refining Corporation, Inc., and Leonard Pipeline Company, it used the device of requesting a clearance from the Antitrust Division. This permission was quickly given because, "the merger will enable the four companies to offer more effective competition to the very large oil companies whose sales dominate the state of Michigan."[8] The situation was different when Sohio, a major oil company with little business in the state, wanted to take over the largest independent one. Moving swiftly to interdict the marriage, the government charged that the union would substantially lessen competition and tend to create a monopoly. It noted that Sohio was one of the largest integrated companies in the petroleum industry, ranking fourteenth in size in terms of domestic refining capacity. The government also considered the Michigan market, observing that Sohio had made several forays into the state and that, projecting expansion there, the merger would probably lessen competition between the two enterprises in the future. Furthermore, it would enhance Sohio's competitive advantage over other small concerns in the field. It would serve to concentrate the market and would stimulate other mergers which would also concentrate the industry.[9] Exactly three weeks after the government expressed its intention to oppose the merger, the companies abandoned their plans.

The Sohio case became a model for the Justice Department. In a memo entitled "Lessons to be learned," Robert Hummel, Chief of the Great Lakes Field Office, emphasized that a lot of time was spent in a concentrated period but that the expenditure saved many man-hours in the long run. While normally there is danger of the companies in question stalling and trying to scramble assets, by filing the action before consummation of the merger, "they [Sohio and Leonard . . . had to] cooperate in bringing the case to a fast trial" if they wished to bring their plans to fruition. Finally Hummel noted that the Department had made good use of the material it had already amassed on the industry.[10]

From the perspective of its authors, the acquisition by Texaco, Incorporated, of the Superior Oil Company was ideal. Although an integrated oil company, Texaco was a crude-deficit firm since it never had enough crude oil for its refineries. Conversely, Superior produced more crude than it could refine. Also important was the location of their respective oil reserves. While Texaco's were mainly in Indonesia and the Middle East, most of Superior's were in South America. But since such a marriage definitely would affect the relative concentration of the industry, the Justice Department indicated its opposition. It based its case first upon the fact that Texaco and Superior were "competitors in significant areas, particularly crude oil and natural gas sales." Second, Texaco would be acquiring control of a substantial source of supply that previously had also been available to its refiner competitors. Third, inaction by the Justice Department would set a bad example and might incite a wave of mergers in the industry. Finally, Texaco had a record of prior acquisitions, of which its 1958 takeover of Seaboard Oil Company was the largest, increasing its oil reserves by 12 percent.[11] After a meeting with company officials in which it is very likely that Bicks threatened to include the Seaboard acquisition in any suit, the two oil companies set aside their design; and the government won a major victory without having to waste the time and undergo the expense of a protracted court fight. Had the Eisenhower Administration not had a strong record in the field of antitrust, it is unlikely that the situation would have ended in such a manner.

Not all of the mergers were thwarted so easily. When the eighth largest petroleum company, Phillips Petroleum, disclosed pursuant to the Securities Exchange Act of 1935 that it had become the owner of over 1 million shares of Union Oil Company of California, the fifteenth largest in the field, the Antitrust Division moved rapidly. Although Phillips maintained that the purchase was for investment purposes only, Bicks was not convinced, for he believed that the mere holding of a substantial percentage of Union stock by Phillips impaired competition between the two. When it became evident that Phillips was not willing to negotiate with the Justice Department, Bicks sought an injunction enjoining Phillips from acquiring any more stock in Union or from voting the Union shares that it already held.[12]

The Phillips-Union case is a perfect example of the validity of the contention that a strong antitrust policy does not imply an antibusiness bias. Union did not want to be controlled or acquired by Phillips; indeed, its president, Reese Taylor, characterized the situation as a "raid."[13] After the government action, the company, too, filed a "cross-claim" alleging that the acquisition violated Section 7 and praying for divestiture and treble damages. Ultimately, after intricate legal maneuvering, Phillips agreed to sell its holdings in Union to a third party. In January 1964 on the government's motion, the case was dismissed. In February 1965, Union purchased the block and placed it in the company treasury.[14]

Bicks was very sensitive about the fact that every time an oil company requested a pre-merger clearance, the Justice Department found that the action would violate the Clayton Act and hence denied each one. In early 1960, the Woodley Petroleum Company contemplated liquidation, and Pure Oil Company, a significant factor in the industry, wanted to purchase its assets and business. After minor negotiations resulting in Pure Oil agreeing not to influence the business of a small subsidiary of Woodley operating in the same area as Pure, the Justice Department cleared the merger. In a memorandum to the Attorney General, Bicks wrote that the Department should capitalize on the case because it provided the "precedent" of a "successful merger clearance by a petroleum company."[15]

Not all of the anti-monopoly actions took place in the petroleum industry. The instance of the General Motors Corporation's acquisition of the Euclid Road Machinery Corporation is very instructive because it illustrates the strengthening of antitrust enforcement which took place during the Eisenhower years. In 1953, General Motors completed the takeover, and the Antitrust Division sent out the standard letters of inquiry. Apparently, in late September 1953 there was also a meeting with General Motors officials. The motor giant's arguments that it produced nothing that "could stand up the way Euclid's did," that Euclid did not have the necessary resources for continued expansion, and that all of Euclid's competitors were far more integrated seem to have convinced the antitrusters that the merger was legal because there are no more materials in the files until Hansen moved to reopen the subject in mid-1956.[16] During the interval the results of the marriage became manifest. In their re-evaluation, the antitrusters realized that they had erred in not acting. Victor Kramer, who played such an important role in the Du Pont-General Motors case, wrote, "I feel that *I failed to give sufficient weight to the so-called conglomerate integration issue.*"[17] Yet there were still difficulties, and while Jacobs noted that after acquisition, Euclid's sales rose while those of its main competitor, Cummings Engine, fell, the Antitrust Division felt unable to attack the merger, for after an unsuccessful attempt to prove that General Motors had used its size to force reciprocal dealings, the action once again was put aside.[18]

It is noteworthy that as early as November 1954, Eisenhower was alarmed by the size of General Motors, and he directed that government purchases be made with an eye to "avoiding undue concentration."[19] Although Barnes, Hansen and Bicks all deny that there was an investigation of General Motors as a whole, and while there does not appear to be any material on that subject in the Justice Department records, it is likely that there were antitrusters who did have such a plan in mind. A. I. Jacobs, a staff lawyer, wrote to George

Reycraft concerning the relationship of the Euclid case to an "overall GM monopolization allegation."[20] Later during the preparation of the complaint, the government utilized a great deal of material which would not ordinarily have been included.

Donald Turner, a future chief of the Division and former conferee of the Attorney General's National Committee to Study the Antitrust Laws, was instrumental in formulating one of the main government arguments: "General Motors with its tremendous resources and knowhow, could easily have entered the earth-moving machinery field by building its own new facilities. For GM, any additional costs in following this route would have been relatively negligible. In fact, GM was planning precisely such a step." Turner noted that it had spent $2 million in preparation to enter the field. Thus when it had acquired Euclid, it had "eliminated a potential competitor."[21] Finally, six years after the takeover, on October 15, 1959, the Attorney General gave Bicks permission to file the case.[22]

The crux of the action revolved around the government's contention that the acquisition provided General Motors with an edge over smaller producers. The antitrusters feared that the nation's number one automotive manufacturer would use its power and expertise to build up the Euclid Division, possibly to the point of monopoly. That there was validity in the government's concern was evidenced by the fact that earlier the company had bought into the bus business, and by 1958, it was building 89 percent of all city and interstate busses. A similar but more startling result had occurred in the locomotive industry: In 1958, General Motors had sold *every* passenger locomotive constructed in the United States. It also had the power to exclude its competitors from Euclid's field, for the government noted that General Motors was the major supplier of important components such as diesel engines, and it could squeeze those companies that had to purchase part of their components from General Motors. It could easily become number one in the field by raising the prices of the components, cutting off their supply, or by delivering an inferior quality of goods.[23] To prevent this from happening, the suit had been entered. Bicks characterized it as another example of "prophylactic" antitrust.[24]

The issue did not come to trial during the Eisenhower presidency. Since there is little in the Justice Department files after the action was initiated, possibly the antitrusters were focusing on other cases or perhaps the material was transferred to other files for use in the study of General Motors as a whole. Not until 1968 was the matter settled by a consent judgment whereby General Motors sold several important Euclid properties to White Motor, a large conglomerate.[25]

Of all the antitrust cases, none had more effect than one called the Hand Tool case and the 20 cases filed against various members of the electrical industry. Important because of its influence on the outcome of the Electrical cases, the action against five companies in the hand-tool industry grew out of an investigation into illegal price-fixing in the field.[26] That the government proved its charges and that five company executives pleaded *nolo contendere* is significant only because the judge, Mell Underwood, broke tradition and then sentenced them to jail. Never before in the history of the Sherman Act had anyone been incarcerated after having entered a *nolo* plea. This background definitely influenced the defendants. Additionally, according to F. Bliss Winn, a deal was made in which the Justice Department promised to seek only fines.[27] Allegedly only then did John T. Mains plead *nolo*.[28] While all concurred that "Bicks said that if all of the defendants would plead *nolo* and not quibble about the fines . . . we [the government] would not oppose *nolo* pleas,"[29] there is some difference of opinion regarding whether or not there was any more to the agreement. There is no question that in sentencing the men to jail terms Judge Underwood imposed greater penalties than the prosecution demanded in court. The *Cleveland Plain Dealer* story, while quoting the defendants at length, did not mention the existence of any broken covenants,[30] a charge subsequently made by Peter McDonough, the president of one of the companies which pleaded *nolo*.[31] Nevertheless, the prospect of having to serve a sentence so unnerved Mains that, on the way to jail, he committed suicide in front of a shocked wife and son.[32] The suicide and the jailings had several effects: First, Underwood was criticized for his action and later, in part as a result of a scathing series in the *Cleveland Plain Dealer*,[33] he was forced to resign his post. Second, rightly or wrongly, many people blamed Bicks for the tragedy, and very likely it was one of the reasons why he was not confirmed by the Senate as Assistant Attorney General in charge of the Antitrust Division. Third, the hand tool case and its denouement was very helpful to the government, especially in the electrical investigations because suddenly there were more executives who were willing to tell all they knew before a grand jury in return for immunity from prosecution as provided by federal statutes.[34]

No case or series of antitrust cases has ever garnered as many headlines as the group of 20 actions which have come to be known collectively as the Electrical cases. Although no new interpretations of the corpus resulted from them, by their very scope the actions were enough to illustrate the vigor of the antitrusters' program.

For years the Antitrust Division had been watching the various members of the heavy electrical industry.[35] There were several instances during the 1940s when the companies were caught for fixing prices, but each time when they agreed to abandon the practice, the charges were dropped.[36] In 1949 the Division launched an inquiry into the business of electrical transformers. Although by 1951 not enough evidence had been uncovered to support criminal indictments, the action was kept alive in the civil sphere. Barnes subsequently closed the investigation.[37] In mid-1954, there was another inquiry which focused on the problems of identical bidding and allocation of customers. It studied a total of 1,989 bids and concluded that 1,048 "were identical with one or more companies."[38] But the mere existence of identical bids by themselves proves neither price-fixing nor collusion. In certain instances conscious parallelism in pricing is both explainable and permissable.

As a result of large increases in the prices of heavy electrical equipment, in 1957 the Tennessee Valley Authority (TVA) enlarged the number of companies eligible to bid on its jobs. Several of the companies admitted to the bidders' lists were foreign and they consistently submitted prices which, even after adjustments for the "Buy American" laws, were far lower than those of the American manufacturers.[39] Almost immediately there was agitation to limit the importation of foreign electrical generating equipment. The National Electrical Manufacturers' Association and General Electric Corporation spearheaded the attack using such devices as an avalanche of letters to public officials and intense lobbying efforts, all endeavoring to prove that the high price of American labor led inexorably to the cost differentials. Not to "Buy American" was unpatriotic and, worse, it denied jobs to deserving citizens. Even some unions boarded the band wagon.[40] But after extensive economic analysis, Albert Fitzgerald, president of the United Electrical, Radio, and Machine Workers of America, was able to counter the argument and prove that the difference in bid prices "would cover the actual wage cost differential almost 17 times over."[41]

Undoubtedly the publicity had an effect on the Justice Department investigation. The TVA had to reply to the electrical equipment company attacks, and it released a statement noting the similarity in bids it had been receiving over the previous few years. An enterprising newspaperman, Julian Granger, picked up the material. Unaware that the Antitrust Division was studying the subject, he wrote a series of articles in the *Knoxville News-Sentinel*.[42] Subsequently, the *Washington Daily News*, its Scripps-Howard sister paper, carried the story.[43] This account may have been responsible in part for the inquiry instigated by Senator Estes Kefauver's Subcommittee on Antitrust and Monopoly. Being from Tennessee, his interest may have been sparked by the possibility of making some home-state headlines in time for the presidential primary election in 1960. The Antitrust Division also was interested and contacted the TVA on June 1, 1959.

The material supplied by the TVA, plus the publicity, convinced the antitrusters that enough improprieties did exist to merit a full-scale investigation. This yielded results which suggested that a grand jury be impaneled to inquire into the practices of the industry. At this juncture, Kefauver dropped his investigation and turned over his findings to the Justice Department.[44] The amount of material uncovered by the grand jury was so great that two others were impaneled. The number was increased until at one point there were actually five separate grand juries probing the electrical industry.

The investigations found 20 separate conspiracies, and General Electric was a member of all but one. Some of the violations were long-lived, one being traceable to the heyday of NRA,[45] but the Justice Department concentrated on the most recent evidence to prove its charges.[46] The violations were so blatant that one group of perpetrators had even formulated a set of rules for themselves:

1) Minimize phone calls;
2) Use plain envelopes if mailing materials;
3) When registering at a hotel, do not include the company's name;
4) Endeavor not to travel together;
5) Do not eat together;
6) Leave no wastepaper behind after a meeting in a hotel room.

When the final numbers were tabulated, a total of 32 corporations were involved as defendants or co-conspirators, and 48 individual defendants were also included. Almost every large manufacturer of electrical equipment was cited at least once.

In these cases especially, Bicks' enthusiasm and vigor were apparent as he personally handled large segments of the project. That the government was determined to block the easy escape route for the electrical companies was illustrated by its opposition to the court's acceptance of a *nolo contendere* plea. In this situation undoubtedly private suits would ensue, and like consent judgments in civil action, *nolo* pleas could not be entered as *prima facie* evidence in subsequent private treble damage suits. In an unprecedented move, both Bicks and William Rogers, the new Attorney General, went before the court and urged Chief Judge J. Cullen Ganey not to accept any *nolo* pleas. Bicks personally argued that since the cases included charges that ranked them among the most serious in the entire 70-year history of the Sherman Act, the acceptance of a *nolo* plea would be highly inappropriate. Second, he wanted the record to be available so that injured parties could sue to recover treble damages. Finally, he noted that there was more stigma attached to the plea of guilty than to that of *nolo*.[48] Attorney General Rogers stated by affidavit that each conspirator knew he was violating the law and that, in view of the severity of the crime, acceptance of a *nolo* plea would essentially mean that in the future there could be no other plea.[49] The power of the government's argument was such that Judge Ganey rejected most of the *nolo* pleas.

The third largest electrical manufacturer, Allis-Chalmers, then decided to cooperate fully with the government. After conferences, the company agreed to plead guilty to each charge. What Allis-Chalmers was doing was disclosing everything and aiding the government in hopes that its cooperation and record of 50 years without any other violations of the antitrust laws would militate in its behalf at the time of sentencing. When compared to the list of prior infractions of General Electric, some 36 actions by the government after 1941, the record of Allis-Chalmers seemed pristine. Later, when the government recommended fines, "virtue" was rewarded, for it consistently suggested a lower figure for the cooperative company.[50]

The importance of the Electrical cases is illustrated by the prestigious counsel employed by the various manufacturers. Bruce Bromley, who had previously been a member of the Attorney General's National Committee to Study the Antitrust Laws, represented Westinghouse. As the actions progressed, it became obvious that additional aid was necessary. He therefore persuaded his former superior, Herbert Brownell, to join the Westinghouse team. It was a brilliant coup on Bromley's part, for Brownell and his firm, Lord, Day and Lord, had an enviable record in antitrust defense actions. Moreover, until three years earlier, Brownell had been Attorney General and thus had intimate knowledge of the thought patterns of many in the Antitrust Division. Brownell's acceptance of the position has been attacked as approaching a conflict of interest or as being hypocritical, inasmuch as he had helped set down strict rules of conduct forbidding anyone, within *two* years of his severance from the government payroll, to work for a company having legal dealings with the government.[51] To be fair, Brownell had waited more than the requisite time, and then he had requested clearance from the Department of Justice based upon his contention that the cases had begun "after I left and I knew nothing about [them]."[52] Because of his background, Brownell became the leader for the defendants and he often acted as liaison with the Justice Department in unsuccessful efforts to obtain a negotiated settlement with the government.

In the end, not one company or any executives pleaded "not guilty." The burden of recommending sentences then fell on the shoulders of the Justice Department. This was complicated by the fact that the Democrats had won the presidential election and the sentencing was scheduled to be handed down after John F. Kennedy had taken the oath of office.

After a lengthy prolegomenon, the sentencing was begun on February 6, 1961. Two days were necessary to hear all the arguments for mitigation of the sentences; the actual sentencing came after that. On the first day alone, $931,500 in fines were levied. In all, penalties of nearly $2 million were imposed. The companies were punished to the extent of $1,785,500 and their executives personally had to pay $139,000. In addition, seven defendant executives were sent to jail for 30-day periods. Others were much luckier— although they were to have been chastened by jail, the terms were suspended and long periods of probation were substituted. That made it possible for the government to keep a watchful eye on their activities.[53] In December 1961, Judge Ganey canceled the probation period. Had the administration-supported bill raising the Sherman Act fines not been passed,[54] the total would have been closer to $200,000, rather than the nearly $2 million which were assessed.

For the companies, however, the worst was yet to come. One of the recommendations of the Attorney General's National Committee to Study the Antitrust Laws made was that the government be entitled to sue for the recovery of damages incurred as a result of antitrust violations. Even single damages would involve a large sum. Others could sue for treble damages, and the TVA endeavored to prove that as a government corporation it belonged in the latter and not the former group. Furthermore, under the False Claims Act,[55] the government could sue for "double the amount of actual damages and in addition may recover a $2,000 forfeiture for each violation of the Act."[56]

The government employed several criteria in settling on the size of the awards. First, "the recovery should bear a direct relationship to the damages suffered by the Government on account of the defendants' conspiratorial activity"; and second, "account must be taken of the defendants' ability to pay and still maintain the position of an effective competitor in the industry."[57] Luckily for the smaller and weaker companies, the government recognized that in many cases to apply the first principle too vigorously might well defeat the purpose of the second. Yet, it recognized that too much attention to the second might rob the case of its deterrent effect. Lee Loevinger, Kennedy's chief of the Antitrust Division, also believed that the guilty companies should be left with enough funds to be able to pay off other injured parties.[58] Finally, it was obvious that those who had exercised initiative in the formation and continuation of the conspiracy should be penalized more heavily than those who had been "fellow travelers." Therefore, different formulae were applied to each company in assessing damages.

Not wishing to be closed out by the statute of limitations, the government filed damage suits almost immediately. The first occurred in March 1961. In order to facilitate negotiations, General Electric hired the politically potent Clark Clifford. That he was "persuasive" in his negotiations was illustrated by the low cost of the settlement which was reached. The electrical giant agreed to pay the TVA $6.47 million and an additional $1 million to the government to compensate it for any damages done to other federal agencies. The government rationalized the figure of roughly 10 percent of sales by citing the fact that the principle of price during conspiracy minus price before conspiracy equals damages "is not necessarily sound nor binding upon the court or a jury."[59] The smallest payments were made by Southern States, Inc., which settled with the government and TVA for $11,645.36.[60]

The federal claims were miniscule compared to those emanating from the state, local and private sectors. There were at least 344 separate "state and local public agencies affected by the charged conspiracies."[61] Few private utilities were unaffected. Throughout the various federal courts, 1,912 damage suits were filed and in all but a handful, General Electric was a defendant. The charges ranged from the small and picayune to what was the largest private suit in antitrust history. Milton Handler of Kaye, Scholer, Fierman, Hays and Handler represented a group of 44 utilities in a suit to gain treble compensation for damages sustained. Although he was unable to secure full repayment, he was able to get "pretty close to $100 million for my clients."[62] On May 13, 1969, with but four cases left unsettled, Senator Philip Hart of Michigan claimed that the "total paid [by the defendant electrical manufacturers] or agreed to "was $405,274,016.07."[63]

The expenses accruing to the defendants were actually even larger than the costs cited by Senator Hart. Not only did the companies have to pay the settlements, but they also had to defend against all the claims throughout the United States. They had to expand their legal, accounting, and engineering staffs and hire additional counsel. For General Electric the outlay was so large "that [no] attempt was ever made to keep track of all that expense."[64] Allis-Chalmers paid $34,346,556.00 in settlements, but the company hazards that the total cost was between $40 and $50 million.[65] In the end, for all the parties, estimating all the expenses, including those of the Antitrust Division, the uncollected damages, the company costs, and the lost man-hours, a total of $1 billion would be a more reasonable total.

Although all manner of publications enunciated pious hopes that now a chastened business community would behave itself, it is difficult to ascertain whether or not that was true. Not for this reason then are the Electrical Cases so important. The suits stand out because the Antitrust Division fought head-on with some of the most politically potent corporations in America; the Division did this in an election year, and it won. The 20 cases were a fitting capstone to a period of vigorous antitrust enforcement in America.

There was also a secondary benefit which accrued from the cases. Until the time of the Eisenhower Administration, the group of lawyers specializing in the subject of antitrust was small and the topic interested few others. With minor exceptions, all the lawyers were defense-oriented; that is, since the government brought most of the suits, a private antitrust suit was a rarity. Thus there were few antitrust lawyers outside the government with much nongovernmental experience as plaintiffs. It was not until 1952 that the Antitrust Section of the American Bar Association was organized. It took until mid-1955, after the appearance of the *Report of the Attorney General's Committee to Study the Antitrust Laws*, for the field to have a journal of its own. It was then that *The Antitrust Bulletin* made its debut; it has flourished ever since. The suits filed as a result of the government's victory in the Electrical cases increased the need for antitrust lawyers, not only by the government but by industry as well. As a consequence many lawyers entered the field and have remained there ever since. The number of private treble damage cases which had begun to increase during the Eisenhower Administration and which skyrocketed because of the Electrical cases has continued at a high level to this very day.

Private treble damage suits are in many ways the most effective means of antitrust enforcement. Allowing such actions adds a host of interested and well-informed parties to the enforcement field. Instead of the Antitrust Division having to spend precious time and manpower amassing the requisite information, private litigants, who usually better understand the complexities of their industry, do the work. Furthermore, private actions deal with real or sometimes imagined injuries; governmental action is that of a third party based on what a bureaucrat interprets as a wrong. When comparing settlements, those with the government are much more likely to be of a preventive nature than aimed at repairing an injury. Finally, in crass monetary terms, the settlements are generally higher in private actions, thus probably increasing the deterrent effect. This has been recognized by all parties; and in many government actions the Justice Department has followed a course which insured that the public would be able to utilize government material in its own suits. It has been estimated that, absent private antitrust actions, the Antitrust Division would need at least four times as large a budget.[66]

The antitrust record of the closing years of the Eisenhower Administration is stellar. In the Clayton Act area of mergers, it includes extension of the ambit of the Celler-Kefauver amendment, and in the Sherman Act sphere it encompasses major prosecutions, which, while not forging new precedents, did make antitrust a major factor to consider when making corporate decisions.

OVERVIEW: ELECTRICAL CASES

	Power Switchgear	*Oil & Air Circuit Breakers*	*Low Voltage Circuit Breakers*	*Bushings*	*Insulators*	*Open Fuse Cutouts*	*Lightning Arresters*	*Distributors (Count I)*	*Intermediate & Station (Count II)*	*Arrester Cutout Combinations (Count III)*	*Distribution Transformers*	*Power Transformers*	*Instrument Transformers*	*Network Transformers*	*Power Switching Equipment*	*Navy & Marine Switchgear*	*Isolated Phase Fuse*	*Industrial Control Equipment*	*Low Voltage Distribution Equipment*	*Turbine Generators*	*Steam Condensors*	*Power Capacitors*	*Watt Hour & Demand Meters*
General Electric	G	G	N	N	N	N		N	N	N	G	N	N	G	N	N	G	G	N	G		N	N
Westinghouse	G	G	N	N		N		N	N	N	G	N	N	G	N	N	G	G	N	G	G	N	N
Allis-Chalmers	G	G									N	G	G	G						G	G		
Federal Pacific	G	N													G				N				
ITE	G	N	N	N	N										G	N	N		N				
McGraw-Edison						N	N	N	N	G	N											N	
Lapp				N	N																		
Ohio Brass				N	N	N	N															N	
Porcelain I.				N																			
Joslyn						N	N	N							N								
Hubbard						N	N	N															
A.B. Chance				N	N																		
S. States Equip.						N									G								
H.K. Porter				N		N									G		N						
Molony Elect.												N	G	N									
Wagner Elect.												N	G	N									
Kuhlman Elect.												N											
Schwager-Wood														N									
Allen-Bradley																		G					
Clark Controller																		G					
Cutler Hammer																		G	N				
Square D																		G	N				
Foster Wheeler																					G		
Carrier																					N		
Ingersol Rand																					G		
C.H. Wheeler																					G		
Worthington																					G		
Sangamo Elect.																						N	N
Cornell-Dubilier																						N	

N = Nolo Plea, G = Guilty Plea   Source: *Herling*, 332-3.

CONVICTIONS: ELECTRICAL CASES*

U. S. v. Westinghouse Electric Corp. et al (Power Transformers)

Corporate Defendants	Plea	Imposed Fine &/or Sentence
General Electric	Guilty	$40,000
Westinghouse	Guilty	40,000
Allis-Chalmers	Guilty	25,000
McGraw-Edison	Guilty	20,000
Wagner Electric	Guilty	10,000
Moloney Electric	Guilty	15,000

Individual Defendants	Plea	Imposed Fine &/or Sentence
J.H. Chiles, Jr., V.P., Mgr. Trans. Div., Westinghouse	Guilty	$2,000 & 30 days
W.S. Ginn, V.P., Gen. Mgr. Trans. Div., General Electric	Guilty	5,000 & 30 days
R.N. McCollum, Mgr., Pwr. Trans. Dept., Westinghouse	Guilty	2,000 & 30 days (susp.)
J.W. McMullen, V.P. & Gen. Mgr. Pwr. Equip. Div., Allis-Chalmers	Guilty	3,000 & 30 days (susp.)
J.W. Seaman, Gen. Mgr. Pwr. Trans. Dept., General Electric	Guilty	2,500 & 30 days (susp.)
W.R. Swoish, Sales Mgr. Penn. Trans. Div., Moloney Electric	Guilty	5,000 & 30 days (susp.)
R.W. Smith, V.P., Gen. Trans. Div., General Electric	Guilty	3,000 & 30 days (susp.)

U.S. v. Westinghouse Electric Corp., et al (Power Switchgear Assemblies)

Corporate Defendants	Plea	Imposed Fine &/or Sentence
General Electric	Guilty	$30,000
Westinghouse	Guilty	20,000
Federal Pacific	Guilty	10,000
Allis-Chalmers	Guilty	10,000
I-T-E	Guilty	10,000

Individual Defendants	Plea	Imposed Fine &/or Sentence
L.J. Burger, Gen. Mgr., Switchgear & Control Div., General Electric	Guilty	$2,000 & 30 days
G.E. Burons, V.P., Gen. Mgr. Switchgear & Control Div., General Electric	Guilty	4,000 & 30 days

CONVICTIONS: ELECTRICAL CASES*

U.S. v. Westinghouse Electric Corp. et al (Power Switchgear Assemblies)

Corporate Defendants	Plea	Imposed Fine &/or Sentence
L. Fuller, Asst. Gen. Mgr. E. Pittsburgh Div., Westinghouse	Guilty	3,000 & 1 mo. (susp.)
H.F. Hentschel, Gen. Mgr. Medium-Voltage Switchgear Dept., General Electric	Guilty	2,000 & 1 mo. (susp.)
H. Jones, Mgr. Drawout Load Center Sales Sub-section Low-Voltage Switchgear Dept., General Electric	Nolo	1,500
L.W. Long, Asst. Gen. Mgr., Pwr. Equip. Div., Allis-Chalmers	Guilty	2,000 & 30 days (susp.)
F.M. Nolan, Mgr. Sales, Switchgear Dept., Pwr. Equip. Div., Allis-Chalmers	Guilty	1,000
A.W. Payne, Sales Mgr. Assembled Switchgear Dept., Westinghouse	Guilty	1,000
F.E. Stehlik, Gen. Mgr. Low-Voltage Switchgear Dept., General Electric	Guilty	3,000 & 1 mo. (susp.)

U.S. v. Allen-Bradley Co. et al (Industrial Control Equipment)

Corporate Defendants	Plea	Imposed Fine &/or Sentence
General Electric	Guilty	$35,000
Westinghouse	Guilty	40,000
Allen-Bradley	Guilty	40,000
Cutler-Hammer	Guilty	30,000
Square D	Guilty	35,000
Clark Controller	Guilty	35,000

Individual Defendants

	Plea	Imposed Fine &/or Sentence
J.M. Cook, V.P., Marketing, Cutler-Hammer	Guilty	$2,000 & 30 days
T.C. Finnell, Sales Mgr. Systems Control Dept., Westinghouse	Guilty	1,500
E.R. Jung, V.P., Marketing, Clark Controller	Guilty	2,000 & 30 days
F.F. Loock, Pres., Gen. Mgr., Sales Mgr., Allen-Bradley	Guilty	7,500
W.F. Oswalt, Gen. Mgr., Gen. Purpose Control Dept., General Electric	Guilty	4,000 & 30 days (susp.)

J.T. Thompson, Sales Mgr. Assembled Switchgear Dept., Westinghouse — Guilty 2,000

D.W. Webb, Mgr. Switchgear Dept. Pwr. Equip. Div., Allis-Chalmers — Guilty 1,000

U.S. v. General Electric Co. et al (Turbine-Generators)

Corporate Defendants	Plea	Imposed Fine &/or Sentence
General Electric	Guilty	$50,000
Westinghouse	Guilty	35,000
Allis-Chalmers	Guilty	25,000

Individual Defendants

	Plea	Imposed Fine &/or Sentence
W.S. Ginn, V.P., Gen. Mgr. Turbine Div., General Electric	Nolo	7,500
C.I. Mauntel, Sales Mgr. Steam Div., Westinghouse	Nolo	1,000 & 30 days
W.C. Rowland, V.P., Steam Div., Westinghouse	Nolo	4,000 & 1 mo. (susp.)
W.E. Saupe, Gen. Mgr., Large Steam Turbine-Generator Dept., General Electric	Nolo	5,500 & 1 mo. (susp.)

U.S. v. Federal Pacific Electric Co. et al (Power Switching Equipment)

Corporate Defendants	Plea	Imposed Fine &/or Sentence
General Electric	Guilty	$30,000
H.X. Porter	Guilty	25,000
Westinghouse	Guilty	20,000
I-T-E	Guilty	15,000
Southern States	Guilty	20,000
Schwager-Wood	Nolo	15,000
Federal Pacific	Guilty	15,000
Joslyn Mfg.	Nolo	10,000

Individual Defendants

	Plea	Imposed Fine &/or Sentence
J.E. Cordell, V.P., Sales Electrical Southern States	Guilty	$1,500 & 1 mo. (susp.)
W.T. Pyle, Sales Mgr., Switchgear Devices Section, Assembled Switchgear Dept., Westinghouse	Guilty	1,000
G.L. Roark, Mgr. Pwr. Switching Equip. Sales (3-1-57 to 5-1-59); Mgr. Mktg. H.V. Switchgear Dept. (5-1-59), General Electric	Guilty	1,500
J. Romano, Gen. Sales Mgr., Delta Star Div., H. K. Porter	Guilty	1,500 & 1 mo. (susp.)

CONVICTIONS: ELECTRICAL CASES*

U.S. v. Federal Pacific Electric Co. et al
(Power Switching Equipment)

Corporate Defendants	Plea	Imposed Fine &/or Sentence
H.K. Wilcox, Div. Mgr., Greensburg Div., I-T-E	Guilty	1,500 & 1 mo. (susp.)
W.M. Wood, Sec. Treas. (V.P. & Asst. Sec., NWL Corp., 3-31-59), Schwager-Wood	Guilty	7,500 & 1 mo. (susp.)

U.S. v. Foster Wheeler Corp. et al
(Condensers)

Corporate Defendants	Plea	Imposed Fine &/or Sentence
Westinghouse	Guilty	$25,000
Foster Wheeler	Guilty	20,000
Ingersoll-Rand	Guilty	20,000
Worthington	Guilty	20,000
C.H. Wheeler	Guilty	20,000
Allis-Chalmers	Guilty	10,000
Carrier	Nolo	7,500

Individual Defendants

	Plea	Imposed Fine &/or Sentence
C.I. Mauntel, Sales Mgr., Steam Div., Westinghouse	Guilty	$1,500

U.S. v. General Electric Co. et al
(Distribution Transformers)

Corporate Defendants	Plea	Imposed Fine &/or Sentence
W.R. Swoish, Sales Mgr., Penn. Trans. Div., Moloney Electric	Nolo	3,500
A.R. Waehner, Director of Trans. Sales, Moloney Electric	Nolo	1,500
J. Watkens, V.P. & Mgr. Trans. Div., Kuhlman Electric	Nolo	2,500

U.S. v. General Electric et al
(Circuit Breakers)

Corporate Defendants	Plea	Imposed Fine &/or Sentence
General Electric	Guilty	$40,000
Allis-Chalmers	Guilty	20,000
Federal Pacific	Nolo	15,000
I-T-E	Nolo	10,000
Westinghouse	Guilty	30,000

Individual Defendants

	Plea	Imposed Fine &/or Sentence
H.G. Conkey, V.P., Gen. Mgr Sales, Ingersoll-Rand	Guilty	4,000 & 30 days (susp.)
L.G.L. Thomas, President, C.H. Wheeler	Guilty	4,000 & 1 mo. (susp.)
M.H. Howard, Production Mgr., Equip. Div., Foster Wheeler	Guilty	2,000
A.M. Tullo, Group V.P., Worthington	Guilty	3,000 & 30 days (susp.)

Individual Defendants

	Plea	Imposed Fine &/or Sentence
C.E. Burke, Gen. Mgr., H.V. Switchgear Dept., General Electric	Guilty	$3,500 & 1 mo. (susp.)
R.C. Crawford, Mktg. Mgr., H.V. Switchgear Dept., General Electric	Nolo	2,000
L.W. Long, Asst. Gen. Mgr., Pwr. Equip. Div., Allis-Chalmers	Nolo	1,500 & 1 mo. (susp.)
W.H. Schick, Mgr., Pwr. Ct. Brk. Sales, H.V. Switchgear Dept., General Electric	Nolo	1,500
J.W. Stirling, Mgr. Pwr. Ct. Bkr. Dept., Westinghouse	Guilty	1,500 & 1 mo. (susp.)

U.S. v. General Electric Co. et al (Distribution Transformers)

Corporate Defendants	Plea	Imposed Fine &/or Sentence
General Electric	Nolo	$30,000
Westinghouse	Nolo	30,000
McGraw-Edison	Nolo	25,000
Allis-Chalmers	Nolo	20,000
Wagner Electric	Nolo	15,000
Moloney Electric	Nolo	15,000
Kuhlman Electric	Nolo	10,000

Individual Defendants

	Plea	Imposed Fine &/or Sentence
M.A. DeFerranti, Gen. Mgr. Dist. Trans. Dept., General Electric	Nolo	$3,500 & 30 days (susp.)
G.C. Hurlbert, Mgr. Dist. Trans. Dept., Westinghouse	Nolo	2,000 & 30 days (susp.)

U.S. v. I-T-E Circuit Breaker Co. et al (L.V. Circuit Breakers)

Corporate Defendants	Plea	Imposed Fine &/or Sentence
I-T-E	Nolo	$ 5,000
General Electric	Nolo	10,000
Westinghouse	Nolo	5,000

CONVICTIONS: ELECTRICAL CASES*

U.S. v. Federal Pacific Electric Co. et al (Power Switching Equipment)

Corporate Defendants	Plea	Imposed Fine &/or Sentence
Individual Defendants		
R.W. Ayers, Mgr. Air Ct. Bkr. Subsect., L.V. Switchgear Dept., General Electric	Nolo	1,500
W.T. Pyle, Sales Mgr. Switchgear Devices Sect., Assembled Switchgear Dept., Westinghouse	Nolo	1,500
F.E. Stehlik, Gen. Mgr., E.V. Switchgear Dept., General Electric	Nolo	2,500
J.T. Thompson, Sales Mgr., Assembled Switchgear Dept., Westinghouse	Nolo	2,000

U.S. v. Cutler-Hammer Inc. et al (L.V. Distribution Equipment)

Corporate Defendants	Plea	Imposed Fine
General Electric	Nolo	$40,000

U.S. v. Cornell-Dubilier Electric Corp. et al (Power Capacitors)

Corporate Defendants	Plea	Imposed Fine
General Electric	Nolo	$20,000
Westinghouse	Nolo	10,000
McGraw-Edison	Nolo	15,000
Ohio Brass	Nolo	7,500
Cornell-Dubilier	Nolo	20,000
Sangamo Electric	Nolo	7,500

U.S. v. McGraw-Edison Co. et al (Lightning Arrestors)

Corporate Defendants	Plea	Imposed Fine
General Electric	Nolo	$15,000
Westinghouse	Nolo	15,000
Ohio Brass	Nolo	7,500
McGraw-Edison	Nolo	10,000
H.K. Porter	Nolo	10,000
Hubbard	Nolo	7,500
Joslyn Mfg.	Nolo	10,000

Corporate Defendants	Plea	Imposed Fine
Square D	Nolo	40,000
Westinghouse	Nolo	35,000
Cutler-Hammer	Nolo	10,000
Federal Pacific	Nolo	25,000
I-T-E	Nolo	25,000

U.S. v. Allis-Chalmers Mfg. Co. et al
(Instrument Transformers)

Corporate Defendants	Plea	Imposed Fine
General Electric	Nolo	$10,000
Westinghouse	Nolo	7,500
Allis-Chalmers	Nolo	7,500

U.S. v. Sangamo Electric Co. et al
(Watthour Meters)

Corporate Defendants	Plea	Imposed Fine
General Electric	Nolo	$20,000
Westinghouse	Nolo	15,000
Sangamo Electric	Nolo	10,000

U.S. v. McGraw-Edison Co. et al
(Network Transformers)

Corporate Defendants	Plea	Imposed Fine
General Electric	Nolo	$15,000
Westinghouse	Nolo	10,000
Allis-Chalmers	Nolo	10,000
McGraw-Edison	Nolo	5,000
Moloney Electric	Nolo	5,000
Wagner Electric	Nolo	2,000

U.S. v. Ohio Brass Co. et al
(Insulators)

Corporate Defendants	Plea	Imposed Fine
General Electric	Nolo	$20,000
Ohio Brass	Nolo	20,000
McGraw-Edison	Nolo	10,000
H.K. Porter	Nolo	10,000
I-T-E	Nolo	10,000
Lapp Insulator	Nolo	10,000
Porcelain Insulator	Nolo	7,500
A.B. Chance	Nolo	7,500

U.S. v. Lapp Insulator Co., Inc. et al
(Bushings)

Corporate Defendants	Plea	Imposed Fine
General Electric	Nolo	$10,000
Westinghouse	Nolo	10,000
Ohio Brass	Nolo	10,000
Lapp Insulator	Nolo	5,000

CONVICTIONS: ELECTRICAL CASES*

U.S. v. H.K. Porter Co., Inc. et al
(Isolated Phase Buses)

Corporate Defendants	Plea	Imposed Fine.
General Electric	Nolo	$10,000
Westinghouse	Nolo	7,500
I-T-E	Nolo	5,000
H.K. Porter	Nolo	5,000

U.S. v. I-T-E Circuit Breaker Co. et al
(Navy & Marine Switchgear)

Corporate Defendants	Plea	Imposed Fine
General Electric	Nolo	$5,000
Westinghouse	Nolo	7,500
I-T-E	Nolo	7,500

U.S. v. A.B. Chance Co., et al
(Open Fuse Cutouts)

Corporate Defendants	Plea	Imposed Fine
General Electric	Nolo	$ 7,500
Westinghouse	Nolo	10,000
A.B. Chance	Nolo	10,000
Southern States	Nolo	10,000
I-T-E	Nolo	5,000
Hubbard	Nolo	2,500
Joslyn Mfg.	Nolo	5,000

* Source: John Herling, The Great Price Conspiracy (Washington, D.C., 1962), pp. 335-351.

NOTES

1. Robert Bicks to author, June 10, 1971.
2. Stephen Spingarn to author, Apr. 22, 1971; Mark Green, *The Nader Study Group Report on Antitrust Enforcement*, p. 134; *The New York Times*, Oct. 4, 1956 and Oct. 25, 1956.
3. Richard Austin Smith, "What Antitrust Means under Mr. Bicks." *Fortune*, 54 (Mar. 1960), 123.
4. Hansen to author, Nov. 30, 1972.
5. Rogers to author, Oct. 22, 1974. According to Harold Brayman, after about a year with Bicks still in the position of Acting Assistant Attorney General, an executive of a "fairly substantial corporation" protested Bicks' possible appointment and stated that if it were to come to pass, "the Republican Party would never get another dime of contributions from him or from his company associates and friends." On the following day the President sent Bicks' nomination to the Senate. *Corporate Management in a World of Politics* (New York: 1967), pp. 96-7. Rogers' reaction to this story was that if the official had said that directly to Eisenhower, the President would have "thrown him out of the office" and sent up the nomination immediately. (Rogers to author, Oct. 2, 1974).
6. Bicks to author, June 10, 1971.
7. Quoted in "Antitrusters Show Their Claws," *Business Week* (Oct. 3, 1959), p. 34.
8. Memo to Jacobs, initialed by Barnes, Sept. 6, 1955, Antitrust Papers: Leonard, Acc. 70A4771, file 60-0-37-77.
9. Memorandum for the Attorney General, Dec. 28, 1959, Antitrust Papers: Sohio, Acc. 70A4771, file 60-0-37-332.
10. Hummel to Bicks, Jan. 21, 1960, Antitrust Papers: Sohio.
11. Bicks to Rogers, Sept. 29, 1959, Antitrust Papers: Texaco-Superior, Acc. 70A4771, file 60-0-37-302.
12. Bicks memorandum to Rogers, Dec. 5, 1960 with Rogers' initialed approval Dec. 8, 1960, Antitrust Papers: Phillips, Acc. 70A4771, file 60-0-37- 473.
13. Earl M. Welty and Frank J. Taylor, *The Seventy-Six Bonanza: the Fabulous Life and Times of the Union Oil Company of California* (Menlo Park, Calif., no date), p. 276.
14. 1964 Annual Report of the Union Oil Company, p. 19.
15. Bicks to Rogers, Mar. 23, 1960, Antitrust Papers: Pure Oil, Acc. 70A4771, file 60-0-37-379.
16. Memos Sept. 23, 1953 and Feb. 21, 1956, Antitrust Papers: General Motors-Euclid, Acc. 71A6389, file 60-0-37-212.
17. Kramer to Jacobs, Mar. 9, 1956. It is likely that the emphasis was added at a later date because one copy of the note did not have the underlining. Antitrust Papers: General Motors-Euclid.
18. "Not one company showed any reciprocity except Southern Railways which prefers to buy from companies which use its facilities," Special Agent Robert Herrington Report, July 3, 1958, in FBI Reports to the Justice Department, "Section O," Antitrust Papers: General Motors-Euclid.
19. Papers of the President of the United States: 1963-61, Ann Whitman Deary, Menco of Conference, Nov. 9, 1954. Those present included Brownell, George

Humphrey (Sec. of the Treasury), Anderson, Peke, Barnes (either Wendell of the Small Business Administration or Stanley of the Antitrust Division) and Col. Goodpaster.

20. Oct. 5, 1959, Antitrust Papers, General Motors-Euclid.

21. Turner to Bicks, Aug. 27, 1959, Antitrust Papers: General Motors-Euclid.

22. Memo to the Attorney General, Sept. 29, 1959, and approved Oct. 15, 1959.

23. Memo for the Attorney General, Sept. 29, 1959, Antitrust Papers: General Motors-Euclid.

24. Robert Bicks to author, June 10, 1971; Richard Austin Smith, "What Antitrust Means under Mr. Bicks," *Fortune* 59 (Mar. 1960), 270.

25. 1968 Trade Cases par. 72,356.

26. Hansen to Rogers, Feb. 25, 1958, Antitrust Papers: Hand Tools, Acc. 70A4771, file 60-186-21.

27. F. Bliss Winn to author, Oct. 6, 1971. (Winn was president of the O. Ames Company, one of the five companies.)

28. Peter McDonough statement, minutes of meeting with antitrust officials, Nov. 24, 1959, Antitrust Papers: Hand Tools.

29. McCareins to files, Aug. 19, 1959, Antitrust Papers: Hand Tools.

30. *Cleveland Plain Dealer*, Nov. 17, 1959.

31. Minutes of Nov. 24, 1959, meeting between officials of the McDonough Company and the Antitrust Division, Antitrust Papers: Hand Tools.

32. It is also likely that Mains had expected that Judge Underwood would reduce the sentence or change it to probation. The judge was known for exacting heavy fines, and then, after the publicity had died down, reducing them. (*Cleveland Plain Dealer*, June 4, 1965.)

33. June 2-13, 17, 19, 20, 25, 26 and 29, 1965.

34. 18 U.S.C. 6001, 6002.

35. The earliest file is dated 1902. An index as of Mar. 5, 1956, is located in Antitrust Papers: Heavy Electrical Power Equipment Industry (Electrical), file 60-230-27.

36. Memo dated Jan. 27, 1956, Antitrust Papers: Electrical.

37. Barnes memo dated Nov. 21, 1953. Antitrust Papers: Transformers and Power Line Lightning Arresters, file 60-9-78.

38. Barnes memo to files dated July 22, 1954; Hansen memo to J. Edgar Hoover dated July 18, 1957, Antitrust Papers: Electrical.

39. A non-American manufacturer had to pay 15% customs duty; 50% of the machinery had to be delivered in high-cost American ships; additionally, a 20% differential was allowable (6% for Buy American, 6% for a contract to a company located in areas of high unemployment, 8% "to cover the cost of sending men to make a general factory inspection"), testimony of Alan Barraclough of English Electric, Ltd., before Grand Jury #4/ empaneled Apr. 21, 1960, *in re* Electrical Suppliers Industry, located in Antitrust Papers: Electrical, Acc. #64A580, file 60-230-45.

40. See folders of letters, Official File 149-B-2, Box 789, folder entitled "Heavy Electric Power Equipment"; 102-I, Box 439, 1959, Folder I; Box 440, 1959, Folder II, Eisenhower Library.

41. Albert Fitzgerald to author, Dec. 8, 1971; letter to all public officials dated Mar.

23, 1959 (copy in Antitrust Papers: Electrical, file 60-230-27) and made public at press conference Mar. 26, 1959.

42. *The Knoxville News-Sentinel*, May 17, 1959; May 18, 1959; May 19, 1959.

43. *Washington Daily News*, May 20, 1959.

44. U.S. Senate, Subcommittee on Antitrust and Monopoly of the Committee on the Judiciary, 87th Cong., 1st Sess., *Administered Prices: Hearings . . .* (Washington, D.C., 1961), Pt. 13.

45. "A Theory for Computing Damages Sustained by the United States and Tennessee Valley Authority in the Direct Purchase of Power Transformers," 2 (a memorandum dated July 25, 1961) Antitrust Papers: Electrical, file 60-230-55.

46. Bicks to William Maher (Chief of the Philadelphia office which was the headquarters for the investigation), Apr. 30, 1960, Antitrust Papers, file 60-230-29.

47. U.S. Senate, *Administered Prices: Hearings. . .* , Pt. 28, 17,394-17,396.

48. Bicks to Rashid, Mar. 17, 1960, Antitrust Papers: Electrical, file 60-230-29.

49. Rogers to author, Oct. 22, 1974. Also in Charles A. Bane, *The Electrical Equipment Conspiracies* (New York, 1973), pp. 1-22; Attorney General Rogers' affidavit is reprinted in Clabault & Burton, *Sherman Act Indictments: 1955-1965* (New York, 1966), pp. 58-62.

50. M. Wallace Kirpatrick to Robert Kennedy, Jan. 27, 1961, but formulated by Bicks, and Government's Recommendations for Sentences, Antitrust Papers.

51. John Herling, *The Great Price Conspiracy*, pp. 167-8; Eisenhower Papers, Central Files, OF-5, Department of Justice release dated Mar. 27, 1957, citing the rule from an April 1956 "handbook for employees" which set forth standards of conduct; see also "Post-Employment Conflict of Interest Regulations," Staff Files: Rogers, Box 32 (Eisenhower Library).

52. Brownell to author, Apr. 11, 1974.

53. See chart of total sentences appended to end of chapter.

54. Reports to the President on Pending Legislation prepared by the White House Records Office, July 4-11, 1955, Box 53, folder "7/7/55 to Amend the Clayton Act . . . HR 4954."

55. 31 U.S.C. 15a.

56. "A theory for Computing Damages Sustained by the United States and Tennessee Valley Authority in the Direct Purchase of Power Transformers," 31 (dated July 25, 1961), file 60-230-55.

57. "Guide Lines for Damage Case Settlements," Oct. 30, 1962, file 60-230-29.

58. Lewis Markas to Fred Turnage, Feb. 28, 1963, Antitrust Papers: Moloney Electric, Acc. 70A4771, file 60-230-53.

59. Administratively Confidential Memorandum to the Attorney General from Loevinger, July 23, 1962, Antitrust Papers: Electrical, file 60-230-29.

60. Memo dated Nov. 6, 1962, Antitrust Papers: Southern States, Acc. 71A6389, file 60-230-60.

61. Appendix B, Confidential Memorandum for Members of the American Public Power Association drawn up by Ely, Duncan, and Bennell, Mar. 1, 1961.

62. Handler to author, Apr. 6, 1971.

63. U.S. Senate , 91st Cong., 1st Sess., *Record* (Washington, D.C., 1969) CXV, Pt 9,

12,277. (This does not include any figure for the Worthington Corporation.)

64. James Bruce (litigation and antitrust counsel to General Electric) to author, Mar. 11, 1975.

65. William Beringer (Counsel and Director of Allis-Chalmers General Law Department) to author, Jan. 27, 1975.

66. Lee Loevinger to author, July 8, 1971; H. Graham Morison to author, July 15, 1971; Lee Loevinger, "Private Action—The Strongest Pillar of Antitrust," *The Antitrust Bulletin* 3 (Mar.-Apr. 1958), 167-177.

CHAPTER VII

The Eisenhower Administration's Antitrust Activism

NOWHERE was the commitment of the Eisenhower Administration to the concept of antitrust more evident than in its attempts to extend the antitrust ambit. This was especially apparent in two broad areas: first, the Justice Department's treatment of the relationship of antitrust to the exempted industries; and, second, the administration's efforts to expand the body of laws itself.

The question of exactly how free from antitrust laws were the exempted industries has perplexed the Justice Department and puzzled numerous defendants since the passage of the first bill granting immunity. Perhaps the most difficult problems have occurred in the fields of agricultural cooperatives, broadcasting, transportation and labor.

There were several laws governing the activities of agricultural cooperatives, the most important being the Capper-Volstead Act. It was its interaction with the Clayton Act that was significant in determining the limitations of the exemptions accorded cooperatives.

The 1954 acquisition of the assets of the Embassy Dairy, Inc., by the Maryland and Virginia Milk Producers' Association, Inc. (MVPA), triggered an investigation of the new entity, which uncovered enough evidence of restraint of trade to warrant impaneling a grand jury.[1] Although both criminal and civil cases were filed, it was the latter which was the more important. Very wary about the exact extent of the Capper-Volstead exemption in the merger field, the Antitrust Division charged that the milk company had violated Sections 1, 2, and 3 of the Sherman Act, for the association had "attempted to monopolize and has monopolized interstate trade and commerce in the supplying of milk for resale as fluid milk . . . in a manner and to an extent not permitted by law to agricultural cooperative associations."[2] In addition, the suit alleged that the association had engaged in predatory pricing and discriminatory practices.

Although Barnes felt that the chances of victory in the Clayton Act Section 7 area were "doubtful," in a separate action MVPA was accused of transgressing that statute for the acquisition of the Embassy Dairy. Until the takeover, Embassy had served as an outlet for farmers who were not members of the cooperative; it had consistently made a profit by underselling the Maryland and Virginia Milk Producers' Association, and by so doing it had been able to obtain much of the business of supplying government installations in the area. According to Hansen, "The elimination of Embassy Dairy as a competitive factor in the milk industry in the Washington metropolitan area resulting from the acquisition of its assets by the Association is alleged to have substantially lessened competition in the production and sale of milk in the area. In requesting the Court to order the Association to divest itself of the Embassy assets, it is our intention to seek to restore the competition of an independent outlet to the Washington milk market."[3] As the first Section 7 suit against a Capper-Volstead organization, it is important, for it refuted the contention that agricultural cooperatives were free to engage in practices which were designed to monopolize trade or restrain and suppress competition.[4] It is fortunate, too, that there was no rivalry between the Department of Agriculture, which had primary jurisdiction, and the Department of Justice. Indeed, Brownell received a letter from Ezra Taft Benson, the Secretary of Agriculture, stating, "it is the desire of this Department to cooperate with your Department . . . feel free to raise any questions with our people which may be a matter of concern . . . regarding this problem."[5] The files indicate that subsequent to this communication, there was a series of interdepartmental exchanges.

The district court sustained the cooperative in its contention that it was not violating Sherman Act Section 2 ("attempting to monopolize and monopolizing interstate trade and commerce in the supply of raw milk") because the producers' association was covered by the Capper-Volstead Act exemption,[6] but later it was found guilty of transgressing Section 7 of the Clayton Act for its acquisition of Embassy Dairy.[7] Upon appeal to the Supreme Court, in the former case in a major victory for the government the opinion was reversed, and in the latter action the lower court's finding was sustained. In short order, a consent judgment was entered, in which, among other clauses, the milk producer agreed to divest itself of another acquisition, the facilities of the Richfield-Wakefield Dairy, as well as those of Embassy. It is noteworthy that earlier, the court had found that the Richfield-Wakefield acquisition did not violate the Clayton Act.[8]

There always is difficulty in bringing actions against industries which suppose themselves to be exempt. When an administration which, rightly or wrongly, was labeled "business" by its opponents chose to take action against labor unions, it brought upon itself a tidal wave of criticism. This reaction happened each time the Eisenhower Administration charged a labor union with antitrust infractions.

From the beginning, labor unions have been held to be covered by the Sherman Act.[9] However, under the Clayton Act and the Norris-La Guardia Act, a labor union was immunized from the operation of the Sherman Act if it was acting alone and in its own self-interest.[10] The exemption was not all-inclusive, and any combination with a non labor group rendered its position legally precarious. In 1945, a union, employing means sanctioned by the Clayton Act, was found to have no exemption when it combined with businessmen to eliminate competition.[11] Should a union combine with a non-labor group to fix prices, that, too, was an unlawful restraint of trade.[12] Similarly, when an association of businessmen made an agreement which restricted competition and controlled prices and markets, the simple inclusion of labor provisions in the agreement did not immunize it from the act.[13]

The parameters of labor-union coverage had been drawn long before the Eisenhower Administration assumed office and they were well defined in the Attorney General's *Report*.[14] In the application of antitrust laws to labor unions, the Republican administration followed the guidelines of the *Report* and did not break new ground; but, as in other aspects of the antitrust field, it was most vigilant. In its eight years in office it instituted a total of 19 cases having labor-union defendants, compared to 15 during the previous eight years.[15]

One of the more interesting infractions of union power was provided by the Seafarers Sea Chest Corporation which was owned by the Seafarers International Union of North America, Atlantic and Gulf District. On August 20, 1954, after a private complaint,[16] the government filed a civil suit seeking an injunction against monopolistic practices of the corporation and the union in the furnishing of "slop chest" supplies for seamen on board foreign-bound American merchant vessels. The term "slop chest" is the historic name for the ship's store which carried such articles as clothing, tobacco and other gear which the seamen might wish to purchase during the voyage. The complaint charged that the union used its power as a labor organization to compel vessel owners to buy their supplies from the defendant corporation and to refuse to purchase them from other dealers who offered the goods at a competitive rate.[17] Barnes was very careful to emphasize that the suit was not intended to break the union, stating to the press, "While a labor union is involved as a defendant in this action, it is not being sued for any activity in connection with its legitimate objectives. The Union here has joined with a business corporation which it owns to further its business interest and obtain a monopoly of furnishing slop chest supplies to vessels. Such activity, involving as it does a conspiracy between a labor and a non-labor group, is not exempted from the antitrust laws."[18] The defendant corporation moved to have the complaint dismissed on the grounds that the union and the corporation were immune from antitrust laws; but on April 5, 1955, the government was upheld by the court in its contention that when a union entered into a business enterprise, it became subject to the same antitrust principles as any other business activity. At that point the two parties began negotiations leading toward a consent decree.

The final judgment, entered on March 20, 1956, required the defendant union to cancel the provisions of the collective-bargaining contracts relating to the purchase of slop chest supplies from the defendant corporation. The decree also contained a "sword of Damocles" provision which enjoined the defendants from continuing to engage in the sale of slop chest supplies after five years, unless after three years they were able to prove that there was effective competition in the field.[19] Brownell summarized the administration's position, stating, "The antitrust laws are applicable to labor unions when they depart from their ordinary functions and engage in a business enterprise. The judgment entered today takes cognizance of the right of the defendant union to bargain with the vessel owners . . . , but prohibits the union from using its collective bargaining powers to force the owners to purchase slop chest supplies exclusively from the defendant corporation."[20] In June 1961, the union ended its slop chest business; but it continued to operate its retail sales establishments in its union halls. On December 31, 1967, it closed these as well.[21]

Whether it was the moving of theatrical scenery and equipment or the export of yellow grease, the situation was similar.[22] In each instance the Antitrust Division alleged that the union had overstepped the boundary of legal activities. This usually had been achieved by the threat or actual use of the strike power.

As important as the filing of new actions was the policing of old ones. Already emphasized as a vital element of the Eisenhower Administration's antitrust program,[23] the review of previous judgments was coincident in all fields, including that of labor. An outstanding example was the July 30, 1954, filing of contempt proceedings against a Chicago Milk Drivers' Union, its president and its treasurer.[24]

Not all the regulatory agencies took such strong antitrust positions as did the Justice Department. In June 1955, the National Broadcasting Company (NBC), a wholly owned affiliate of the Radio Corporation of America (RCA), and the Westinghouse Broadcasting Company sought the approval of the Federal Communications Commission (FCC) for an exchange of stations. The proposed deal consisted of Westinghouse's trading its Philadelphia outlets, KYW Radio and WTPZ Television, to NBC for its Cleveland stations, WTAM Radio (also WTAM-FM) and WNBK Television. To sweeten the exchange, NBC also included $3 million. Following an investigation, but without a hearing by the FCC, on December 21, 1955, the FCC voted to allow the switch, and within one month the actual exchange was made.

Although the FCC had notified the Justice Department concerning the transaction on August 19, 1955, no effective liaison bridged the two governmental agencies because no communications took place between them subsequent to September 26, 1955.[25] When the Justice Department review of the facts was complete, Barnes wrote a letter to the FCC stating that "There appears to be a serious question as to whether or not the proposed transfer is unreasonably restrictive, and thus violates the Sherman Act."[26] Some of the material later uncovered by the antitrusters convinced them to file a civil complaint asking that the court find the exchange in violation of the Sherman Act and requesting divestiture of some assets of NBC.

Network affiliations are very valuable properties for a local television station. The transmission of programs supplied by either Columbia Broadcasting System or NBC often made the difference between profit and loss for the outlets.[27] Westinghouse found itself in a very difficult situation. Having just purchased KDKA Radio and KDKA-TV in Pittsburgh from the Dumont Broadcasting Corporation, it wanted to keep its NBC affiliation for those stations, but the network "made it clear that Westinghouse was not assured of . . . affiliation . . . until the deal [the station switch] went through."[28] Moreover, NBC also threatened to buy a station in Philadelphia reducing the value of WPTZ-TV. NBC also applied similar pressure in Boston against Westinghouse's twin stations, WBZ and WBZA (Springfield). Although Westinghouse did not seek Justice Department aid and indicated, probably out of fear, that it "would prefer that the government do nothing," it did promise to cooperate fully. This it did, to the extent of turning over its files on the subject. They were entitled "Operation Blackmail."[29]

The district court held that the government's suit could not be entertained since the FCC had primary jurisdiction in this matter. In dismissing the case, the judge stated that the FCC must have determined that there was no antitrust violation.[30]

Luckily, however, the Antitrust Division had a more vigorous conception of the antitrust laws than did the District Court or the FCC. Consequently it appealed to the Supreme Court emphasizing the extreme network power wielded by NBC and the coercive actions it had taken. This excessive power, the antitrusters claimed, violated the Sherman Act. Even though they felt that the transfer also transgressed the Clayton Act, they did not make that charge, for communications as a regulated industry are not subject to its rule.[31]

In the government's view, the exchange meant a further concentration of NBC into the nation's top markets, for while the Cleveland locale was rated as the number-ten area, Philadelphia was fourth, the NBC already owned stations in the other top three, New York City, Chicago and Los Angeles. Of paramount importance to the government was the fact that had Westinghouse not agreed to the switch, it would have lost its NBC affiliations; and without the network tie-in, especially on such short notice, the value of Westinghouse's broadcasting properties would have fallen precipitously.

The antitrusters were victorious in the Supreme Court because the justices unanimously reversed the dismissal, acknowledging that the Antitrust Division did have the right to object to the change. Later in the year a consent decree was negotiated in which RCA and NBC were enjoined from coercing "any person to otherwise transfer any ownership interest in any broadcast station." In addition, the defendants were ordered to divest themselves of the Philadelphia broadcasting station.[32]

The civil suit filed against Pan American World Airways (Pan Am), a major American airline with routes to the east coast of South America, W. R. Grace and Company (Grace), a company engaged in shipping to South America, and Pan American-Grace Airways (Panagra), an air carrier on the west coast of South America with routes as far north as Panama, is another illustration of the vitality of the Antitrust Division during the Eisenhower period. Although the chairman of the Civil Aeronautics Board (CAB) had written in mid-1945 to the Attorney General expressing his concern about the status of Panagra and its relationships with other transportation companies, the Antitrust Division had done nothing.[33] In late 1946, the next chairman of the CAB requested that, if the Division were contemplating a suit, they hold it in abeyance because the Board was working on some new route divisions.[34] The files on the case include several internal memos written in 1951 and 1952 on the topic of a possible action against Pan Am, Grace, and Panagra. There is also a letter from the chairman of the CAB to Attorney General James McGrath.[35] Nothing was done, however, until Barnes became Division chief.

The Panagra situation was very complicated. Formed in 1928 as a joint venture by Pan Am and Grace, the company was owned equally by the two transportation concerns. Although the CAB consistently held that it was not in the public interest for a common carrier in one form of transportation to control one in another, it believed it was unable to handle the Panagra situation because the company antedated the board by nine years. In the suit, the government argued that Pan Am had used its 50 percent ownership in Panagra to insure that the company would not endeavor to parallel its routes. The government alleged that the two airlines had attempted to monopolize air travel to South America. Because of the concept of reasonable interchangeability, the authorities also charged that Grace's steamships and Panagra's airplanes were in direct competition. The part of the action against Panagra claimed that the company had opposed Braniff's plans for South American routes. The government also questioned Panagra's price-cutting policy which had driven a non-American competitor into bankruptcy. In the district court, the portions of the case against Grace and Panagra were dismissed, but the court found that while the Pan Am actions had acted lawfully in the beginning, subsequent conduct had been in violation of the antitrust laws. Therefore, it ordered that Pan Am be forced to divest itself of the holdings.[36]

Both the government and Pan Am appealed the decision to the Supreme Court. After nine years, it finally decided all the questions. While it upheld the district court in dismissing the actions against Grace and Panagra, the high tribunal did emphasize that the "grandfather" clause which had protected Panagra from the CAB policy was not valid and that the board could force divestiture.[37] The court also directed Pan Am to dispose of its holdings in the company.

During the Eisenhower period, the antitrusters pressed for a negotiated settlement in which both Pan Am and Grace would sell their equity to another company. Although Pan Am expressed a willingness to sell its share to Braniff Air Lines on condition that Grace would do the same, the shipper refused.[38] In an effort to force compliance by Grace, the Division spent weeks trying to interpret the Panama Canal Act, which denies the use of the canal to antitrust law violators, in a way which would be "a bargaining tool for negotiating a consent decree."[39] Luckily for Grace, a large volume user of the canal, the antitrusters were unable to find the necessary loopholes.

The divorce finally did come to pass as the CAB finally issued Grace with the requisite directive. Both Pan Am and Grace sold their holdings on March 18, 1966, to Braniff Air Lines, already the possessor of many routes to South America. While this outcome did not appear to have produced the results which the antitrusters had in mind when they originally filed the suit, the denouement was definitely in line with the Eisenhower transportation policy. On March 1, 1954, Brownell stated during a conference with the CAB that if Panagra were sold to Braniff, "We would dismiss our complaint."[40] Additionally, the conclusion was in accord with government policy as set forth in the *Air Coordinating Committee's Report on Civil Air Policy* in May 1954. The document stated "competition between United States flag carriers is desirable only in areas where traffic is sufficiently dense that competition can be economically supported."[41] Unfortunately, the South American market had not developed enough for competition to be feasible.[42]

One of the longest cases was the one initiated against El Paso Natural Gas Company for its acquisition of the Pacific Northwest Pipeline Corporation. In November 1956, the two companies announced their plan: an exchange of stock in which Pacific Northwest was to become a wholly owned and operated subsidiary of El Paso. The method of acquisition was extremely important because it avoided the necessity of obtaining a clearance from the Federal

Power Commission (FPC). By May 1957, El Paso owned 99.8 percent of the outstanding stock of Pacific Northwest, and in July the Justice Department filed suit claiming that the acquisition eliminated competition in the purchase and distribution of, and exploration for, natural gas. The antitrusters finally decided that the market in question should include much of western United States.[43] Very likely spurred on by the government's suit, El Paso then applied to the FPC for permission to merge the assets of the two companies. El Paso must have decided that it had a far better chance of obtaining sanction from the FPC than from the Justice Department, for an asset merger involved sizable extra costs, such as the refunding of several issues of debt securities that had been floated at a time when interest rates were lower. The gamble was worthwhile because on December 23, 1959, over the Department's vocal objections, the FPC allowed the merger. Before the end of the year it was consummated. The case is another example of vigilance on the part of the Antitrust Division and indifference to the subject of antitrust displayed by the regulatory commissions.

While the FPC was deliberating on the merger, the antitrusters had gone to court to interdict the marriage. Little was accomplished because first, FPC matters seemed to take precedence, and then the government tried to secure a satisfactory consent decree. After obtaining the FPC's blessings, El Paso refused to negotiate an acceptable decree, and the case finally went to trial. In late 1962, it was dismissed by the District Court without even a written opinion.

In the meantime, in 1958, at the behest of the man who was then Attorney General and subsequently became governor, Edmund Brown, the State of California had also endeavored to block the merger. Rebuffed at the district level, the state then appealed to the Supreme Court. This aspect of the case is significant because the difficulties illustrate the new directions of the Justice Department during the Kennedy regime. Although it is true that the Solicitor General represents all agencies of the government before the Supreme Court, it is rare for the Department of Justice to go before the Supreme Court and argue one side of the case, while at the same time pleading the other side of the case in a district court. Even though the perspectives of the regulatory agencies and the Antitrust Division are often at variance, the differences of opinion usually do not get out of hand. In the El Paso situation, the attorneys involved in the Antitrust Division action were not even consulted before Solicitor General Archibald Cox argued in *California* v. *Federal Power Commission*, that the FPC had acted correctly. Morale in the Division was shattered, and several members of the Division recommended dropping the case.[45]

Disturbed by the course of events, Lee Loevinger, Kennedy's chief of the Antitrust Division, pleaded with Cox, emphasizing that the "payscale here is such that we cannot attract or hold lawyers on the basis of salary. The only real attraction . . . is the sense of participation in a noble cause and contribution to the public welfare. But this will not last long unless the staff feels assurance that its efforts will be aided, not frustrated, at the highest levels. . . . [T]o have efforts thwarted by officials of the Department tends to create a feeling of futility." The "feeling of futility" also must have affected Loevinger deeply, for the final sentence of his memo to Cox, a former professor of labor law and an expert on labor relations, was abnormally harsh, "If nothing else, you may be interested in this . . . as another aspect of labor relations."[46] That antitrust was not as important to the Kennedy and Johnson Administrations is further borne out by the fact that arguing the case with Cox was William Orrick, soon to be appointed chief of the Antitrust Division! In the end, even after a Supreme Court decision which was favorable to the antitrusters,[47] it would take nearly a decade until all parties could agree on an acceptable plan of divestiture, and it was not until April 15, 1974, that participation certificates in the successor company, Northwest Pipeline, Inc., were publicly traded.

Not all of the expansion of the ambit of antitrust during the Eisenhower era was made by means of judicial interpretation of the laws. The administration made a concerted effort to extend the sweep of the laws by amendments to the antitrust corpus and also by backing and proposing new legislation.

With the exception of raising the maximum fine for violating the Sherman Act from $5,000 to $50,000, there was little innovative accomplished in the field in the first few years. This inactivity was understandable for any proposed change in the antitrust laws of necessity took a long time to be ratified by Congress.[48] Also important was the activity of the Attorney General's National Committee to Study the Antitrust Laws. Until that body had submitted its *Report*, the administration was unlikely to propose any major alterations.

One of the most notable recommendations of the Attorney General's National Committee was that the Attorney General be empowered to issue a civil investigative demand (CID). Supported almost immediately by Barnes, at that time the Assistant Attorney General in charge of the Antitrust Division, the concept was first introduced to Congress in the form of HR 7309. That the administration wholeheartedly backed the demand was illustrated by President Eisenhower's recommendation in the 1956 *Economic Report of the President* to Congress: "When civil rather than criminal proceedings are contemplated, the Attorney General should be empowered to use a civil investigative demand, compelling the production of documents before the filing of a complaint, and without having to invoke grand jury proceedings."[49] From this time onward, obtaining congressional acceptance of CID was a part of the Eisenhower program and often an important point made in speeches by the Antitrust Division chiefs and cabinet officers.[50]

There was a clear need for the device. Under the existing law, the Division had no means by which to obtain the requisite documents for its investigation. Although it could seek the voluntary cooperation of those under scrutiny, obviously few would willingly produce incriminating materials. In order to force their production, the Department had to resort to the use of the grand jury. Thus many a criminal case was filed which, had there been CID, would have been civil. In other instances, the government filed a criminal case, used the grand jury, and then employed its findings in a subsequent civil suit. Perhaps the most utilized weapon, it was snatched from the government's arsenal by an adverse Supreme Court decision. The Proctor and Gamble Company had challenged the circumvention, and the Supreme Court ruled that "criminal procedure is subverted" by this means.[51] After that, enactment of CID was imperative. Even before the Proctor and Gamble case, in the Section 7 merger cases, the Justice Department was in a difficult position, for the antimerger statute had no criminal provisions, and thus it was impossible to resort to the use of the grand jury. CID, therefore, was a logical request for an administration which was so enforcement-oriented. CID was moderate, already the Securities and Exchange Commission and the FTC had similar powers, yet at the same time it would achieve its purpose.

Despite its efforts the Eisenhower Administration never was able to obtain passage of a bill containing CID. The most obvious explanation was that the Republicans did not control Congress after 1954. It was not until the Kennedy years that the law was finally approved. It is notable that during the period from 1958 to 1961, when Robert Bicks was especially vigorous in lobbying for the bill, the Democrats controlled more seats in the Congress than they did when the bill was finally approved. The credit for securing passage of CID must be given to Loevinger, Kennedy's Assistant Attorney General in charge of the Antitrust Division. Working on the project at least as diligently as his precedessor, he was successful because he had more influence with the Congress.[52] For his efforts, he was awarded the pen used by President Kennedy to sign the bill into law.

A second change proposed was that of pre-merger notification. In 1956, when the idea was first presented in the *Economic Report of the President*, the staff on the monopoly section devoted much time to ferretting out mergers before they occurred.[53] With pre-merger notification, their efforts could be more constructively directed.[54] Given the same emphasis as the CID, especially during the Hansen years, it also was not passed during the Eisenhower era; but unlike CID, it was not approved during the subsequent Democratic administrations.

Not all Republican proposals to strengthen the antitrust laws were turned down by a hostile Congress. Even after the Celler-Kefauver 1950 Amendment to the Clayton Act, there were still loopholes left in the anti-merger act.

Due to the insistence of Congressman Wright Patman, the influential chairman of the Select Committee on Small Business and member of the Banking and Currency Committee, the bill had been redrawn in such a way as to leave uncovered any asset acquisitions by banks.[55] Although that provision's stock acquisition barrier applied to all corporations "engaged in commerce," in contrast, Section 7's asset acquisition portion covered only those corporations "subject to the jurisdiction of the Federal Trade Commission."[56] Since Section 11 of the Clayton Act exempted banks from FTC jurisdiction by specifying that the Federal Reserve Board had authority to enforce compliance with Section 7, the Department of Justice as early as 1952 had concluded that there was no way that an asset acquisition by a bank could be covered by Section 7.[57] Therefore it became the objective of the Antitrust Division, and especially of Hansen, to apply the standards of the Clayton Act to mergers in the banking industry.[58]

There was an obvious need for legislation covering bank mergers. During the Eisenhower years, there were a large number of consolidations in the banking field. In New York City almost all the leading institutions were involved in at least one merger. In December 1954, the Chemical Bank and Trust Company combined with the Corn Exchange Bank and Trust Company. In March and April of the following year, there were three significant consolidations: The combination of Chase National Bank with the Bank of Manhattan Company created a new entity which, in terms of total assets, was the largest in the nation's financial capital; also the merger of National City Bank of New York with First National Bank of New York to become the First National City Bank, ranking second in New York City; the absorption by Bankers Trust Company of New York of Public National Bank and Trust Company. In 1959 J.P. Morgan Company merged with Guaranty Trust Company of New York to form the Morgan Guaranty Trust Company of New York. These consolidations seemed to presage a wave of mergers beyond the reach of the antitrusters.[59] The Division established a special file for those bank mergers to which it could not apply the Clayton Act.[60] Open, after being asked for clearance, the Assistant Attorney General was forced to reply, "After a complete consideration of this matter, we have concluded that this Department would not have jurisdiction to proceed. . . . For this reason this Department does not presently plan to take any action on this matter."[61] The loophole allowing bank marriages was so large that after Marine Midland Trust Company and Auburn Trust Company were refused a merger preclearance, they "got around the law" by completing the combination by means of stock acquisition.[62]

Many of the proposed bills provided for pre-merger consent by a banking agency, such as the Board of Governors of the Federal Reserve Board, the Comptroller of the Currency or the Federal Deposit Insurance Corporation. Hansen vigorously opposed these pieces of legislation, describing them as deficient for two reasons; first, they would set up competitive tests for bank mergers different from those that apply to other sectors of American business. Second, they might, even beyond the banking area, seriously dissipate enforcement efforts by decentralizing responsibility for enforcement of the Clayton Act Section 7.[63]

While the Antitrust Division was unsuccessful in obtaining responsibility for enforcing the new statute in the banking field, the law (Public Law 86-463), when it was signed on May 13, 1960, did contain a necessary safeguard: that the agency deciding on the mergers had to request from the Attorney General a "report on the competitive features involved." The new law, known as the Bank Merger Act, therefore extended the scope of the antitrust statutes, and while it did not provide every item desired by the Antitrust Division, it did have the immediate effect of slowing down the merger rate of banking institutions.

The Eisenhower antitrusters expended a significant amount of energy in the area of regulated industries. Their first task was to persuade the regulatory body in question that antitrust was a factor which deserved consideration. Here they met with varying degrees of success; the Department of Agriculture, run by Eisenhower appointee Ezra Taft Benson, quickly came to understand the value of competition as, for example, in the marketing and production of milk. In other fields, success was slower, either perhaps because of the more entrenched position of the regulators, as in the case of the FPC, or because of different agency objectives, as in the case of the CAB.

Nevertheless, the Eisenhower record in the field is not completely stellar. It did not treat the problem of the other statutes which encouraged mergers. Nothing was done to modify inheritance taxes or the procedures which forced many a closely held small business to seek takeover by a larger company whose securities were more liquid. In like manner, no legislation was backed to stimulate voluntary corporate divestitures. For instance, if General Motors were to have decided that it wanted to spin off its Chevrolet Division, without a specific tax ruling the new shares would be taxed as dividend income. Had tax incentives been adopted in this area, undoubtedly there would have been some deconcentration in several major industries.

When considering efforts to obtain passage of supplementary laws to facilitate the tasks of the Antitrust Division, the record is harder to assess. Certainly the amount of legislation is small, but that amount does have to be viewed in the context of the ever-stronger legislative position of the opposition party. Even here, however, gains were made, such as bringing the banking industry within reach of the enforcers.

NOTES

1. Memo for the Attorney General, Feb. 21, 1955, Antitrust Papers: Maryland and

Virginia Milk Producers' Association, Inc. (MVPA), Acc. 70A4771 and 71A6389, file 60-0-37-31.

2. Dept. of Justice, "Immediate Release," Nov. 21, 1956.

3. Dept. of Justice, "Immediate Release," Nov. 21, 1956.

4. Hansen to author, June 16, 1971; Hansen, "Antitrust and the Dairy Industry," speech delivered to the National Independent Dairies Association in Washington, D.C., on Apr. 22, 1958, and "The Administration of Federal Antitrust Laws," speech delivered to the New York State Bar Association Section on Antitrust Laws in New York, N.Y., on Jan. 29, 1959.

5. Benson to Brownell, June 26, 1958, Antitrust Papers: MVPA.

6. 167 F. Supp. 45 (1958).

7. 167 F. Supp. 799 (1958).

8. 1960 Trade Cases, par. 69,860; also Antitrust Papers: MVPA-Richfield-Wakefield, Acc. 70A4771, file 60-0-37-164.

9. Even before the passage of the Sherman antitrust law in 1890, efforts had been made to apply the common-law principles of antitrust of the labor field. In 1809, in the case of the Journeyman Cordwainers of the City of New York, a labor combination was found to be a criminal conspiracy; Edwin Smith and Ernest Hitchcock, *Reports of Cases Adjudged and Determined in the Supreme Court of Judicature of the State of New York* (Newark, N.Y., 1884), p. 153. In 1835 the Supreme Court of Judicature of the State of New York watered down the charge and found a conspiracy to raise wages to be only a misdemeanor; John L. Wendell, *Report of Cases Argued and Determined in the Supreme Court of Judicature and in the Court for the Correction of Errors of the State of New York*, 14 (Albany, N.Y.: 1837), 9. By 1842, in Commonwealth v. John Hunt & others, the Massachusetts Supreme Court acknowledged the legality of concerted action by labor unions. Theron Metcalf, *Reports of Cases Argued and Determined in the Supreme Judicial Court of Massachusetts* (Boston, 1864), p. 111. It was easy to apply the Sherman Act's language "combination in restraint of trade" to labor unions, and the Cleveland Administration brought four cases against labor organizations (Thorelli, p. 386). Although the Clayton Act, the Norris-La Guardia, and the Taft-Hartley acts provided exemptions for unions, they still were covered in certain instances.

10. 29 U.S.C. 101-115.

11. Allen Bradley Co. v. Local 3, International Brotherhood of Electrical Workers, 325 U.S. 797 (1945).

12. Gulf Coast Shrimpers' and Oysterman's Association v. United States, 1956, Trade Cases, par. 68,469.

13. U.S. v. Women's Sportswear Manufacturers' Association, 336 U.S. 460 (1949).

14. *A.G. Report*, p. 293-305; see above, p. 48; but see Archibald Cox, "Labor and the Antitrust Laws—A Preliminary Analysis," *University of Pennsylvania Law Review*, 104 (Nov. 1955), 252-284.

15. ANTITRUST CASES IN WHICH UNIONS WERE DEFENDANTS:
Walton Hauling & Warehouse Corp., et al. (Civil and Criminal)
Chattanooga Chapter, NECA, Inc., et al.
Louisiana Fruit and Vegetable Producers Union, Local 312, et al.
Cigarette Merchandisers Assn., Inc., et al. (Civil and Criminal)

Milk Wagon Drivers' Union, Local 753, International Brotherhood of Teamsters, Chauffeurs, Stevedores and Helpers of America, et al.

Seafarers Sea Chest Corp. and Seafarers Union of North America, Atlantic Gulf Division

Fish Smokers Trade Council, Inc., et al. (Civil and Criminal)

Operative Plasterers and Cement Masons International Association of the United States and Canada, et al.

United Scenic Artists, Local 829

Hamilton Glass Company, et al.

Greater Blouse, Skirt & Neckwear Contractors' Assn., Inc., et al.

Meyer Singer, et al.

Los Angeles Meat and Provision Drivers' Union 626. (Civil and Criminal)

Gasoline Retailers' Assn., Inc., et al. (Civil and Criminal)

The author would like to thank Baddia Rashid of the Dept. of Justice for supplying the list of cases in which unions were defendants.

16. Letter dated Mar. 23, 1933, from Weill Brothers Seamen's Supplies, Inc., to the Justice Department, Antitrust Papers: Slop Chest, Acc 70A4771, file 60-258-2; *Seafarers' Log*, Mar. 30, 1956.

17. Memo for the Attorney General, Aug. 16, 1954, Antitrust Papers: Slop Chest.

18. Dept. of Justice, "Immediate Release," Aug. 20, 1954.

19. 1956 Trade Cases, par. 68,298.

20. Dept. of Justice, "Immediate Release," Mar. 20, 1956.

21. Francis X. Pecquex (historian-archivist of the Seafarers' International Union) to author, Sept. 12, 1975, Jan. 13, 1976, and Jan. 27, 1976.

22. Dept. of Justice, "Immediate Release," June 23, 1953, July 15, 1953, and May 27, 1959.

23. See above, p. 84.

24. Dept. of Justice, "Immediate Release," July 30, 1954.

25. Antitrust Papers: NBC-Westinghouse, Acc. 70A4771, file 60-211-69.

26. Barnes to FCC, Dec. 27, 1955, Antitrust Papers: NBC-Westinghouse.

27. The American Broadcasting Company affiliation was not so important, since ABC ran a poor third in the ratings. In 1953, Westinghouse placed the value of the NBC network affiliation at $5 million when it paid Philco Corporation $2 million for the land and equipment of WPTZ-TV, $1.5 million for goodwill and $5 million for the affiliation. U.S. House, 84th Cong., 2nd Sess. Antitrust Subcommittee of the Committee on the Judiciary, *Monopoly Problems in Regulated Industries: Hearings* . . . (Washington, D.C., 1957), Pt. 2, I, 3117-3120; Victor R. Hansen, "Broadcasting and the Antitrust Laws," *Law and Contemporary Problems*, 22 (Autumn, 1956), 575-578.

28. Memo reporting Bernard Hollander, interview of E. V. Higgins, Vice-President of Westinghouse, Oct. 24, 1955, in Antitrust Papers: NBC-Westinghouse.

29. Memos to Barnes, Jan. 12, and 13, 1956, Antitrust Papers: NBC-Westinghouse.

30. 1957 Trade Cases, par. 68,913, and 158 F. Supp., 333.

31. 15 U.S.C. 18.

32. 1959 Trade Cases, par. 69,459.

33. L. Welch Pogue to Wendell Berge, July 6, 1945, Antitrust Papers: Panagra, Acc. 70A4771, file 60-228-16.

34. James Landis to Berge, Oct. 1946 (no specific date), Antitrust Papers: Panagra.
35. Donald Nyrop to James H. McGrath, Oct. 3, 1951, Antitrust Papers: Panagra.
36. 193 F. Supp. 18.
37. 371 U.S. 296, 311-313.
38. Henry Friendly (Vice-President of Pan Am) to Hansen, Nov. 19, 1956, Antitrust Papers: Panagra.
39. Internal memo, Oct. 1, 1958, Antitrust Papers: Panagra.
40. Memo of conference with CAB, Mar. 1, 1954, Antitrust Papers: Panagra.
41. "Air Coordinating Committee's Report on Civil Air Policy," 15, Antitrust Papers: Panagra.
42. Memo to the Solicitor General, June 29, 1961, Antitrust Papers: Panagra.
43. Memo for the Attorney General, June 11, 1957, Antitrust Papers: El Paso, Accs. 71A6389, 60-74-157, 60-73-112, file 60-0-37-158.
44. 369 U.S. 482.
45. See, for instance, memo to George Reycraft, Sept. 28, 1961, Antitrust Papers: El Paso.
46. Loevinger to Cox, Nov. 13, 1961, Antitrust Papers: El Paso.
47. U.S. v. El Paso Natural Gas Co., 376 U.S. 651 (1964).
48. Reports to the President on Pending Legislation prepared by the White House Records Office, Box 53, July 4-July 11, 1955, "increase criminal penalties under the Sherman Antitrust Act HR 3659."
49. *Economic Report of the President: 1956* (Washington, D.C., 1956), p. 79.
50. Brownell, "Address," delivered to the 1956 Executive Conference on Administrative Policies and Problems, Philadelphia, Pa., June 20, 1956; Rogers, "Address," delivered to the meeting of the Antitrust Section of the New York State Bar Association, New York, N.Y., Jan. 26, 1956; Hansen, "Proposed Civil Investigative Demand: A More Precise Method for Antitrust Investigation," delivered to the Michigan State Bar Association, Detroit, Mich., Apr. 25, 1958.
51. U.S. v. Proctor and Gamble and Company et al., 356 U.S. 677, 684 (1958).
52. Lee Loevinger to author, July 8, 1971.
53. Victor Hansen to author, June 16, 1971.
54. Victor Hansen, "Current Programs and Policies of the Antitrust Division," delivered to the Association of the Bar of the City of New York, N.Y., Nov. 13, 1956.
55. Patman envisioned that such regulation would be included in an amendment to a banking act; H. Graham Morison to author, Aug. 11, 1975.
56. 17 U.S.C. 18.
57. Hansen to author, June 16, 1971.
58. Although Barnes, Hansen, and Bicks did not believe that Section 7 was applicable to bank mergers, in 1963 in the Philadelphia Bank case (374 U.S. 321), the Supreme Court decided that it was, thus making the Bank Merger Act of 1960 unnecessary.
59. See Antitrust Papers: Chase National Bank and Bank of Manhattan, Acc. 71A6389, file 60-0-37-55; First National Bank of New York and National City Bank of New York, Acc. 64A580, file 60-0-37-65; Bankers Trust Company of New York and Public National Bank and Trust Company, Acc. 70A4771, file 60-

0-37-64; J.P. Morgan Company and Guaranty Trust Company of New York, Acc. 70A4771, file 60-0-37-243.

60. File 60-111-0 and following.

61. Barnes to Lawrence Bennett (one of the attorneys in the firm of Milbank, Tweed, Hope and Hadley handling the Chase National Bank merger), Mar. 23, 1955, Antitrust Papers: Chase National Bank and Bank of Manhattan.

62. Foote to Barnes, Nov. 4, 1955, Antitrust Papers: Marine Midland, Acc. 70A4771, file 60-0-37-83.

63. Hansen, "Current Programs and Policies of the Antitrust Division," speech of Nov. 13, 1956, delivered to the Association of the Bar of the City of New York, N.Y.

CHAPTER VIII

Conclusion

IN the context of the mid-twentieth century, the Eisenhower Administration, incontrovertibly, oversaw a period of vigorous and innovative enforcement of the antitrust laws by the Justice Department's Antitrust Division. How good a record the Federal Trade Commission had in its performance of similar assignments will be the subject of a companion book; but because of its mandated composition, the Commission probably will not be seen to have achieved comparable accomplishments. Not until April 1953 did it have a Republican chairman, and it was even later than that before the Republicans had a majority of commissioners; and when they did, they had only the specified three of five.

Perhaps castigating Arnold and the TNEC for having achieved little is unfair since the intervention of World War II did change the whole face of American life. However, with the advent of peace came opportunities to resume his crusade. The country must have been in a new mood that was also shared by the Truman Administration; otherwise there would be no explanation at all for the government's sale of the massive Geneva Steel Works to the number-one steel producer in the nation. Perhaps the administration was still basking in the afterglow of the World War II victory which the Allies won thanks to the enormous power of American industry.

It is ironic that an administration that began life with a cabinet composed of "seven millionaires and a plumber" (and which soon lost the plumber), had such an affinity for a body of laws previously viewed as anti-business. The Eisenhower Administration took the hitherto unused Celler-Kefauver amendment to the Clayton Act and molded it into a useful statute. They did this carefully and without the overzealousness which often accompanies a crusade. Thus, when there were opportunities to achieve their goals via consent judgments in several of their earlier cases, such as the Hilton or General Shoe actions, they happily negotiated decrees and waited for new opportunities. In the brilliance of subsequent victories, often forgotten is Bethlehem's attempt to merge with Youngstown, a marriage halted by the antitrusters. This helped lay the groundwork for Bicks' successful prophylactic antitrust program. Although it is true that the nation had to wait some time

155

for the denouement of several of the more spectacular cases, for example *Brown Shoe*, without the strong antitrust philosophy and diligence of the Eisenhower Department of Justice, America would have had to wait much longer for the precedents. A perusal of the Sherman Act enforcement record shows that the Antitrust Division continued to prosecute the actions it inherited and to find new ones of its own, the most notable of which were the Electrical cases. They alone changed the complexion of antitrust enforcement. Ever since then there has been an awareness of the laws and of the consequences of transgressing them which could not have occurred had several powerful corporations and their executives not felt the full brunt of the statutes they had violated. Furthermore, the Electrical cases spawned many private actions, further increasing the application of the laws.

What explains the outstanding record of the Eisenhower Administration in the antitrust field? First, and probably of least importance, is the historic Republican record in the area. Second, and also probably of minimal import, is the psychological reason of overcompensation by the party of "big business." Neither simplistic answer is satisfactory; antitrust was and is far too complicated a subject to be explained away by the mere evocation of historical precedent or psychological quirk. Instead, and of the greatest magnitude, is the fact that antitrust laws had been for the twentieth-century American an expression of one of the country's goals: economic freedom in a democratic society. The underlying ideology was based on the American principle of limited power which was not only the cornerstone of the governmental system, but also the foundation of American business. The antitrust laws protected the American businessman; he could carry on his endeavors without being subjected to organized group pressures or monopoly power, but if he was injured by the violation of one of the laws, the antitrust corpus afforded him a chance for redress.

Aside from certain special activities, such as public utilities, atomic energy, and communications, most business was not subject to public regulation. Many Americans, especially members of the Republican Party, believed that a stronger, more productive economy could be built by relying on the competitive system of free enterprise. According to this line of reasoning, government regulation should be kept to a minimum, and be resorted to only in situations in which experience had already shown it necessary for the national welfare. Usually regulation was necessary because of a *lack* of competitive forces—such as in the field of public utilities. Without effective competition, the need for government regulation was immediately apparent, and that need ran counter to the Republican philosophy of avoiding expansion of the federal government's powers.

The businessman had a vital stake in the antitrust laws, for they protected his freedom and ability to act. While they proscribe certain actions, they did not prescribe anything. They were not aimed at any one company or group of companies, and where the laws were invoked, they benefited more corporations than they hurt. Antitrust, thus, was pro-business.

For these reasons, on December 5, 1953, Attorney General Brownell announced a program for attracting outstanding law-school graduates into the Department of Justice.[2] The project entailed admitting 30 of the best-qualified law-school graduates each year. To be sure of attracting the most talented, the salaries offered were competitive with those of the best law firms in the country.[3] This recruitment effort was the first ever undertaken by the Justice Department. The dividends were enormous since the "honors program" proved an immediate success. While it aided the entire Department, its influence was most resounding in the Antitrust Division. The results of the honors program, the "happy coming together" of Robert Bicks, Marcus Hollabaugh and Ephraim Jacobs, plus the general attitude of the administration, all played a part in making the section the "glamor division of the Department."[4]

Despite the fact that it was during the Kennedy-Johnson terms that the civil investigative demand was finally passed and first utilized, and that such top scholars as Lee Loevinger and Donald F. Turner headed the Antitrust Division, the Democratic record pales when compared to that of the preceding administration. In the 1960s, antitrust was all but forgotten.

Actions bravely begun in the mid-1950s were either dropped or were settled in ways that did little to stimulate competition. A good example here is the container industry; compare the resolution of either the suits against Continental Can Corporation for its acquisitions of the Hazel Atlas and Robert Gair Corporations, or the action against Owens-Illinois for its takeover of National Container, with the Du Pont-General Motors story. For the Eisenhower Administration, the "pass through" solution whereby Du Pont stockholders would vote the proxies of the General Motors stock held by Du Pont was no solution at all because "any conscientious management must . . . take into consideration the interests of those investors . . . even if formal power to direct them or fire them is absent."[5] Continental Can was allowed to keep 20 percent and sell 80 percent of its Hazel Atlas Division to the Brockway Glass Company, not for cash or a loan, but for nonvoting stock. Surely this had the effect of actually increasing concentration. And in the next year the suit against the Robert Gair acquisition was dropped. In similar manner, although Owens Illinois agreed to divest itself of most of the properties it had acquired in the National Container takeover, the method of financing the sale to Alton Box Board was in line with the weak enforcement in the former container case. As part payment Owens received warrants to buy Alton stock. In each case, then, ownership was not truly divested, it was only diluted—and as a result, the companies in question owned a smaller percentage of a larger factor in the business!

In the 1960s, the term "glamor section" of the Justice Department became the Civil Rights Division, and with the downplaying of antitrust came a concomitant surge in the "urge to merge." The concept of synergism gripped Wall Street and many a small company quickly became an extremely large multiproducted conglomerate. Even though the Celler-Kefauver Amendment to Section 7 of the Clayton Act was drafted with the idea of including conglomerate mergers,[6] nothing in that area was accomplished until after Richard M. Nixon had taken office. The man who, as Vice President, had suggested Judge Stanley Barnes as the first chief of the Antitrust Division in 1953 was the same man who, as President, chose Richard B. McLaren to head the Division in 1969. Within three years, the antitrusters attacked the largest of the conglomerates; cases were initiated against Ling-Temco-Vought, Inc., for its acquisition of the Jones and Laughlin Steel Corporation, against the International Telephone and Telegraph Corporation for its takeovers of the Canteen Corporation, Hartford Fire Insurance and Grinnell Companies, and against Northwest Industries for its newly amassed holdings in the B. F. Goodrich Company. Although the outcome of several of the cases has been shrouded in the controversy and suspicion bred of Watergate, and even though the deteriorating economic conditions probably played an important role in the decline, there is no question that the Nixon-Ford years saw a precipitous reduction in "conglomerate" mergers.

During the Eisenhower years, in both the Sherman and Clayton Act phases of trade regulation the antitrusters were active and innovative. Not only were many Sherman Act cases entered and vigorously prosecuted, but the bounds of the anti-merger provisions of the Clayton Act were also delineated. Although many of the important antimerger cases were not decided until well into the 1960s, their roots lay in the Eisenhower antitrust program. The *Brown Shoe* and *Von's Grocery*[7] cases, both of which ended with landmark opinions for the Justice Department, were formulated during the 1950s. That they and the Du Pont-General Motors precedents stayed little or totally unused for the next years illustrates more than anything else the vitality of the Eisenhower policy—especially in comparison to that of its successors.

NOTES

1. Richard McLaren (Assistant Attorney General in charge of the Antitrust Division, 1969-71) to author, Jan. 6, 1971.
2. H. Brownell, address delivered at the Univ. of Texas Law School, Austin, Tex., Dec. 5, 1953.
3. Lino Graglia to author, Nov. 18, 1971. Mr. Graglia was a member of the first group, which began its orientation under the leadership of Charles Goodell on Oct. 1, 1954.

4. Robert Kaufman to author, Aug. 16, 1971. Mr. Kaufman was an attorney in the Dept. of Justice (1957-1958) and then served as legislative assistant to Jacob Javits, a Republican senator from New York.
5. U.S. v. DuPont, 353 U.S. 586. Brief for Plaintiff at 43.45, 54 (Oct. 1960).
6. H. Graham Morison to author, July 17, 1971.
7. 384 U.S. 270.

Bibliography

Unpublished Sources and company statements

Allis-Chalmers Company. "Prospectus". Delaware, May 6, 1965.

Barnes, Stanley. "Annual Report of the Antitrust Division: Fiscal Year Ending June 30, 1954". Washington, D.C., 1954. Also other years.

Bethlehem Steel Corporation. "Prospectus". Delaware, October 1, 1920. Also other years.

Fogarty, Thomas C. "The Outlook for 1965". Speech delivered to the annual meeting of the stockholders of Continental Can Company. April 27, 1965.

General Electric Company. "Prospectus". New York, April 25, 1967.

Greenewalt, Crawford H. "Letter to the Stockholders". Delaware, May 31, 1962.

Martin, Edmund F. "The Promise for the Future". Speech delivered at the National Newcomen Dinner of the Newcomen Society in North America. April 20, 1967.

Mueller, Willard F. "Du Pont: A Study in Firm Growth". Diss. Vanderbilt Univ., 1956.

Shaffroth, Morrison. "Papers Pertaining to the Attorney General's National Committee to Study the Antitrust Laws." (private collection)

Union Oil Company. "Annual Report". California, 1964.

United States Shares Corporation. "Special Analysis on the Proposed Youngstown-Bethlehem Merger". n.p., March 22, 1930.

Westinghouse Electric Company. "Prospectus". Pennsylvania, March 29, 1967.

Wilkey, Malcolm R. Letter to Herbert Vogel, chairman of the T.V.A. June 1, 1959.

Government Documents

Congressional Record 51st Cong., 1st sess. Washington, D.C., 1889.

Economic Report of the President: 1956. Washington, D.C., 1956. Also other years.

U.S. Federal Trade Commission. *Annual Report . . . 1927.* Washington, D.C., 1927.

————— *Large Mergers in Manufacturing and Mining: 1948-1971.* Washington, D.C., 1972.

Supreme Court of the United States. "Transcript of Record". No. 3. October term, 1956.

————— "Transcript of Record". No. 54. October term, 1958.

U.S. Attorney General. *Annual Report, 1955.* Washington, D.C. 1955. Also other years.

U.S. Attorney General's National Committee to Study the Antitrust Laws. *Report.* Washington, D.C., 1958.

U.S. Congress House. Antitrust Subcommittee of the Committee on the Judiciary. *Current Antitrust Problems: Hearings.* 84th Cong., 1st sess. 3 pts. Washington, D.C., 1955.

_____. *Consent Decree Program of the Department of Justice: Hearings.* 85th Cong., 1st and 2nd sess. 2 pts., 6 vols. Washington, D.C., 1957-1958.

_____. *Consent Decree Program of the Department of Justice: Report.* 86th Cong., 1st sess. Washington, D.C., 1959.

_____. *Monopoly Problems in Regulated Industries: Hearings.* 84th Cong., 2nd sess. 2 pts., 4 vols. Washington, D.C. 1957.

U.S. Congress. House. Rep. No. 1191. 81st Cong., 1st sess. Washington, D.C., 1949.

_____. Rep. No. 627. 63rd Cong., 2nd sess. Series 6559. n.p., 1914.

U.S. Congress. House. Select Committee on Small Business. *Hearings Pursuant to House Resolution 114.* 84th Cong., 1st sess. Washington, D.C., 1955.

U.S. Congress. Senate. Subcommittee on Antitrust and Monopoly of the Committee on the Judiciary. *A Study of the Antitrust Laws: Hearings.* 84th Cong., 1st sess. 8 pts. Washington, D.C., 1955.

_____. *Administered Prices: Hearings.* 87th Cong., 1st sess. 28 pts, Washington, D.C., 1961.

U.S. Temporary National Economic Committee. *Monograph No. 16, Antitrust in Action.* Washington, D.C., 1940.

_____. *Investigation of Concentration of Economic Power, Final Report and Recommendations.* Washington, D.C., 1941.

Papers and Records

Philip Areeda (Eisenhower Library, Abilene, Kansas)

Herbert Brownell (Oral History Collection, Columbia University, New York, N.Y.)

Department of Justice, Antitrust Division (Federal Records Center, Suitland, Maryland, and Department of Justice Building, Washington, D.C.)

E.I. du Pont de Nemours Co. (Eleutherian Mills Historical Library, Greenville, Wilmington, Delaware)

Irénée du Pont (Eleutherian Mills Historical Library)

Pierre S. du Pont (Eleutherian Mills Historical Library)

Dwight D. Eisenhower Papers as President of the United States (Eisenhower Library)
    Administration Series
    Ann Whitman Diary Series
    Cabinet Series
    Eisenhower (DDE) Series
    Legislative Meetings Series
    NSC series
    White House Office: Cabinet Secretariat
    White House Office: Records Office
    White House Office: Staff Records Group

Christian Herter (Eisenhower Library)
Robert Jackson (in possession of his heirs)
Neil Jacoby (Eisenhower Library)
Thomas Jefferson, The Papers of. Ed. Julian P. Boyd. 18 vols. N.J.: Princeton, 1950—.
National Association of Manufacturers (Eleutherian Mills Historical Library)
Joseph Rand (Eisenhower Library)
John J. Raskob (Eleutherian Mills Historical Library)
William Rogers (Eisenhower Library)

Federal Court Cases

Allen Bradley Co. v. *Local 3, International Brotherhood of Electrical Workers,* 325 U.S. 797. 1945.
California v. *Federal Power Commission.* 369 U.S. 482. 1961.
Carter v. *Carter Coal Co.* 298 U.S. 269. 1936.
F.T.C. v. *Cement Institute.* 333 U.S. 683. 1948.
F.T.C. v. *Western Meat Co.* 272 U.S. 554. 1926.
Ford v. *Chicago Milk Shippers Association.* 39 N.E. 651. 1895.
International Shoe Company v. *F.T.C.* 280 U.S. 291. 1930.
Klor's v. *Broadway-Hale Stores.* 359 U.S. 207. 1959.
Pan American World Airways, Inc. v. *United States.* 371 U.S. 296. 1963.
Panama Refining Company v. *Ryan.* 293 U.S. 388. 1935.
Schechter Poultry Corp. v. *United States.* 295 U.S. 495. 1935.
Schwegmann Bros. v. *Calvert Distillers Corp.* 341 U.S. 384, 1951.
United States v. *Bethlehem Steel Corp.* 168 F. Supp. 576. 1958.
United States v. *Brown Shoe Co.* 370 U.S. 294. 1962.
United States v. *Butler, et al.* 297 U.S. 61. 1936.
United States v. *Columbia Steel Co.* 344 U.S. 495. 1948.
United States v. *E.I. Du Pont de Nemours and Company, et al.* 118 F. Supp. 41. 1953.
United States v. *E.I. Du Pont de Nemours and Company, et al.* 126 F. Supp. 235. 1954.
United States v. *E.I. Du Pont de Nemours and Company, et al.* 351 U.S. 377. 1956.
United States v. *E.I. Du Pont de Nemours and Company, et al.* 353 U.S. 586. 1957.
United States v. *E.I. Du Pont de Nemours and Company, et al.,* 366 U.S. 316. 1961.
United States v. *Gulf Coast Shrimpers' and Oysterman's Association.* S.D. Miss. 1953.
United States v. *Joint Traffic Association.* 171 U.S. 505. 1898.
United States v. *Maryland and Virginia Milk Producers Association.* 167 F. Supp. 799. 1958.
United States v. *Maryland and Virginia Milk Producers Association.* 362 U.S. 458. 1960.
United States v. *Henry S. Morgan, et al.* 118 F. Supp. 621.
United States v. *Otis Elevator Co.* 9th Cir. 1906.
United States v. *Paramount Pictures, Inc.* 334 U.S. 131. 1948.
United States v. *Proctor and Gamble and Company, et al.* 356 U.S. 677. 1958.
United States v. *Socony Vacuum Oil Co.* 310 U.S. 150. 1940.
United States v. *The Standard Oil Co. et al.* 221 U.S. 1. 1911.

United States v. *Trenton Potteries Co.* 273 U.S. 392. 1926.
United States v. *Women's Sportswear Manufacturers Association.* 336 U.S. 460. 1949.

Articles by Participants

Adelman, Mark A. "Economic Aspects of the Bethlehem Decision." *Virginia Law Review,* 45 (June 1959), 684-696.
_____. "General Comment on the Schwartz Dissent." *The Antitrust Bulletin,* 1 (April 1955), 71-79.
_____. "The Du Pont-General Motors Decision." *Virginia Law Review,* 43 (October 1957), 873-879.
Arnold, Thurman. "Fair Fights and Foul." *The Antitrust Bulletin,* 10 (September-December 1965), 655-666.
Barnes, Stanley. "Background and Report of the Attorney General's Committee." *University of Pennsylvania Law Review,* 104 (November 1955), 147-152.
_____. "Settlement by Consent Judgment." 4 *A.B.A. Antitrust Section* (1-2 April, 1954), 8-13.
_____. "The Consent Judgments against IBM and AT&T." *Antitrust Law Symposium*—1956. Chicago, 1956, pp. 45-55.
_____. "The Judge Looks at Antitrust." 3 *A.B.A. Antitrust Section* (26-27 August, 1953), 13-19.
Bicks, Robert A. "Antitrust Goals and Current Enforcement Programs." *University of Miami Law Review,* 15 (Spring 1961) 225-236.
Brownell, Herbert. "Antitrust Today." *Catholic University of America Law Review,* 6 (May 1957), 129-138.
_____. "Justice Policy: Vigorous Action." *Nation's Business,* 44 (January 1956), 32-33.
Clark, J. M. "The Orientation of Antitrust Policy." *American Economic Review,* 40 (May 1950), 93-99.
Handler, Milton. "Annual Review of Antitrust Developments." *The Record of the Association of the Bar of the City of New York,* 10 (October 1955), 332-350. Also other years.
_____. "Antitrust—New Frontiers and New Perplexities." *The Record of the Association of the Bar of the City of New York,* 6 (February 1951), 59-82.
_____. "Industrial Mergers and the Antitrust Laws." *Columbia Law Review,* 32 (February 1932), 178-271.
Hansen, Victor R. "Broadcasting and the Antitrust Laws." *Law and Contemporary Problems,* 22 (Autumn 1957), 572-583.
_____. "The Current Federal Policy on Antitrust Matters." *The Antitrust Bulletin,* 4 (July-August 1959), 541-555.
Loevinger, Lee. "Antitrust and the New Economics." *Minnesota Law Review,* 37 (June 1953), 505-568.
_____. "Private Action—The Strongest Pillar of Antitrust." *The Antitrust Bulletin,* 3 (March-April 1958), 167-177.
Morison, H. Graham. "Is the Sherman Act Outdated?" *Journal of Public Law,* 1 (Fall 1952), 323-334.

Oppenheim, S. Chesterfield. "Federal Antitrust Legislation: Guideposts to a Revised National Antitrust Policy." *Michigan Law Review*, 50 (June 1952), 1139-1244.

———. "Highlights of the Final Report of the Attorney General's National Committee to Study the Antitrust Laws." *The Antitrust Bulletin*, 1 (April 1955), 5-36.

———. "The Organization of the Attorney General's National Committee to Study the Antitrust Laws." 3 *A.B.A. Antitrust Section* (26-27 August. 1953), 20-28.

Orrick, William. "The Clayton Act: Then and Now." 24 *A.B.A. Antitrust Section* (16-17 April, 1964), 44-53.

Rostow, Eugene. "The New Sherman Act." *University of Chicago Law Review*, 14 (June 1947), 567-600.

Schwartz, Louis B. "The Schwartz Dissent." *The Antitrust Bulletin*, 1 (April 1955), 37-70.

Smith, Blackwell. "Precedent, Public Policy and Predicatability." *The Georgetown Law Journal*, 46 (Summer 1958), 633-645.

Turner, Donald F. "Antitrust Policy and the Cellophane Case." *Harvard Law Review*, 70 (December 1956), 281-318.

Zimmerman, Edwin M. "Regulated Industries and Antitrust." 32 *A.B.A. Antitrust Law Journal*, (7-10 August, 1966), 239-250.

Author Interviews and Correspondents

Adelman, Mark A.
Anderson, Cyrus V.
Anonymous Members of the Attorney General's National Committee
to Study the Antitrust Laws (2)

Austin, Cyrus	Galligan, Joseph	Kittelle, Sumner
Barnes, Stanley	Giarrusso, Armand	Kramer, Victor
Barthold, Walter	Gordon, Eugene	Lamb, George P.
Barton, Edgar	Graglia, Lino	Levy, Jack
Beringer, William	Graham, Robert	Loevinger, Lee
Bicks, Robert	Griffin, Clare	Lofton, Thomas
Brady, Thomas	Hale, G.E.	Loos, Karl
Brownell, Herbert	Handler, Milton	Marquis, Robert
Bruce, James	Hansen, Victor R.	Mason, Lowell B.
Budge, R.W.	Harsha, E. Houston	McAfee, William
Cary, Frank	Hotchkiss, Willis L.	McAllister, Breck
Chaffetz, Hammond	Johnston, Edward	McDermott, R.B.
Cummings, Walter J.	Jones, W.K.	McLaren, Richard
Curtis, S.R.	Kahn, Alfred	Morison, H. Graham
Deadman, Homer	Kahn, Arthur H.	Murchison, David
Derenberg, Walter	Kaufman, Robert M.	O'Donnell, James O.
Fenhagen, F.D.	Kimble, Kenneth	Oppenheim, S. Chesterfield
Fitzgerald, Albert	Kintner, Earl	Pecquex, Francis
Fuller, Fred	Kirkham, Francis R.	Rahl, James A.

Rashid, Baddia
Robinson, David
Rogers, William
Rostow, Eugene
Sayre, William
Searls, David T.

Seay, Dudley
Segal, Bernard
Shafroth, Morrison
Smith, Blackwell
Spingarn, Stephen

Stevens, John Paul
Thomas, Robert
Van Cise, Jerrold
Wallace, Charles
Winn, F. Bliss

Speeches

Barnes, Stanley
Bicks, Robert
Brownell, Herbert

Hansen, Victor R.
Kintner, Earl V.

Martin, Edward F.
Rogers, William

Secondary Works

American Bar Association. *An Antitrust Handbook*. Chicago, 1958.

Antitrust Section of the American Bar Association. *Antitrust Developments 1955-1968: A Supplement to the Report of the Attorney General's National Committee to Study the Anti-Trust Laws March 31, 1955*. Chicago, 1968.

_____ "Antitrust Developments: 1968-1970." n.p., n.d.

_____ "Antitrust Law Developments." n.p., 1975.

Bane, Charles. *The Electrical Equipment Conspiracies*. New York, 1973.

Belden, Thomas and Marva. *The Lengthening Shadow: The Life of Thomas J. Watson*. Boston, 1962.

Brayman, Harold. *Corporate Management in a World of Politics.* New York, 1967.

Chandler, Jr., Alfred D. and Stephen Salsbury. *Pierre S. Du Pont and the Making of the Modern Corporation*. New York, 1971.

Clabault, James and John Burton. *Sherman Act Indictments 1955-1965*. New York, 1966.

Commerce Clearing House, comps. *1954 Trade Cases*. Chicago, 1955. Also subsequent years.

Fuller, John. *The Gentlemen Conspirators: The Story of the Price-Fixers in the Electrical Industry*. New York, 1962.

Gerassi, John. *The Great Fear: The Reconquest of Latin America by Latin Americans*. New York, 1963.

Green, Mark (Project Editor and Director). *The Nader Study Group Report on Antitrust Enforcement: The Closed Enterprise System*. Washington, D.C., 1971.

Handler, Milton. *Cases and Other Materials on Trade Regulation*. 3rd ed. Brooklyn, 1960.

Hawley, Ellis. *The New Deal and the Problem of Monopoly: A Study in Economic Ambivalence*. Princeton: 1966.

Herling, John. *The Great Price Conspiracy*. Washington, D.C., 1962.

Hoar, George F. *Autobiography of Seventy Years*. 2 vols. New York, 1903.

Lieuwen, Edwin. *U.S. Policy in Latin America*. New York, 1965.

Link, Arthur S. *Woodrow Wilson and the Progressive Era: 1910-1917*. New York, 1954.

Loevinger, Lee. *The Law of Free Enterprise*. New York, 1949.

Lynch, David. *The Concentration of Economic Power*. New York, 1946.

Metcalf, Theron. *Reports of Cases Argued and Determined in the Supreme Judicial Court of Massachusetts*. Boston, 1864.

Parkes, Henry B. and Vincent P. Carosso. *Recent America: A History*. 2 vols. New York, 1963.

Porter, Kirk and Donald Bruce Johnson, comps. *National Party Platforms: 1840-1956*. Urbana, Ill., 1956.

Seagle, William. *Men of Law from Hammurabi to Holmes*. New York, 1947.

Shale, Roger, comp. *Decrees and Judgments in Federal Antitrust Cases: July 2, 1890-January 1, 1918*. Washington, D.C., 1918.

Smith, Edwin and Ernest Hitchcock. *Reports of Cases Adjudged and Determined in the Supreme Court of Judicature of the State of New York*. Newark, N.Y., 1884.

Taft, William Howard. *The Anti-Trust Act and the Supreme Court*. New York, 1914.

Thorelli, Hans. *The Federal Antitrust Policy: Origination of an American Tradition*. Baltimore, 1955.

Thornton, W.W. *A Treatise on Combinations in Restraint of Trade*. Cincinnati, 1928.

Tugwell, Rexford G. *The Democratic Roosevelt: A Biography of Franklin D. Roosevelt*. Baltimore, 1969.

Welty, Earl M. and Frank J. Taylor. *The Seventy-Six Bonanza: The Fabulous Life and Times of the Union Oil Company of California*. Menlo Park, Calif., n.d.

Wendell, John L. *Report of Cases Argued and Determined in the Supreme Court of Judicature and in the Court for the Correction of Errors of the State of New York*. 26 vols. Albany, N.Y., 1837.

Periodical Articles

"Antitrust: Age of Consent." *Newsweek*, 47 (20 February, 1956), 79.

"Antitrust: More Clamor to Come." *Newsweek*, 45 (13 June, 1955), 77-78.

"Antitrust: The Barnes Era" (editorial). *Fortune*, 53 (March 1956), 93-94.

"Antitrusters Score a Patent Victory in the AT&T Case." *Business Week* 28 January, 1956, p. 160.

"Antitrusters Show Their Claws." *Business Week*, 3 October, 1959, p. 34.

Barnes, Irston. "Competitive Mores and Legal Tests in Merger Cases: The Du Pont-General Motors Decision." *The Georgetown Law Journal*, 46 (Summer 1958), 564-632.

"The Bethlehem-Youngstown Case." *Barron's,* 10 (29 September, 1930), 24.

"Bethlehem-Youngstown—Controversial Engagement." *Fortune*, 55 (June 1957), 145, 188-190.

"Billion Dollar Steel Merger Enjoined." *Barron's*, 11 (5 January, 1931), 21.

Buttle, Edgar. "Analysis of the Antitrust Laws." *Bar Bulletin*, 13 (September 1955), 44-50.

Cecil, Lamar. "Remedies in Antitrust Proceedings: Fines and Imprisonment." 5 *A.B.A. Antitrust Section* (18-19 August, 1954), 113-128.

Chamberlain, John. "The Lost Merger: A Bethlehem-Youngstown Marriage Would Have Helped Steel Competition." *Barron's,* 34 (11 October, 1954), 3, 23-24.

"The Changing of the Corporate Board." *Newsweek*, 47 (25 June, 1956), 77.

"Consent Decree: Both Sides Win." *Business Week*, 3 March, 1956, p. 80.

Cox, Archibald. "Labor and the Antitrust Laws—A Preliminary Analysis." *University of Pennsylvania Law Review*, 104 (November 1955), 252-284.

Crider, John. "New Look at Antitrust: Mr. Barnes Speaks Softly but Carries a Big Stick." *Barron's*, 34 (23 August, 1954), 3, 17-18.

Dirlam, Joel B. and Irwin Stelzer. "The Cellophane Labyrinth." *Antitrust Bulletin*, 9 (February-April 1956), 633-651.

_____. "The Du Pont-General Motors Decision in the Antitrust Grain." *Columbia Law Review*, 48 (January 1958), 24-43.

Donovan, William J. and Breck McAllister. "Consent Decrees in the Enforcement of Federal Antitrust Laws." *Harvard Law Review*, 46 (April 1933), 885-932.

Edwards, Corwin. "Thurman Arnold and the Antitrust Laws." *Political Science Quarterly*, 58 (September 1943), 338-355.

"Fortune Perspective." "A Note to Mr. Brownell." *Fortune*, 51 (February 1953), 107-108.

"Government: Quick Action." *Newsweek*, 45 (3 January, 1955), 49-50.

"Government: The New Trust Buster." *Time*, 62 (7 September, 1953), 86.

Haines, Wilder. "Youngstown-Bethlehem and Other Proxy Contests." *Barron's*, 11 (5 January, 1931), 20-21.

Kilgore, William D. "Antitrust Judgments and Their Enforcement." 4 *A.B.A. Antitrust Section* (1-2 April, 1954), 102-131.

Limbaugh, Rush. "Historic Origins of Antitrust Legislation." *Missouri Law Review*, 18 (June 1953), 215-248.

Lupton, George W. "New Route Certificates under the Civil Aeronautics Act of 1938." *Air Law Review*, 12 (April 1941), 103-152.

Markham, Jesse. "The Du Pont-General Motors Decision." *Virginia Law Review*, 43 (October 1957), 881-888.

McDonald, John. "Businessmen and the Sherman Act." *Fortune*, 41 (January 1950), 104-114.

Noakes, John. "Exemption for Cooperatives." 19 *A.B.A. Antitrust Section* (7-11 August, 1961), 407-421.

Pusey, Merlo J. "F.D.R. *vs.* the Supreme Court." *American Heritage*, 9 (April 1958), 24-27, 105-107.

Schefter, John E. "Historical Public Policy of the United States Toward Monopoly." *North Dakota Law Review*, 43, (Fall 1966), 17-52.

Smith, Richard Austin. "What Antitrust Means under Mr. Bicks." *Fortune*, 61 (March 1960), 119-123, 256-270.

Stedman, John. "New Look at Antitrust: The Report of the Attorney General's Committee." *Journal of Public Law*, 4 (Fall 1955), 223-284.

Stocking, George W. "The Attorney General's Committee Report: The Businessman's Guide through Antitrust." *Georgetown Law Journal*, 34 (November 1955), 1-57.

_____. "The Du Pont-General Motors Case and the Sherman Act." *Virginia Law Review*, 44 (January 1958), 1-40.

_____. "Economic Tests of Monopoly and the Concept of the Relevant Market." *Antitrust Bulletin*, 2 (March 1957), 479-493.

Stocking, George W. and Willard F. Mueller. "The Cellophane Case and the New Competition." *American Economic Review*, 45 (March 1955), 29-63.

Sunderland, Thomas E. "The Robinson-Patman Act: Go Out and Compete But Don't Get Caught At It." *Chicago Bar Record*, 34 (September 1953), 447-459.

"Trustbusters Flay GM Again." *Business Week*, 24 October, 1959, pp. 141-142.

"The United States and Business: Era of Good Feeling?" *U.S. News and World Report*, 35 (24 July, 1953), 69-73.

Votaw, Dow. "Antitrust in 1914: The Climate of Opinion." 24 A.B.A. *Antitrust Section* (16-17 April, 1964), 14-28.

Weston, Glen E. "Restatement of Antitrust Law: Salient Features of the Attorney General's Report." *The George Washington Law Review*, 24 (October 1955), 1-19.

Wham, Benjamin. "The Growth of Antitrust Law: A Revision Is Long Overdue." *American Bar Association Journal*, 38 (November 1952), 934-935.

"What the Merger Law Means." *Business Week*, 9 October, 1954, pp. 25-27.

Newspapers and Magazines

Barron's (1928-1931, 1951-1961).
Business Week (1951-1961).
Cleveland Plain Dealer (1957-1965).
Forbes (1951-1961).
Fortune (1951-1961).
Kodak News (1951-1959).
The Knoxville News Sentinel (May 1959).
Newsweek (1951-1961).
New York American (1927).
New York Evening Post (1927).
The New York Times (1951-1961).
New York World (1927).
The Seafarers Log (1953-1961).
The Wall Street Journal (1927, 1951-1961).
The Washington Daily News (May 1959).
UE News (1959-1961).
U.S. News and World Report (1951-1961).

The Reaction of the Antitrust Division to Corporate Mergers during the Eisenhower Administration

THE Antitrust Division of the Department of Justice monitors all mergers or plans thereof. Many of such actions involve corporations which are too small to be important except to those directly involved; their records are filed by date under the number 60-0-37 in the Justice Department papers stored in the Federal Records Center at Suitland, Maryland. Each merger involving a more significant factor is the subject of an individual file numbered 60-0-37-11 *et sequi*. (Most, but not all, banking mergers are numbered 60-111-0 *et sequi*.) Below is a listing of all the 60-0-37-11 *et sequi* mergers studied by the Antitrust Division and assigned an individual file.

The raw data is useful in proving antitrusters' vitality in the 1950s. Innumerable companies dropped or altered their plans after receiving the standard letter of inquiry from the Department of Justice. Had the Division not possessed a reputation for vigorous enforcement, many of the mergers which were dropped might have been consummated. In addition, by providing valuable insight into the thinking of the lawyers in the Division, the material can be useful today in corporate planning.

Although approximately chronological, the order is that used by the Justice Department in indexing its files; thus, for example, the number of the International Shoe-Florsheim merger is 60-0-37-11, and below it is cited as 11. The date in parentheses after the company name is the date of the first entry in the file. This first file entry might be a newspaper clipping, an item from Standard and Poor's Daily Record of Corporate News, a letter from a competitor or private citizen, or a memo from an Antitrust field office. The category "market" does not include all the products of the companies in question, but only the areas in which they overlap. Where necessary, for a better understanding of the issues, the entire product lines of the merging companies are included.

11.   International Shoe Co.
      Florsheim Shoe Co. (2/2/53)
          MARKET: Shoe Sales
          OUTCOME: The merger was cleared (no date) because there are
                       many different shoe markets; and Florsheim is in
                       the "quality shoe market," an area in which
                       International is not represented*
12.   Westinghouse Electric Corp.
      Houghton Co. (4/12/53)
          MARKET: Elevator Equipment
          OUTCOME: Clearance denied (5/12/53) because Westinghouse
                       has size, diversification, and a history of ac-
                       quisitions. Most of Houghton's business is within
                       500 miles of Toledo; therefore, merger would lead
                       to increased concentration in the area.
13.   Ross Carrier Co.
      Clark Equipment Co. (3/25/53)
          MARKET: Truck parts, straddle carriers, and construction
                       machinery
          OUTCOME: Although no written clearance was given, apparent-
                       ly verbal clearance was supplied (4/27/53).
14.   Congoleum-Nairn, Inc.
      Sloane Blabon Co. (4/15/53)
          MARKET: Different types of floor covering
          OUTCOME: Cleared (no date). Sloane is in difficult financial
                       straits.
15.   American District Telegraph Co. of Mass. [Grinnell]
      General Alarm Corp. (No date)
          MARKET: Alarms (burglar and fire)
          OUTCOME: Clearance originally denied, but later given when
                       Device Division was disposed of, clearing the
                       Boston market (7/15/55).
16.   White Motor Co.
      Autocar Co. (7/23/53)
          MARKET: Trucks
          OUTCOME: Cleared, probably at a meeting, because the merged
                       entity would be able to compete more effectively
                       with larger entities in the field.
17.   Crown Cork & Seal Corp. [subsidiary]

---

* In the material below, where the "OUTCOME" is in the present tense, the material is derived from Justice Department files; where it is in the past tense, the sources are court records, newspaper accounts and company files.

Mitchell & Smith [Crown Division] (8/11/53)

> MARKET: Closures
>
> OUTCOME: File closed 10/7/53, no action taken even though Crown has 43 percent of the market and Mitchell & Smith's Division has 2.8 percent. But it has been losing money and been up for sale for some time, and Crown Cork made the only bid.

18. Honolulu Construction & Draying Co., Ltd.

The Collins Co. [Honolulu division of Concrete & Steel Pipe Co.] (6/29/53)

> MARKET: Sewer construction
>
> OUTCOME: "No action contemplated" (No date). The sewer construction market has shrunk because the building program is 80 percent completed.

19. South States Portland Cement Co.

Marquette Cement Manufacturing Co. (12/16/53)

> MARKET: Cement
>
> OUTCOME: Merger not attacked because of the age of the president and the other stockholders of South States. Their plant is old; reconstruction would cost $4 million. Marquette wants to increase its share in the Atlanta area; therefore, the merger will lower costs.

20. [Changed to 60-207-2]

Bensing Bros. & Beeney

California Ink Co. (12/11/53)

> MARKET: A joint venture to sell flexographic and related types of ink
>
> OUTCOME: Clearance denied, and the planned joint venture is dropped.

21. Nash Kelvinator

Hudson Motor Car—See Chapter IV.

22. General Shoe

Regal Shoe—See Chapter IV

23. Allied Chemical & Dye Corp.

Mutual Chemical Co. of America (3/15/54)

> MARKET: Chemicals (Mutual makes special chromium chemicals, Allied does not)
>
> OUTCOME: Cleared 5/5/54. Allied has many competitors. (Du Pont and Union Carbide are much bigger). American Cyanimid, smaller than Allied, has chromium chemicals; and it has not helped them to grow.

24. Harris Seybold Co.
    C. B. Cottrell & Sons Co. (12/11/53)
    Intertype Corp. (2/26/57)
    Lithoplate, Inc. (1/6/56)
        MARKET: All in printing business
        OUTCOME: File never closed. No action taken because market share of acquiring company is decreasing, ease of entry exists, line of commerce presents problems, and competitors not complaining; a better first Section 7 case is required (12/1/54).

25. Washington Post Co.
    Washington Times Herald, Inc. (5/4/54)
        MARKET: Washington morning newspapers
        OUTCOME: No suit opposing the merger. Brownell feared that the administration would be accused of playing politics. Besides, the concentration figures are worse in other cities, and *Times Herald* is losing money (5/28/54).

26. Koppers Co., Inc.
    American Lumber & Treating Co. (5/11/54)
        MARKET: Pressure-treated wood, roofing
        OUTCOME: Cleared 11/12/54. Wood-treating is a very localized industry and plants in the same area compete— this is not a nationwide market (Last Koppers acquisition in 1939).

27. Studebaker
    Packard —See Chapter IV.

28. W. T. Grant & Co.
    G. C. Murphy Co.
    S. H. Kress & Co.
    J. J. Newberry Co.
    H. L. Green Co.
    McCrory Stores Corp.
    Neisner Bros., Inc.
    McLellan Stores Co. (7/6/54)
        MARKET: Chain variety stores
        OUTCOME: The plan which was conceived to compete more effectively with Woolworth and Kresge falls apart after letters of inquiry from the Justice Department.

29. Bethlehem
    Youngstown—See Chapter IV.

30. National Steel Corp.
    Republic Steel Corp. (9/3/54)
       MARKET: Steel
       OUTCOME: Plans were dropped after opposition from Justice
                  Department (11/4/54).

31. Virginia & Maryland Milk Producers' Assn.
    Embassy Dairy—See Chapter VII.

32. Republic Steel Corp.
    Follansbee Steel Corp. (9/15/54)
       MARKET: Steel
       OUTCOME: Justice Department opposes takeover; in the end
                  Cyrus Eaton, who is a major shareholder of Inland
                  Steel, purchases most of Follansbee's assets.

33. Koppers Co.
    Western Precipitation Corp. (9/29/54)
       MARKET: Precipitators, dust collectors, driers
       OUTCOME: Companies drop plans 11/30/54. John Crimmins
                  (president of Koppers) wrote to the Justice
                  Department, "[We will] base expansion on research
                  rather than acquisition . . . the risk of possible
                  actions on the part of the Department of Justice,
                  even though this present question was decided
                  favorably to Koppers, was a risk we prefer not to
                  run."

34. Textron, Inc.
    Robbins Mills, Inc.
    Newmarket Manufacturing Co. (8/17/54)
    American Woolen Co. [45 percent equity]
       MARKET: Textiles
       OUTCOME: No action 12/14/54. American would liquidate
                  without merger and Newmarket is too small to
                  compete. Robbins was sold by J. P. Stevens in
                  accordance with Antitrust Division directive.

35. National Alfalfa Dehydrating & Milling Co.
    Quaker Oats' Cerophyl Laboratories
    CarO-Green, Inc. (4/54)
       MARKET: Alfalfa processing
       OUTCOME: CarO-Green has one plant using a new method to
                  store alfalfa meal. File closed because National did
                  not acquire CarO-Green's patent, and competition
                  is supplied by 700 other factors in the field (8/6/54).

36. Colson Corp.
    Service Caster & Truck Co. (5/11/54)
        MARKET: Casters
        OUTCOME: File closed 12/28/54. There are different types of casters and the two companies do not compete; many new firms are entering the field. Service Caster was available very cheaply especially because they lost a large contract and would be in possible financial difficulty as a result.

37. B. F. Goodrich Co.
    The Sponge Rubber Products Co. (7/14/54)
        MARKET: Sponge rubber
        OUTCOME: While not attacked in a Section 7 action, the Justice Department began a Sherman Act Section 1 case on monopolization of sponge-rubber industry (the other company involved is Dayton Rubber). Settled by consent decree 12/57.

38. Hydraulic Press Manufacturing
    Birdsboro Steel Foundry & Machine Co. (8/31/54)
        MARKET: Heavy machinery
        OUTCOME: Hydraulic's stockholders fail to ratify the deal; therefore, it does not go through.

39. Ideal Cement Co.
    Spokane-Portland Cement Co. (8/18/54)
        MARKET: Cement
        OUTCOME: Cleared 9/30/54, because although Ideal is a large factor, the two companies do not compete, and the cost of freight makes selling over long distances uneconomical.

40. Certain-Teed Corp.
    Wm. Cameron & Co. (8/17/54)
        MARKET: Building materials
        OUTCOME: "Not within Justice Department jurisdiction."

41. J. P. Stevens & Co.
    John P. Maguire & Co. (8/16/54)
        MARKET: Textiles
        OUTCOME: Merger (no date) goes through and there are no further entries in the government files.

42. Pressed Steel Car Co. [U.S. Industries]
    Clearing Machine Corp. (9/24/54)
    Fray Machine Tool Co. (1/5/55)

MARKET: Presses for use in auto, appliance and aircraft industries.

OUTCOME: Cleared 2/16/55. The two will continue to sell to all. Their products are not competitive, all have larger competitors and competition from used machine tools. Pressed Steel Car diversified out of railroad car manufacturing; Clearing Machine makes presses for use in the auto, appliance and aircraft industries.

43. American Linen Supply's subsidiary, Steiner Co.
    Paper Corp. of America (9/27/54)
    MARKET: Cloth and paper-linen goods
    OUTCOME: Cleared 10/19/54. Paper Corp. is a failing company, loaded with debt.

44. Stokley Van Camp, Inc.
    Pictsweet Foods Co. (8/10/54)
    MARKET: Canned fruits and vegetables
    OUTCOME: Inquiry closed 9/19/55. There was no way to show lessening of competition; Barnes felt it "would be a tough case to win."

45. Container Corp. of America
    Mengel Corp. (11/30/54)
    MARKET: Container goods
    OUTCOME: No action taken by Justice Department since Container increased its investment in Mengel to 96.8 percent and began to operate it as a separate division.

46. Merritt, Chapman & Scott Corp.
    Marion Power Shovel Co. (8/2/54)
    Tennessee Products & Chemical Corp. (4/19/55)
    Devoe & Raynolds Co. (4/19/55)
    New York Shipbuilding Corp. (4/19/55)
    Sharp Voting Machine Corp. (4/19/55)
    Newport Steel Corp. (4/19/55)
    Savin Construction Corp. (7/19/56)
    Whaling City Dredge & Dock Corp. (7/19/56)
    MARKET: Involved in many areas, especially marine insurance
    OUTCOME: Justice Department takes no action but observes only because of fear of "intercompany use giving unfair advantages." It decides to do nothing as of 9/6/56.

47. Bigelow, Sanford Carpet Co.
    Mohawk Carpet Mills, Inc. (No date)
    MARKET: Carpets
    OUTCOME: Companies request clearance. Justice Department asks many questions and on 9/5/54 merger is called off.

48. Statler Hotels Corp.
    Hilton Hotels Corp.—See Chapter IV.

49. Hart Schaffner & Marx
    Society Brand Clothes, Inc. (9/15/54)
    MARKET: Men's clothing
    OUTCOME: Closed 10/26/54 because there are all types of clothing, and there are many factors in the industry.

50. International Minerals & Chemicals Corp.
    Riverton Lime & Stone Corp. (6/16/54)
    MARKET: Joint venture in aplite
    OUTCOME: Dropped 2/8/55 after receiving letters requesting information.

51. Minute Maid
    Snow Crop Division of Clinton Foods—See Chapter IV.

52. Ideal Cement Co.
    Superior Portland Cement, Inc. (12/30/54)
    MARKET: Cement
    OUTCOME: Plans are abandoned "when we say we will sue" (Foote to Barnes, 4/22/55).

    Ideal Cement Co.
    Northwest Portland Cement Co. (2/13/57)
    MARKET: Cement
    OUTCOME: During meeting with Antitrust Division over above merger case, material was requested, but on 2/27/57 merger plans "withdrawn" because "Northwest not worth as much as we thought."

53. General Shoe
    Delman—See Chapter IV.

54. Sylvania Electric Products
    National Union Electric Corp. (1/6/55)
    MARKET: Sylvania to purchase National's tube manufacturing facilities
    OUTCOME: The facilities were not profitable, and National Union Electric would have closed down its plant.

55. Chase National Bank
    Bank of Manhattan—See Chapter VII.

56. Los Angeles Mirror
    Los Angeles Daily News (1/7/55)
    MARKET: Los Angeles newspapers
    OUTCOME: Closed; no action. the *News* is a failing company.
57. Schenley
    Park & Tilford—See Chapter IV.
58. Inland Steel Co.
    Arthur Harvey Co. (1/7/55)
    MARKET: Steel warehousing
    OUTCOME: Cleared 2/24/55. Harvey planning to leave the business anyway.
59. Lodge & Shipley Co.
    Hydraulic Press Mfg. Co. (1/3/55)
    MARKET: Machine tools
    OUTCOME: Companies drop plans 3/15/55 after request for information.
60. National Radiator Corp.
    United States Radiator Co. (12/30/54)
    MARKET.   Air-temperature control
    OUTCOME: Clearance denied 3/17/55. After appeal, noting the changes transpiring in the heating industry and that U.S. Radiator is in financial difficulty, the companies are given a "go ahead" but no clearance (3/28/55).
61. Gould National Batteries, Inc.
    Hobbs Battery Co. (1/17/52).
    MARKET: Batteries
    OUTCOME: Merger plans were dormant until 1/31/55. Hobbs cannot go it alone. Gould plans to close its plant in Los Angeles and use the Hobbs facility. Therefore there is no real change in competition. Merger allowed but not cleared (3/6/55).
62. Consolidated Grocers Corp. [Consolidated Foods]
    Libby McNeill & Libby (1/24/54)
    Kitchens of Sara Lee, Inc. (3/10/56)
    Piggly Wiggly Midwest Co. (3/7/56)
    MARKET: Foods
    OUTCOME: 3/17/55—"Libby merger dropped because of unfriendly attitude of Department of Justice and attendant banking problems." Department of Justice would like to attack the others but cannot, because the Attorney General's *Report* opposed "quantitative substantiality" (10/28/59).

63. Corning Glass Works
     Sylvania Electric Products, Inc. (2/7/55)
        MARKET: Picture tubes and electronic components
        OUTCOME: Clearance denied 8/12/55 and merger is dropped.
64. Bankers Trust Co.
     Public National Bank & Trust Co. (2/21/55)
        MARKET: New York City banking
        OUTCOME: Justice Department memo states: "doubtful
                     whether we have jurisdiction"; therefore, no action
                     (3/23/55).
65. First National Bank of New York
     National City Bank of New York—See Chapter VII.
66. S.M. Frank & Co.
     Kaywoodie Co. (3/22/55)
        MARKET: Pipes for smoking tobacco.
        OUTCOME: No opposition to merger (no date). Kaywoodie is
                     failing. Also Kaywoodie makes expensive pipes,
                     Frank makes cheap ones; hence, they do not
                     compete.
67. Champ Hats, Inc. [Byrndum Corp.]
     Hat Corp. of America
     Barton Rough Hat Co.
     Champ Hat Sales, Inc.
     Five Main Street, Inc.
     Greenough Sewing Co.
     Sunbury Products Corp. (9/4/56)
        MARKET: Hats
        OUTCOME: File closed 8/27/62 in view of the lapse of time and
                     the fact that the Justice Department was unable to
                     ascertain whether or not the acquisitions had been
                     cleared.
68. Campbell Soup Co.
     C.A. Swanson & Sons, Inc. (9/15/55)
        MARKET: Prepared foods
        OUTCOME: Material missing, but merger does come to pass
                     (May 6, 1955).
69. Allied Chemical & Dye Corp.
     Niagara Alkali Co. (12/22/54)
        MARKET: Chemicals
        OUTCOME: Merger plans dropped. Niagara subsequently
                     merged into Hooker Chemical 11/30/55.
70. Whirlpool Corp., Seeger Refining Corp. and Radio Corporation of

American transfer their stove and air-conditioning business to a new company. (4/18/55)

> MARKET: Stoves and air-conditioning equipment
> OUTCOME: Cleared 7/21/55. It creates a new vigorous competitor in the field, but the Justice Department plans to watch the new entity.

71. Federal-Mogul Corp.
Bower Roller Bearing Co. (5/11/55)

> MARKET: Bushings & bearings
> OUTCOME: Matter turned over to the Federal Trade Commission, and the merger is consummated.

72. General Dynamics Corp.
Stromberg-Carlson Co. (4/25/55)

> MARKET: Telephone, radio, TV and other sound equipment
> OUTCOME: Cleared 7/21/55. Although both manufacture electronic equipment, they are not competitors. Both are heavy defense contractors.

73. Allstate Insurance Co. ownership of stock in Montgomery Ward & Co. (4/12/55) [Sears Roebuck & Co., owns Allstate]

> MARKET: Retail merchandising
> OUTCOME: Allstate's 8,000 shares subsequently liquidated (Theodore Seyfarth, Senior Attorney at Allstate to author, 1/13/75).

74. Wilson Athletic Goods Mfg. Co.
Ohio-Kentucky Mfg. Co. (6/8/55)

> MARKET: Sporting goods
> OUTCOME: No action against the transaction. No other company wanted to buy Ohio-Kentucky (12/16/55).

75. Peabody Coal Co.
Sinclair Coal group (6/1/56)

> MARKET: Coal
> OUTCOME: No action (9/12/56) because of the present state of the coal industry.

76. Koppers Corp.
American Aniline Products, Inc. (5/7/55)

> MARKET: Dye stuffs
> OUTCOME: Koppers acquires all stock 3/31/55. No action by the Justice Department; no reasons given (7/15/55).

77. Leonard Refineries
Midwestern Refineries

Roosevelt Oil & Refining Corp.
Leonard Pipelines—See Chapter VII

78. First National Bank of Buffalo
   Manufacturers & Traders Trust Co. (No date)
   MARKET: Western New York banking
   OUTCOME: Buffalo bank requests clearance and are advised that the Department of Justice lacks jurisdiction (8/2/55).

79. Crown Zellerbach Corp.
   Gaylord Container Corp. (7/1/55)
   MARKET: Containers
   OUTCOME: Allowed 12/2/55 because Crown Zellerbach will dispose of its one-half interest in Field Fibreboard Corp., a competing company.

80. The Pennsylvania Co.
   First National Bank [Philadelphia] (7/1/55)
   MARKET: Philadelphia banking
   OUTCOME: No action (7/1/55) due to lack of jurisdiction.

81. Brown Shoe Co.
   G. R. Kinney Co. (11/8/55)
   MARKET: Shoe manufacturing and sales
   OUTCOME: Complaint filed 11/28/55 charging that Brown's acquisition of Kinney would lessen competition or tend to create a monopoly in the production, distribution and sale of shoes. Brown has a history of acquisitions. On 12/8/59 the District Court found the merger to be in violation of Section 7. In 1962 the Supreme Court affirmed the decision and on 2/21/63 the District Court directed divestiture. On 8/26/63, it approved the sale of Kinney to F. W. Woolworth Company.

82. Monsanto Chemical Co.
   Lion Oil Co. (7/28/55)
   MARKET: Chemicals
   OUTCOME: No action (1/27/56). The chemicals are different, and there is no lessening of competition.

83. Auburn Trust Co.
   Marine Midland Trust Co.
   MARKET: Upper New York State banking
   OUTCOME: Clearance requested 7/22/55 and refused 9/12/55. Therefore, by means of a stock acquisition, the companies avoided the jurisdiction of the Justice Department (11/4/55).

84. Melville Shoe Corp.
　　Edison Brothers Stores, Inc. (8/22/55)
　　　　MARKET:　　Retail sales
　　　　OUTCOME:　After receiving standard letters of inquiry from the
　　　　　　　　　　Justice Department, companies reply that they
　　　　　　　　　　have dropped plans to merge (8/30/55).
85. Winn & Lovett Grocery Co.
　　Dixie-Home Stores Co. [New entity is Winn-Dixie Stores, Inc.]
　　(9/30/55)
　　　　MARKET:　　Supermarkets
　　　　OUTCOME:　According to a Justice Department memo of
　　　　　　　　　　3/27/56, "We could not show that the merger has
　　　　　　　　　　caused a substantial lessening of competition, but
　　　　　　　　　　we should carefully scrutinize any further expan-
　　　　　　　　　　sion."
86. Whirlpool-Seeger Corp.
　　International Harvester Co. (9/29/55)
　　　　MARKET:　　White goods
　　　　OUTCOME:　Purchase by Whirlpool of International
　　　　　　　　　　Harvester's white-goods line was not attacked by
　　　　　　　　　　the Justice Department. According to a Justice
　　　　　　　　　　Department memo of 3/9/56, "International lacks
　　　　　　　　　　the distribution and full line ability to merchandise
　　　　　　　　　　the goods. They looked for eight months for a buyer
　　　　　　　　　　and lost a lot of money."
87. Alexander Smith, Inc.
　　Mohawk Carpet Mills, Inc. (9/29/55)
　　　　MARKET:　　Carpeting
　　　　OUTCOME:　Merger consummated 12/31/55. The surviving
　　　　　　　　　　entity is known as Mohasco Industries. No
　　　　　　　　　　clearance is given, but no action is taken
　　　　　　　　　　(12/16/55).
88. White Motor Co.
　　Diamond T. Motor Co.
　　Reo Motors, Inc. (9/29/55)
　　　　MARKET:　　Trucks
　　　　OUTCOME:　They cannot compete with the big companies;
　　　　　　　　　　perhaps by merging, they will be able to do so.
　　　　　　　　　　4/17/57.
89. Julius Kayser & Co.
　　Holeproof Hosiery Co. (8/17/55)
　　　　MARKET:　　Women's clothing
　　　　OUTCOME:　According to a Justice Department memo of

2/4/57, "There is a great deal of competition in the field and both companies buy from the same suppliers. But we must watch Kayser in the future."

90. Prince Macaroni Mfg. Co.
   V. Viviano & Brothers Mfg. Co. (11/30/55)
      MARKET: Macaroni products
      OUTCOME: Companies too small (12/4/56); Viviano was in financial straits, and the merger plan was subsequently dropped (Armand Giarrusso, Vice-President of Prince, to author, 11/22/74).
   Prince Macaroni Mfg. Co.
   Ideal Macaroni Co., Inc. (9/16/57)
      MARKET: Macaroni products
      OUTCOME: Merger plans dropped because the seller placed too high a valuation on the company (Armand Giarrusso, vice president of Prince, to author, 11/22/74).

91. Standard Pressed Steel Co.
   Cleveland Cap Screw Co., Inc. (11/4/55)
      MARKET: [No overlap]
      OUTCOME: Cleared 4/4/56. Companies were not competitive in purchases or sales; no lessening of competition.

92. American Radiator & Standard Sanitary Corp.
   Mullins Mfg. Corp. (11/10/55)
      MARKET: Kitchen and bathroom fixtures
      OUTCOME: Merger attacked 3/26/56 because Mullins, the largest manufacturer of steel kitchen sinks and cabinets, had facilities which American Standard could use to enhance its position in cast-iron sinks and bathtubs. On 9/20/60, American Standard signed a consent decree, agreeing to divest the properties in question and to obtain government or court permission for any acquisitions in the field.

93. Inland Steel Co.
   Cleveland Steel Barrel Co. (10/17/55)
      MARKET: Steel products
      OUTCOME: Conditionally cleared (no date) "on the basis of present facts."

94. First Western Bank of San Francisco
   Citizens National Bank of Los Angeles (1/10/56)
      MARKET: California banking
      OUTCOME: Merger dropped when Citizens realizes the merger is not in its best interests.

95. W. R. Grace & Co.
    Smith Douglass Co. (No date)
        MARKET: Chemicals and fertilizers
        OUTCOME: After inquiry, Grace replied, "There are no such negotiations."

96. Carthage National Exchange Bank
    Northern New York Trust Co. (No date)
        MARKET: New York State banking
        OUTCOME: Folder reassigned; transferred to bank mergers (60-111).

97. Fluor Corp., Ltd.
    Sante Fe Tank & Tower Co. (1/15/56)
        MARKET: Water-cooling towers
        OUTCOME: Cleared 2/8/56. No monopolization; the field is easy to enter. All jobs are done on a competitive bid basis.

98. Consolidated Cigar Corp.
    P. Lorillard Co. [Cigar Div.] (1/26/56)
        MARKET: Cigars
        OUTCOME: No action taken; no further information desired (7/27/57). The transaction will help competition in cigar business.

99. Western Auto Supply Co. [Missouri]
    Gamble-Skogmo, Inc. [Western Auto Supply Div.] (11/29/54)
        MARKET: Specialized stores selling auto supplies and consumer hard goods
        OUTCOME: In 1945 the Gamble-Skogmo predecessor company purchased 19.1 percent of Western Auto's stock preparatory to a merger bid. The Justice Department objected, and the merger plans were dropped. In 1956, Gamble sold the stock to National Management, Ltd. (instead of Western Auto Supply Co.); but in 1958, Gamble repurchased the securities and others constituting a 41.8 percent equity in the company. On 4/1/60, after conferences between the company and the Justice Department, antitrusters filed a complaint seeking divestiture. Gamble sold its Western Auto stock to Beneficial Finance, and a consent decree was entered on 7/18/60.

100. Falstaff Brewing Co.
    Mitchell Brewing Co. (2/29/56)
        MARKET: Beer and malt liquor

OUTCOME: Takeover of the Mitchell brewing facility was consummated with no further Justice Department action.

101. American Cyanimid Co.
Formica Co. (3/7/56)
MARKET: Plastic materials
OUTCOME: Merger consummated 4/16/56.

102. Charles Eneu Johnson Co., Inc. [div. of Union Carbon Co.]
Interchemical Corp. (2/29/56)
MARKET: Business-printing work
OUTCOME: Sale of assets cleared 3/23/56 because it will not increase Interchemical's productive capacity (Johnson needs a new plant). There is no reduction in competition and no adverse effect on purchasers or sellers.

103. Libby, McNeill & Libby
Rockfield Canning Co. (3/14/56)
MARKET: Canned fruits and vegetables
OUTCOME: Cleared 4/11/56. Rockfield wanted to sell out or liquidate. Others in the area have closed. There were no other purchasers. Besides, the takeover will have no substantial effect on competition, and Libby will continue to use Rockfield's suppliers.

104. Sears Roebuck & Co.
United Wall Paper, Inc. (2/28/56)
MARKET: Wallpaper
OUTCOME: Cleared 4/17/56 because United is potentially bankrupt, and Sears is the only company interested in purchasing it without planning liquidation.

105. Allied Chemical & Dye Corp. [stock holdings in]
United States Steel Corp.
Virginia-California Chemical Corp.
Libbey-Owens-Ford Glass Co.
Owens Illinois Glass Co.
American Viscose Corp. (2/8/55)
MARKET: Chemicals
OUTCOME: File closed 5/10/56. The holdings are for investment purposes, and Allied recently sold Virginia-California to Socony-Mobil Oil Co.

106. P. R. Mallory Co.
General Dry Batteries, Inc. (3/22/56)
MARKET: Batteries

OUTCOME: No action (5/3/56). They are in two different types of market and General is in need of aid.

107. Liquid Carbonic Corp.
Standard Vanilla Co. (4/12/56)
MARKET: Flavorings
OUTCOME: Cleared 6/29/56. These are two small companies in different areas of the flavor business (Liquid sells to bottlers; Standard to ice cream makers); therefore, there is no effect on competition since the two service different areas, and serve different geographic areas as well.

108. B.B. Crystal Co.
Perfit Crystal Corp. (9/11/56)
MARKET: Watch crystals
OUTCOME: Cleared 5/7/56 because the companies are so small that they are not even listed in the guides of the top-27 glass watch-crystal makers. They make inferior plastic crystals.

109. Draper Co.
Wildman Mfg. Co. (4/10/56)
MARKET: Automatic-weaving looms
OUTCOME: Justice Department defers to the FTC which is also interested. (4/25/56)

110. International Telephone & Telegraph Corp.
Underwood Corp. (4/24/56)
MARKET: Diversified products
OUTCOME: Although not objecting immediately to the merger in question, the antitrusters were antipathetic to the tie. "The companies are planning ten years ahead and this is of interest to us as they already have complementary or parallel products." On 5/15/56 merger was called off for "personal reasons."

111. Penn-Texas Corp.
Union Twist Drill Co. (4/26/56)
MARKET: Heavy industrial equipment
OUTCOME: File closed 12/3/56 since the merger falls through.

112. Textron American, Inc.
Carolina Bagging Co. (4/13/56)
MARKET: Packaging
OUTCOME: Cleared 10/15/56 because merger will help Textron to offer a full line of felt padding, etc. It

will not lessen competition (Textron is a small number 3 in the field), and the product is being replaced by foam rubber anyway.

113. Anacostia Federal Savings & Loan
     Perpetual Building Assn. (5/8/56)
         MARKET: Banking/savings and loan
         OUTCOME: File closed 5/21/56 because merger was accomplished by transfer of assets and "there is nothing we can do."

114. Borg-Warner Corp.
     York Corp. (4/19/56)
         MARKET: Air-control equipment
         OUTCOME: Nonclearance but no action taken (6/18/56); "Although Borg-Warner has a record of many acquisitions, we cannot win against this conglomerate merger in court without a rather extensive investigation," and "our case is speculative at best."

115. File changed to no. 24

116. Manufacturers & Traders Trust Co.
     Liberty Bank of Buffalo (5/11/56)
         MARKET: Buffalo banking
         OUTCOME: Merger not attacked because of lack of jurisdiction under Section 7. (7/17/56)

117. Hertz Corp.
     Jolly's Motor Livery Corp.
     Metropolitan Distributors, Inc.
     Robinson Auto Rental, Inc.
     Rentways, Inc.
     Uttal Rentals, Inc.
     Northern California Truck Rental Co.
     Carey Drive-ur-self, Inc.
     Boynton Cab Co.
     Atlantic National Insurance Co.
     Drive-A-Car, Inc.
     New York Truck Renting Corp.
     Storch Leasing Corp.
     Rental Properties [including Avis Rent-A-Car System] (5/18/56)
         MARKET: Auto and truck renting and leasing
         OUTCOME: Complaint filed 5/1/59 seeking divestiture of some of the acquired corporations. On 6/29/60, the matter was settled by consent judgment

providing for divestiture of the auto-rental business in Miami Beach, Florida, and the truck-rental and leasing business in New York City. Within three years, the New York City firm was in severe financial difficulty, and Hertz was given permission to reacquire it.

118. Owens-Illinois Glass Co.
     National Container Corp.—See Chapter IV.

119. American Laundry Machine Co.
     Western Laundry Press Co.
     Ajax Pressing Machine Co. (5/1/56)
     > MARKET: Laundry machines
     > OUTCOME: Cleared 11/5/56. Western has falling sales. The acquisition of Ajax will not change the market picture.

120. Standard Oil Co.
     Pate Oil Co.
     Files removed for use in a case against Standard Oil and never returned.

121. Corn Products Refining Corp.
     Refined Syrups & Sugars, Inc. (6/7/56)
     > MARKET: Sweeteners
     > OUTCOME: According to a Department of Justice memo of 2/13/57, "the merger has potentially anti-competitive effects, they are extremely difficult to predict, and therefore it would be difficult to bring an action under Section 7, at this moment." A letter was sent to Corn Products stating that the situation would be monitored carefully "to check for any anticompetitive effects".

122. Dan River Mills, Inc.
     Iselin-Jefferson Co., Inc.
     I-J Financial Co.
     Woodside Mills Co.
     Alabama Mills Co. (5/28/56)
     > MARKET: Textiles and fibres
     > OUTCOME: Although this is a backward integration move, the field is highly competitive. Taking into account the pressure from imports and the fact that "at the present time all available staff is occupied with what would seem to be more significant mergers," the Department of Justice took no action (9/19/56).

123. A.P. Green Fire Brick Co.
    Pyro Refractories Co.
    Portsmouth Clay Refractories Co.
    Durex Refractories (6/20/56)
        MARKET: Refractories and fire brick
        OUTCOME: No action (6/29/56). There is no lessening of competition. Concentration is high but there are many substitutes.
    A.P. Green Fire Brick Co.
    Standard Brick Co. (4/22/58)
        MARKET: Refractories and fire brick
        OUTCOME: No action. There is no lessening of competition. Concentration is high but there are many substitutes.
    A.P. Green Fire Brick Co.
    Richard Remmey Son Co. (1/9/57)
        MARKET: Refractories and fire brick
        OUTCOME: Cleared 2/6/57. There is no lessening of competition. Concentration is high but there are many substitutes.

124. Detroit Bank
    Detroit Wabeck Bank & Trust
    Birmingham [Michigan] National Bank
    Ferndale [Michigan] National Bank (5/15/56)
        MARKET: Detroit area banking
        OUTCOME: No action (8/30/56) because the merger is not subject to Department of Justice jurisdiction and there is no violation of Sherman Act.

125. Admiral Corp.
    Raytheon Mfg. Co. [Television & Radio Div.] (6/19/56)
        MARKET: Radio and television manufacturing
        OUTCOME: Inquiry closed 9/21/56 because "merger is good for competition. It will help Admiral cut into Radio Corp. of America and General Electric share by offering a competitive product at lower prices."

126. Electric Auto-Lite Co.
    Reading Batteries Co. (6/26/56)
        MARKET: Batteries
        OUTCOME: Cleared (no date) because there is no lessening of competition (local or national). There are 246 makers of storage batteries.

127. Atlantic Refining Co.
    Houston Oil Co. [Texas] (1/16/56)
        MARKET: Petroleum products
        OUTCOME: The takeover was consummated with no further action by the Justice Department.

128. Sheraton Corp. of America
    Eppley Hotels Co. (5/29/56)
        MARKET: Hotels
        OUTCOME: Cleared 7/11/56. Sheraton acquires old hotels and makes them profitable. It does not have others in the area, therefore there is no lessening of competition.

129. Continental Can Corp.
    Hazel Atlas Glass Co.—See Chapter IV.

130. Borg-Warner Corp.
    Humphreys Mfg. Co. (7/2/58)
        MARKET: Tubs and cabinets
        OUTCOME: Borg-Warner sells steel tubs and cabinets; Humphreys sells enameled ones and fixtures (Borg-Warner purchases some of this type for resale). No letter of clearance was granted, but no suit was filed because the merger does not have sufficient foreseeable anticompetitive effects to warrant injunctive proceedings.

131. Fairchild Aerial Surveys, Inc.
    Gray McKinnon Surveys Co. (7/2/56)
        MARKET: Airmapping
        OUTCOME: No action (7/13/56). There is no violation of the merger act. No patents are involved. Gray McKinnon is in unsatisfactory financial situation.

132. Whiting Milk Co.
    Maverick Mills (5/8/56)
        MARKET: [See Outcome]
        OUTCOME: No action (7/25/56). Although Whiting had previously purchased two small dairies, they were not big enough for a Section 7 case. This purchase was not of a dairy; it was a textile plant which needed major alterations.

133. Wrigley Stores, Inc.
    Big Bear Stores Co.
    ACF Brill Co.
    Abner Wolfe Co. (9/19/55)

MARKET: Wholesale and retail groceries

OUTCOME: According to Antitrust Division memorandum of 6/27/58, "The merger has taken place and there have been no problems or complaints." At this point the file was closed.

134. Jos. Schlitz Brewing Co.
Muehlebach Brewing Co. (7/9/56)
MARKET: Beer and malt liquor
OUTCOME: Case closed 7/26/56. Schlitz is very large and the merger would have violated Section 7, but Muehlebach is almost bankrupt. Therefore the union was not attacked.

135. Borg-Warner Corp.
Dittmer Gear & Mfg. Co. (7/2/56)
MARKET: Gears and transmissions
OUTCOME: Clearance request denied 9/17/56, but no action is taken to halt the acquisition.

136. Marquette Cement Mfg. Co.
Louisville Cement Co. (11/19/57)
MARKET: Cement
OUTCOME: The Antitrust Division refused to grant clearance 1/11/60. The merger would violate Section 7 of Clayton Act because the two companies compete in a wide market. According to the secretary-general counsel for Marquette, the merger fell through "for economic reasons . . . not due to the opposition of the Justice Department" (Robert Thomas to author, 12/19/74).

137. Brown Foreman Distillers Corp.
Garneau Co. of New York
Jack Daniels Distillery (8/26/56)
MARKET: Scotch whiskey and wines
OUTCOME: Purchases allowed because Brown Foreman is small compared to the four giants in the industry. It needs them to round out its product line; therefore, there is no lessening of competition (2/26/57).

138. Standard Oil Co. of Indiana
Braun Bros. Oil Co. (9/20/56)
MARKET: Home-heating oil
OUTCOME: Standard has few acquisitions in its history and a bad reputation in servicing furnaces. They plan to

use the Braun name to help upgrade their reputation. There is no competition between the two companies since they operate in different marketing areas.

139. Philco Corp.

Avco Mfg. Corp. [patents and trademarks of Bendix home-appliance division] (9/18/56)

MARKET: Home laundry machines

OUTCOME: Merger not viewed as a violation (12/7/56) because there was no transfer of assets; Avco had decided to quit the business, and Philco, which had only a small percentage of the market, will help ex-customers by honoring all old Avco warranties.

140. Continental Can Corp.

Robert Gair Co.—See Chapter IV.

141. Sylvania Electric Products

Argus Cameras, Inc. (9/26/56)

MARKET: Cameras, camera accessories (Argus) and photographic-lighting products (Sylvania)

OUTCOME: Inquiry closed 3/14/57. "The two companies are complementary." The addition of Argus' assets to Sylvania will not affect the lighting market because there are only two other major producers, General Electric and Westinghouse. The addition of Sylvania's assets to Argus will not affect competition much either as the major competitors are Kodak and General Precision Equipment's Graflex Division. Therefore "no difference will be manifested in the industry from what it was previous to the merger."

142. American Can Co.

Bradley Container Corp. (10/11/56)

Dixie Cup Co. (5/9/57)

Marathon Corp. (10/18/57)

MARKET: Containers

OUTCOME: In order to avoid antitrust problems, Marathon divested itself of its hot-cup line, selling it to Potlatch Forests, Inc., on 12/6/57.

143. General Electric Co.

Schick Shaver Co. (9/19/56)

MARKET: Shavers

OUTCOME: According to General Electric, there was "no basis for this report" (9/28/56).

144. Permacel Tape Co. [subsidiary of Johnson & Johnson]
Le Page's, Inc. (10/31/56)
MARKET: Glue, tape, mucilage and paste
OUTCOME: The merger allowed 6/18/57 because Permacel will not receive much competitive advantage over its less-diversified competitors; neither company is dominant, there is much competition, and entry into the field is relatively easy.

145. The Armstrong Co.
The Dicks-Pontius Co. (11/20/56)
MARKET: Putties and caulking compounds
OUTCOME: Merger clearance granted 1/18/57 because they will be able to compete more effectively with the larger firms in the industry. As a result of their increased size, they may be able to break into the automobile market.

146. Kroehler Mfg. Co.
Mengel Furniture [division of Container Corp.] (11/7/56)
MARKET: Furniture
OUTCOME: No action by Justice Department and file closed 3/18/58. There is low concentration in the field and much competition.

147. General Instrument Corp.
Micamold Radio Corp. (11/5/56)
MARKET: Capacitors, resistors, filters
OUTCOME: The two companies do not compete. It is a conglomerate type of acquisition, and there is a lot of competition in the field. Therefore case closed on 4/18/57.

General Instrument Corp.
Radio Receptor Co. (5/2/57)
MARKET: Radio parts
OUTCOME: The merger was consummated and the Antitrust Division took no further action.

148. *Chicago Tribune Co.*
Chicago Daily and Sunday American (10/24/56)
MARKET: Chicago newspapers
OUTCOME: Because "the *American* is suffering huge financial losses" and "we might more profitably use our personnel in other Section 7 investigations" the

investigation closed 10/24/57. This avoided "stir[ring] up . . . [the] fuss such an inquiry would mean."

149. Stauffer Publications Co.

Capper Publications (10/4/56)

    MARKET: Small-town newspapers and magazines

    OUTCOME: File closed 12/10/56 because Capper apparently is in dire financial straits. The only place they compete is Topeka, where they are operated as one company anyway.

150. General Tire & Rubber Co.

Lawrence Process Co., Inc. (11/27/56)

    MARKET: Plastics

    OUTCOME: General Tire's reply to Hansen's letter of inquiry: "Negotiations were voided" (12/7/56).

151. Drexel Furniture Co.

Morgantown Furniture Co.

Heritage Furniture Co. (11/29/56)

    MARKET: Furniture

    OUTCOME: File closed 8/23/57. The companies will be kept unintegrated and there are many other small companies. The cost of transportation is a key factor in price; there is great ease of entry into the field, and the merger will not hurt competition.

152. H. P. Hood & Sons, Inc.

F. P. Mallory, Inc. (12/10/56)

    MARKET: Dairy products in Connecticut and Massachusetts

    OUTCOME: Request for clearance granted 12/31/56 because Mallory is a failing company and no company other than Hood would buy it.

153. Permanente Cement Co. [div. of Kaiser Gypsum Co.]

Fir-Tex Insulating Board, Inc. (10/30/56)

    MARKET: Two types of wall board manufactured in Oregon

    OUTCOME: Although Kaiser makes gypsum board (leader in six states) and Fir-Tex makes insulating board (leader in same area) and the two products are nearly competitive, the merger would appear to imply Section 7 violation; but the entry of Johns-Manville into the area will lead to increased competition. Therefore no action (2/25/58).

154. The Gillette Co.

Schick, Inc. (1/9/57)

MARKET: Shaving products
OUTCOME: Clearance denied, therefore merger dropped 2/1/57.

155. Cudahy Packing Co.
Seattle Packing Co. (1/17/57)
MARKET: Meat packing
OUTCOME: No action taken (5/1/57). The merger will enable Cudahy to complete more efficiently with Swift and Armour. The bulk of Seattle's sales are in Washington-Oregon and most of the big companies are in the area so "it seems that Cudahy's acquisition . . . will not create any problems."

156. Kaiser Aluminum & Chemical Corp.
Wire and Cable division of United States Rubber Co. (1/22/57)
MARKET: Insulated and covered aluminum conductor
OUTCOME: After extensive negotiations, a complaint was filed 4/28/61, attacking the takeover. On 2/23/65, in a consent judgment, Kaiser agreed to sell the Bristol plant. After nine months of efforts to sell it, Kaiser petitioned the government to be relieved of the obligation. The consent decree was then so modified.

157. Miehle Printing Press & Mfg. Co.
Goss Printing Co. (4/11/57)
MARKET: Printing presses
OUTCOME: File closed (no date) because much time passed and there are not enough facts; besides, divestiture might not expand competition anyway.

158. El Paso Natural Gas Co.
Pacific Northwest Pipeline Co.—See Chapter VII

159. Grain Elevator Warehouse Co. [controlled by National Alfalfa Dehydrating & Milling Co.]
Saunders Mills, Inc. (1/31/57)
Midland Industries, Inc. (12/20/57)
Central Mills, Inc. (1/31/57)
MARKET: Alfalfa powder and pellets
OUTCOME: On 6/27/58, the acquisitions were attacked in court. Although Saunders operated 15 mills, and Midland was a sizable factor in the field, on 3/15/63, a consent decree was entered in which National Alfalfa agreed to sell 7 plants, plus abide by certain minor stipulations.

160. File changed to no. 24
161. Wood Newspaper Machinery Corp.
     Walter Scott & Co. (3/20/57)
         MARKET: Newspaper printing presses and equipment
         OUTCOME: No action taken (2/6/59) because the two companies are the smallest in the field and are dwarfed by their competitors, Hoe and Goss.
162. Technicolor, Inc.
     Two processing laboratories of Warner Bros. Pictures, Inc. (4/24/57)
         MARKET: Professional film processing
         OUTCOME: Cleared 9/13/57 despite the opposition of several members of the Antitrust Division.
163. Anheuser-Busch Brewing Co.
     Jacob Ruppert Brewing Co. (6/10/57)
         MARKET: Beer and malt liquor
         OUTCOME: After receiving the Department of Justice request for information on the takeover, Anheuser-Busch loses interest (6/20/57).
164. Maryland and Virginia Milk Producers Assn.
     Richfield Dairy Corp. and Simpson Bros., Inc. (6/3/57) [trading as Wakefield Dairy]
         MARKET: Washington, D.C., area dairy
         OUTCOME: Richfield and Simpson have operated jointly as the Wakefield Dairy since May 1955. The failure of an independent Richfield-Simpson is "inevitable" (11/20/57). Although neither attacked nor cleared, the takeover was undone in the settlement of the Maryland & Virginia-Embassy merger case. (For details, see Chapter VII.)
165. File changed to no. 164
166. Dow Chemical Co.
     Dobeckmum Co. (6/14/57)
         MARKET: Films, foils
         OUTCOME: Dobeckmum is unable to compete with the titans in field; furthermore, the merger will help Dow compete with some of its larger rivals. Therefore, the deal will strengthen competition (3/7/58).
167. Screen Gems, Inc. [Columbia Pictures]
     Universal Picture Co., Inc.
         MARKET: Film distribution
         OUTCOME: Screen Gems had acquired for 14 years the

exclusive right to distribute for television exhibition 600 Universal films. The government saw this as an asset purchase and sued under Section 7 of the Clayton Act and Section 1 of the Sherman Act (the licensing agreement fixed prices). On 6/29/60, the court found for the defendants and the government did not appeal.

168. Columbia Broadcasting System, Inc.
    Westinghouse Electric Corp. (6/26/57)
        MARKET: Broadcasting
        OUTCOME: In reply to the Justice Department request for information, Frank Stanton of CBS answered that there was "nothing to it."

169. General Telephone Corp.
    Peninsular Telephone Co. (6/17/57)
        MARKET: Telephone service
        OUTCOME: In view of the nondivestiture in the ATT case (above, Chapter III), "it would be hard to oppose this merger" (9/22/57).

170. Bensing Brothers & Beeney, Inc.
    Sun Chemical Corp. (7/2/57)
        MARKET: Printing ink
        OUTCOME: Action deferred until the 1958 census of manufacturers (4/9/58). No action after that date.

    Sun Chemical Corp.
    Ansbacher-Siegel Corp. (10/26/58)
        MARKET: Pigments
        OUTCOME: "We must review this with the other case for market effect." File removed for review on 8/17/60 and returned on 8/21/61 with no additions or recommendations for action.

171. United Artists Theatre Circuit, Inc.
    United California Theatres, Inc. (6/27/57)
        MARKET: Motion-picture display
        OUTCOME: After a letter from Justice Department requesting information, California says no merger is planned (7/22/57).

    United Artists Theatre Circuit, Inc.
    Associated Prudential Theatres Co. (6/27/57)
        MARKET: Motion-picture display
        OUTCOME: After letter from Justice Department requesting

information, Associated says no merger planned
(7/1/57).
United Artists Theatre Circuit, Inc.
  Rowley United Theatres, Inc.
  Randforce Amusements, Inc.
  Skouras Theatres Corp. (6/27/57)
    MARKET: Motion-picture display
    OUTCOME: The group of companies is described by Universal
            as being closely allied but not merging; the deal is
            just a "rearrangement of stock."

172. Pittston Co.
  Brink's, Inc. (3/12/56)
    MARKET: Protective-trucking service
    OUTCOME: After a vicious proxy battle won by Pittston, the
            Interstate Commerce Commission gives its ap-
            proval 7/58.

173. Lucky Lager Brewing Co.
  Fisher Brewing Co. (3/20/58)
    MARKET: Beer in Utah
    OUTCOME: Complaint filed 2/18/58, settled by a consent
            decree (10/6/58) providing for sale of Fisher
            Brewing or a consolidated entity selling no more
            beer in Utah than Fisher had sold prior to the
            merger. In 1962, Lucky moved to modify the
            decree, but it was denied.

174. S&W Fine Foods, Inc.
  United Vintners, Inc. (7/16/57)
    MARKET: Canned foods for S&W, wines for United
    OUTCOME: File closed 11/13/57 because there are no
            common products and neither company supplies
            the other. Antitrusters view it as an investment
            only.

175. Union Tank Car Co.
  Phoenix Manufacturing Co. (7/18/57)
    MARKET: Commercial forgings, pipe and tank flanges
    OUTCOME: Cleared (no date). Union is the smallest of the
            three tank-car manufacturers.

176. Sunshine Biscuits, Inc.
  Mann Potato Chip Co. (7/22/57)
    MARKET: Biscuits and potato chips
    OUTCOME: File closed 10/20/57. There is no competition

between Sunshine and Mann. Mann will not achieve a decisive advantage over competitors. There are many other companies in the area, including Lay and Wise, and Mann is a minor factor.

177. Armour & Co.
Nampa [Idaho] plant of the King Packing Co. [owned by Safeway Stores] (7/25/57)
MARKET: Meat packing
OUTCOME: According to Justice Department memo (10/19/59) there is no violation of Section 7 because there is no change in Armour's competitive position: 1) Plant will supply customers previously supplied from elsewhere; 2) Others of the Big Four (Swift, Cudahy, Merrill) serve the same area.

178. American Excelsior Co.
Western Wood Excelsior Mfg. Co. of California
Roesner Bros., Inc.
Oroville Excelsior Co.
Western Wood Excelsior Mfg. Co. of Arizona
Western Aspen Excelsior Mfg. Co., Inc.
Angelus Supply Co.
Suburban Sales Corp.
Western Aspen Excelsior Mfg. Co. of Colorado
Western Wood Excelsior Mfg. Co. of Utah
Western Timber & Development Corp. (6/3/57)
MARKET: Excelsior production
OUTCOME: No action (1/9/58) because
1) excelsior padding is not a separate line of commerce;
2) there is great ease of entry in the field;
3) the companies are still in existence and only the ownership has changed;
4) the excelsior industry will probably decline in the future;
5) the companies' sales are rather small.

179. Lever Bros.
ALL [division of Monsanto Chemical Co.] (5/24/57)
MARKET: Detergent for washing machines
OUTCOME: On 5/22/57, Monsanto sold to Lever Bros. all trademarks, patents and copyrights. On 7/8/58,

the Justice Department filed a complaint charging that actual and potential competition between the two companies had been eliminated, and that Lever had gained a decisive competitive advantage over others in the field. On 4/30/63, the District Court found the acquisition to be lawful and dismissed the complaint. Despite Loevinger's pleas, Solicitor General Cox refused to file an appeal (9/4/63).

180. Texas Eastern Transmission Corp.
    La Gloria Oil & Gas Co. (8/19/57)
        MARKET: Oil wells (La Gloria), pipelines (Texas Eastern)
        OUTCOME: No action (10/24/57). There are no plans to change customers and much of La Gloria's petroleum products are committed under long-term contracts. Texas Eastern is without plans to acquire others in petroleum refining. La Gloria is very small.

181. Certified Grocers of California Co.
    Spartan Grocers, Inc. (8/22/57)
        MARKET: Supermarket supply
        OUTCOME: File closed 4/12/61. No substantial lessening of competition.

182. Atlas Corp.
    Rio de Oro Uranium Mines Corp.
    Lisbon Uranium Corp.
    Mountain Mesa Uranium Corp.
    Radorock Resources, Inc. (8/30/57)
        MARKET: Uranium mining
        OUTCOME: In response to a Department of Justice letter requesting information, Atlas stated that the merger plans had been dropped. (12/10/57).

183. Halliburton Oil Well Cementing Co.
    Welex Jet Services, Inc. (9/9/57)
        MARKET: Oil-well servicing
        OUTCOME: The merger is consummated 10/15/57.

184. Electric Storage Battery Co. [now known as ESB Corp.]
    Ray-O-Vac Co. (9/30/57)
        MARKET: Batteries
        OUTCOME: ESB is an electric storage-battery maker; Ray-O-Vac manufactures dry cells. Therefore they are in two separate markets. Although the inquiry on the

merger was closed 3/13/58, the material in the file was used in the battery industry investigation which was dropped 5/2/61.

185. Falstaff Brewing Co.
Griesedeck Bros. Brewing Co. (10/25/57)
MARKET: Beer and malt liquor
OUTCOME: According to Justice Department memo of 12/17/57, Griesedeck is in major financial difficulties, but Falstaff is growing too much via acquisitions. As a result of government opposition, Griesedeck then sold its brewing assets to Carling Brewery and became a closed-end investment fund.

186. National Gypsum Co.
Connecticut Adament Plaster Co. (10/25/57)
American Encaustic Tiling Co. (5/28/58)
MARKET: Building materials
OUTCOME: No action (no date). The companies are too small.

187. United States Gypsum Co.
Ruberoid Co. [Indiana gypsum deposits] (10/25/57)
OUTCOME: According to United States Gypsum, the purchase was completed in 1956 with no government opposition (Homer Deadman to author, 12/24/74).

188. Outboard Marine Corp.
Cushman Motor Works, Inc. (10/24/57)
Midland Co. (11/20/58)
MARKET: Motor scooters (Cushman), tractors for gardens (Midland)
OUTCOME: The mergers are consummated.

189. Pennsylvania RR
New York Central RR (11//57)
MARKET: Railroading
OUTCOME: Department of Justice defers to the ICC on this merger. On 2/1/68, the merger was finally consummated and on 6/21/70, the court approved the resultant company's petition for bankruptcy.

190. Litton Industries, Inc.
Monroe Calculating Machine Co. (11/18/57)
Airtron, Inc. (6/13/58)
Westrex, Inc. [division of American Telephone & Telegraph]

MARKET: Office equipment and sound transmission
OUTCOME: No apparent Antitrust Division opposition. The Westrex division was sold with the permission of the Justice Department.

191. National Telefilm Associates, Inc.
    Associated Artists Productions, Inc.
    Elliot Hyman Co. (11/15/57)
        MARKET: TV film production
        OUTCOME: Neither merger consummated.

192. Monsanto Chemical
    Plax Corp. [division of Owens Illinois Glass Co.] (11/13/57)
        MARKET: Plastic sheet and bottles
        OUTCOME: File closed 3/23/64. "By this time Plax totally absorbed into Monsanto . . . therefore no possible relief."

193. American Metal Co.
    Climax Molybdenum Co. (11/8/57)
        MARKET: Lead, copper, zinc, gold, silver, etc.
        OUTCOME: File closed 12/17/57, because it would be a difficult and long case.

194. Parker Pen Co.
    Eversharp, Inc. [Writing Instrument Division] (12/4/57)
        MARKET: Writing instruments
        OUTCOME: File closed 12/30/58. Eversharp's division is losing a lot of money, and while both manufacture the same products, the price and quality difference between them is significant.

195. Hamilton Watch Co.
    Gruen Industries, Inc. (12/6/57)
        MARKET: Timepieces
        OUTCOME: In response to Department of Justice letter requesting information, the two stated, "When the merger outcome is finalized, we will seek clearance" (11/12/58). Subsequently the merger plans were dropped.

196. United Drill & Tool Corp.
    Greenfield Tap & Die Corp. (12/12/57)
        MARKET: Hand tools and dies
        OUTCOME: File closed 5/12/58. Although merged entity is a leader, there is good competition; but we should allow no more mergers among the top companies in this industry.

197. United Artists Corp.
    C & C Television Corp.
    Associated Artists Productions, Inc. (11/15/57)
    Distribution rights to backlog of pre-1948 Paramount Pictures
    Corp. feature films (1/20/58)
    ZIV Television Promotions, Inc. (3/30/60)
        MARKET: Feature films
        OUTCOME: A complaint was filed on 9/15/59 seeking divestiture of the compan's. As a result of the government's motion, the case was dismissed on 2/5/62.

198. Pickering Lumber Corp.
    Westside Lumber Co. (1/21/58)
        MARKET: Lumber
        OUTCOME: Cleared 2/12/58 because the merger will not lessen competition.

199. Julius Kayser & Co.
    C.H. Roth Co. (2/5/58)
    Phoenix Hosiery Co. (12/5/58)
    A. Stein & Co. (10/5/60)
    Cole of California (11/15/60)
        MARKET: Garments
        OUTCOME: No action (4/14/60). Already pending are Von's and Brown-Kinney cases which deal with interpretations of lessening of the market, such as the Kayser-Roth case. "We must watch them . . . One more merger and we must file. Right now we can't" (5/22/61).

200. Aluminum Co. of America
    Huyler Corp. [div. of Basca Mfg. Corp.] (2/6/58)
        MARKET: Milk bottle closures
        OUTCOME: FTC refers the case to Justice Department because of its previous work on Alcoa. Sale dropped after Justice Department's letter requesting information (8/12/58).

201. American Automobile Assn.
    Keystone Auto Club (2/14/58)
        MARKET: Automobile service
        OUTCOME: The merger is consummated and the government takes no further action.

202. Music Corp. of America
    Paramount Pictures Corp. [750 pre-1948 feature films] (2/25/58)

MARKET: Feature films

OUTCOME: As MCA was not previously in the business, the Justice Department does not object and the purchase is effected in the same month.

203. Anheuser Busch, Inc.

City Products Corp. [Florida brewery] (2/13/58)

MARKET: Beer brewing

OUTCOME: A complaint was filed 10/30/58 charging violation of Section 7, and on 1/11/60 the parties signed a consent decree providing for divestiture of the acquired brewery and forbidding Busch to sell its low-priced beer in the area in question until after the disposition. In mid-1961, Busch sold the brewery to National Brewing Co., which used the facility to replace its outdated plant in Orlando, thus avoiding antitrust difficulties. According to National, the Orlando plant was demolished in December 1963 (F.D. Fenhagen to author, 12/10/74).

204. Julio Lobo

Cuban Atlantic Sugar Co. (8/3/55)

MARKET: Sugar

OUTCOME: Cuban Atlantic complains to Justice Department that Lobo's attempt to take over the company violates Section 7. On 4/30/56, Lobo was beaten in a proxy battle, and the plan was dropped.

205. Cheseborough Ponds, Inc.

Helena Rubenstein (2/26/58)

MARKET: Health and beauty aids

OUTCOME: The merger plans are dropped. Subsequently Colgate-Palmolive-Peet Corp. acquired Helena Rubenstein.

206. American Potash & Chemical Co.

Lindsey Chemical Corp. (2/25/58)

MARKET: Rare earth and thorium compounds

OUTCOME: The merger was consummated, and Lindsey Chemical became a division of American Potash.

Textron American, Inc.

Cleveland Pneumatic Tool Co.

Bell Intercontinental Corp. (7/26/60)

MARKET: Aircraft gears and control mechanisms

OUTCOME: There appears to have been no Justice Department opposition to these mergers.

207. Empire Millwork Corp.
     E.L. Bruce Co. (5/8/58)
          MARKET: Lumber, especially oak
          OUTCOME: No action (5/21/59). Oak has a nationwide market. There are many suppliers; therefore, the merger creates negligible effect on competition. There is minimal competition between the two companies.

208. Security Banknote Co.
     Columbian Banknote Co. (12/26/57)
          MARKET: Printing of stock certificates
          OUTCOME: File closed 5/20/60, because both companies are very small in a very limited market. They only deal with new issues and that field is very competitive. (Reorders go to the original company.)

209. General American Industries Co. [Tandy Leather Co.]
     Craftool Co. (5/9/58)
          MARKET: Home leather products
          OUTCOME: The merger was consummated, but the file on Tandy Corp. (GAI changed its name in 1960) was kept open until 1966; then it was closed 3/23/66 because
                          1) the leathercraft industry is small, and public interest would be better served by using our resources elsewhere;
                          2) too much time has elapsed since the merger took place.

210. United Press
     International News Service (5/23/58)
          MARKET: News gathering and dispersal
          OUTCOME: File closed 6/3/58 because "We had a meeting and there seems no need of further action." (Although not included in the file, UP and INS are distant competitors to Associated Press.)

211. National Theatres, Inc.
     National Telefilm Associates, Inc. (4/1/58)
          MARKET: Feature films
          OUTCOME: No action (12/1/58). Conglomerate types merger; both companies are in different areas of entertainment.

212. General Motors Corp.
     Euclid Road Machinery Co. — See Chapter VII

213. McLean Trucking Co.
     Hayes Freight Lines, Inc. (6/12/58)
          MARKET: Trucking
          OUTCOME: On 6/12/58, the Justice Department went before
                      the ICC opposing the merger, but the acquisition
                      was completed on 1/4/60.

214. Times-Picayune Publishing Co.
     New Orleans Item (4/2/58)
          MARKET: Both publish New Orleans newspapers
          OUTCOME: No clearance (6/29/58), "but we don't intend to
                      take action."

215. General American Transportation Co.
     Piggy-Back, Inc. (6/20/58)
          MARKET: Railroad equipment (General), transportation of
                      trailers via rail (Piggy-back)
          OUTCOME: As the FTC is already investigating the merger, the
                      Antitrust Division files are turned over to them
                      (8/15/58). The merger was allowed to stand.

216. No file

217. Pabst Brewing Co.
     Blatz Brewing Co. [owned by Schenley] (no date)
          MARKET: Beer
          OUTCOME: On 10/1/59, a complaint against Pabst, Blatz and
                      Schenley was filed charging that the acquisition
                      and its method of payment (cash, debentures,
                      stock and warrants to buy stock) violated Section
                      7. On 10/13/64, the District Court dismissed the
                      case, but on appeal, the Supreme Court reversed,
                      directing divestiture of brand, trademarks, and
                      brewery. On 9/2/69, the Blatz trademarks and
                      brand name were sold to G. Heilemann Brewing
                      Co., but the brewery itself was not sold. On
                      2/11/71, the District Court ordered Pabst to make
                      a "bona fide effort" to sell the property, but it was
                      not sold. On 10/9/74, with no government
                      opposition, the provisions for sale of the plant
                      were vacated.

218. Lever Brothers Co. distribution of the products of Airwick Industries,
     Inc. (7/31/58)
          MARKET: Air fresheners
          OUTCOME: After having terminated their distribution con-
                      tract with Seeman Bros., Inc., Airwick utilized

Lever Bros. distribution system. There were never any discussions relating to merger or takeover. In 1963, the contract was canceled and from that time onward, Airwick has distributed directly. (Joseph Galligan, vice president of Airwick, to author, 9/5/75).

219. Ruberoid Co.
Funkhouser Co.
    MARKET: Roofing materials
    OUTCOME: While the request for clearance was denied on 9/30/58, on second request, based on the small size of Funkhouser and the magnitude of its competitors, permission was granted 12/12/58.

Mastic Tile Corp. of America (8/14/59)
    MARKET: Floor tiles
    OUTCOME: File closed 12/8/59, because Ruberoid's principal competitors have been involved in floor-tile manufacture for years. "This is really just catching up for it." In February 1960, Bicks initiated a review of the deal, and on 4/14/61 the file was closed again.

220. Hilton Hotels Corp.
Diners Club, Inc. (9/24/58)
    MARKET: Credit cards
    OUTCOME: Negotiations were discontinued because of "problems." (N. Whitehorn, counsel for Hilton, to Hansen, 10/9/58)

Sheraton Corp. of America
Diners Club, Inc. (10/16/58)
    MARKET: Credit cards
    OUTCOME: Although the merger was cleared on 2/13/59 because it would not give Sheraton any advantages over its competitors, there was a change in plans, and eventually Diners Club acquired the Sheraton credit card subsidiary, Central Credit Co.

221. Sheraton Corp. of America
American Express Co. (9/26/58)
    MARKET: Travel arrangements and credit
    OUTCOME: The merger was abandoned as a result of the agreement with Diners Club (#220).

222. Dover Corp.
Shepard Warner Elevator Co. (8/18/58)

MARKET: Elevators and lifting equipment

OUTCOME: No action (1/4/60). Antitrust Division decides to use Brown Shoe decision for other cases that are stronger, even though, by delineating the market in question as hydraulic elevators, the companies come to control a large percentage of the market.

223. No file.

224. Schenley Industries, Inc.

Austin Nichols & Co. (10/24/58)

MARKET: Alcoholic products

OUTCOME: Schenley stated that the purchase of shares in Austin Nichols was for investment purposes only. Austin Nichols remained independent until Liggett and Meyers acquired it on 1/24/69.

225. Seven banks form a trade association which was determined to be beyond the jurisdiction of the Antitrust Division. (8/28/58)

226. Kennecott Copper Corp.

Okonite Co. (10/24/58)

MARKET: Insulated electrical wire and cable

OUTCOME: A complaint was filed on 6/22/59 "to divorce fabrication from production" by a divestiture of Okonite. In November 1965, Okonite became an independent company only to be immediately taken over by one of the most voracious of all conglomerates, the Ling-Temco-Vought Corp. [LTV].

227. Thompson Products, Inc.

Federal Industries, Inc. (8/27/58)

MARKET: Pumps and gears

OUTCOME: Case dropped 11/25/59 because Federal was operating at a loss prior to acquisition. Besides the two companies do not compete; therefore, "all the merger means is a substitution of owners."

228. General Telephone Corp.

Sylvania Electric Products, Inc. (10/7/58)

[surviving company called General Telephone & Electronics Corp.]

MARKET: General Telephone: largest independent telephone system in United States. Sylvania: lighting, radio, TV manufacture and photo equipment

OUTCOME: Merger consummated 3/5/59; must be viewed in context of AT&T-Western Electric problem. The relationship between General and Sylvania appears to be analogous to the General Motors-

Euclid merger. "While foreclosure of access to the General Telephone market appears to be inevitable . . . the problem of evidencing . . . would be very difficult" (10/6/59). File not closed.

General Telephone & Electronics Corp.
California Water & Telephone Co.
West Coast Telephone Co.
Southwestern States Telephone Co.
Western Utilities Corp.

MARKET: Telephone service
OUTCOME: The Antitrust Division headed by William Orrick wanted to attack the merger because "the probable effects . . . would substantially and adversely injure competition in the furnishing of telecommunications services and in the manufacture, distribution . . . [of] such services" (Orrick to Attorney General, 6/24/64). It was decided that no action be taken until a case was filed against AT&T. One was filed against AT&T on 4/25/67 but it was not until 1/30/69 that Assistant Attorney General Turner submitted a General Telephone case to Attorney General Mitchell; it was never filed.

229. Minneapolis Honeywell Regulator Co.
Marion Instrument Co. (11/29/58)
American Sentry, Inc. (9/22/59)
H. Belfield Co. (9/14/59)
Heiland Research Corp. (8/5/60)
Davies Laboratories, Inc. (1/5/61)

MARKET: Temperature controls
OUTCOME: File closed 6/21/61 because of the small size of all the acquisitions and the "lapse of time" which had occurred.

230. McGraw-Edison Co.
National Electric Coil Co. (7/15/58)

MARKET: Electrical elements
OUTCOME: Case dropped 3/16/59 because there is little vertical or horizontal integration, no patents involved, and both companies will operate separately.

231. Avco Mfg. Corp.
Pre-Flite Industries Corp. (10/31/58)

MARKET: Diverse aviation materials

OUTCOME: File closed 11/10/58 because Pre-Flite is very small and unprofitable.

232. Cunningham Drug Stores, Inc.

    Kinsel Drug Store Co.

        MARKET: Detroit area drug stores

        OUTCOME: Complaint filed on 6/30/60, claiming that Cunningham as the largest drug store in the Detroit area had violated Section 7 in its acquisition of Kinsel, the second largest in the city. Case dropped by the government 3/21/63, because Cunningham had closed a number of Kinsel stores and competition by other chains had increased.

233. Shampaine Electric Co.

    W.D. Allison Co.

    Carrom Industries, Inc.

    Harley Corp.

    O.E.M. Corp.

    Shampaine Co.

    Richard Phillip Co.

    Professional Specialties Co.

    Crown Products, Inc. (11/25/58)

        MARKET: Hospital supplies

        OUTCOME: File closed because there are no antitrust implications and no single line of commerce. There is little interstate commerce and the merger will strengthen the financial picture of the group, thus stimulating competition.

234. Schering Corp.

    American Scientific Laboratories, Inc. (12/6/60)

        MARKET: Veterinary biologics, medicinals, pesticides and specialties

        OUTCOME: No action. "When the field office did the job, they found no violations." "Now, (1/27/61) we find that the investigation was sloppy, . . . it is too late."

235. International Business Machines Corp.

    Simplex Time Recorder Corp. (10/21/58)

        MARKET: Time-recording equipment

        OUTCOME: Prior to the transfer, IBM accounted for 50 percent of industry sales, with Simplex accounting for 25 percent. But "the assets involved in the acquisition are machinery, customer lists, sales personnel, the rights to license patents, and not a going business" (Bicks to Rogers, 6/2/59). The relief sought was

1) to sell "assets to one not in the business" and

2) to "split up the assets among existing firms" (Bicks' handwritten addenda to 6/9/59 memo to Rogers).

Apparently, Rogers did not wish to pursue the matter since on 1/29/60, Bicks wrote to the president of Simplex, "although we believe that it [the merger] raises certain questions under the antitrust laws, we contemplate no action under Section 7 at present."

236. Rexall Drug Co.
   Tupper Corp. (10/8/58)
   MARKET: Manufacturer and operator of drug stores (Rexall), containers and dishes (Tupper)
   OUTCOME: There is only a remote possibility that a Section 7 case could emerge. There is little competition between the two companies. Therefore case closed 1/28/59.

237. Midland Ross Corp.
   Consolidated Metal Products Corp. [Door Operating Div.] (10/28/58)
   MARKET: Railroad door fixtures
   OUTCOME: File closed 5/10/60 because there is little competition. There is no injury and the competitor who complained has obtained more business since the purchase.

238. Food Fair, Inc.
   Best Markets, Inc. (10/20/58)
   MARKET: Supermarkets in Philadelphia area
   OUTCOME: Matter turned over to the FTC (7/27/59).

239. Perloff Bros., Inc.
   Alfred Lowry & Bros., Inc. (10/10/58)
   MARKET: Food wholesaling
   OUTCOME: File closed 4/20/60 because the companies are small and cater to small businesses. "There is no reason to move in this matter especially when we haven't done so with the big ones." The economics involved do not warrant a move and there will be

an investigation of the food industry (See below, no. 247).

240. Mages Sporting Goods Co.
Cushman Motor Products, Inc. (12/11/58)
    MARKET: Small motor products
    OUTCOME: File closed 4/9/59. "Too insignificant for further action" since the entire transaction involves only $25,000.

241. Hearst Corp.
The Nashville Banner
The Nashville Tennessean (7/30/58)
    MARKET: Newspapers
    OUTCOME: After the Justice Department refuses to grant clearance, Hearst drops the plans (No date).

242. Houdaille-Hershey Corp.
Buffalo-Eclipse Corp. (10/17/58)
Provincial Engineering, Ltd. (11/5/58)
    MARKET: Assorted hardware and motors
    OUTCOME: Although there is some duplication of customers and suppliers, it does not involve the same product. There has been no combination of sales forces; therefore, there is no objection to the merger and the file is closed 4/1/59.

243. Guaranty Trust Co.
J.P. Morgan & Co., Inc. (12/19/58)
    MARKET: New York City banking
    OUTCOME: "We can't touch it because of the bank law. They did it via assets transfer."

244. Worthington Corp.
Well Machinery & Supply Corp. (1/7/59)
    MARKET: Machinery and pumping equipment
    OUTCOME: Although Worthington has broadened its line by acquisitions, the move is not "significantly significant to justify our challenging any of them by action under the Clayton Act." Case closed (8/13/59).

245. Chase Manhattan Bank
Clinton Trust Co. (12/22/58)
    MARKET: New York City banking
    OUTCOME: No coverage by Clayton Act "Sherman Act action not justified" (12/22/58).

246. General Cable Corp.
      General Insulated Wire Works, Inc.
      New England Cable Co.
      Cornish Wire, Inc.
      Alphaduct Wire & Cable Co.
      Hathaway Patterson Corp.
      Indiana Steel & Wire Co.
      Clifton Conduit Co., Inc. of Maryland
      Clifton Conduit of Tennessee Corp.
      Metal Textile Corp. (10/30/58)
      MARKET: Electric wire and cable industry
      OUTCOME: The takeovers were attacked in a complaint filed
                 on 1/19/61, seeking divestiture of the companies.
                 In a consent decree entered on 2/28/64, no
                 divestitures were required and General Cable was
                 enjoined for eight years from any acquisitions of
                 United States companies in the field.
247. Quaker City Wholesale
      Penn Mutual (11/24/58)
      MARKET: Food wholesaling
      OUTCOME: Merger plans dropped 10/24/59. In November
                 1961, the companies resumed negotiations and on
                 1/22/64 they consummated the merger. (See no.
                 239).
248. Johns Manville Corp.
      Libbey-Owens-Ford Glass Fibres Co. (10/1/58)
      MARKET: Insulation fibres and fibre glass
      OUTCOME: Takeover consummated 12/31/58 and Libbey is
                 now operated as a division of Johns Manville.
249. American Cable & Radio
      RCA Communications
      Western Union Cable Co. (10/8/58)
      MARKET: Communications
      OUTCOME: Federal Communications Commission ordered
                 Western Union to divest its international
                 operations. Western Union appealed the decision
                 and finally formed Western Union International.
                 RCA never disposed of its communications
                 subsidiary. American Cable was subsequently
                 taken over by International Telephone and
                 Telegraph.

250. Aluminum Co. of America
  British Aluminum
   MARKET: Aluminum
   OUTCOME: Material "classified" and thus file was unavailable.

251. Foremost Dairies, Inc.
  Borden, Inc.
  Carnation Corp. (10/30/58)
   MARKET: Dry milk
   OUTCOME: File closed 3/23/59. The patent interchange is nonexclusive and at reasonable rates. Besides, the three companies sell less than 1 percent of the annual output of dry-milk products in the United States, and the patented process does not appear to be superior to any other method.

252. *Chicago Sun-Times*
  Chicago Daily News (1/6/59)
   MARKET: Chicago newspapers
   OUTCOME: No action (3/30/59). Merger in part due to increased competition from the *Tribune-American* merger and "we couldn't win."

253. Colgate-Palmolive Co.
  Wildroot, Inc. (no date)
   MARKET: Hair products
   OUTCOME: Department of Justice planned as of 6/3/59 to wait six months and then interview competitors. Since there is no further material in the file, either no interviews were conducted or there were no problems worthy of note. On 4/27/61 the file was closed.

254. H.W. Lay & Co.
  Halter's Pretzels, Inc. (1/9/59)
   MARKET: Snack foods
   OUTCOME: File closed 7/17/59. Lay does not manufacture pretzels. Halter's does not make potato chips. The merger will help Lay into new territory. There is great ease of entry, therefore no violation.

255. American Boxboard Co.
  Wolverine Carton Co. (10/16/58)
  Central Fibre Products Co. (12/24/58)
  Ohio Boxboard Co. (12/24/58)
   MARKET: Boxboard

OUTCOME: File closed 9/21/62. The acquired companies were small, and there do not seem to have been any problems. Besides, too much time has passed.

256. Aluminum Co. of America
  Rome Cable Corp. (1/23/59)
   MARKET: Wire and cable
   OUTCOME: A complaint was filed on 4/1/60 seeking divestiture of Rome Cable. The District Court found for Alcoa. The government appealed and on 6/1/64 the Supreme Court reversed the decision, remanding the case to the District Court for a divestiture decree. Alcoa disposed of Rome on 4/27/66.

257. General Electric Corp.
  A.O. Sutton (9/30/58)
   MARKET: Air-conditioner parts, fans, motors and coils
   OUTCOME: In response to standard letter of inquiry, Sutton replied that it had been trying to sell out, not just to General Electric. On 11/4/59 it merged with Two Guys from Harrison, Inc., and the new entity became known as Vornado, Inc.

258. Electric Auto Lite Co.
  Crane Co. [293,300 shares of stock] (11/5/58)
   MARKET: No overlap
   OUTCOME: Crane opposed the investment and when it offered to repurchase its stock, Electric Auto Lite tendered (7/23/59).

259. Columbia Gas System
  Gulf Interstate Gas Co. (5/23/58)
   MARKET: Gas transmission
   OUTCOME: File closed 8/20/59 because Gulf only supplies gas to a subsidiary of Columbia.

260. Standard Oil Co. [New Jersey]
  Texas Gulf Producing Co. (11/18/58)
   MARKET: Texas produces crude oil and gas in the Gulf area
   OUTCOME: On 3/17/59 they deny plans (after letters from Department of Justice). Therefore file closed 3/25/59.

261. Standard Oil Co. [New Jersey] [via Oklahoma Oil Co.]
  Gaseteria, Inc. (2/25/58)
   MARKET: Gasoline stations
   OUTCOME: Acquisition goes through 3/31/58. Oklahoma is

small in the area and all other major companies
are there.

262. Moran Towing Co.
Curtis Bay Towing Co. (2/19/59)
MARKET: Harbor work along the East Coast
OUTCOME: File closed 6/17/59. The two companies do not
compete in harbor work. The only area in which
they compete is coastwise haulage (Curtis Bay has
1.8 percent, Moran has 10 percent of the market).
Therefore there is little damage to competition.

263. Harsco Corp.
Capitol Mfg. & Supply Co.
MARKET: Pipe fittings (Capitol), gas cylinders (Harsco)
OUTCOME: Merger is essentially conglomerate. There is ease
of entry. The transaction is not of sufficient
importance and file is closed 6/8/59.

264. Esso Oil Co.
Metropolitan Petroleum [division of Pittston] (10/9/58)
MARKET: Fuel-oil supply
OUTCOME: Clearance denied, therefore plans dropped
1/16/59.

265. H.K. Porter Co., Inc.
Thermoid Co. (12/11/58)
MARKET: Rubber goods (Porter), auto parts, belting,
textiles, shoe heels and soles (Thermoid)
OUTCOME: Complaint prepared by the Justice Department
but not approved by Attorneys General Rogers or
Kennedy. On 5/4/61 the Justice Department
indicated its "disapproval" and nothing further
was done.

266. Grinnell Corp.
Hajoca Corp. (10/6/58)
MARKET: Fire protection, iron and brass foundry products,
heating and plumbing goods
OUTCOME: File closed 11/22/60. All the material on Grinnell
should be in one case (which is now being studied).

267. Carrier Corp.
Appliance Buyers Credit Corp [20 percent interest therein]
(12/16/58)
MARKET: Appliance Buyers Credit formed by Whirlpool in
1956 to finance purchases
OUTCOME: File closed 2/18/60. Whirlpool intends to keep
control and there have been no complaints.

268. Kerr McGee Oil Industries
    Texas Pipeline Co. [Oklahoma "gathering line"] (10/13/58)
      MARKET: Oklahoma pipeline
      OUTCOME: The transfer took place and there was no further action by the Department of Justice.
269. Sunray-Mid-Continent Oil Co.
    Mid-Continent facilities of Tidewater Oil Co. (12/12/58)
      MARKET: Oil refineries and distribution
      OUTCOME: Takeover consummated December 1958.
270. Texaco, Inc.
    Seaboard Oil Co. (7/7/58)
      MARKET: Crude oil
      OUTCOME: File closed 9/29/59. Texaco has owned one-third of the company for 26 years. Courts would be unlikely to order divestiture; Seaboard sells mostly to Texaco anyway. Seaboard has little in the way of reserves; therefore the Justice Department planned to use this case only if there was to be a major action against Texaco.
271. Kerr-McGee Industries
    Gulf Oil Co. [crude-oil "gathering lines" in Oklahoma] (10/13/58)
      MARKET: Oil pipeline and distribution
      OUTCOME: File closed 10/5/60 because of small size of deal and its local character.
272. Magnolia Petroleum
    Freeport Sulphur Co. [Lake Wash., La., oil and gas properties] (7/22/59)
      MARKET: Oil and gas
      OUTCOME: There have been no complaints subsequent to the acquisition. The companies are small (Magnolia has 2.2 percent, Freeport 0.6 percent of the oil market in the area). "We have limited manpower which can be better used on other cases."
273. National Gypsum Co.
    Huron Portland Cement (12/31/58)
      MARKET: Cement products
      OUTCOME: File closed 4/5/60. The merger "gives another basic line of essential building materials . . . it is part of National's diversification program." Also Huron is very small.
    National Gypsum Co.
    Union Gypsum (4/13/60)

Allentown Portland Cement Co. (7/6/60)
    MARKET: Gypsum and cement products
    OUTCOME: File closed 2/28/61. "We can't win here." Huron,
                Union and Allentown are located in different
                areas, and while they are significant factors, there
                is no competition with National's products.
274. Kerr McGee Industries
    Magnolia Petroleum [crude-oil gathering line system in Oklahoma]
    (10/10/58)
    MARKET: Pipeline
    OUTCOME: File closed 10/12/60. The acquisition went
                through and the Justice Department took no
                action, regarding the transaction as inconsequen-
                tial.
275. Wheeling Steel
    Follansbee Steel Co. [some assets of] (1/8/59) [Also see no. 32]
    MARKET: Sheet- and strip-making facilities
    OUTCOME: File closed 9/15/59. Follansbee's properties were
                working at 10 percent or less of capacity. They cost
                $4.5 million.; therefore, they are economically
                insignificant.
276. Sunray-Mid-Continent Oil Co.
    Gafil Oil Co. (12/10/58)
    MARKET: Oil products
    OUTCOME: The takeover was consummated in December
                1958.
277. The Standard Oil Company of Ohio [Sohio]
    Atlas Powder Co. (2/19/59)
    MARKET: Explosives and chemicals
    OUTCOME: After a letter of inquiry from the Justice
                Department, the companies change plans. Atlas
                and Sohio will own jointly several facilities (to be
                run by Atlas with the marketing handled by
                Sohio).
278 &
279. Continental Oil Co.
    International Refineries
    Western Oil & Fuel Co. (3/3/59)
    MARKET: Petroleum products
    OUTCOME: Justice Department has a problem: should a
                lesser, major, integrated firm be permitted to
                expand? Therefore regional office requested

further instructions from Washington. On 1/5/61 they were told, "Keep on back burner while we work on Continental-Malco case." File subsequently closed 10/21/63. (See no. 299).

280. H.K. Porter Co.
National Electric Products Corp. (2/4/59)
  MARKET: Electric products (Porter), steel conduit wire and steel cables (National)
  OUTCOME: No action (9/15/59). They are not competitors in the electrical products field, and there are no patents involved.

281. H.K. Porter Co.
Herron Zimmers Moulding Co.
Southern Mouldings, In⌐ (3/3/59)
  MARKET: Metal moldings
  OUTCOME: File closed 9/17/59, because they are not competitors; there are no patents involved nor product interchangeability. Furthermore, there is no loss of buyers or sellers.

282. Waste King Corp.
Cribben & Saxton Co. (2/3/59)
  MARKET: Household appliances
  OUTCOME: File closed 5/11/59. While both make household appliances, Waste King's are built in; Cribben's are movable. The only competition is in the small area of gas ranges and dishwashers.

283. Consolidated Copper Mines
Cerro de Pasco (3/4/59)
  MARKET: Copper mining in South America
  OUTCOME: "Very hard to deal with . . . therefore send warning letter" (4/29/59). The merger plans were dropped after receipt of letter.

284. Bayuk Cigars, Inc. being acquired by either
Cullman Bros., Inc. [a leader in wrapper-leaf tobacco] or
Philip Morris, Inc. (3/23/59)
  MARKET: Tobacco products
  OUTCOME: Bayuk opposes the offers and wins against both attempts. File closed 1/23/61.

285. L.H. Shingle Co.
Johnson Belting Co. (1/30/59)
  MARKET: Leather for mechanical purposes
  OUTCOME: Although Shingle had acquired seven companies

before, each was losing money. File closed 3/4/59 because the acquisitions are of little economic significance; the companies are in a declining industry, and they themselves are declining. There is no monopolization.

286. Utah-Idaho Sugar Co.
Layton Sugar Co. (2/21/59)
    MARKET: Sugar
    OUTCOME: File closed 3/23/59. Layton is a very small, losing company, and there are many other sugar companies in the area.

287. California Bank of Los Angeles
Norwalk Commercial Savings Bank (6/3/59)
    MARKET: California banking
    OUTCOME: Action included in the case of California Bank being taken over by First America Corp. (2/26/59). That action was litigated and there was a consent judgment with First America either setting up another company and selling it, or spinning it off to its shareholders. (9/27/60).

288. American Security & Trust Co. of Washington, D.C.
The City Bank (4/1/59)
    MARKET: Washington banking
    OUTCOME: "We feel it violates Section 7 in that it eliminates competition (American's position rises from 11 percent to 18 percent) in Washington, D.C." American had to acquire City via the stock route. Three other large companies in the Washington area expanded via the asset-acquisition method. "It is not fair that we should penalize the bank for using this route." Merger is effected 5/29/59.

289. J. Paul Getty
Skelly Oil Co.
Tidewater Oil Co. (4/27/59)
    MARKET: Oil
    OUTCOME: Most of the file is missing. The takeover does not take place until much later. On 9/30/67 Getty took over Tidewater. (In 1975 Skelly was still controlled by Mission Corp. [owned by Getty] but not consolidated.)

290. Standard Oil Co. of New Jersey
        Globe Fuel Products, Inc. (4/3/59)
            MARKET: Globe a very small entity in the oil industry
            OUTCOME: "Let's add this to their takeover of Pate Oil Co.,
                         Perfect Power Co., Oklahoma Oil Co.'s takeover
                         of Gasteria for a Section 7 case" (7/11/60). File
                         closed 10/21/63 because of lack of manpower and
                         passage of time.
291. Continental Oil Co.
        San Jacinto Petroleum Co. (3/24/59)
            MARKET: Petroleum products
            OUTCOME: Sellout takes place on 5/20/59. The rest of the
                         material was probably placed in the Continental
                         Malco file.
292. Continental Oil Co.
        Coastal Oil Co. (5/11/59)
            MARKET: Petroleum products
            OUTCOME: No action (11/8/61). "Too late . . . even if we
                         won, it would be a tough divestiture problem."
                         Only a small section of country is involved; there is
                         competition; and the other cases against Con-
                         tinental are stronger.
293. Emerson Western Co. [div. of Emerson Electric]
        Universal Electric Co. [Colorado plant] (5/12/59)
            MARKET: Electric motors
            OUTCOME: File closed 3/28/60 because purchase is insignifi-
                         cant.
294. Electrical & Musical Industries
        Capitol Records, Inc. (12/24/58)
            MARKET: Phonographic supplies and records
            OUTCOME: File closed 10/17/59. EMI has lost RCA and
                         Columbia licenses. There is ease of entry, active
                         price competition, and no evidence of adverse
                         effect. Also there are two different markets
                         involved, classical and pop records.
295. Black & Decker Mfg. Co.
        Master Pneumatic Tool Co. (4/20/59)
            MARKET: Electric tools (Black & Decker), air power tools
                         (Master)
            OUTCOME: File closed 11/12/59. Actually there are two
                         different noncompetitive markets. "We can't get

them now." The two companies sell to different purchasers. "Maybe we can work on this later."

296. United States Gypsum
American Rock Wool Corp. (4/24/59)
    MARKET: Rock wool and glass fibre products
    OUTCOME: File closed (no date). There are others in the field. American is too small.

297. Pure Oil
Wisconsin Independent Oil Co.
Pure Oil Products of Michigan
Shaw Bros. (5/12/59)
    MARKET: Petroleum products
    OUTCOME: File closed 7/5/60. Acquisition not of enough economic significance.

298. Continental Oil Co.
F.P. Kendall Oil Co. (6/2/59)
    MARKET: Oil products
    OUTCOME: File closed 6/5/60. Kendall is not a substantial marketer where Continental operates (the only area of competition is Tennessee and Continental is very small there). There is little wholesale competition and no retail. "But the merger does enlarge a major. However, it would be better to act against the Malco takeover and use this for background."

299. Continental Oil Co.
Malco Refineries (5/8/59)
    MARKET: Malco is the leading independent oil marketer in New Mexico
    OUTCOME: Antitrust Division recommends filing complaint (8/8/60), but Bicks took no action. The complaint filed 5/16/61 asked that a new corporation be formed to replace Malco. On 9/27/63, the District Court dismissed the complaint, the government appealed, and the Supreme Court remanded the case back to the District Court for trial on the merits (5/4/64). On 9/20/65, the District Court found for the defendants. The Justice Department appealed, and on 5/26/67 the Supreme Court vacated the final judgment of 9/20/65, ordering reconsideration. On 10/11/68 Judge Payne of the

District Court announced that he was constrained to enter a judgment in favor of the government and ordered divestiture of the Malco Refineries. In 1969 the Malco properties were sold to the newly-formed Navajo Refining Co.

300. Seeman Bros., Inc.

Francis Leggett & Co. [including Premier Foods subsidiary] (4/3/59)

Seabrook Farms Co. (5/26/59)

Lewiston, Idaho plant for frozen peas from Minute Maid (7/9/54) [See Chapter IV]

Reliable Food Distributors (8/24/60)

J.W. Myers & Co. (5/12/61)

MARKET: Food processing and distributing

OUTCOME: File closed 8/20/62. All factors are small and in different areas of the country. J.W. Myers is not even engaged in the food industry and it has decreasing sales.

301. Esso Standard Oil Co.

General Automatic Fuel Oil Co.

Smedley & Mehl Co. (7/1/59)

OUTCOME: "While we could take an action against these acquisitions, they are very small, when Jersey makes a sizeable acquisition . . . [t]hen all acquisitions over the past few years could be included in a case against Jersey." (8/2/60)

302. Texaco [The Texas Co.]

The Superior Oil Co. — See Chapter VI

303. Maryland Shipbuilding & Dry Dock Co.

Charleston Shipyards, Inc. [some assets]

Charleston Marine Corp. (5/13/59)

MARKET: East-coast shipbuilding and repair

OUTCOME: File closed 10/23/59. Merger does not create a Section 7 action. The companies are in different areas.

304. Aluminum Corp. of America [Alcoa]

Tapas y Envases, S.A. de C.V. of Mexico [interest in] (7/23/59)

MARKET: Bottle tops

OUTCOME: No action but the merger is consummated.

Aluminum Corp. of America [Alcoa]

Imperial Chemical Industries (7/13/59)

MARKET: Joint venture to form Imperial Aluminum, Ltd.

OUTCOME: The plans were modified; on 5/6/50, they each bought 50 percent of Almin Ltd. which owned several companies.

305. Otis Elevator Co.
Northland Equipment Co. (5/19/59)
MARKET: Northland sells Otis's products. It used to sell Baker industrial trucks, but has lost that business.
OUTCOME: File closed 8/12/59. "Insignificant acquisition," "no real changes in the market," "Northland is not even listed in any reference book."

306. Texas Instruments, Inc.
Metals & Controls Corp. (1/6/59)
MARKET: Clad-metal products (Metals & Controls)
OUTCOME: File closed 9/28/59. Neither of the companies competed before the acquisition. Metals & Controls is not dominant in its field.

307. Atlantic Refining Co.
Major Petroleum Co. (7/21/59)
MARKET: Philadelphia heating oil distribution (Major)
OUTCOME: File closed 12/10/63. Atlantic has only one of seven large refineries in the area. Major is only one of ten fuel retailers. There are hundreds of other competitors. "The action is not worth the cost of an FBI investigation to turn up evidence."

308. Diebold, Inc.
Herring-Hall Marvin Safe Co. (8/6/59)
MARKET: Bank vaults and related equipment
OUTCOME: Complaint filed 8/24/59 seeking divestiture. On 3/8/61, the District Court dismissed the case, and the government appealed to the Supreme Court which reversed the decision (5/14/62). On 5/10/63, Diebold agreed to a consent judgment in which it would try, for a period of 12 months, to sell the acquired properties. If after that time divestiture was not accomplished, Diebold would be allowed to keep them. In 1964 litigation was terminated, with Diebold being allowed to retain its holdings.

309. Flintkote Co.
Calaveras Cement (8/5/59)
Blue Diamond Corp. (3/18/59)
H.J. Grove Lime Co. (6/29/60)

Harry T. Campbell Sons (6/30/60)
Diamond Portland Cement Co. (7/18/60)

MARKET: Cement and gypsum in various areas of the country.

OUTCOME: File closed 9/21/60. The acquired companies are not potential competitors or customers; all operations are unchanged. Besides, the Antitrust Division is "having trouble developing a case." The last three companies are owned by people "who are getting on in years and who need to have a more liquid type security."

310. Falstaff Brewing Co.
Miller Brewing Co. (8/14/59)

MARKET: Beer brewing

OUTCOME: Takeover falls through due to the opposition of one of the ten Miller stockholders and the Justice Department. On 8/24/66, W.R. Grace and Co. bought 53 percent from the Miller family.

311. Kar-Go System
Arcoa, Inc.

MARKET: U-haul trailers (Arcoa), tractors (Kar-Go)

OUTCOME: File closed 2/19/60. Kar-Go is in difficult circumstances. It is a sole proprietorship, therefore Justice Department cannot use the Clayton Act. Many of Kar-Go's people have left the fold since the takeover, hence there is competition. The leasing of car trailers is a young, growing and changing industry.

312. J.P. Stevens & Co., Inc.
Green River Mills [spinning plant] (4/20/59)
Angle Silk Mills (9/3/59)
Virginia Mills Corp. (12/9/59)

MARKET: Textiles

OUTCOME: File closed 12/9/59. Green River had not been operating for one year and had been losing money before then. The principal stockholder of Angle had died and there was need to sell stock to settle the estate and cover the taxes. "The other acquisitions are not serious either."

313. Du Pont Corp.
Remington Corp. — See Chapter V.

314. American Crystal Sugar Co.
Holly Sugar Corp. [properties in Arkansas River Valley] (8/5/59)

MARKET: Sugar cultivation

OUTCOME: File closed 1/15/60 because there is no effect on beet-sugar growers or competition. Holly is not enjoined in the contract from reentry into the area. It had been incurring losses there and American Crystal needed a new facility. Also there is competition between beet and cane sugars. The West is one sugar market, and the Department of Agriculture controls the market via controls on imports.

315. Wurlitzer Corp.
    Miessner Inventions, Inc. (5/28/59)

MARKET: Electric pianos

OUTCOME: File closed (no date). Miessner had tried to "peddle the patents for years." Wurlitzer is big in other areas and number one in pianos. Wurlitzer will not lessen competition because no one else is interested in the field.

316. Armour & Co.
    Mississippi River Fuel Corp. [ammonia plant] (9/2/59)

MARKET: Ammonia

OUTCOME: File closed 1/10/60. Armour is not planning to sell the ammonia; it needs it for own use. The plant produces 2 percent of the nation's needs, therefore there is no tendency to create a monopoly. "We can't prove anti-competitive effects."

317. Dan River Mills, Inc. [via Woodside Mills]
    Norris Cotton Mills Co. (8/21/59)

MARKET: Cotton textiles and print cloths

OUTCOME: File closed 1/23/61. Norris is not big and is insignificant in cotton prints.

318. Pure Milk Assn.
    Hawthorn Mellody Farms Dairy (4/16/59)

MARKET: Dairy products

OUTCOME: None recorded

319. San Francisco *Call Bulletin*
    San Francisco *News* (8/10/59)

MARKET: San Francisco newspapers

OUTCOME: No action (10/5/59). The *News* was in financial stress, and the takeover took place in 1933.

320. National Steel Corp. [via Stran-Steel Corp.]
    Metallic Building Co. (7/14/59)

MARKET: Structural steel

OUTCOME: Government goes to court to block the merger (2/15/60). The case was dismissed by the District Court on 3/30/65, and the government appealed. Upon motion of the parties before the Supreme Court, the case was referred back to the District Court for settlement. A consent judgment was entered 4/10/67, requiring divestiture, and Metallic was sold in May 1967 to MAT Corp.

321. Electric Storage Battery Co.
Chemical Linings Co. (9/8/59)
MARKET: Storage batteries
OUTCOME: On 8/1/60, ESB also purchased from McGraw Edison Co. the property, plant, etc., to make nickel-iron storage batteries. The file was closed 1/20/64 because size does not warrant the expenditure of time, effort and money to initiate an action.

322. Electric Auto Lite Co.
C&D Batteries, Inc. (9/18/59)
MARKET: Storage batteries
OUTCOME: File closed 7/18/63. C&D manufactures industrial batteries; Electric Auto Lite makes them for autos and aircraft. They are allied but not competitive fields. Also "we are already involved with Electric Auto Lite and Ford for Electric Auto Lite having sold one company to Ford."

323. First New Haven National Bank
Union and New Haven Trust Co. (8/26/59)
MARKET: New Haven banking
OUTCOME: After the Justice Department sent the standard letter of inquiry to the two companies, on 10/14/59 they abandoned their plans and so informed the Justice Department on 10/16/59.

324. Joy Mfg. Co.
Western Precipitation Corp. (9/2/59)
MARKET: Dust collectors
OUTCOME: File closed 12/11/59. There is little direct competition since there are many companies in the field of wet scrubbing of air and gas and that is not even a line of commerce. Therefore, "we will lose because the two have a very small percentage of the total market."

325. Standard Oil of Indiana.
>> True Oil Co. (9/18/59)
>>> MARKET: Petroleum products in the Northwest (True)
>>> OUTCOME: Merger does not seem significant based on figures, but "Standard is the largest purely domestic oil company." Nevertheless, the file was closed 10/21/63 due to the passage of time and the transaction's relative insignificance.

326. National Homes Corp.
>> Thyer Mfg. Corp. (7/59)
>> W.G. Best Factory-Built Homes, Inc. (7/59)
>> Lester Bros., Inc. (7/59)
>> Fairhill, Inc. (7/59)
>> Western Pacific Homes, Inc. (8/13/59)
>> Knox Corp. (5/59)
>> American Homes [recently acquired by Knox] (6/59)
>>> MARKET: Prefabricated housing business
>>> OUTCOME: A complaint was filed 11/20/59 seeking divestiture. The court permitted National to liquidate three of the companies and to operate them as divisions of National with the proviso that they be operated separately. On 12/1/62, the case was terminated by a consent judgment in which National agreed to divest itself of four of the acquired companies.

327. Clevite Corp.
>> Walco Products, Inc. (2/8/59)
>>> MARKET: Small needle makers (Walco)
>>> OUTCOME: File closed 6/21/60 because Clevite could develop Walco's potential fully; Clevite produces transducers and they can go with Walco's needles, but there is already a government action against Clevite in the piezoelectric transducer field and thus "our leverage could be cut here." Clevite tried unsuccessfully to cancel the deal and later (7/60) sold off the division.

328. Olivetti Corp.
>> Underwood Corp. (10/2/59)
>>> MARKET: Typewriters
>>> OUTCOME: On 4/11/60, William Rogers approved the filing of a complaint charging that the acquisition might lessen competition, etc. and violate Section 7 of

the Clayton Act. In a memorandum dated 4/6/60, Robert Bicks noted that although Underwood "may have been a failing company," there were other possible purchasers, thus necessitating the filing of the suit. Staff note 757 reveals that the entire administration was interested in the case. (5/2/60 in Papers of the President of the United States: 1953-61, Eisenhower Diaries Series, Box 32, Staff notes.) On 5/20/60, after conferences between the State Department and the Italian Embassy, the proposed complaint was withdrawn.

329. Budd Co.
American Machine & Foundry Co. [Cleveland Welding Div.]
Lewyt Mfg. Co. (10/2/59)
   MARKET: Welding (Cleveland), mechanical and electrical products (Lewyt)
   OUTCOME: File closed 11/5/63. Cleveland plant closed down and its business has been intermingled with that of other Budd divisions. "The proposed case needs more investigation." "It would be difficult to define a line of commerce."

330. Home Mutual Savings & Loan Assn.
Arrowhead Savings & Loan Assn.
Pico-Rivera Savings & Loan Assn. (10/13/59)
   MARKET: California savings and loans
   OUTCOME: This merger does not appear to have taken place. Although *Moody's Bank and Finance Manuals* for 1959 and 1961 do not include Arrowhead or Pico, Home is listed as being held by the First Charter Financial Corp.

331. Diana Stores Corp.
Ralph Miller, Inc. (8/21/59)
   MARKET: Women's apparel stores
   OUTCOME: File closed 9/28/59. Ralph Miller has been a losing company; there is grave possibility of a business failure.

332. The Standard Oil Co. of Ohio (Sohio)
Leonard Refineries, Inc.—See Chapter VI

333. Bank Stock Corp. of Milwaukee [a holding company]
Bank of Commerce
Marshall & Ilsley Bank
Northern Bank (no date)

MARKET: Wisconsin banking

OUTCOME: Bank Stock acquires control of Bank of Commerce 1/26/61 and, in compliance with consent judgment, on 6/26/69 it sells the company. The other acquisitions were not attacked and in July 1962, Bank Stock changed its name to Marshall & Ilsley Bank Stock Corp.

334.   National Steel & Shipbuilding Corp. [sale of assets to]

Henry J. Kaiser Co.

Macco Corp.

Morrison-Knudsen Co., Inc.

F.E. Young Construction Co. (10/19/59)

    MARKET: Structural steel production products

    OUTCOME: File closed 11/16/59. National needs more capital. This will strengthen it against Bethlehem Steel, and the sales do not have that negative an effect.

335.   Chemical & Industrial Corp.

Chemtron Corp. [Girdler Construction Div.] (no date)

    MARKET: Chemical construction

    OUTCOME: File closed 12/31/59. Girdler has been losing money since 1956; Chemical has been doing well and merger will help it become a stronger competitor. Besides, buyers of chemical plants are substantial and are "able to take care of themselves and are not at the mercy of builders."

336.   American Pipe & Construction Co.

Nukem Products Corp. (7/30/59)

    MARKET: Coatings for pipes and floors

    OUTCOME: File closed 10/5/71. Very small merger with little effect on commerce. Nukem is only in the Northeast and American is nationwide.

337.   Allis Chalmers Mfg. Co.

Ohio Brass Co. (7/17/59)

    MARKET: Joint affiliate OBAC, Inc., to manufacture power capacitors

    OUTCOME: File closed 3/2/62 because there is no change in the competitive situation.

338.   Allis Chalmers Mfg. Co.

Valley Iron Works Co. (9/29/59)

    MARKET: Special industry machinery

    OUTCOME: No action (4/12/60). Valley accounts for 3 percent of total industry dominated by six companies (two control 75 percent of the output). Valley buys supplies from other companies than Allis Chalmers. Allis Chalmers does not sell to the industry so suppliers will not be hurt or competition hindered. There will be no noticeable changes in the market structure.

339. American Smelting & Refining Co.
General Cable Corp.
Revere Copper & Brass, Inc.
Newmont Mining Co. (10/15/59)

    MARKET: Action attacks acquisitions, corporate interrelationships, interlocking directorships and joint ventures.

    OUTCOME: A complaint was developed and sent by Bicks to Rogers on 7/22/60; Rogers approved its filing on 1/17/61. The action sought to require American Smelting to divest its stock holding in General Cable and Revere and to enjoin future acquisitions. On 3/15/67, the case was terminated by a consent judgment in which American Smelting was enjoined from casting stockholder votes at meetings of General Cable and Revere. It placed limitations on future acquisitions and sales of American Smelting. These were to last for five years, at which time American Smelting could request the court to terminate the judgment, which it did, and on 3/21/72, the judgment was terminated.

340. A.E. Staley Co.
Hubinger Co. (10/12/59)

    MARKET: Staley obtains license for the sole right to sell Hubinger's quick elastic starches.

    OUTCOME: File closed 2/17/61. Insufficient evidence.

341. Kalamazoo Vegetable Parchment Co.
Sutherland Paper Co. (10/13/59)

    MARKET: Paper products

    OUTCOME: On 1/4/60, the companies merged with the successor being the KVP Sutherland Paper Co. The Justice Department files were closed on 5/10/62 with no reason given.

342. Von's Grocery Co.
  Shopping Bag Food Stores (10/26/59)
    MARKET: Supermarkets in California
    OUTCOME: A complaint was filed 3/20/60 seeking to prevent the merger. An injunction was denied on 6/13/60. On 9/16/64, the District Court found for Von's, with findings of fact and conclusions of law being filed on 12/16/64. The government appealed and on 5/31/66 the Supreme Court reversed and directed divestiture, and on 1/30/67 the District Court so ordered. On 2/27/67, agreement in principle was reached for E. F. MacDonald Co. to purchase the firm's 108 supermarkets in the Los Angeles area. (E.F. MacDonald is in the trading stamp and incentive plan business.) Many of the markets were subsequently sold to Fisher Foods, Inc., a midwestern supermarket chain (9/19/72).

343. California Packing Corp.
  Van Camp Seafood Co. (10/13/59)
    MARKET: Food canning
    OUTCOME: Request for clearance denied 3/31/60, merger plan dropped.

344. Bridgeport Brass Co.
  Seymour Mfg. Co. (10/12/59)
    MARKET: Bridgeport Brass: brass products Seymour: special machinery and equipment for manufacture of nonferrous alloys
    OUTCOME: No action taken because Seymour "is very small and there is no overlap between the companies" (undated). On 6/30/61, Bridgeport Brass was merged into National Distillers & Chemical Co.

345. Bell & Howell Co.
  Consolidated Electrodynamics Corp. (10/28/59)
    MARKET: Photographic equipment, tape recorders and microfilm products (Bell & Howell), spectrometers and specialized electronic equipment (Consolidated)
    OUTCOME: File closed 2/4/60. No competition between the two; no tendency to create a monopoly.

346. Howard Stores Corp.
  Ripley Mfg. Corp. (10/29/59)

MARKET: Men's clothing manufacture and sales
OUTCOME: Much material missing from Justice Department files; but the merger is consummated in December 1959 and the Justice Department appears to have taken no action.

347.   Kaiser Aluminum & Chemical Corp.
      Mexico Refractories Co.
      A.P. Green Fire Brick Co.
      Climax Fire Brick Co. (2/9/59)
          MARKET: Refractories
          OUTCOME: File closed 1/17/64. Although both Mexico and Green are located in Mexico, Mo., the Antitrust Division closed the file, saying that the mergers did not lessen competition (Also see no. 123).

348.   John Morrill & Co.
      Hunter Packing Co. (10/15/59)
          MARKET: Beef, pork and sausage packing house products
          OUTCOME: File closed 12/27/60. "Weak case." Hunter is small and becoming increasingly weak. (There is only one place where there is competition—St. Louis—and both companies are very small there.)

349.   Certain-Teed Products Corp.
      Central Commercial Co. (11/13/59)
          MARKET: Roofing materials
          OUTCOME: Clearance request denied 1/11/60. Central then tried to sell out to Ruberoid, and that was also denied (12/14/60).

350.   Standard Slag Co.
      Cleveland Builders Supply Co. (10/20/59)
          MARKET: Slag, sand, gravel and stone
          OUTCOME: Clearance denied 8/2/62, but there is a memo dated 4/12/60 closing the case.

351.   Harbison-Walker Refractories Corp.
      Carborundum Co. (11/6/59)
          MARKET: A joint venture in fused refractory products
          OUTCOME: File closed 12/31/63 because of small size of money-losing venture. Besides, no one else is involved in the business at all.

352.   [Changed to 60-156-37]
      Vulcan Materials Corp.
      Union Chemicals & Materials Corp. (no date)
          MARKET: Chemicals

OUTCOME: The merger took place on 12/31/57 and the matter was turned over to the FTC.

353.   Lucky Stores, Inc.
        Market Basket Supermarkets (11/10/59)
        MARKET: California supermarkets
        OUTCOME: After receiving letters of inquiry from the Justice Department, the companies terminated negotiations 12/24/59.

354.   Controls Co.
        Electrosnap Corp. (no date)
        MARKET: Hermetically sealed switches and components (Electrosnap), switches, etc. (Controls)
        OUTCOME: The merger was consummated 12/31/59. The file was closed 7/11/63 "because it would be hard to get relief."

355.   Midland-Ross Corp.
        Surface Combustion Corp. (11/1/59)
        MARKET: Auto supplies (Midland), engineering space technology (Surface)
        OUTCOME: File closed 4/1/60. The two companies are not competitive; they produce different types of atmospheric controls for different markets and deal with different sellers and purchasers.

356.   United Gas Improvement Co.
        A.C. Horner, Inc. (11/6/59)
        MARKET: Pennsylvania gas and electricity supply (United)
        OUTCOME: File closed 9/14/62. Little change of competitive picture. Furthermore, there are many other operators in the area.

357.   *New York Journal American*
        New York World Telegram & Sun (10/22/59)
        MARKET: New York City evening newspapers
        OUTCOME: The antitrusters were prepared to allow the merger but they were worried about a possible tie between the Hearst and Scripps-Howard organizations. On 9/12/66 the papers, along with the *New York Herald Tribune*, merged to form the *World Journal Tribune*, a morning paper. On 5/5/67, it folded.

358.   Ashland Oil & Refining Co.
        Louisville Refining Co. (11/7/59)
        MARKET: Oil refining in Kentucky

OUTCOME: File closed 2/8/60. Louisville cannot compete at a profit, has small capacity, and Ashland was its major customer anyway.

359. Boeing Airplane Co.
    Vertol Aircraft Corp. (12/1/59)
        MARKET: Helicopters
        OUTCOME: File closed 4/26/60. There is no horizontal competition between Boeing and Vertol. Competitors will not be hurt by Boeing's entry into the field. Although Boeing will supply motors now, there will be no major effect because Vertol bought so few before.

360. Wells Fargo Bank
    American Trust Co. (12/2/59)
        MARKET: California banking
        OUTCOME: "We can't sue under Section 7, therefore we should try Section 1 of the Sherman Act—but if we do that we should attack the Morgan Guaranty merger" (1/26/60). Although a proposed complaint was drawn up 3/21/60, it was not filed; there were conferences in which Wells Fargo persuaded the Justice Department that it was essentially a "wholesale" bank and that American was a retail bank (R.W. Budge, attorney for Wells Fargo, to author, 12/13/74).

361. Changed to no. 24
362. Chance Vought Aircraft, Inc.
    General Coach Works, Inc.
    Mid States Corp.
    ABC Coach (12/11/59)
        MARKET: Mobile-home manufacturers
        OUTCOME: The mobile-home business is bad, and there is difficulty in defining the market. They make not only homes but also travel trailers. Therefore, file closed 10/3/60.

363. Fairchild Camera & Instrument Co.
    R.C. Allen Business Machines, Inc. (12/4/59)
        MARKET: Adding machines, typewriters, cash registers and aircraft instruments
        OUTCOME: After standard letter of inquiry from the Justice Department, the merger was dropped 12/7/59, and R.C. Allen remains an independent entity today.

364. Theodore Hamm Brewing Co.
    Gunther Brewing Co. (12/16/59)
        MARKET: Beer and ale
        OUTCOME: File closed 1/5/60. There is little competition. Gunther is in worsening financial condition.

365. Air Products & Chemical Corp.
    Southern Oxygen Co. (no date)
        MARKET: Compressed gasses
        OUTCOME: File closed 3/30/62. There is no competition except in Philadelphia, and there they have a low market share. But "we must watch Air Products."
    McKesson & Robbins, Inc.
    Barada & Page, Inc. (8/17/59)
        MARKET: Distribution of industrial chemicals
        OUTCOME: Cleared 12/14/59. The merger will give McKesson a nationwide wholesaler of chemicals. Barada is in distribution, not manufacture. But "watch McKesson; they could make problems."

366. Lipsett, Inc. [division of Luria Bros.]
    Corsicana oil-field equipment plant [owned by Bethlehem Steel Corp.] (12/17/59)
        MARKET: Oil-field maintenance equipment and scrap metals
        OUTCOME: Material turned over to the FTC for its case against Luria.

367. Henry Holt & Co.
    John Winston Co.
    Rinehart Co. (12/10/59)
        MARKET: Book publishing
        OUTCOME: File closed 2/29/60. The anticompetitive impact is minimal; they publish in separate fields except for college texts where they only overlap in 11 subjects. Even after the merger, the company would be number three in college publishing, having half the sales of number one.

368. Aluminium Ltd.
    Apex Smelting Co. (1/11/60)
        MARKET: Aluminum products
        OUTCOME: After the Justice Department letter of inquiry, merger plans dropped on 6/8/60.

369. Loblaw, Inc.
    National Tea Co. (equity interest in)
    Sparkle Market Stores, Inc.
    Star Markets, Inc. (no date)

MARKET: Supermarkets in the Midwest and Pittsburgh area
OUTCOME: There is little overlap between the companies, therefore the file is closed 1/25/61.

370. Bliss & Laughlin, Inc.
Sierra Drawn Steel Corp. (1/14/60)
MARKET: Cold-finished steel bars
OUTCOME: Complaint filed 6/28/60 seeking divestiture of business and assets of Sierra. On 3/27/62, the District Court found for the defendants. The government appealed to the Supreme Court. On 11/5/62, it remanded the case to the District Court to reconsider in light of the Brown Shoe decision. On 3/27/63, the District Court again found for the defendants and the government did not appeal.

371. Aluminum Corp. of America
Cupples Products Corp. (2/1/60)
MARKET: Extruded aluminum products
OUTCOME: A complaint was filed 4/27/61 charging that the acquisition would lessen competition in the manufacture and sale of aluminum residential and nonresidential windows, doors, door frames, entrances and curtain walls. On 12/4/64, the District Court found for the government and ordered divestiture. On 10/11/65, the Supreme Court affirmed the order of divestiture, and on 2/18/66, the District Court approved the sale of Cupples to H. H. Robertson Co.

372. General Dynamics Corp.
Material Service Corp. (no date)
MARKET: Quarries, coal
OUTCOME: The merger was consummated and no further action was taken.

373. Great Lakes Carbon Corp.
Crescent Carbon Corp. (1/26/60)
MARKET: Synthetic graphite electrodes, anodes and molds
OUTCOME: File closed 6/3/60, but there is a problem; substantial competition is eliminated since there is an increase in concentration among the sellers, indicating a probable violation of Section 7 which could be established by further investigation. However, Crescent's dollar volume is low and the

company has been operating at a loss for several years. According to the memo, "To undertake the work necessary to the preparation of such a case would require the expenditure of manpower which could be put to more beneficial and productive uses on other matters."

374. Federal Pacific Co.
Cornell Dubilier Electric Co. (1/12/60)
    MARKET: Devices for distribution and control of electrical energy (Federal), capacitors, vibrators, TV-antenna rotators (Cornell)
    OUTCOME: There is no competition between the two. They do not buy from each other; they sell compatible gear to electric utilities; and their technology may be of use in the future. The only anticompetitive aspect would be that they could "package their products," but the two giants are already integrated. Therefore, the merger will increase competition and will help Cornell, which is in an economic tailspin.

375. Eaton Mfg. Co.
American Metal Products (1/26/60)
    MARKET: Miscellaneous fabricated tubular and stamped metal assemblies
    OUTCOME: After letter of inquiry from the Justice Department, merger terminated 2/23/60.

376. *Cleveland Press*
Cleveland News (1/23/60)
    MARKET: Cleveland newspapers
    OUTCOME: File closed 9/1/60. The *News* has had substantial losses for a very long time.

377. Aluminum Corp. of America
REA Magnet Wire Co. (1/21/60)
    MARKET: Wire
    OUTCOME: Merger consummated 1/19/60.

378. Sinclair Refining Co.
Patterson Oil Co. (2/11/60)
    MARKET: Philadelphia oil distribution
    OUTCOME: File closed 6/13/60. Sinclair is number five in the market and the takeover would have no effect on competitive structure.

379. Pure Oil Co.
   Woodley Petroleum Co. — See Chapter VII
380. General Contract Finance Corp.
   Topeka Morris Plan Co.
   Morris Plan Co. (of Wichita, Kansas) (1/29/60)
   MARKET: Finance and loans
   OUTCOME: File closed 4/11/60. General Contract is in business finance, insurance and loans. The Morris Plan companies are in the personal loan business. They are very small and there would be no change in any competitive relationships.
381. H.K. Porter Co., Inc.
   Peerless Electric Co. (9/29/59)
   MARKET: Electric motors and fans
   OUTCOME: File closed 7/1/60. Peerless makes electric motors, but they are not competitive with those purchased by Porter from other outside firms. Therefore, there is no anticompetitive effect, and anyway Porter only purchased 76,000 of the units in question.
382. Texas Natural Gasoline Corp.
   Union Oil & Gas Corp. of Louisiana (2/19/60)
   MARKET: Crude oil and petroleum products in Texas and Louisiana
   OUTCOME: No action. Companies merged 3/3/60 to form Union Texas Natural Gas Corp.
383. Sunbeam Corp.
   John Oster Mfg. Co. (2/19/60)
   MARKET: Barber supplies
   OUTCOME: Merger consummated 9/7/60 and no further action taken.
384. Federal Paper Board Co., Inc.
   Manchester Board & Paper Co. of Virginia (12/15/59)
   MARKET: Paperboard
   OUTCOME: No action (4/28/60), because there is no substantial competition between the two companies. There will be little change in the paperboard market. Both companies were supplied in large measure by West Virginia Pulp & Paper Co. Even taking into account Federal's acquisitions, "it isn't enough for a Section 7 action." "But we should watch Federal closely."

385. Humble Oil & Refining Co. [via subsidiary Carter Oil Co.]
    Lincoln Oil Co.
        MARKET: Small wholesaler in Lincoln, Nebraska (Lincoln)
        OUTCOME: File closed 4/11/60. Lincoln is a wholesaler of petroleum products and its owner is 77 years old. Carter has no sales in Lincoln, Nebraska. Therefore there is no competitive impact. "We will take no separate action on this acquisition but we can use the material in an overall action against Standard Oil of New Jersey, the parent company of Humble."

386. Pennsalt Chemicals Corp.
    Olin Mathieson Chemicals Corp. (2/15/60)
        MARKET: Joint venture to manufacture sodium chlorate
        OUTCOME: The case was viewed by many in and out of the Justice Department as an excellent means of testing whether or not the antitrust laws covered joint ventures.

                "The combination of Pennsalt and Olin Mathieson in Penn-Olin offers a particularly strong case for testing the applicability of Section 7 (as well as Section 1) to the popular joint venture form of merger-acquisition. The venture is in its incipient stages. It involves large companies with a substantial volume of competitive sales. It forecloses the potential competition of Olin Mathieson from broadening the production base of a highly concentrated industry and increases barriers to entry by keeping productive capacity well ahead of current demand. It involves a unique product of substantial and growing importance to both national defense and the paper industry. It is spawned by Olin Mathieson which already ranks among the foremost exponents of growth through merger, acquisition and joint venture. And it takes place in the chemical industry whose history and pattern of joint ventures is probably second to none" (Memorandum for the Attorney General, 12/23/60).

                On 5/1/63, even though the District Court adopted many of the government's findings of fact, it ruled that the joint venture did not violate any antitrust laws. The government appealed to the Supreme Court, which affirmed the lower court's Sherman Act dismissal, but remanded the case for further proceedings on the Clayton Act charges (6/22/64). On 10/12/65, the District Court dismissed the case. The government appealed again, but the District Court decision was upheld by an equally divided Supreme Court (12/11/67).

387. Siegler Corp.
    Magnetic Amplifier, Inc. (2/12/60)
        MARKET: Sound equipment
        OUTCOME: File closed 4/12/61. The acquisition does not appear to violate Section 7.

388. Reichold Chemicals, Inc.
    Alsynite Corp. of America (3/1/60)
        MARKET: Translucent fiberglass building panels (Alsynite)
        OUTCOME: The merger is consummated 8/7/60 and no further action is taken.

389. Revlon, Inc.
    Pinex Co., Inc.
    Pinex Co. Canada
        MARKET: Cosmetic Products
        OUTCOME: File closed 4/28/60. The companies are too small and no competitive products are involved.

390. Diamond Gardner Corp.
    United States Printing & Lithography Co. (12/16/59)
        MARKET: Paper goods, cartons, lumber products (Diamond), printing (United States)
        OUTCOME: Merger consummated 9/28/59 to form Diamond National Corp.

391. Crane Co.
    Briggs Mfg. Co. [some stock of] (12/22/59)
        MARKET: Plumbing and heating equipment (Crane), vitreous chinaware and plumbing fixtures (Briggs)
        OUTCOME: File closed 5/16/60. "Nothing left for us to do." The FTC has filed suit and stockholders have filed suit against Crane acquisition.

392. California Canners & Growers [agricultural cooperative]
    San Jose Canning Co. (3/8/60)
        MARKET: Food processing
        OUTCOME: File closed 4/4/60. This plus the acquisition of the

Thornton Canning Co. gives a strong position in tomato products but there is a lot of competition in the field. Additionally, the "legal position of the growers' cooperative under the various agricultural laws" rules out further work on the merger.

393. Shell Oil Co.
Buckley Oil Co.
MARKET: Petroleum products
OUTCOME: File missing.

394. Continental Carbon Co.
Columbian Carbon Co. (2/17/60)
MARKET: Joint interest in European plants
OUTCOME: File closed 12/1/60. The two companies did not compete before; therefore, it would be impossible to prove that the merger eliminates or may lessen competition.

395. Motorola, Inc.
Lear, Inc. [personal aircraft production business] (12/10/59)
MARKET: Aircraft production
OUTCOME: File closed 10/4/60. There is no lessening of competition. Motorola is new to the field but has radio expertise.

396. Chance Vought Aircraft Co.
Information Systems, Inc. (1/23/60)
MARKET: Data retrieval
OUTCOME: File closed 6/21/61. The takeover is part of Chance Vought's effort to minimize the cyclical nature of armament production; therefore, it is a diversification. Information Systems will be supplemental to Genesys Corp., hence the merger will be beneficial.

397. Harris Trust & Savings Bank
Chicago National Bank (2/25/60)
MARKET: Chicago banking
OUTCOME: File closed 4/20/60. Merger accomplished by asset acquisition, and since the new entity will still be competing with two substantially larger banks, there is no Sherman Act Section 1 action possible.

398. Farmers & Mechanics Trust Co. [of Childress, Texas]
First National Bank [of Paducah, Texas] [5 percent equity] (1/13/60)

MARKET: Texas banking

OUTCOME: File closed 3/10/60. Section 7 does apply. The purchase is of stock, not assets, "but the situation involves no critical concentration of capital funds that opposition to the Federal Reserve Board is warranted." The Federal Reserve Board found that alternative services are available. Farmers now owns only 10 percent of the stock. No action, but "watch."

399. Inland Steel Co.

Allied Structural Steel Co. (1/19/60)

MARKET: Structural steel

OUTCOME: Clearance denied 6/29/60 and merger abandoned.

400. Falstaff Brewing Co., Inc.

Miller Brewing Co. (1/29/60)

MARKET: Beer and ale

OUTCOME: File closed 3/1/60. In reply to Justice Department's letter of inquiry, the "reports are without substance."

401. Wachovia Bank & Trust Co. of Greensboro, N.C.

Guaranty Bank & Trust Co. [Greensville, N.C.] (2/12/60)

MARKET: Consolidation of two North Carolina banks

OUTCOME: File closed 3/22/60. There is no competition between the two companies since branches of both are not in the same city. The only way to touch it is with the Sherman Act — but the merger results in little real percentage increase in the market share throughout North Carolina.

402. Brunswick-Balke-Collender Co.

Sheridan Catheter & Instrument Corp. (3/31/60)

MARKET: Diversified manufacturer (Brunswick), small mechanical and surgical equipment manufacturer (Sheridan)

OUTCOME: File closed 4/5/60. Of no interest to the Justice Department since there is no competition between the two companies.

Brunswick-Balke-Collender Co.

Bowl-Mor (3/2/60)

MARKET: Bowling pinspotter machine makers

OUTCOME: After the standard letter of inquiry from the Justice Department and an investigation was authorized to uncover all facts, merger plans were dropped.

403. Prudential Life Insurance Co.
  Fireman's Fund Insurance (3/9/60)
    MARKET: Insurance
    OUTCOME: The merger plans were dropped. (No date)

404. American Cable & Radio Corp.
  Globe Wireless, Ltd. (2/26/60)
    MARKET: Communications manufacture
    OUTCOME: File closed 4/27/60. Clayton Act exempts acquisitions approved by FCC. Also, Globe is a failing company and a noncommunications carrier purchaser could not be found. "Therefore we won't object to the transfer."

405. International Harvester Co.
  Solar Aircraft Co. (3/9/60)
    MARKET: Missile and aircraft components, gas turbine engines
    OUTCOME: File closed 10/25/61. There is no competition between the two companies: Solar is a small factor in the military craft and missile field. Solar's gas turbine motor is complementary. It is hoped that the motor can be developed by International Harvester's superior resources.

406. American Auto Accessories Stores, Inc.
  Dean Phipps Stores, Inc. (3/16/60)
    MARKET: Retail chain store dealing in household goods, hardware and auto accessories (Phipps)
    OUTCOME: File closed 8/10/60. In larger towns the companies compete with Sears and Montgomery-Ward. Only in the automotive area do the two compete with each other. Phipps is not in "robust health"—its earnings have been down since Mr. Phipps died. It suffered its first loss in 1956. There would be a difficulty in defining a line of commerce. The lines were due to variety of product sold. If wide enough, their sales would be a small percentage of total industry sales. Therefore, there is little competition between the two.

407. Papercraft Corp.
  LaPage [division of Johnson & Johnson]. (3/17/60)
    MARKET: [See Outcome]
    OUTCOME: File closed 5/6/60 because Papercraft makes and sells decorative paper foil ribbons and tags; Le

Page makes pressure-sensitive tapes and glue. The acquisition will enhance competition.

408. Pendleton Tool Industries
Vicheck Tool Co. (3/3/60)
MARKET: Mechanics' hand tools
OUTCOME: File closed 7/30/62. "We could not dissolve them now if we wanted to." "There are a lot of companies in the tool field. There have been no complaints up to now."

409. Fidelity Baltimore National Bank & Trust Co.
Maryland Trust Co. of Baltimore (3/4/60)
MARKET: Baltimore banking
OUTCOME: The merger by asset acquisition was consummated on 6/24/60. The Antitrust Division considered attacking the merger on Sherman Act Section 1 grounds, but nothing substantive appears to have been done after 8/1/60.

410. Raymond International, Inc.
Western Concrete Pipe Co. [interest in] (3/18/60)
MARKET: Concrete pipes and conduits
OUTCOME: File closed 7/25/60 as Justice Department turns the case to the FTC to be part of their inquiry into acquisitions in the concrete pipe field.

411. Inspiration Consolidated Copper Co.
International Smelting & Refining Co. (3/18/60)
MARKET: Copper smelting
OUTCOME: Inspiration (28.17 percent owned by Anaconda Corp.) planned to buy a smelter from International (100 percent owned by Anaconda). Although several in the Antitrust Division wanted to attack Anaconda's holdings on the basis of the Du Pont-General Motors decision, nothing was done in this area, and on 9/1/64, the Division decided to take no action on the sale itself.

412. Ingersoll Rand Co.
Black & Decker Mfg. Co. (3/29/60)
MARKET: Hand and machine tools
OUTCOME: File closed 8/24/60. In reply to the standard letter of inquiry by the Justice Department, the companies say that they "will advise before anything is consummated." Nothing further transpired.

413. Chicago Title & Trust Co.
    Kane County Title Co. (3/29/60)
        MARKET: Title guarantee, abstract of title, trust and escrow
        OUTCOME: Chicago had a long list of acquisitions, and in 1962, the Justice Department attacked it for its takeover of Kansas City Title Insurance Co. On 5/23/66, the action was terminated by a consent judgment in which Chicago agreed to divest itself of five small title companies.

414. Republic Aviation Corp.
    Fokker Aircraft Co. [one-third interest] (3/22/60)
        MARKET: Aircraft construction
        OUTCOME: File closed 8/8/60. As part of the agreement, Republic has right to acquire no more than 49 percent. Fokker has licensed Fairchild Aviation to make its turboprop planes and Republic does not make those. Therefore, the purchase will have no significant effect on vertical or horizontal competition.

415. Rockwell Standard Corp.
    Murray Co. (3/23/60)
        MARKET: Auto parts and hangers
        OUTCOME: File closed 4/5/60. After the standard letter of inquiry, Rockwell Standard replied in a letter to the Antitrust Division, "The negotiations have ceased and no further ones are expected—but we will inform you if so."

416. J.P. Stevens, Inc.
    Exposition Cotton Mills Co. (1/12/60)
        MARKET: Textiles
        OUTCOME: File closed 8/16/60. Stevens had been selling agent for Exposition, and the customers had bought other Stevens lines. The purchase maintains the status quo and protects the Stevens position. Also Exposition is very small.

417. J. J. Newberry Co.
    Hested Stores Co. (3/29/60)
        MARKET: Variety chain
        OUTCOME: File closed 6/31/61 [sic], based on memo dated 6/27/60. There are only two cities where direct competition exists between the companies. Where there is only one variety store there is a natural

monopoly as the town would not support two. Where there are other variety stores, there is competition. Therefore there is no elimination of competition.

418. Great Western Malting Co.
California Malting Co. (4/1/60)
MARKET: Malt
OUTCOME: File closed 4/8/65. If the market is California, they do not compete; if it is regional, the merger gives the companies a better chance to compete with Froedent Malt which had acquired Bauer Schweitzer, "We took no action here, therefore to act would be to stop a smaller entity when we did nothing against a larger one." (Some of the material is filed in no. 532)

419. Flintkote Co.
Harry T. Campbell Sons Corp. (4/1/60)
[All material in no. 309.]

420. American Biltrite Rubber Co.
National Shoe Products Corp. (4/7/60)
MARKET: Rubber soles
OUTCOME: File closed 6/13/60. There is no horizontal or vertical relationship between the two companies. Merger will help American to capitalize on National's consumer acceptance. Competitors make over 80 percent of sales. The transaction will strengthen competition.

421. American Greetings Corp.
Ostrander-Sams Corp. (4/11/60)
MARKET: Greeting cards
OUTCOME: File closed 4/20/60. FTC is working on the merger already, so the file is turned over to them.

422. McGraw Edison Co.
American Laundry Machines Co. (4/19/60)
MARKET: Laundry machines
OUTCOME: File closed 3/25/65. "Material promising but the investigation is old and has low priority."

423. Hunt Foods & Industries
Wesson Oil & Snowdrift Co., Inc. (4/20/60)
MARKET: Cottonseed oil (Wesson)
OUTCOME: File closed 8/10/61. Justice Department memo on 8/25/60 states, "The merger would have little

effect on competition," but the file was not closed for nearly one more year.

424. Suburban Gas Service, Inc.
American Laundry Calor Gas Co.
Various liquid propane gas plants in Washington and Oregon
13 liquid propane gas plants in Arizona (4/15/60)
MARKET: Liquid propane gas production and distribution
OUTCOME: A complaint was filed on 7/11/61, alleging that all the acquisitions tended to lessen competition and to create a monopoly. The case was disposed of on 9/17/62 by a consent decree providing for divestiture of Calor and three small companies in Oregon and Washington.

425. Twentieth Century Film Corp.
Skiatron of America [equity interest in]
[Metro Goldwyn Mayer Corp. to negotiate purchase of an interest in the company] (4/25/60)
MARKET: Special TV systems and radar products
OUTCOME: File closed 1/23/61. Negotiations fall through, partially because of antitrust interest.

426. Standard Oil of California
Standard Oil of Kentucky (4/21/60)
MARKET: Oil and gasoline products in southeastern United States
OUTCOME: Clearance denied 7/11/60 because merger would foreclose competition. On 6/5/61, despite the "surprise of Standard Oil of New Jersey" (*Wall Street Journal*, 6/7/61), the Department of Justice agreed to the merger if:
1) KYSO terminated its contract to buy 80 percent of its petroleum products from Standard of Jersey
2) KYSO agreed not to purchase any products from Standard of Jersey in its 11-state market after 7/11/66,
3) there be no allocation of sales territories.
According to Robert Kennedy, the rationale for allowing the merger was that it was expected that Standard of Jersey would enter the market with its own distributor. Thus, even though increasing concentration would result, the ensuing competition would more than offset the disadvantages.

427. Neptune Meter Co.
     Power Equipment Co. (4/22/60)
     MARKET: Electronic or magnetic amplifiers, D-C power
                supplies for specific applications (Power)
     OUTCOME: File closed 5/9/60. After standard letter of inquiry
                from the Justice Department, the proposal was
                withdrawn.

428. First Bank Stock Corp.
     Eastern Heights State Bank of St. Paul (4/5/60)
     MARKET: Twin Cities banking
     OUTCOME: Merger denied by the Federal Reserve Board after
                protest by Justice Department (4/22/60)

429. E.J. Gallo
     Pio, Inc.
     Melody Hill, Inc.
     RWL Wine & Liquor Co. (3/29/60)
     MARKET: Bottler (Pio), distributors (Melody and RWL)
     OUTCOME: File closed 10/5/61. Since they have been tolerant
                of other distributors and have not insisted on
                exclusivity of dealing, no Clayton Act coverage is
                possible.

430. American Hoist & Derrick Co.
     Industrial Brownhoist Co. (4/20/60)
     MARKET: Lifting equipment
     OUTCOME: The merger was consummated on 4/4/60 (In-
                dustrial Brownhoist was in financial difficulties),
                and no further action was taken.
     Ohio Locomotive Crane Co.
     Wellman Engineering Co. [locomotive crane business] (9/8/60)
     MARKET: Lifting equipment
     OUTCOME: File closed 7/26/61, despite Chicago office
                protests, because no effective relief was possible,
                there was a delay in the case, customers have had
                no problems, and "Chicago can't handle
                everything."

431. National Gypsum Co.
     Union Gypsum Co. (4/15/60)
     [Also see no. 273]
     MARKET: Gypsum and cement
     OUTCOME: File closed 2/10/61. There is no horizontal
                competition. Neither is a supplier or customer of
                the other. It is a conglomerate merger; tile,

cement, gypsum are separate products and ownership in one does not help in other fields.

432. Marine Midland Corp. [via subsidiary Marine Midland Trust Co.]
   Windsor National Bank (9/13/60)
   MARKET: Western New York banking
   OUTCOME: File closed 8/30/60. It is an asset acquisition. Therefore there is no Clayton Act coverage and no probable substantial competitive effects. According to the Justice Department, "We are not strong enough here for a test case."

433. Sperry Rand [via Remington-Rand]
   Clary Corp. [adding machines and cash register business]
   MARKET: Office machines
   OUTCOME: On 10/21/60, the Justice Department recommended action against the merger, but no action was taken because the adding machine division was allegedly losing money. In 1964, the Justice Department considered taking action again, but decided not to because divestiture was impracticable and the possibility of adequate relief had been frustrated.

434. Texas Industries, Inc.
   J.C. Brownell [Irving Concrete Div.] (4/12/60)
   MARKET: Concrete
   OUTCOME: File closed 11/21/60 because the companies represent an insignificant percentage of cement business (3.7 percent). The market is the Dallas area where there is competition. Also, Texas is not in the cement business—except for one subsidiary.

435. Borg-Warner Corp.
   Elgin Metalformers Corp. (5/10/60)
   MARKET: Metal cabinets for electronic installations (Elgin)
   OUTCOME: File closed 7/20/60. There is no competition between them.

   Borg-Warner Corp.
   Brummer Seal, Inc. (no date)
   MARKET: Engine seals
   OUTCOME: Merger consummated in 1960 (*Standard and Poor's*) with no Justice Department opposition.

436. Emerson Electric Co.
   Day Brite Lighting, Inc. (4/20/60)
   MARKET: Lighting fixtures

OUTCOME: File closed 12/15/60. A bona fide attempt at diversification. Where there is overlap in products, most of Emerson's output is sold to Sears.

437. Nationwide Check Co.

Money Order Corp. of America (3/17/60)

MARKET: Money transmission

OUTCOME: Companies are so small that they are not even listed in *Poor's Register*.

438. Cleveland Cliff's Iron [acquisition of 50 percent interest in iron properties held by]

Thompson-Lundmark Gold Mines

Quebec Cobalt & Exploration (4/19/60)

MARKET: Iron ore properties

OUTCOME: According to Cleveland Cliffs, it never sought to own either company, but it did "[acquire] an undivided, partial interest in some mining claims from a company, who leased the property from Quebec Cobalt." After a length of time, the lease was terminated (S.R. Curtis, secretary and resident counsel of Cleveland Cliffs to author, 12/10/74).

439. Anthony Pools, Inc.

Swimming Pool Supply & Engineering Co. of Los Angeles (5/11/60)

MARKET: Swimming pools

OUTCOME: File closed 6/10/60. The acquisition is insignificant. Swimming Pool makes $400,000 in sales per year.

440. Vermont Marble Co.

Gray Knox Marble Co. [of TN] (5/6/60)

MARKET: Marble quarries and processing

OUTCOME: File closed 1/2/62. Gray Knox's owners are old and its sales are falling. Vermont needed their type of marble. Their "counsel did not understand the Clayton Act and was surprised at our interest." The industry is declining and is not that important. It would be difficult to define a line of commerce.

441. Lockheed Aircraft Corp.

Grand Central Rocket Co. [50 percent interest]

Lockheed and Petroleum Chemical Co., [which own the rest of the company will operate it jointly.] (3/17/60)

MARKET: Aerospace

OUTCOME: File closed 7/21/60. No reason to go further. Lockheed's food machinery and chemical corporation has a 50 percent interest in Petrotex. Lockheed's other rocket work is with solid propellants.

442. West Virginia Pulp & Paper, Inc.
United States Envelope Co.
Virginia Folding Box Co. (5/16/60)
MARKET: Paper products
OUTCOME: On 5/24/60, West Virginia acquires Virginia Folding Box Co; and on 8/25/60, it acquires U.S. Envelope and no further action is taken. West Virginia is now known as Westvaco Corp.

443. BancOhio Corp.
Hilliard Bank (4/1/60)
MARKET: Columbus-based bank holding company (BancOhio)
OUTCOME: On 4/10/61, the Board of Governors of the Federal Reserve Board denied the request to merge. A large part of their order used the material supplied by the Antitrust Division in their opposition to the takeover.

444. Chesapeake & Ohio Railroad
Baltimore & Ohio Railroad (5/27/60)
MARKET: Mid-Atlantic states railroading
OUTCOME: Justice Department felt that the proposed merger "raises substantial questions of an antitrust nature." The Interstate Commerce Commission ruled favorably and stock exchange was effected. By 1964 C&O controlled 90 percent of B&O stock.

445. Black & Decker Mfg. Co.
De Walt, Inc. [div. of American Machine & Foundry] (5/27/60)
MARKET: Power tools
OUTCOME: File closed 7/11/61. The companies are involved in different but related lines of commerce. Therefore, a case would be a problem for us, especially because each has too small a portion of the market.

446. King-Seeley Corp.
American Thermos Products Co. (5/20/60)
MARKET: Automotive gauges, fans and iron castings (King-

Seeley), vacuum insulated containers (American Thermos)

OUTCOME: Merger consummated 11/9/60. No further Justice Department action.

447. American Metal Climax Co.
Pyron Corp. (5/18/60)
MARKET: Hydrogen iron powders (Pyron)
OUTCOME: File closed 8/5/60. Other steel companies have like subsidiaries. Therefore there would be no competitive advantage for either.

448. United Aircraft Corp.
Hiller Aircraft Corp. (6/1/60)
MARKET: Aircraft construction
OUTCOME: File closed 8/30/60. When the requested clearance was not forthcoming, the merger plans were "suspended."

449. Changed to no. 53.

450. Turpentine & Rosin Factors, Inc. [via Nelio Resins, Inc.]
Gum Naval Stores [div. of Glidden Corp.] (5/12/60)
MARKET: Naval stores
OUTCOME: File closed 6/27/61. "Together the two companies are insignificant factors."

451. [Changed to 60-111-58]
First National Bank of Portland
First National Bank of Bath (5/9/60)
MARKET: Maine banking
OUTCOME: The Justice Department reported to the Controller of the Currency that the takeovers would have little detrimental effect on competition.

452. Reliance Varnish Co.
Coast Paint & Lacquer Co. (5/13/60)
MARKET: Paints and varnish
OUTCOME: On 6/1/60 the purchase took place for $1.7 million. The implication is that the two factors were insignificant in the industry, and the merger would have no effects whatsoever.

453. General Instrument Co.
General Transistor Co. (5/25/60)
MARKET: Semiconductors
OUTCOME: File closed 12/5/61. "The merger can be viewed as one between two companies each with small market shares in different branches of an industry

neither of which offered a strong program for developing new products or marketing present lines." Therefore the merger strengthens competition. Also there has been no opposition from competitors.

454. Spencer Chemical Co.
    Pittsburgh & Midway Coal Mining Co. (5/23/60)
        MARKET: Chemicals (Spencer), coal mining (Pittsburgh & Midway)
        OUTCOME: File closed 10/7/60. The two companies had had preexisting relationships dating back to 1911. Had they not already existed, the reciprocal nature of the tie would have been the basis of opposition.

455. Rapid American Corp. [via McCrory-McLellan Stores Corp.]
    H.L. Green Co. (6/58)
    Lerner Stores
    Spartans Industries
        MARKET: Variety stores (Green); women's and children's wear (Lerner); discount hard, soft and white goods (Spartans)
        OUTCOME: Although on 9/6/60 the Antitrust Division felt that the tie between McCrory and Green increased the market share in the variety store line of commerce and eliminated competition enough to embark upon a full-scale investigation, on 7/23/63, the inquiry was closed because "Rapid American has lost much of its steam." Citing the facts that there had been a net loss the previous year, and that the Spartans merger had been abandoned, the Division allowed the Green and Lerner acquisitions to remain unscathed.

456. Weyerhaeuser Co.
    Roddis Plywood Corp. (6/7/60)
        MARKET: Lumbering
        OUTCOME: File closed 6/10/60. The investigation was turned over to the FTC.

457. Automatic Canteen Co. of America
    One Thousand Corp. (2/12/60)
    A.B.T. Mfg. Co. [div. of Atwood Mfg.] (6/24/60)
    Nationwide Food Services (2/7/60)
    Hubshman Factors Corp. (10/10/60)
        MARKET: Vending machines

OUTCOME: File closed 7/20/60. The investigation was turned over to the FTC.

458. Maremont Corp.
Saco-Lowell Corp. (no date)
MARKET: Exhaust parts (Maremont), mufflers (Saco-Lowell)
OUTCOME: According to Robert Bicks, Maremont purchased 27 percent of Saco's stock with the intent of eliminating competition. Therefore, two cases were filed: one on 6/23/60 (dismissed 8/15/60 for lack of jurisdiction), the other on 12/9/60 in a different district court. In the first case, the government prayed for divestiture of all stock interest in Saco, while in the second, the government wanted Saco to divest itself of all assets used to manufacture automobile mufflers. In a consent judgment filed 12/9/60, Saco agreed to the government's wish and started to search for a buyer. When none could be found, on 1/2/63 it was relieved of the divestiture obligation.

459. Northern Electric Co.
Power Equipment Co. (no date)
MARKET: Power Equipment sells a sizable percentage of its output to IBM on a cost-plus basis; Northern Electric furnishes telephone supplies to independent telephone companies.
OUTCOME: File closed 9/8/60. The two companies do not compete and they purchase from 20 different companies. There is no tendency to monopolize.

460. Hibbard, Spencer, Bartlett & Co.
Buhl & Sons (5/19/60)
MARKET: Hardware wholesaling
OUTCOME: File closed 8/26/60. Although Hibbard wholesales hardware in 16 states, including Michigan, and Buhl wholesales in Michigan, the latter has been losing money and there are 32 other wholesalers in the area.

461. Richardson Co.
Plastics Corp. of America (3/2/60)
MARKET: Laminated and molded plastics
OUTCOME: File closed 5/19/60. There never was any competition between the two companies. Both are

very small. Richardson never bought Plastics' products. Richardson has diversified a great deal.

462. Midwest Piping Co.
Flori Pipe Co.
Houston Pipe & Steel Co.
T.T.S. Metal Products, Inc. (5/26/60)
MARKET: Piping
OUTCOME: File closed 10/16/61. Flori was a failing company, and had it not been acquired by Midwest (from Sparton Corp.) Flori "would not exist today" (10/16/61). In closing the file, no mention was made of Houston Pipe or T.T.S. Metal.

463. Columbian Carbon Co.
Ander Chemical Co. (6/2/60)
MARKET: Chemicals, petroleum, paint, gases, inks (Columbian); inks (Ander)
OUTCOME: File closed 6/6/60. Matter turned over to the FTC.

464. H.K. Porter Co.
Allied Paint Mfg. Co. (6/3/60)
MARKET: Paints
OUTCOME: File closed 8/26/60. The merger is part of Porter's diversification plans. It will not lessen competition.

465. International Latex Corp. [div. of Stanley Warner Corp.]
Sarong, Inc. (5/23/60)
MARKET: Girdles (Sarong), rubberized products and undergarments (International Latex)
OUTCOME: Merger is consummated. All other material, including rationale for allowing the action, is missing from file.

466. John B. Stetson Co.
Frank H. Lee Co. (5/25/60)
MARKET: Hats
OUTCOME: Lee owners want to sell out and Stetson will buy. Lee is a failing company. Bicks verbally promises he will not sue (7/19/60).

467. Glass-Tite Industries, Inc.
Advanced Vacuum Products, Inc. [div. of Indiana General Corp.] (6/13/60)
MARKET: Hermetic seals for semiconductors and aircraft

(Glass-Tite), magnets and vacuum seals (Advanced)

OUTCOME: File closed 7/12/61. There is no horizontal competition and both companies do a low volume of business.

468. American Seal-Kap Corp.
Potlatch Forest, Inc. [container business]
Herz Mfg. Corp. (8/19/60)
MARKET: Containers and caps
OUTCOME: File closed 5/12/61. No reason for action. Potlatch's division was losing money; the Antitrust Division did not object to American Can Company's acquisition of Dixie; American Seal-Kap will still be small. The takeovers will lead to more competition.

469. General Steel Castings Corp.
St. Louis Car Co. [sale of assets] (7/1/60)
MARKET: Metal fabrication
OUTCOME: Transaction completed. No further material in the files.

470. GIT Financial Corp.
Home Finance Service Corp. (5/25/60)
MARKET: Financial services
OUTCOME: File closed 12/28/60. Home is a very small company and the competition between the two companies is minimal.

471. Stauffer Chemical Co.
American Synthetic Rubber Co. (7/7/60)
MARKET: Joint venture to make synthetic rubber (American Rubber & Chemical Co.)
OUTCOME: File closed 12/29/60. This is not significant enough to make it "an attractive Section 7 opportunity." There are other much larger joint ventures.

472. Minerals & Chemicals Corp. of America
Philipp Bros., Inc.
Philipp Bros. Ore Co. (5/2/60)
MARKET: Import and export of ores (Minerals & Chemicals), Fuller's Earth (Philipp Bros., Inc.)
OUTCOME: File closed 5/25/60. Products of the companies are not competitive nor will there be any foreclosure of the market to any.

473. Phillips Petroleum Co.
   Union Oil Co. of California—See Chapter VI

474. Inland Steel Products Co. [subsidiary of Inland Steel Co.]
   Steelcraft Mfg. Co. (7/21/60)
   MARKET: Steel products
   OUTCOME: Acquisition consummated (no date) and there is
              no further action by the Justice Department.

475. The Koppers Co.
   United States Hammered Piston Ring Co. (6/9/60)
   MARKET: Pistons and related products
   OUTCOME: Clearance granted 7/26/60. Hammered Piston is
              in bad financial shape; its operations are limited; it
              has no hope of diversification, and no other
              company than Koppers would buy it.

476. Textron, Inc.
   Cleveland Pneumatic Industries (6/8/60)
   MARKET: Gears, pumps, aircraft parts (defense-oriented)
   OUTCOME: This takeover leads to a survey of Textron's
              acquisitions to see if they violate the antitrust laws.
              Cleveland is not acquired because its stockholders
              do not accept the offer. The Textron inquiry dies
              slowly, the last memo being dated 2/1/61.

477. Changed to no. 476.

478. Dan River Mills [via Iselin Jefferson Co., Inc.]
   Jacob S. Bernheimer & Bros., Inc. (7/28/60)
   MARKET: Textiles
   OUTCOME: File closed 12/14/60. Bernheimer principally
              converts or finishes cotton goods. Dan River
              needs a converter and Bernheimer is very small.
              The merger is probably beyond the reach of the
              antitrust laws.

479. AP Parts Corp.
   Heckethorn Mfg. & Supply Co. (7/26/60).
   MARKET: Seat cushions and shock absorbers (Heckethorn),
              exhaust-system parts (AP)
   OUTCOME: File closed 12/6/60 since there seems to be no
              vertical foreclosure. [Much of the material is
              misfiled in no. 478.]

480. Universal Container Corp.
   Six small barrel-reconditioning firms (7/29/60)
   MARKET: Containers
   OUTCOME: None. Material missing.

481. Tennessee Gas Transmission Corp.
   Renwar Oil Corp. (7/21/60)
      MARKET: Oil exploration (Renwar)
      OUTCOME: File probably closed, but no documentation
                 thereof. The subject too small for action.
                 Tennessee itself is a minor factor in the oil
                 industry.

482. Humble Oil Co.
   Monterey Oil Co. (6/9/60)
      MARKET: Crude petroleum and petroleum products
      OUTCOME: Clearance denied 12/13/60 but merger takes place
                 with no further Justice Department opposition.
                 Robert Bicks wrote to Sen. Estes Kefauver
                 (12/13/60), explaining that Monterey was very
                 small, was operating in only two states, and had
                 less than 1 percent of the market. Monterey's total
                 production was sold to the majors anyway. It had
                 long-term contracts in the natural gas business,
                 therefore there were no foreclosures possible; thus
                 it would not lessen competition, and besides "we
                 felt we would not win."

483. Changed to no. 522
484. Rexall Drug & Chemical Corp.
   Kraloy Plastic (1957)
   Granada Corp.
   Tupper Corp.
   Chippewa Plastics
   E-Z Packaging Co.
   E & A Plastic Fillings
   Chemtrol Corp.
   Injection Moulding Co. (7/1/60)
      MARKET: Plastics
      OUTCOME: File closed 11/23/60. None of the companies is
                 sufficiently big to warrant action, and one of them
                 was failing.

485. Allied Chemical Corp.
   American Potash & Chemical Corp. (8/16/60)
      MARKET: Chemicals
      OUTCOME: File closed 8/18/60. After receiving the standard
                 letter of inquiry from the Justice Department, the
                 companies stated the merger idea had been
                 dropped.

486. Lamb Industries Corp.
  Thomson Mfg. Co., Inc.
  B.C. Thomson, Inc.
  Hurrycane Harvesting
  Teche Tractor (1/60)
    MARKET: See Outcome
    OUTCOME: File closed 10/18/60. The companies are so small they are not even in directories. The acquired companies are in sugar cane harvesting and Lamb makes vacuum cleaners, water heaters, and products for the home. The companies acquired are still one-tenth the size of the biggest factory in the sugar harvesting industry.

487. Highway Trailer Industries, Inc.
  Weber Trailer & Mfg. Co. (7/29/60)
    MARKET: Trailer construction
    OUTCOME: File closed 4/6/61. Weber is closely held and the owner is over 65. The company has lost money and there is no way to restore the business. It needs a capital infusion. Together Highway and Weber have a small percentage of the market.

488. Motor Wheels Corp.
  Foreman Mfg. Co. (8/25/60)
    MARKET: Motor Wheels manufactures wheels and drums for mobile home assemblies, and Foreman uses them in its construction.
    OUTCOME: File closed 2/12/61. There appears to be a violation here but "we can't win the suit"; "We can't restore Foreman" (2/9/61). There is a lot of competition from large companies.

489. Anderson Prichard Oil Co. [sale of assets]
  Brookston Oil Co.
  Apco Oil Corp.
  Union Texas Natural Gas Corp. (9/7/60)
    MARKET: Petroleum products
    OUTCOME: The assets were sold to two newly formed companies: Brookston and Apco, as well as to Union Texas.

490. G.B. Macke Corp.
  29 acquisitions (8/10/60)
    MARKET: Vending machines
    OUTCOME: File closed 11/29/61 and turned over to the FTC for its vending-machine investigation.

491. American Radiator & Standard Sanitary Corp.
    Rochester Mfg. Co., Inc. (9/14/60)
        MARKET: Temperature and pressure gauges and warning devices.
        OUTCOME: Acquisition consummated 5/5/61.

492. McKay Machine Co.
    Federal Machine & Welder Co. (9/13/60)
        MARKET: Welding equipment and tire chains (McKay), resistance welders, mechanical power presses (Federal)
        OUTCOME: File closed 10/21/60. While there is a little competition between two subsidiaries of the two companies, it is not substantially affected and their competitors are bigger.

493. Dow Chemical Co.
    Allied Laboratories (9/14/60)
        MARKET: Veterinary pharmaceutical drugs (Allied)
        OUTCOME: On 4/20/61 the Antitrust Division decided to adjourn the case for a year to find out the effects on the smaller manufacturers. Eight months later the case was closed (12/13/61).

494. Glen Alden Corp.
    Hudson Coal Co. (9/15/60)
        MARKET: Coal
        OUTCOME: File closed 10/20/60. While this will lead to more concentration in the coal industry, Hudson is a failing company. Therefore no action for the time being.

495. Flintkote Co.
    Sealzit Co. of America (8/12/60)
        MARKET: Spray gun for glass fibre and resin coating (Sealzit)
        OUTCOME: Memo (no date): "We are having trouble developing a case." There is no further material in the file.

496. Minnesota Mining & Mfg. Co.
    Warner Lambert Pharmaceutical Co. (9/7/60)
        MARKET: MMM owns Mutual Broadcasting and General Outdoor Advertising, among other companies. Proprietary drugs (Warner Lambert)
        OUTCOME: Merger clearance denied because it would give Warner Lambert a decisive competitive advantage in advertising its products. In March 1961 the

companies announced that they had dropped their plans.

497. Continental Oil Co.
Pyramid Oil Co. (9/16/61)
MARKET: Petroleum products distribution (Pyramid)
OUTCOME: Pyramid has seven out of 957 stations in the Kansas City area and has a declining income. Continental will sell two of the seven stations. Pyramid has sold products under Continental's label for 30 years. Pyramid's chief wants to retire. Therefore file closed 11/30/60 but "use material in the International Refineries and Malco cases."

498. Changed to no. 547

499. Coca-Cola Co.
Minute Maid Co. (9/13/60)
MARKET: Soft drinks and juices
OUTCOME: Thurmond Arnold persuaded the Antitrust Division that the two companies were not competitive. It appears that in late 1960 there was an investigation into the anti-competitive aspects of the merger, but there was no follow-up. On 2/20/63, the file was officially closed.

500. Ryder Systems, Inc.
Yellow Rental, Inc.
Baker Truck Rental
Lincoln Transport System, Inc. [Truck leasing assets only]
Columbia Truck Leasing Cos. [in six different states]
Indiana Truck Leasing Corp.
Barrett Garages, Inc.
Motorent, Inc.
U-Drive-It Co.
Truck Leasing Corp.
Truck Maintenance, Inc.
Russell M. Young, Inc.
Mountain States Truck Lease, Inc.
Monumental Truck Rental
Barrett Truck Leasing
MARKET: Truck renting and leasing
OUTCOME: The Justice Department attacked Ryder Corp. for the series of acquisitions which lessened competition and tended toward monopoly in a complaint filed 10/3/60. On 6/15/61, the case was ter-

minated by the entry of a consent judgment in which Ryder agreed to divest itself of a specified number of trucks in five cities. On 8/7/62, the judgment was modified, reducing the number of trucks to be divested and lengthening the period of time to fulfill the agreement.

501. American Stores
Alpha Beta Food Markets (9/30/60)

MARKET: Supermarkets. American mainly in the East, Alpha Beta in the Los Angeles area.

OUTCOME: At first the Division viewed the case as a good one "to test the ability of the Department to successfully institute preliminary injunction proceedings" (Coyle to Whittinghill, 10/28/60), the rationale being the increasing concentration in food distribution. "Although Alpha is a major factor in the Los Angeles area, its percentage of sales is small, and it would be better to look at other more significant mergers in the industry" (Owens to Whittinghill, 12/15/60). File kept open until 12/29/69, but nothing of consequence was added.

502. General Telephone Corp.
General Cable Corp. [13.5 percent equity in] (7/26/60)

MARKET: Cable production

OUTCOME: General Telephone decided "to dispose of our holdings in General Cable . . . prior to the time that we were aware that the Department of Justice had any interest in our investment" (Theodore Brophy, president of General Telephone & Electronics Corp., to author, 1/28/75).

503. Simplex Wire & Cable Co.
Hitemp Wire, Inc. (10/14/60)

MARKET: Insulated wire

OUTCOME: The merger was ratified on 9/26/60. The last entry in the file is dated 4/26/61, but the file was not closed.

504. Harcourt Brace & Co.
World Book Co. (10/7/60)

MARKET: Publishing

OUTCOME: Clearance denied 11/18/60, but the merger is consummated on 12/30/60.

Crowell-Collier Publishing Co.

Macmillan Co. (11/1/60)

> MARKET: Publishing
>
> OUTCOME: Although the Justice Department opposed the merger in principle, it took no action; and the marriage was consummated on 12/13/60.

505. Standard & Poor's Corp.

Fitch Publishing Co. (10/11/60)

> MARKET: Financial publishing
>
> OUTCOME: Clearance granted 9/12/61. The merger was allowed because Fitch was a failing company.

506. Continental Oil Co.

Calvert Petroleum Co. (10/31/60)

> MARKET: Petroleum products
>
> OUTCOME: Although there is no material in the file indicating that the merger was cleared by the Justice Department, it appears that a verbal clearance was given 12/23/60.

507. Diversa, Inc.

Merritt Gas Co. (11/3/60)

> MARKET: Distribution of liquified petroleum gas
>
> OUTCOME: Diversa really wanted to acquire one of Merritt's facilities. No action was taken (1/27/61), and the merger was consummated.

508. Changed to No. 92

509. *Detroit News*

Detroit Times (11/9/60)

> MARKET: Detroit newspapers
>
> OUTCOME: File closed 1/24/61, because the *Times* is a failing company and the government would be unable to formulate effective relief.

510. [Changed to 60-358-112]

International Business Machines Corp.

Texas Instruments, Inc.

International Telephone & Telegraph Co. (11/10/60)

> MARKET: Transistors
>
> OUTCOME: Not a merger question, rather an inquiry into IBM's purchase of part of its transistor requirements from Texas and ITT. The inquiry was dropped 3/14/62 because while "both purchased items from Texas, many others had entered the

field of diodes and transistors since the contracts. Further, Texas has similar contracts with 14 other companies."

511. Marquette Cement Mfg. Co.
     National Cement Corp. (11/21/60)
     MARKET: Cement
     OUTCOME: File closed 12/13/60, because there is little competition between the two companies.
     Marquette Cement Mfg. Co.
     Green Bay Cement Co. [from Pittsburgh Coke & Chemical Co.] (no date)
     MARKET: Cement
     OUTCOME: File closed 1/15/61, because there is little competition between the two companies.

512. Burgemeister Brewing Corp.
     Joseph Schlitz Brewing Co.
     Miller Brewing Co. (no date)
     MARKET: Beer
     OUTCOME: According to the Justice Department card catalogue, Burgemeister was to be acquired by either Schlitz or Miller. The file has been lost.

513. Changed to no. 199

514. Ampex Corp.
     Telemeter Magnetics, Inc. (6/28/60)
     MARKET: Electronics (Ampex), memory components (Telemeter)
     OUTCOME: Telemeter, 75 percent owned by Paramount Pictures, is a very small company which is not in competition with Ampex. As a result of the merger, Paramount will own shares in Ampex; it already owns stock in Fairchild Camera & Instrument Corp. Ampex purchases semiconductors from Fairchild occasionally, but envisions no difficulties from the new interrelationship (9/27/60). File closed 4/9/65; last entry 6/61.

515. Purex Corp.
     Turco Products, Inc. (10/11/60)
     MARKET: Cleaning compounds
     OUTCOME: No action (4/13/61) taken against the merger because the two companies make different types of cleaning compounds, one for industry (Turco) and

the other for households (Purex). Were the companies larger, it is likely that the Justice Department would have developed a "cleaning compound" market; as it was, the two companies were minor factors anyway.

516. Avi-Sun Corp.
    Shin Nippon Chisso-Hiriyo, H.K. (11/29/60)
    MARKET: A technological agreement for importing and producing polypropane from Japan
    OUTCOME: No action taken (1/13/60) to halt the tie. The Justice Department believed that "Chisso won't go anywhere without this."

517. Koppers Co., Inc.
    Thomas Flexible Coupling Co. (12/6/60)
    MARKET: Flexible couplings [metal devices used in transmitting power by joining together rotating shafts] (Thomas)
    OUTCOME: The matter was first brought to the attention of the Justice Department by a disgruntled minority stockholder who had also filed suit claiming fraud by management in the negotiations for merger. The Antitrust Division prepared a complaint for filing on 1/16/61, but it did not receive the go-ahead until 2/16/61. On 1/24/62, the District Court ordered Koppers to dispose of Thomas as a working entity. Koppers appealed to the Supreme Court on 3/9/62 but filed a motion to dismiss the appeal after it sold Thomas to the Chain Belt Co. in September 1962.

518. *Albany Knickerbocker News*
    Albany Times Union (11/21/60)
    MARKET: Albany, New York, newspapers
    OUTCOME: The merger was not attacked (4/11/61) because *Knickerbocker* was losing a great deal of money.

519. Seagram & Sons, Inc.
    Jim Beam Distilling Co. (12/9/60)
    MARKET: Alcoholic beverages
    OUTCOME: After the standard letter of inquiry from the Justice Department, the merger plans were dropped.

520. Changed to no. 199.

521. Webcor, Inc.
    Dormeyer Corp. (12/21/60)
        MARKET: Sound systems and defense contracts (Webcor), small electrical appliances (Dormeyer)
        OUTCOME: The merger was consummated, and while the Justice Department file was not closed, there is no material therein dated later than 2/1/61, indicating that the antitrusters saw no future in the case.

522. Champion Paper & Fibre Co.
    Carpenter Paper Co. (No date)
        MARKET: Paper and paper products
        OUTCOME: After Champion had also acquired Whitaker Paper Co. and Sample-Durick Co., the Justice Department filed a complaint on 4/19/65 seeking divestiture of the three companies. On 8/28/68, the parties agreed to a consent decree in which Champion agreed to divest itself of a number of paper merchant houses with sales of at least $7.5 million. In July 1969, Carpenter Paper Co. of Nebraska was incorporated in order to acquire and operate nine wholesale paper distribution outlets previously owned by United States Plywood-Champion Papers, Inc. (the successor company, and now known as Champion International Corp.).

523. Pearl Brewing
    M.K. Goetz Brewing Co. (11/9/60)
        MARKET: Malt and hops beverages
        OUTCOME: File closed 10/17/61 because there was no competition between the two companies.

524. Varian Associates
    Eastern Industries, Inc. (11/14/60)
        MARKET: Microwave tubes and components, and radar equipment. (Varian), Radar and advanced control system equipment (Eastern)
        OUTCOME: No file entries suggesting course of action. Merger abandoned 1/28/61. On 3/14/61, Eastern was merged into Laboratory for Electronics, Inc.

525. Wilson Bros. [via Lawson Mfg. Co.]
    Clayton & Lambert Co. [Hoffman Water Heater Div.] (12/7/60)
        MARKET: Water heaters

OUTCOME: File closed 1/25/61. Hoffman is a failing company. Although Wilson has a history of acquisitions, "If anything, Wilson has acquired a group of failing companies and is creating a vital competitor to the industry."

526. [Changed to 60-153-10]
Standard Brands, Inc.
Planters Nut & Chocolate Co. (10/15/02)
MARKET Food products (Standard), peanuts and candy (Planters)
OUTCOME: In 1902 there was fear that Armour was monopolizing corn production, but no action was taken. On 8/25/53, Barnes requested an investigation of the yellow-corn-milling industry, but nothing came of it. The merger in question took place in 1961 after Standard Brands had privately bought a block of Planters stock in mid-1960. (All explanations missing.)

527. Jewel Tea Co.
Osco Drug Co. (1/9/61)
MARKET: Supermarkets (Jewel), drug stores (Osco)
OUTCOME: File closed 7/14/61. The relevant market shows little change in concentration.

528. Cheseborough Ponds, Inc.
Northam-Warren Co. (12/9/60)
MARKET: Manicure and toilet preparations (Northam)
OUTCOME: File closed 8/29/61 because we would have a "problem of defining markets."

529. Seaboard Airline Railroad Co.
Atlantic Coastline RR. Co. (12/23/60)
MARKET: Southeastern railroading
OUTCOME: On 7/1/67, the merger was consummated.

530. Von's Grocery Co.
Thriftimart, Inc.
Alexander's
Market Basket Supermarkets
Jerseymaid (11/1/60)
MARKET: California supermarkets purchasing dairy products from Jerseymaid
OUTCOME: Jerseymaid is a joint venture by the four supermarkets who purchase most of their dairy products from it. Additionally, it sells to other

> grocers. File closed 9/6/61 because Safeway Corp., the largest supermarket in the state, owns dairies and because there does not appear to be any interstate commerce.

531. C. Brewer & Co., Ltd.
    Fajardo Eastern Sugar Associates (11/18/60)
        MARKET: Sugar
        OUTCOME: File closed 5/5/61, because there is no lessening of competition in the industry.

532. Bauer-Schweitzer Malting Co.
    Charles Bach Malting Co. (10/27/60)
        MARKET: Malt
        OUTCOME: No memo closing the file. Bach was very small and inefficient and could not compete. After the merger Bach's old plant was closed and the business transferred to Bauer-Schweitzer. Even today it is small compared to its competitors (Dudley Seay, chairman of the board of Fleischmann Malting Co., Inc., which acquired Bauer-Schweitzer, to author, 1/29/75).

533. Southern Pacific Co.
    Western Pacific Railroad Co.
    Atchison, Topeka & Santa Fe Railway System (10/20/60)
        MARKET: Southwestern railroading
        OUTCOME: On 10/12/60, after purchasing 10 percent of the Western Pacific stock, SoPac applied to the ICC for permission to control Western by purchase or exchange of stock. Santa Fe countered by purchasing 20 percent and making a similar application. Although the Justice Department was interested, no action was taken before the change of administrations took place in 1961. Hearings before the ICC began on 7/17/61, and on 9/9/63, it recommended that Santa Fe be allowed to take control. This created such a furor that on 1/27/65 the ICC denied all applications for control of Western.

534. American Viscose Corp.
    Monsanto Chemical Co.
    Chemstrand Corp. (11/1/60)
        MARKET: Chemical textured fibres
        OUTCOME: American Viscose exchanged stock held in

Chemstrand for stock in Monsanto, enabling Monsanto to own 100 percent of Chemstrand. The file was closed in 1963 when FMC Corp. acquired all the assets of American Viscose.

535. File concerns a merger totally treated after the end of the Eisenhower Administration

536. Federated Dept. Stores [via Sanger's Dept. Stores]
A. Harris & Co. (1/17/61)
    MARKET: Dallas department stores
    OUTCOME: Merger cleared during the Kennedy years. "Harris is a failing company."

537. ⎫ File concerns a merger
538. ⎪ totally treated after
539. ⎬ the end of the Eisenhower
540. ⎭ Administration

541. Douglas Oil Co. of California
Continental Oil Co.
[All materials missing.]

542. Michigan Plating & Stamping Co.
Beard & Stone Electric Co. (12/60)
[surviving company Gulf and Western Corp.]
    MARKET: Auto bumpers and parts (Michigan), automotive electric systems (Beard)
    OUTCOME: From 1957 to 1962 G&W made 23 acquisitions—17 in auto-parts distribution. Few competed with each other and all were small, but there was a tendency for G&W to make increasingly larger acquisitions as it purchased New Jersey Zinc and Paramount Pictures. On 2/9/67, the Antitrust Division concluded that the series of acquisitions in the auto-parts field had been *pro*-competitive; on 3/8/67 the files were put into storage.

543. Texaco
Paragon Oil Co. (12/22/60)
    MARKET: Petroleum products
    OUTCOME: The merger was consummated June 1959. The Justice Department took no action after 12/22/60.

544. File concerns a merger totally treated after the end of the Eisenhower Administration

545. File concerns a merger totally treated after the end of the Eisenhower Administration

546. Electronic Specialty Co.
    D.S. Kennedy Co. (2/24/58)
        MARKET: Avionics, electronics, radar (Electronic) (Kennedy).
        OUTCOME: The merger was consummated in 3/61 but was not attacked because while both entities were in the microwave field, there were many competitors and the companies were small.

547. Liquidation of Honolulu Oil Corp. (12/2/60)
        MARKET: Petroleum products
        OUTCOME: The properties were sold chiefly to Tidewater Oil Co. and Pan American Petroleum Co. (owned by Standard Oil Co. of Indiana). The Justice Department filed a motion to halt the sale, but when it was dismissed, the liquidation was allowed to take place.

548. Parker-Hannifin Corp.
    Span Brass Mfg. Co.
    Spanco Brass Sales Co. (12/1/60)
        MARKET: Fittings for fluid systems
        OUTCOME: File closed 5/26/61 due to "lack of evidence to show that the acquisitions are illegal."

549. Dover Corp.
    OPW Corp. [privately owned] (3/8/60)
        MARKET: Gas nozzles
        OUTCOME: File closed 6/22/61. Sales are small. No action was taken in 1960.

1953 Annual Report of Assistant Attorney General, Stanley Barnes*

MEMORANDUM for the President and the Attorney General

Antitrust Enforcement Program for 1953

This report will review the activities of the Antitrust Division for the period from July 1, 1952 to June 30, 1953. While the Division continued during the year to concern itself with the special problems arising out of defense mobilization, the principal effort was directed toward the broader objectives of antitrust policy. This effort took the form of an expanding program of antitrust enforcement which had as its objective a well-rounded attack upon all phases of the national economic structure where restraints and monopolies were found. Special emphasis was placed on those situations which had the most substantial effect upon the public interest.

Perhaps the most significant development of the past year was the initial consideration given to methods of simplifying the administration of the antitrust laws, both procedurally and substantively, in order to facilitate the impartial and effective enforcement of those laws. With this objective in view, the Attorney General announced in late June a proposal to set up the "Attorney General's Committee to Study the Antitrust Laws," charged with the duty of considering and analyzing criticisms, suggestions and proposed procedures for the modernization and strengthening of the whole body of antitrust law. This committee, it is proposed, will attempt to clarify, possibly for congressional approval, an agreeable statement of national antitrust policy that will confirm the principles of private competitive enterprise, and in so far as possible, combine certainty with flexibility.

Enforcement of the Antitrust Laws

During the past year, the Antitrust Division filed a total of 32 cases, of which 15 were

---

* Typed copy in Justice Department Library, Washington, D.C. Starting in 1955, the report was published by the United States Government Printing Office.

civil actions. Within the same period, a total of 23 civil and 13 criminal cases were terminated, of which the Government won 31 and lost 5. At the close of the fiscal year there were 143 antitrust cases pending as against 147 pending at the beginning of the year.

There are presently being conducted 139 preliminary inquiries, 70 FBI investigations, and 13 grand jury investigations. Some of these inquiries and investigations relate to such important fields as housing, clothing and food. Others include such things as automobile distribution, gasoline, insurance, and newspapers.

Seventeen consent judgments were obtained in cases involving a variety of commodities such as electrical equipment, automobile financing, fish, denture plastic, flowers, hosiery, phonograph records, fluid milk, printers' rollers, ball bearings, outdoor advertising, plumbing and heating supplies, steel culverts, rolling mills and rolling mill machinery, watch cases and linen supplies.

The past year saw the institution of an unusually large number of major antitrust cases as well as several significant decisions by the Supreme Court and federal district courts.

Cases Filed During Year

Among the major cases filed during the year, two in particular attracted considerable public interest. The first involved *Standard Oil Company* (New Jersey) and four other major oil producers. The civil complaint charges a conspiracy beginning in 1928 to (a) secure and exercise control over foreign production and supplies of petroleum, (b) regulate imports in order to maintain a level of domestic and world prices agreed upon by defendants, and (c) divide world foreign producing and marketing territories. The complaint sets forth seventeen separate terms of the conspiracy and lists twenty-one contracts and agreements which allegedly were used to effect the conspiracy and monopolization.

The second such case was a civil action against the "Big Three" in soaps and detergents, *Proctor & Gamble, Colgate-Palmolive-Peet,* and *Lever Brothers.* That complaint alleges that the three companies have successfully sought to attain, maintain, augment and exploit positions of dominance over all others engaged in producing and selling household-soap and household-synthetic-detergents; it further alleges that the three companies have sought successfully to restrict and control competition among themselves and with others. The complaint also states that defendants have succeeded in selling at least 75 percent of the national sales of household-soap for the past twenty years and more than 90 percent of the national sales of the newer products, household-synthetic-detergents, during the past three years. The court is asked to split up each of the three companies into separate independent organizations so as to prevent continued monopolization and to restore competitive conditions.

In another major civil action brought against *Twentieth Century-Fox* and eleven other motion picture producers and distributors, the complaint alleges a conspiracy to prevent 16 mm. feature films from being exhibited so as to compete with established motion picture theatres. Defendants are charged specifically with refusing to allow television stations to exhibit 16 mm. feature films despite the wide demand for their use. They are further charged with refusal to permit the exhibition of such film within ten miles of an established theatre and the placing of severe limitations on exhibitions in schools, churches, hospitals and USO centers.

In the newspaper field, both a criminal and civil action were filed against the *Kansas City Star* and two of its officers. The indictment alleges that the *Star* has attempted to monopolize and has monopolized dissemination of news and advertising in the area. This was effected, it is charged, by forcing subscribers to subscribe to, and advertisers to advertise in, the *Times* and *Star* in combination. It is also alleged that advertisers were either prevented entirely from advertising in competing media or were prevented from using advertisements as large as they desired in such competing media because of threats by *Star* representatives. Discriminatory discounts and rates are alleged to have been given to persons using various combinations of defendants' newspapers, or advertising on defendants' radio station and in one of its publications. The indictment also charges that defendants refused television facilities to non-users of its newspapers. The civil complaint asks injunctive relief and the revocation of defendants' radio and television licenses.

Another civil case was filed against *American News Company*, which handles more than half of the magazines sold through national independent distributors, and its subsidiary, *Union News Company*, the world's largest operator of newsstands. Defendants are charged with an agreement whereby Union refuses to handle magazines, unless they are distributed by American, and discriminates in the sale and display of magazines which are exclusively distributed by American on a national basis. It is further charged that American uses this arrangement to induce publishers to enter into contracts giving to American exclusive national distribution rights, in order that the magazines of such publishers may be sold on Union newsstands.

Four cases involving labor unions were instituted during the year. One involved a local of the Milk Drivers and Dairy Employees Union, and charges price fixing and an attempt to monopolize the sale and distribution of milk in Minneapolis. A second was an indictment against Theatrical Drivers, Chauffeurs and Helpers Local 817 of the Teamsters Union for antitrust violations in the hauling of scenery and equipment used by theatres, motion picture producers and television stations in New York City. The third and fourth cases were civil actions against plastering and lathing local unions in Chicago, charging conspiracies to suppress competition among plastering and lathing contractors, to restrict and exclude persons from engaging in business, and to monopolize the installation of plastering and lathing materials in the Chicago area.

Investigations

Grand jury investigations were being conducted in several important fields at the close of the year. Among those is an investigation of the entire New England railroad system and two major bus lines. This investigation followed complaints that a New England railway had been forced to enter into illegal traffic agreements.

An investigation of the machine tool industry is continuing and it is possible that additional cases will be forthcoming. Two civil suits and one criminal case already have resulted from this investigation.

There is currently in progress an investigation of charges that newspaper feature syndicates have conspired with metropolitan newspapers to give such newspapers a monopoly of readership audiences in certain areas. This investigation also is expected to produce information relating to existing relationships between newspaper features syndicates and newspaper chains and to the licensing practice of such syndicates.

Another grand jury is investigating a possible conspiracy among the four largest manufacturers of lead pencils to fix and maintain prices on sales of pencils at wholesale, and to submit rigged bids on Government purchases.

Investigations of milk, electrical equipment, cigarette vending machines, linen supplies, school supplies and wool also are in progress.

In addition to the above-referred to grand jury investigations, some twenty summaries of suggested industrial surveys have been prepared as a basis for future investigations.

Cases Decided During Year

The most important antitrust case decided by the Supreme Court during the year was the *Times Picayune* case. A civil complaint was filed in 1950 charging that defendants had obtained a monopoly in the newspaper and advertising business in the New Orleans area through combination advertising sales, exclusive news vendors, and the subsidization of evening paper losses with morning paper income. The District Court found the defendants guilty. On appeal, the Supreme Court held that defendants, who publish both a morning and evening newspaper, had not violated the Sherman Act in refusing to sell certain types of advertising in one of the two papers only and in requiring advertisers to purchase such advertising in both papers as a unit. The Court, in a 5-4 decision, held (1) that defendants' advertising contracts did not constitute illegal "tying" agreements since the evidence did not show that the morning paper (the "tying" product) was "dominant" in the New Orleans advertising market; and (2) that such contracts had not otherwise unreasonably restrained trade since there had been no showing that such contracts had injuriously affected the competing New Orleans paper or that they had been adopted for that purpose. The court stated specifically that it was not passing upon the legality of similar advertising arrangements "in other circumstances or in other proceedings." A dissenting opinion by four justices held that "the Times Picayune enjoys a distinct, conceded and complete monopoly of access to the morning newspaper readers in the New Orleans area" and that the doctrine of the "tying" cases (*International Salt Co. v. U.S.*) was accordingly applicable.

The Supreme Court also passed upon three of the four cases constituting the first attempt by the Government to enforce Section 8 of the Clayton Act which forbids a person from holding at the same time directorships in two or more competing corporations if any one of the corporations has capital, surplus and undivided profits of more than $1,000,000. All three cases involved John M. Hancock, who at the same time served as a director of Kroger and Jewel Tea Company; as a director of W. T. Grant Company and S. H. Kress & Company; and as a director of Sears, Roebuck & Company and Bond Stores. Hancock resigned one of the directorates in each case after the filing of the suits. The district court granted defendants' motions to dismiss on the grounds that the resignations had rendered each of the cases moot. On the Government's appeal to the Supreme Court, that court held that the resignations did not render the cases moot, but that the district court had not been shown to have abused its discretion in determining that there was "no reasonable expectation" that defendants would renew their violation of the statute and hence that there was no need to award injunctive relief.

The fourth Clayton Act case concerned Sidney J. Weinberg who at the same time served as a director of Sears, Roebuck & Co. and B.F. Goodrich Company. The district court granted the Government's motion for summary judgment, ruling that Sears and Goodrich are competitors within the meaning of Section 8, and that the section forbids the holding of simultaneous directorates therein.

One of the most significant antitrust cases decided by a district court during the year was the *United Shoe Machinery* case. In a complaint filed in 1947, United was charged with monopoly in the manufacture of shoe machinery, shoe machinery parts and shoe factory supplies. The monopoly was alleged to have been acquired through acquisition of competitors by inducing competitors to use only certain types of machines and to distribute their machinery through United, by the misuse of patents, by preventing distribution of secondhand machinery, by requiring lessees to purchase from United all parts for shoe machinery leased by it, and by using its monopoly of shoe machinery to monopolize the distribution of shoe factory supplies. The complaint sought to compel United to sell all of its plants used in the manufacture of shoe factory supplies and some of its plants engaged in the manufacture of shoe machinery, and to require it to offer to sell its machinery to shoe manufacturers instead of leasing such machinery only. The prayer also asked that United be required to make available to its competitors all patents and know-how relating to shoe machinery.

The district court in a judgment entered in February of this year granted a substantial part of the relief sought by the Government. United is required to offer for sale each and every type of machine that it has heretofore leased. While the court declined to order divestiture of United's shoe machinery plants, it directed United to divest itself of certain branches and subsidiaries engaged in the manufacture of shoe factory supplies and to discontinue acting as distributor of other companies' supplies. The judgment also orders United to make its patents available upon a reasonable royalty basis to anyone desiring to manufacture shoe machinery and shoe factory supplies. United has noted an appeal to the Supreme Court.

Transportation Cases

The Antitrust Division also represents the interest of the United States in litigation arising under federal regulatory laws in the field of transportation and communication. During the past year, there were several important Supreme Court decisions in this field. In the *American Trucking Association* case, the Court sustained the validity of regulations of the Interstate Commerce Commission with respect to the leasing of motor vehicles by common carriers subject to Part II of the Interstate Commerce Act. In *King* v. *United States*, it upheld the validity of an ICC order requiring an increase in intrastate rates corresponding to the increase in interstate rates which the Commission had authorized in order to enable the railroads to obtain sufficient revenue to enable them to maintain an adequate national transportation system. In another case, *Baltimore & Ohio R. Co. v. United States*, an ICC order reducing certain freight rates was upheld by the Court against the claim that the prescribed rates were confiscatory.

The Division also successfully defended an order of the Civil Aeronautics Board requiring partners in an investment banking firm to cease and desist from maintaining directors on boards of airlines and airline equipment companies in violation of Section 409 of the Civil Aeronautics Act, even though no one partner was a director of more than one company subject to that section. (*Lehman Bros.* v. *Civil Aeronautics Board*).

During the past few years, the Antitrust Division has been charged with the prosecution of certain claims for the recovery of damages resulting from alleged excessive charges on Government freight during World War II. In the first claim of this kind to come before the courts, the Division secured reversal of an order of the Interstate Commerce Commission denying the Government claim. (*United States* v. *Interstate Commerce Commission*).

Protests have been lodged with ICC during the past year regarding many of the agreements submitted for ICC approval, thereby permitting carriers jointly to make rates under an exemption to the antitrust laws. In addition, the FBI was requested to make investigations of the activities of ten rate making organizations for which applications for immunity from the antitrust laws had not been filed. As a result of these investigations, three rate organizations filed applications with ICC and six other organizations indicated an intention to do so within the near future. It is expected that additional rate organizations will file applications as a result of these investigations.

Other Activities

In addition to its litigative activities, the Antitrust Division performs a number of other functions. These relate to such fields as mergers, interlocking directorships, disposition of property vested by the Alien Property Custodian, small business assistance, and mobilization duties under the Defense Production Act.

There was a sharp increase in activity under the merger program in recent months, with the new language of the recently amended Section 7 of the Clayton Act providing a stricter standard of legality for corporate mergers and acquisitions, and because of the rising rate of such business transactions. Since the beginning of the fiscal year, some 496 mergers or acquisitions have been noted for review, 274 of which warranted preliminary analyses. Of these, 41 were given detailed study, and inquiries were made of the companies concerned regarding 12 of these transactions. Under the clearance phase of the merger program, the Division advises parties whether or not the Division intends to take action to prevent its consummation. Since the beginning of the year, 13 requests have been considered, resulting in 5 clearances.

As for interlocking directorships, there has been considerable work done in connection with Section 8 of the Clayton Act which forbids the same person to hold directorships in two or more competing corporations of a certain size. A review of approximately 1,550 directorships was made during the year; of these, 40 directorships were studied, resulting in 7 letters of inquiry being sent to directors concerned. In addition, a sample survey of 2,475 directors was undertaken.

The Division also is continuing its program to break up foreign cartel arrangements affecting property seized by the Office of Alien Property. During the past year, it advised OAP as to the legality of 15 such agreements in which the enemy interest had been vested. Moreover, some modification of cartel arrangements was secured in 20 cases as a condition precedent to the return of vested property. The eligibility of prospective purchasers from an antitrust standpoint also was examined by the Division in the sale of 5 companies by OAP. Furthermore, Division personnel reviewed 500 claims for the return of vested property which were referred to the Division by OAP.

In connection with legislation authorizing disposal of synthetic rubber plants, the Division has urged a provision requiring an expression of the Attorney General's views as to whether disposal would be inconsistent with the antitrust laws. It is anticipated that, with enactment of the Rubber Producing Facilities Disposal Act, the Attorney General's responsibilities in consultation with the disposal Commission will be increased.

Defense Mobilization Activities

Since the inception of the defense program in 1950, this Division has considered one of its primary responsibilities to be the prevention of injuries to the nation's competitive enterprise system which might occur by virtue of the pressure of the military build-up. The principal mobilization activities of the Division during the past year have involved the approval of voluntary agreements under Section 708 of the Defense Production Act, and consultation with Federal defense agencies on defense matters having antitrust implications.

The total number of voluntary agreements submitted for approval declined from the previous year. One voluntary agreement involving foreign petroleum was approved and two plans for the formation and use of integration committees by the Ordnance Corps of the Army—both involving committees studying problems in the manufacture of ammunition—were endorsed. A number of consultations were held with respect to problems which arose under previously approved voluntary agreements. In addition, Division personnel reviewed minutes of meetings of integration committees for the purpose of assuring adherence to plans as approved.

With respect to voluntary agreements enabling small business to participate in the mobilization program, 8 production pools were approved during the year; these pools had an aggregate membership of 21 small business concerns.

Consultations took place during the past year with the Defense Production Administration with reference to applications for accelerated tax amortization on new plant expansion. A closely related matter, the direction of expansion of domestic primary aluminum production capacity, received considerable attention from the Division in connection with its continuing interest in and responsibility for enforcing the judgment in the *Aluminum Company of America* case. Three new applicants, with an annual production potential of 214,000 tons of primary aluminum, were authorized by DPA to commence construction under the plant expansion program.

During the past year the Division was consulted by a number of Federal agencies with reference to problems posed by the use of industry advisory committees. One such matter concerned the extent to which the organization of the Civil Air Reserve, sponsored jointly by the Department of the Air Force and Department of Commerce, should be governed by the Attorney General's views on the use of advisory committees.

Similarly, the General Services Administration, which first consulted the Division with reference to the use of advisory committees in defense matters, subsequently asked assistance in developing general regulations to govern the use of advisory and technical committees which regularly advise GSA on a wide range of procurement matters.

Respectfully submitted,
STANLEY N. BARNES
Assistant Attorney General

Antitrust Division Annual Report Fiscal Year Ending June 30, 1954

This report will review the activities of the Antitrust Division for the period from July 1, 1953 to June 30, 1954. During that period the Division has actively and effectively sought to uphold the freedom to compete and to remove artificial obstacles to competition, and it carried out an expanding program of antitrust enforcement which had as its objective a well rounded attack upon all phases of the national economic structure where restraints and monopolies were found.

The major work of the Antitrust Division is in litigation, initiated to enforce the antitrust laws. The Division sought, during the past fiscal year, to emphasize the expeditious disposition of pending cases, particularly those that had been pending more than two and a half years. Experience has shown that this period is the average time for an antitrust case to spend in the courts.

Cases brought by the Division have not reflected any concentration of enforcement effort in any particular group of industries, but rather were planned to deal with situations which harmed groups of people, denying them access to the market or forcing them to purchase under rigged conditions. This approach to the enforcement problem is thought to show more appropriately the scope and significance of the antitrust laws than would a concentration of effort in a relatively narrow field.

Enforcement of the Antitrust Laws

At the beginning of the last fiscal year there were 144 cases pending in district courts, and one case pending on appeal. Thirty-two cases (18 civil and 14 criminal) were filed during the year, while 48 civil and 18 criminal cases were terminated. Of these cases terminated, 38 civil cases and 17 criminal cases were won by the Government, 6 civil cases were lost, and 4 civil cases and 1 criminal case were dismissed on the Government's motion. No criminal cases were lost. At the end of the fiscal year, 110 cases were pending in the district courts (76 civil and 34 criminal). In addition, during the past fiscal year, 2 cases in courts of appeals were disposed of, the Government winning in both instances, and 4 cases in the Supreme Court were terminated, 3 by Government victories. At the close of the year, 2 cases were pending in courts of appeal and 3 in the Supreme Court.

The 76 civil cases pending in the district courts is the smallest number of such cases pending since 1946. The termination of 48 civil cases during the year is very much in excess of the number of civil cases terminated in any previous fiscal year since 1938, and reflects the efforts of the Division to dispose of old cases.

On June 30, 1954, 275 major antitrust investigations were under way. This was the largest number of such pending investigations at the close of any one of the last seven fiscal years, and shows the continued activity of the Division. One hundred and eighty-one (181) major antitrust investigations were instituted during this fiscal year and 128 were completed.

Major Cases Filed During Year

One of the major cases filed in the last fiscal year was that against Pan American World Airways and W. R. Grace and Company, seeking to eliminate restraints of trade involved in the joint ownership of Panagra by Pan American and Grace. The complaint in this case alleged that Panagra was formed by Pan American and Grace in order to foreclose a potential air carrier in Latin America which would have competed with Pan American in the field of air transportation and which would have competed with the ocean transportation of Grace and its subsidiaries. It was also alleged that Panagra has been used to combat the growth of a competing air transportation system. The Government seeks a divestiture of Panagra from Pan American and Grace.

A major monopoly case filed during the last fiscal year was that against *American Smelting and Refining Company* and St. Joseph Lead Company, charging that the defendants have restrained, have attempted to monopolize and have monopolized interstate and foreign commerce in the production and sale of primary lead.

Four similar cases were filed against four manufacturers of toilet goods (Guerlain, Inc., Parfums Corday, Lanvin Parfums, Inc. and Empro Corp.) alleging in each case that the defendant had attempted to monopolize and had monopolized interstate and foreign trade by preventing others from importing the line of trademarked toilet goods produced by the defendant's foreign affiliates and sold abroad at substantially lower prices than those charged for the defendant's line of toilet goods in this country. The significance of these cases is in the interrelationship between the trademark law and the antitrust statutes, since the charge basically is that these defendants are misusing the rights given them under the trademark law in order to maintain a monopolistic position and to keep prices higher than competition would dictate.

Civil and criminal contempt cases were instituted against J. Myer Schine, Louis W. Schine, John A. May, the Schine Chain Theatres, Inc., and five of the latter's subsidiary corporations. In the contempt proceedings the Government charged that the defendants, notwithstanding a 1949 decree against them, have maintained and continued their local theatre monopolies and their conspiracy to prevent competition. In addition, the defendants are charged with failing to dispose of 23 of the 39 theatres which the court had ordered the defendants to dispose of, and with violating a number of the injunctive provisions of the earlier decree governing the manner of licensing films for exhibition, and with continuing arrangements for pooling all theatres in a town for non-competitive operation. The proceedings seek to punish the defendants for their disregard of the earlier decree and to force the defendants to carry out its provisions.

Proceedings were also instituted against the American Can Company, based on an alleged violation of a 1950 antitrust judgment entered against it. In the contempt proceedings, it is alleged that American Can had violated the earlier judgment by refusing to sell cans to a packing company except upon condition that the latter lease can closing machinery owned by American. This alleged tie-in between cans and machinery is in direct conflict with one of the principal provisions of the judgment previously entered against American Can.

Contempt proceedings of a somewhat different nature grew out of the case of *United States* v. *Charles A. Krause Milling Company*, in which an indictment was returned on April 20, 1954 at Danville, Illinois, charging eight corn milling corporations with fixing prices for corn grits. On May 27, 1954 the United States filed a petition for citation for contempt against two individuals connected with one of the indicted corporations, charging them with numerous acts of disobedience and misconduct in answering subpoenas issued by the grand jury that returned the indictment. These two individuals were charged with the destruction of reports of price fixing meetings, with erasures, alteration and destruction of expense accounts showing the attendance of one of the men at meetings with co-conspirators, and with refusing and neglecting to return to the grand jury many documents in their possession.

An interesting civil case involving the application of the antitrust laws to the insurance field is *United States* v. *New Orleans Insurance Exchange*. The complaint charged the defendants with conspiring to prevent the selling of fire and casualty insurance in the New Orleans area through outlets other than Exchange members and on any terms other than those set by the defendant Exchange. These objectives were alleged to be accomplished by an effectively policed boycott conducted by Exchange members against non-member agents and their companies, against mutual fire and casualty insurance companies, and against companies selling policies directly to the public through branch offices. The McCarran Act of 1945 provides that the antitrust laws shall not be applicable to the insurance business where this business is subject to regulation by state laws; however it is provided that the Sherman Act shall continue to be applicable where there is any agreement to boycott, coerce or intimidate, or where any such act is committed. This antitrust action aims at correcting illegal activities in the insurance field, and is the second case brought against an association of insurance agents since the passage of the McCarran Act.

Cases Decided During Year

The most important antitrust case decided this year by the Supreme Court was the *United Shoe Machinery* case, in which the Court in May 1954 in a very brief *per curiam* opinion sustained the judgment of the District Court for the District of Massachusetts holding that the United Shoe Machinery Corporation had monopolized the market for shoe machinery and for certain shoe manufacturing supplies. The District Court, in reaching its conclusion, held that a company possessing control of a market violated Section 2 of the Sherman Act if one of the principal sources of its power had been the employment of exclusionary business practices, even though the practices themselves were neither predatory nor illegal *per se*. The decree in that case required, among other things, the elimination of various leasing provisions and practices found to be discriminatory and exclusionary, the giving to customers of an option to purchase shoe machinery offered on lease, the licensing of shoe machinery patents at reasonable royalties, divestiture of the business of producing nails, tacks, and eyelets, and termination of United Shoe's activities as a distributor of shoe factory supplies manufactured by others.

In companion cases brought against the Employing Plasterers Association of Chicago and against the Employing Latherers Association of Chicago and Vicinity, the Supreme Court in March of 1954 handed down opinions which should be helpful in permitting the Government to deal with restraints of competition in the important building trades. In those cases the District Court for the Northern District of Illinois had dismissed the complaints, on the ground that the allegations were insufficient to show a substantial adverse effect on interstate commerce. The Supreme Court, however, held that since wholly local business restraints can produce the effect condemned by the Sherman Act, the complaints in these two cases stated valid causes of action, and the fact that the activities of the defendants were local in character does not immunize them from the Sherman Act if the effects of the defendants' activities adversely affected interstate commerce.

In *United States* v. *Borden Co.*, the Supreme Court held that the District Court for the Northern District of Illinois had abused its discretion in holding that the United States had no right to an injunction against certain Clayton Act violations (price discrimination), because a decree in a private suit against the same defendant enjoined the conduct charged. The Supreme Court pointed out that the respective interests of the Government and the private plaintiff in antitrust litigation were different, and stated that the Government's "right and duty to seek an injunction to protect the public interest exists without regard to any private suit or decree."

Among the significant antitrust cases decided by a district court during the year was the General Electric case involving incandescent lamps. The District Court handed down an opinion holding that General Electric and the other defendants must dedicate to the public their patents on incandescent lamps and lamp parts. In addition, General Electric was required to license its lamp machinery patents at reasonable royalties and to license all patents issued to General Electric within the next five years on incandescent lamps, lamp parts and lamp machinery at reasonable royalties. The order for the dedication of existing patents, entered October 8, 1953, is the first of its kind in a contested antitrust judgment, although such provisions have appeared in consent decrees.

In the Holophane case, charging an illegal cartel dividing world markets for prismatic glassware, the District Court entered a decree against the defendant after making findings of fact and conclusions of law in the Government's favor.

In the National Football League case the District Court held that certain of the restrictions on the broadcasting and telecasting of professional football games enforced by the defendant League and its member clubs violated Section 1 of the Sherman Act. The court distinguished the 1953 decision of the Supreme Court in *Toolson* v. *New York Yankees*, 346 U.S. 356, (which held that the business of professional baseball was not interstate commerce within the meaning of the Sherman Act) on the ground that the decision in *Toolson* relates only to the internal operation of professional baseball, and has no application to the football case, which involves restrictions on the sale of rights to radio and television stations. In January 1954, the court entered in toto the proposed final judgment submitted by the Government and rejected the proposals of the defendants. Neither side appealed.

In the case against du Pont involving cellophane, the defendant was charged with an unlawful monopoly, acquired and maintained through cartel agreements, allocation of world markets, and unlawful patent practices, and the exclusion of actual and potential competitors. After a trial the court held in favor of the defendant and dismissed the action. A petition for appeal to the Supreme Court filed by the Government was allowed and is now being perfected. One principal issue on appeal is whether the court erred in holding that the defendant's monopoly power respecting trade in cellophane is to be determined, not by its control of such trade, but by its control of "the market for flexible packaging materials." This issue involves the substitute products theory, which is of considerable importance.

The most important criminal case in this fiscal year was that against the Chattanooga Chapter, National Electrical Contractors Association, in the Eastern District of Tennessee. In this case an indictment was returned on July 7, 1953 charging a trade association of electrical contractors, a labor union, a corporation, and eight individuals with conspiring to restrain trade in the sale and installation of electrical equipment in the Chattanooga area. Nine of the eleven defendants who were arraigned entered pleas of *nolo contendere* and were fined a total of $16,500. The two remaining defendants, Local 175 of the IBEW, and its business agent, filed a motion to quash the indictment as to them, contending it contained a number of fatal errors. The motion was dismissed. Trial of the two remaining defendants started on January 25, 1954, and on February 5, 1954 they were found guilty. When a motion for a new trial was denied on February 10, 1954, a fine of $3,000 was levied against Local 175 and a fine of $1,000 against the business agent. Defendants have filed an appeal with the Court of Appeals for the Sixth Circuit, which is expected to be heard in the fall of 1954.

Consent Decrees

During the last fiscal year a number of important consent decrees were entered in various cases. The most significant consent judgment, from a legal and economic standpoint, entered during this period was in the case of *United States* v. *United States Rubber Company, et al.*, which was terminated by a consent decree entered on May 28, 1954. The Government's complaint filed December 16, 1948, charged price fixing, restrictive patent cross-licensing agreements and pooling of foreign patents together with division of territories and restraints, supported by joint use and allocation of trademarks relating to elastic yarn, natural latex and latex products. The judgment in effect requires reasonable royalty licensing on a non-exclusive basis of the patents involved and prohibits specific acts in restraint of interstate and foreign trade. In addition, it required the dissolution of one of the jointly-owned companies and the division into two groups of other companies formerly jointly owned. To accomplish this, the judgment divided the English and American companies into two separate and competing organizations without any management control by one over the other, and contained provisions relating to trademarks designed to remove their illegal use to restrain imports and exports of the products involved to or from the United States.

In addition there were four other cartel cases terminated by consent judgments during the fiscal year.

On May 10, 1954, a consent judgment was entered in Pittsburgh terminating the antitrust litigation against Blaw-Knox. This company had been charged in June 1951 with unreasonably restraining foreign and domestic trade in the manufacture, distribution and sale of cast metal rolls through restrictive international cartel agreements with British competitors, the effect of which was to create a division of territories and markets, price fixing and exchange of pricing information, and the use of Blaw-Knox's competitors in foreign countries as their agents for sale and distribution in those countries. In addition to terminating the objectionable agreements and prohibiting their renewal the consent judgment also required that, in licensing technical information, Blaw-Knox may not impose any obstacle against the importation into the United States by the licensing of articles manufactured on the basis of such technical information.

On April 30, 1954, a consent judgment terminated litigation against Scott & Williams, Inc., in the court at New York. The Government had charged in December 1949 that Scott & Williams, a principal manufacturer of seamless hosiery machinery, had entered into restrictive cartel agreements dividing territories and markets with its British competitors. The judgment terminates the illegal agreements and prohibits the use of competitors as sales or distributing agents for the defendant Scott & Williams. The use of competitors as sales or distribution agents was one of the more specific methods by which restraints upon exports and imports had been generated.

On March 26, 1954, a consent judgment terminated the long pending fluorescent electric lamp case against General Electric, Westinghouse, and other corporations. This case had been pending since the filing of the Government's complaint in December 1942 charging General Electric and others with violations of Sections 1 and 2 of the Sherman Act by restraining and attempting to monopolize domestic and foreign commerce in fluorescent lamps. In addition to the fixing of the sale and resale prices on fluorescent lamps sold in the United States it was charged that the defendants had eliminated imports into the United States of such lamps, lamp parts and machinery with which to manufacture them through international cartel agreements with a number of foreign competitors. The consent judgment, in addition to cancelling the illegal cartel agreements, requires General Electric and Westinghouse to license upon application their patents relating to lamps, lamp parts and lamp machinery. Under the judgment, the patents required to be licensed included patents which might hereafter issue upon applications therefor filed up to the date of the judgment.

On January 18, 1954, a consent judgment entered in the court at Philadelphia terminated antitrust proceedings against Servel, Inc. This company had been charged in June 1950 with monopolization of the manufacture and sale of the absorption type refrigerators, and with illegal cartel arrangements with a Swedish refrigeration manufacturer. The judgment requires that Servel license on a reasonable royalty basis to any applicant approximately 175 United States patents which it owned at the date of the judgment and any other patent relating to absorption type refrigerators applied for or acquired within five years thereafter. The judgment further requires Servel to furnish technical assistance and information with respect to its methods and practices under such patents and terminates the restrictive agreement between Servel and the Swedish manufacturer.

Two other consent decrees negotiated during this period deserve mention. One was in the Case of *United States v. Aluminum Company of America*, in which the

Government in July 1953 petitioned the court for relief against a contract entered into between Alcoa and Aluminum Import, a Canadian company, providing that the Canadian company would sell to Alcoa 600,000 tons of aluminum over a period of six years. The Government attacked this contract on the ground that it tied Alcoa to the Canadian company despite an earlier court order providing that ownership and control of the American and Canadian companies should be completely separated. On April 23, 1954, this matter was settled by a consent judgment providing that the Canadian company should make available to independent aluminum users in the United States who do not have facilities for smelting aluminum ingot not less than 110,000 tons of this metal, this obligation to take precedence over the Canadian company's obligations to Alcoa under the contract. In essence the consent decree, while permitting the private contract between Alcoa and the Canadian company to continue, subordinates the contract to the public interest in furthering the national defense and in promoting competition in the United States aluminum industry.

Another important case disposed of by a consent decree was *United States* v. *The New York Great Atlantic & Pacific Tea Company, Inc.*, in the Southern District of New York. The complaint, filed in 1949, charged that the defendants had conspired to restrain and monopolize a substantial part of the business of retailing food, food products and produce. This civil suit was a sequel to an earlier criminal case which had been tried at Danville, Illinois in 1945 and 1946, in which the A & P corporations were accused of substantially the same offenses, were found guilty as charged, and were fined $175,000. The case was settled by a consent decree filed January 19, 1954, which provided for the dissolution of Atlantic Commission Company, Inc., enjoined A & P from acting as broker for the outside trade, limited quantity discounts that A & P may accept, enjoined the defendants from evading state minimum mark-up laws, and enjoined deliberate operations of A & P's business at a loss under certain specified circumstances.

Kindred Law Cases

The Antitrust Division has responsibility to enforce not only the antitrust laws but also a large number of other laws regulating business enterprise (including transportation and communications). Thus, it frequently represents the Government in litigation involving regulations and orders of the following agencies: the Interstate Commerce Commission, the Federal Trade Commission, the Federal Communications Commission, the Civil Aeronautics Administration, the Civil Aeronautics Board, the Federal Maritime Board, and the National Mediation Board. In addition, it is in charge of proceedings to enforce or defend regulatory orders issued by the Secretary of Agriculture under nine statutes, and orders of the Secretary of the Treasury issued pursuant to the Federal Alcohol Administration Act. Broadly speaking, these kindred law cases involve the adjustment of conflicting economic interests and the maintenance of prescribed standards of business conduct. Antitrust policies are frequently an important element in the picture.

Most of the cases arise out of adjudicatory administrative proceedings. Many of these involve a question of licensing or certificating an individual applicant. Others present questions of individual compliance with requirements governing licensees and certificate holders. Cases in these categories cannot readily be singled out as having substantial general importance. Collectively, however, these cases test the fairness and the effectiveness with which regulatory statutes are applied to particular individuals and business enterprises engaged in activities effected with a public interest.

When litigation involves an attack upon the validity of an agency rule or regulation, issues of more obvious general importance are frequently presented. Thus, a series of recent cases challenged the power of the Federal Communications Commission to adopt and proceed under a general plan allocating the available television channels in the nation.

Major litigation involving the tire industry is now pending in the District of Columbia, some twenty manufacturers and distributors having challenged a quantity discount rule prescribed by the Federal Trade Commission pursuant to the Robinson-Patman Act. [(]*B. F. Goodrich Company et al. v. Federal Trade Commission et al.*[)]

Under a number of statutes, suits seeking review of administrative action are required to be brought against the United States rather than against the agency which issued the challenged regulation or order. This emphasizes the duty of the United States to form its independent judgment as to the defensibility of the disputed agency action. Occasionally there are significant differences between the views of the Department of Justice and those of the agency concerned. In most instances, however, such differences have been successfully resolved, and in only a few cases has the Department taken a position in court actively opposing that of another federal agency.

In some instances, two federal agencies other than the Department of Justice are on different sides of a controversy. An instance in point is provided by two cases in which the Postmaster General claimed that the Civil Aeronautics Board had misinterpreted the applicable law and had granted excessive subsidy mail pay to two air carriers in an amount exceeding a million dollars. The Department decided that it should represent the Postmaster, and its position on the merits was unanimously sustained by the Supreme Court. See *Western Air Lines, Inc.* v. *Civil Aeronautics Board*, 347 U.S. 67; *Delta Air Lines, Inc.* v. *Civil Aeronautics Board*, 347 U.S. 74.

The Department has continued its opposition to a position adopted by the Federal Maritime Board in recent years, that a dual rate system of transportation charges is legally permissible. The dual rate system is one by which associated or "conference" lines offer shippers who sign exclusive patronage contracts substantially lower rates than are made available to shippers who fail to contract away their right to patronize independent or non-conference lines. In *Isbrandtsen Co., Inc.* v. *United States and Federal Maritime Board*, 211 F.2d 51 (C.A.D.C.), certiorari denied June 1, 1954, the court of appeals held that in no event could such a system be permitted to take effect without according objecting parties a full administrative hearing in advance. This was the position taken by Isbrandtsen, an independent line, and supported by the United States. Whether the system is *per se* illegal has not yet been judicially determined.

A special category of cases handled by the Antitrust Division consists of the so-called reparations suits. The United States, appearing in its proprietary capacity, has been engaged in prosecuting claims for alleged overcharges by rail carriers. Most of these claims arose out of World War II shipments of military equipment, and they involve, in the aggregate, many millions of dollars. These cases are heard in the first instance by the Interstate Commerce Commission, and most of them are still pending before that agency.

Other Activities

In addition to its litigative activities, the Antitrust Division performs a number of other functions.

The Division has continued its program of granting, under certain circumstances, advance clearance of some types of industry plans and of mergers.

Under the "railroad release" procedure, the Department reviews prospective industry plans or programs with a view toward determining whether or not it will waive its right to institute criminal proceedings with respect to that particular plan or program. This waiver is not granted unless the following conditions are met: (a) full disclosure must be made of all information necessary for consideration of the merits of the plan in relation to the antitrust laws; (b) the submitted plan must be prospective and not in actual operation; and (c) the information submitted must affirmatively disclose that both the plan and the operations contemplated thereunder are not likely to be inconsistent with the antitrust laws. Under this procedure, the Department always reserves the right to institute *civil* proceedings if it decides to test the legality of the plan, and insists upon the understanding that the waiver of criminal prosecution will become inoperative if it appears that actual operations have extended beyond the limits of the proposed plan, or if a full disclosure has not been made.

The Division has also formulated certain "advance" clearance procedures in connection with its merger program. With respect to any proposed merger, the Division permits the parties involved to confer with Division representatives with a view toward obtaining a statement from the Division that the proposed merger would not be made the subject of legal proceedings. Following such conferences, the Division, if it finds that the proposed merger does not raise serious questions under the antitrust laws, may indicate to the parties in writing that it does not intend to take legal action against the merger, but that it reserves its right to take action if subsequent developments and operations so warrant.

The Division expresses views concerning proposed legislation which might have antitrust implications. One important illustration involved the bill to amend the Atomic Energy Act of 1946, particularly with reference to Section 105, concerning certain antitrust provisions, and Sections 151, et seq., relating to non-military use of patents and inventions. With respect to Section 105, we recommended that the Attorney General be consulted by the Atomic Energy Commission prior to the issuance of licenses for non-military use (along the lines provided for in Section 207 of the Federal Property and Administrative Services Act). We also recommended some form of compulsory licensing for private patents for a specified period of years to prevent monopolistic trends. Practically all of our recommendations concerning the antitrust and patent provisions were incorporated in the bill as enacted by the Congress.

The Antitrust Division also opposed the enactment of proposed bills to exempt from the antitrust laws agreements among automobile manufacturers and dealers to prevent the so-called "bootlegging" of automobiles. Our position was that the proposals of the automobile dealers and manufacturers would suppress competition and that these proposed practices should be regulated by the antitrust laws, rather than handled by special *ad hoc* legislation.

The Division also made recommendations concerning the legislation providing for life insurance for Federal employees. Our position was that smaller insurers should have the right to obtain some of this group insurance business, and that the statute should not be so written as to exclude all but a very small number of insurers from the opportunity to participate in this business.

The Antitrust Division is often involved in the clearance of plans for disposing of property by various Federal agencies. Under the Federal Property and Administrative Services Act of 1949, all disposals of surplus property which cost the Government one million dollars or more, and of patents, processes, techniques, and inventions, irrespective of cost, must be submitted to the Attorney General, who is to determine and advise whether such proposed disposition by the Government will tend to create or maintain a situation inconsistent with the antitrust laws. Pursuant to this statute, we have expressed opinions on proposed sales of Government owned properties in a number of significant cases, and on occasions have concluded that the sale proposed would not be consistent with the antitrust laws.

The Rubber Producing Facilities Disposal Act of 1953 authorize the disposal to private industry of the Government owned synthetic rubber producing facilities and sets forth the procedures to be followed by the Disposal Commission in effecting such disposition. These facilities will constitute the nucleus of a private synthetic rubber industry and required an investment by the Government during and after World War II of more than one half billion dollars. This Act requires the Disposal Commission to consult and advise with the Attorney General in order to secure guidance as to the type of disposal program which would best foster the development of a free, competitive synthetic rubber industry, and to secure an opinion from the Attorney General as to whether the proposed disposition will violate the antitrust laws.

The Department of Justice received information that a number of production pools, which were organized under the Defense Production Act, were experiencing difficulty securing defense contracts. Many of the pools alleged that they were discriminated against by procurement officers; on the other hand, certain government officials indicated that the pools were not capable of performing satisfactorily on defense contracts. In accordance with the direction in the Defense Production Act that the Attorney General make surveys for the purpose of "determining any factors which may . . . injure small business," a survey of the production pooling program was undertaken. Members of the Attorney General's staff visited most of the production pool offices to learn firsthand the problems confronting them. Subsequently, interviews were had with procurement officials of the various military services and with officials of other government agencies. As a result a considerable amount of information about the pooling program was obtained.

Upon analysis of this information, the Attorney General concluded, and reported to the President and the Congress in April 1954, that many of the pools had misconceived the purpose of the governmental approval which they received, while at the same time they suffered from certain inherent weaknesses which only the exceptional pools had overcome. The Attorney General also reported that procurement officers were reluctant—perhaps unreasonably so—to accept as responsible bidders for defense supplies these pools. The Attorney General cited the failure of aids provided by legislation to assist the small business groups and recommended reexamination and strengthening of legislation authorizing production pooling.

Respectfully submitted,
STANLEY N. BARNES
Assistant Attorney General

Alphabetical Index of Companies Cited In This Volume

* The number in the right-hand column refers to the entry in Appendix A. When preceded by an "O", the company is cited in the "Outcome" category of Appendix A. Companies treated in the text are indexed according to chapter; companies mentioned in Barnes' 1953 and 1954 annual Antitrust Division reports are indicated as "App. B."

Index